Desert Gardening

FRUITS & VEGETABLES

The Complete Guide
by George Brookbank

Photos by the author and Betsy Iventosch

Revised

FISHER BOOKS

Publishers: Howard W. Fisher
             Helen V. Fisher
             Fred W. Fisher

Editors: Veronica Durie
             Howard W. Fisher
             Fred W. Fisher
             J. McCrary
             E. Thomas Monroe

Art Director: Josh Young

Drawings: Erwin Acuntius
             David Fischer

Published by Fisher Books
P.O. Box 38040
Tucson, Arizona 85740-8040
(602) 292-9080

Library of Congress
Cataloging-in-Publication Data

Brookbank, George, 1925-
    Desert gardening: fruits & vegetables: the complete
    guide/by George Brookbank: photos by the author
    and Betsy Iventosch. -- Rev.
        p.   cm.
    Includes index.
    ISBN 1-55561-002-1: $17.95
        1. Fruit culture. 2. Vegetable gardening.
        3. Desert gardening. 4. Organic gardening.
        5. Hydroponics I. Title.
SB355.B86 1991
635.048--dc20   91-225
                                                      CIP

Printed in U.S.A.
Printing 10 9 8 6 5 4

Notice: *The information in this book is true and complete to the best of our knowledge. It is offered with no
guarantees on the part of the author or Fisher Books. Author and publisher disclaim all liability in connection with
the use of this book.*

TABLE OF CONTENTS

ABOUT THE AUTHOR

Living and working in the desert is a lot different—yet similar—from where George Brookbank started his professional career as an Agricultural Officer in Tanganyika Territory in Africa. A lot of time there was spent figuring out how to protect the crops against monkeys, baboons, pigs and elephants.

Now he's concerned with helping desert gardeners ward off squirrels, rabbits, quail and other birds, javelina and all sorts of other desert critters.

Since 1971 he has been Extension Agent, Urban Horticulture, at the Extension Garden Center of the University of Arizona in Tucson, Arizona. He provides a widely diversified range of educational services to homeowners, garden clubs, the nursery business and landscape-maintenance companies.

George writes a weekly column for the Tucson Daily Citizen, has a Saturday morning radio show on stations KFLT and KGVY and a weekly television program on Channel 4 KVOA. He has a monthly call-in program on radio station KNST.

His popular weekly demonstrations at the Extension Garden Center and at Green Valley are well attended.

He has written a number of publications and prepared several dozen informational audio and video tapes for gardeners.

The term "hands on" really applies to this author. His formal working life started out when he apprenticed as a General Farm Worker, Lord Rayleigh's Farms, Witham, Essex, England. Horses were the source of farmpower.

George was born in England. His Bachelor of Science Degree in Agriculture was obtained at Reading University. He subsequently studied at Downing College, Cambridge. Then he attended the Imperial College of Tropical Agricultural in Trinidad, West Indies.

For 13 years he worked in Tanganyika, helping underdeveloped communities pull themselves up by their bootstraps. This required helping them improve their agricultural productivity. He was promoted to Provincial Agricultural Officer and subsequently became Principal of the Natural Resources School in Tengeru, Tanganyika. This was a two-year residential school for African field advisors and their wives.

Our author came to the United States in 1962. He got his Masters Degree in Agricultural Education at California State Polytechnic College in San Luis Obispo, California in 1966. He did graduate study at the University of Arizona and Arizona State University.

For nine years George taught at the Arizona Western College in Yuma, Arizona where he was Chairman of the Agriculture Department. During three summers he taught citrus husbandry to young farmers from Japan. And he trained unemployed people to become citrus farm hands.

ACKNOWLEDGMENTS

I received a lot of help in writing this book, which is the accumulated wisdom of 15 years of answering questions about gardening in the desert. When people ask questions, they relate their own experiences. Out of their trials and errors came success. and all of these they shared with me. My job as an Extension Agent, Urban Horticulture, with the University of Arizona enabled me to gather much of this information. I now share it with you.

I first shared it with the public through a weekly newspaper article—and those articles were to be the basis of the book. The first article appeared in May 1973 for the *Arizona Daily Star* and they continue today with the *Tucson Daily Citizen*. I am grateful to the Managing Editors of those two newspapers who encouraged me to transform those articles into this book. Many newspaper readers told me they made their own book by saving the more useful articles. I hope this book will replace their faded clippings.

From the first, I was encouraged and guided by my publishers, Howard and Bill Fisher. They taught me how to take pictures and they explained the mysteries of a word-processing system to me. And they taught me how to write without an English accent—turning all my *s*'s into *z*'s— and to write concisely. They were patient and helpful and I am grateful to them.

My daughter, Lesley Cordier, is a well-organized person with a degree in horticulture. She created a system for keeping track of negatives, proof-sheets, enlargements and captions that eliminated frustration and muddle. Her tidy way of doing things saved me a lot of time and worry.

Throughout the writing of this book I received much encouragement from Master Gardeners, the volunteers of the Cooperative Extension Service. While I was training them, their questions and comments provided me with guidelines as to what was of interest and concern to newcomers to desert gardening. As they became more experienced and confident, their comments became more critical and questioning. Eventually, after they themselves became Plant-Problem Solvers, they critiqued the chapter called "When Things Go Wrong" and made helpful suggestions throughout.

To all of these people I say, "Thank you!"

HOW IT ALL BEGAN

Three people influenced my interest in gardening.

The first was my stepmother who made me trim the edges of the grass lawn. I hated it. Mowing was bad enough. The lawn sloped steeply and several flower beds prevented me from taking long efficient runs. The flower beds were the reason for miles of edges that had to be trimmed.

Mrs. James was an eccentric over-weight lady who bred Shetland sheep dogs. She lived in "The Kennels"—originally belonging to a country house—but to me she actually lived in kennels. She wore old doggy clothes, always with a dirty sackcloth apron and she had a doggy smell. She paid me to work around her beautiful and unkempt apple orchard, but it was her flattery that made me work harder than I needed to have. I was the best and most thorough digger she had ever come across.

Jennings—it was never Mr. Jennings or Albert Jennings—was a gardener who almost single-handedly ran the remnants of a country-house estate. The place had been turned into a boarding school and the boys competed with one another to help him. There were abandoned glasshouses where peaches grew against the back walls. There were espaliered fruit trees in the enclosed kitchen garden and in the one functional glasshouse he grew flowers in clay pots for setting out in ancient flower beds on an immemorial timetable that guaranteed constant color.

Jennings was patient and he taught patience to young hotheads. He was knowledgeable and experienced in natural things. He was cunning—in the old English meaning of having understanding. Strawberries were a delicacy but no one knew of those that he grew—in full sight of a hundred little mouths—in the middle of a field of cabbages. He was a good teacher and was kind enough to pass on his skills.

The War came and we boys dug—*Gardens for Victory* they were called—and the camaraderie of team work made it enjoyable.

Gardening was all around me in England during those formative years. Every house and every field was a testament. You couldn't go for a walk without being delighted by the variety of flowers in the gardens, in the woods and the hedgerows.

Tropical agriculture was gardening with a purpose. If you weren't good at sowing seeds, transplanting tobacco or coconuts, making cuttings of sweet potatoes, improving the soil with manures, trimming banana stems or properly digging planting holes for coffee, you weren't good at living. Survival depended on your skills. You had to be good at it.

Home gardening is not so serious but it has meaning. It's a reward—another thing you do well after a lifetime of things done well. Candide, after all his adventures, took up gardening. Gardening calls us. I hope this book helps you enjoy gardening in the desert.

1

DESERT GARDENING CONDITIONS

The desert is a place of extremes. It's dry most of the time—very dry. When it rains, at least during the summer months, the storm's intensity is frightening. Loud with thunder, bright with continuous lightning, the rain comes down in solid sheets and churns up the soil, tearing down river banks. In a day or two it's dry again—almost as if nothing happened.

Air temperatures in the shade reach 110F in summer, and in the same place during winter a nighttime temperature of 12F is possible. Summer soil temperatures can reach 150F on the surface out in full sun where the plants are. Plant surfaces have to put up with a lot of discomfort. It's not just the heat, the sun's radiation and brightness scorch leaves and burn fruit.

Winds

In the spring months the winds are strong. From the east they are dry, from the west they may be moist enough to bring leftover rain from California coastal storms. When winds blow at 50 mph, there's a tremendous moisture loss in plants. Roots of established plants, even if they are in moist soil, cannot replace the loss quickly enough and the plants wilt.

Newly planted vegetables and fruit trees dry out easily because they don't have their new roots out. Tall corn gets blown over, but there's no harvest lost.

Be careful when setting out plants in late spring or early summer. If they have been kept in the shade for a while, they will dry out and burn after a day's wind and sunshine. Make a temporary shade and a screen to keep wind off plants. Generously irrigate such plants and try to anticipate the windstorms by listening to weather reports.

Choose a sheltered spot for your

In summer the thunderclouds build up but don't always produce rain. If they do, it is localized and heavy. Across the street it may be raining, but your garden is dry. Much of the rain runs off the surface of the soil and never reaches plant roots.

citrus because summer winds are hot and dry, and winter winds can be freezing.

Rains

Desert conditions are unpredictable—every year starts differently.

Winter rains are light and gentle with grey skies for several days in a row and morning dew. But they are unreliable. Some years the rains will start on schedule and finish early. Once in a while they go on for weeks and the soil gets a good filling of moisture. Winter gardening is easy, enjoyable and rewarding. After a wet winter there's a gorgeous display of spring wildflowers—and winter weeds. But it's not always so.

Summer rains do not always materialize as expected. They may be late or

never arrive at all. If they do arrive, they can be very localized. It seems that places down the road or across town are getting all the rain while your own garden stays dry and expectant.

Pests

Another desert extreme that works against gardeners is the temporary greening of the natural vegetation. It's green long enough to nourish the growth cycle of birds, rodents and insects. Then the desert suddenly dries up and turns brown. Only green, irrigated gardens remain. Rabbits, ground squirrels, gophers, fruit-eating birds, disease-carrying insects, leaf-chewers and juice-suckers become unwelcome guests in your garden.

Winter rains are slow to develop and fall gently over a wider area. Most of the moisture penetrates the soil. An aftermath of a winter storm is morning mists. These prolong the rain's effect, keeping the soil—as well as plants themselves—moister, longer.

the leaves get hot. Learn this sign; when the leaves feel hot to the touch, the plant needs watering.

If you ignore this signal, the leaves actually burn. Oh, they don't catch fire and give out smoke. But the tissues are killed and a central burn spot appears on the leaves.

Location & Protection
The east side of a wall or a house is a good place for plants. It's sunny in the morning before the sun gets too fierce, and it's shaded during the hot afternoon. The west side of a wall is the reverse and should be avoided—except by heat-loving extremists such as grapes and climbing, tropical, annual beans. A south side gets hot but usually is safe from the heat of a late summer afternoon. A north side is always in the shade and during winter when the sun is low, plants don't get enough light there. A north side becomes the coldest place during a period of winter freezes.

Don't overlook the intensity of the summer sun. Brightness reflected from white walls and heat reflected from blacktop driveways is hard on plants. However, during winter there's a benefit from patio brickwork and blacktop heat reflection.

Keep the sun off plants in summer by putting up shade cloth. Remove it in winter. Strawberries, in particular, benefit from this protection. A natural shade is the sun-loving grapevine that

Soils
Hot soils can be disastrous to plants. Summer irrigations help cool things down and the plants' own shade helps too. We prefer to let tomatoes, for example, grow as sprawling bushes and then harvest from inside a jungle. All the fruit on the outside of the plant will be cracked and sunburned.

A thick mulch of straw or compost that won't blow away works wonders in keeping soil cool and moist during the summer months. It's not recommended for winter because it prevents the sun from warming up the cold soil.

In summer, a thick mulch, corn stalks in this case, keeps the hot sun off the soil. The soil stays cooler than soil which is kept clean and tidy.

Watering
We want plant roots to grow deeply to get them away from the hot surface soil. We lead the roots downward if we irrigate deeply. Always avoid shallow waterings.

Plants try to keep cool, just like we do. They lose moisture from their leaf surfaces and they cool off by evaporation. If, during a hot summer's day, there aren't any moisture reserves in the soil because you forgot to water,

Plastic materials available to use as light shade over plants. This material is particularly helpful on strawberries during the summer. It is light enough to allow plants to push it up as they grow. And it breathes so there is no condensation on its undersides.

Mushrooms suddenly appear after a summer rainstorm. They seem unlikely desert inhabitants and cause concern to newcomers. They will not do any harm to the garden. Even meadow mushrooms come out of lawns after a summer rain, contradicting the notion that they need cool, damp places out of the sunshine.

accommodatingly drops its leaves at the beginning of winter to let the sun come in and warm up a strawberry bed or a patio.

Calcium & Salt

Desert soils are high in calcium. Its main effect is to make other plant nutrients, such as iron and zinc, unavailable to plants. Digging sulphur into the soil and irrigating deeply helps to minimize the role of calcium in denying plants the zinc and iron they need.

Soil salts are common in desert gardens. Salts are dissolved in the water. When your irrigations are shallow, the salts stay in the root zone. It's difficult for plants to take up salty water but they do. Salts are carried to the leaves where they are deposited by evaporation. You can scrape a salt film off the leaves of a plant that has suffered. And you can see salt residue on the sides of clay pots that have held a plant too long. It's helpful to take plants out of such contaminated pots before summer starts. Even change the soil.

Salt accumulation in garden soil is a normal part of summer stress. Affected plants show a slow and stunted growth; they wilt a lot and have dull, bluish leaves. In later stages the leaves develop brown tips and edges. Then they burn all over and fall off. Sometimes whole shoots die back.

Once in a while, in addition to regular freezes, the desert gets a blanket of snow. Snow in itself isn't so bad because it's usually light and doesn't last long. It acts as a sort of insulation and of course it gently melts to provide moisture that slowly penetrates the soil. The bad feature is that a day's snow is followed by freezing nights. That's when the damage is done!

Avoid all this by selecting plants that can take hot weather. Always *irrigate deeply* to wash salts past the roots. Make sure the soil drains well. Don't sprinkle foliage. Keep the soil shaded with a mulch. Set up a temporary shade over the plant to reduce the effects of the sun's radiation.

Don't apply large amounts of fertilizers to plants while they are stressed by summer's heat. It merely puts them under additional stress. It's like trying to cure someone's headache with a turkey dinner when all he wants is to be left alone.

Selection

When selecting varieties of fruit trees and vegetables, choose those kinds that bear their fruit under a leafy canopy. Seed catalogs praise those varieties that display their fruit high above the foliage for all of us to see. That sort of fruit placement is disastrous in the desert.

It's not easy to grow perennials that require two seasons to reach maturity. These include artichokes, rhubarb, strawberries and blackberries. Summer extremes of heat and brightness are hard on them. Further, cold winters put them into dormancy.

Seasons

Summer doesn't go on forever—thank goodness! The desert has its seasons and each one is quite short.

Some winters have hard freezes. Gentle rains may not materialize or last long enough. But the sun is sure to

Winter vegetables survive a freezing night and look horrible in the morning. The sun will melt the ice and the plants will be all right. However, semitropical plants such as citrus are at greater risk and may even be killed.

shine most of the time and the days are delightful. It's a joy to dig the soil for vegetables and holes for planting trees.

Spring, marked by the lengthening days, is as beautiful for gardens as for people. The sun is warm and friendly. Start your summer garden early, before the hot weather arrives. If you delay, the work will be harder and the plants will be off to a late start.

July and August can be a trial, but they are good months for cantaloupe, watermelon, okra, black-eyed peas and Chinese pole beans. They are also good for laziness, swimming and long cool drinks!

September and October are like a second springtime. Start another crop of corn, beans and squash. Your tomato plants come alive again with flowers and fruit-set will follow. Winter gardening begins with high expectations for lettuce, cabbage, cauliflower, carrots, beets, turnips and oriental vegetables.

Experienced gardeners say it's the best time of the year for gardening. Try it—you'll like it.

Winter will arrive suddenly, possibly one night in November. The first frost always takes us by surprise. If we do get continued winter rains, the weather will be warm and frost-free. That makes for good gardening. December is too cold for new plantings, but established vegetables keep growing because the days are sunny.

December is a reflective, relaxing month. Enjoy it, but ready yourself for the hectic month of January.

Clay pots absorb salts from the soil and irrigation water high in chemicals. Soak these pots in water overnight and then scrub them with a wire brush to remove the salt deposit.

Moisture evaporates from ridges in the dry desert air and salt deposits are left at the waterline (white lines). This is dangerously near the root zone of young plants.

Mild winters are a blessing of the desert—ask any Chamber of Commerce booster if you have doubts. For gardeners, a mild winter works both ways; there are good and bad features to it. Mild winters allow you to grow semi-tropical plants such as citrus, figs, and a host of ornamental plants.

Compared with other parts of the country, desert winters are mild. But there are frosts and, though they don't last long, they are damaging to vegetation.

We believe mild weather will last forever and mistakenly try to grow semi-tropical plants such as avocados, bananas and citrus. One afternoon plants are growing happily in the sunshine and that night they are frozen. They weren't ready for the sudden temperature change.

Annual vegetables readily become perennials if our tomatoes, peppers and eggplant are protected from a stray freeze. Each winter is warmer than the last one—it's a documented trend.

On the other hand, our deciduous fruit trees, apples, apricots, peaches and plums, are not chilled enough when we have a mild winter and they produce lightly or not at all the following year. Insect eggs and even some adults survive mild winters.

Year 'Round Gardening

We can't have it both ways—but we almost do.

Plant breeders are coming to our help with new deciduous fruit trees that produce good-quality fruit in spite of warm winters.

Experienced desert gardeners remind us that though you can't grow any one vegetable all through the year, you can grow some vegetable at all times of the year. This means you can make your own Garden of Eden in the desert if you want to—and if you know how.

I've written this book to encourage you and start you in the right direction.

2

LET US COUNT THE DAYS

Gardening is very much like a jig-saw puzzle—you look at the pieces spread out and wonder how they all go together. One or two pieces attract your attention more than others, and some go together quite easily. However, a few assembled clusters don't make the complete picture. Every single piece has its place in relation to all the others. If you're impatient and try to force them together, you spoil the result.

Gardening requires patience and a knowledge of what the picture should look like—a glance at the lid of the box, as it were—before you get the most enjoyment out of it. It's not worth gardening unless you enjoy it.

See the Differences

At first sight, gardening in the desert appears to be just the same as anywhere else, but it's not! Experiences gained elsewhere have only limited value. It usually takes beginners at least a year to discover this. The conditions around us are different—that's quickly learned. But often the ways we did things "back-East" don't seem to work so well. It's not easy to accept if you were successful in other places.

Planting times are different, pruning practices aren't the same, varieties don't perform as they should, familiar fertilizing programs don't apply. The locals laugh at our routine spraying schedules. Dearly bought experience only seems to increase the confusion. We have to go back to the beginning.

Let's take a look at some pieces of the desert puzzle and see how they fit into one another to make the complete picture—a picture that will give you pleasure and satisfaction.

Situation Management

First, we need to recognize the situational pieces and then how our management pieces fit into them. There is flexibility in management but it has to be relevant and appropriate. Here, the pieces are listed briefly. They appear again in later chapters.

Soil

Soil is where gardening begins. Desert soils are short of organic matter, phosphates and nitrogen. Although mostly free-draining, there are localized areas where excessive amounts of calcium carbonate have accumulated under the surface in layers. It is called *caliche* and it prevents drainage. Desert soils are alkaline with a high pH. Some soils are saline, that is, they hold sodium—a poison to plants. Except for the Texas-root-rot fungus, desert soils are relatively free of harmful organisms, though they quickly accumulate after a few years of careless gardening.

Rainfall

Rain in the desert is unreliable, both in its frequency—some years are very dry and others very wet—and in its distribution. Even if you were lucky and got the odd downpour on your garden, there's a likelihood that summer storms ran off the surface and gentle winter rains didn't penetrate deeply.

Humidity is associated with rain and it makes plants comfortable. They relax, stretch and grow.

Pests

Unfortunately, garden pests and diseases come alive and multiply during humid periods so humidity is a mixed blessing.

Pests and diseases are largely the result of our own gardening activities and follow the gardening cycles; pests eat whatever we provide them with. Desert vegetation itself doesn't harbor

It takes time to dig a hole like this, but it's the size you need to grow a tree successfully. Standing on top you don't know whether there is caliche underneath—or how far down it is. Here, 3 feet of good soil overlays a hidden layer of coarse sand.

5

Soil with a lot of clay in it forms clods that are best left to crumble on their own. If you dig wet clay soils, the clods bake hard and don't break down easily. You have to break clods into pieces small enough to allow you to sow seeds or set out plants.

During "Indian Summer" in the fall when temperatures are milder, harvester ants become very active and forage widely on seedlings and new leaves of our vegetable plants.

Fruit ripening in late summer is invariably spoiled by the green fruit beetle which appears with the rains.

many troubles but it follows the natural seasons, growing well with the rains and drying out soon after. In the height of the summer there's no place for insects to go other than our green, irrigated gardens.

Sunshine

Heat and intense radiation from the sun wreak havoc on vegetable plants and fruit trees, especially if we let them dry out too much. Sun exposure, together with a salty soil and a dry wind, usually means poor plant establishment and dubious survival—until we learn to minimize these severities.

Temperature Extremes

Perhaps the biggest factor and one that we don't fully recognize at first, is the enormous temperature range plants have to put up with. Nighttime winter temperatures of 12F are possible in the low-lying areas near drainage channels of washes and rivers. The same places show a daytime summer temperature of 110F in the shade. In full sun, the temperature may be higher than 150F for several hours.

The Desert's Dark Side

Any plant that is able to withstand such temperature extremes coupled with alkaline soil, poor fertility, lack of rain, low humidity, dry winds, intense radiation from the sun, hungry animals, attacks from persistent pests and diseases has indeed found itself a special niche. The palo verdes and the mesquites can survive, but pity our

poor fruit trees!

Day-Length Changes

Another natural factor, scarcely noticed by the average person, is the relentless change in the hours of daylight. It has an effect on plant life and particularly on some vegetable varieties. Winters are dark and summer days are long even as far south as Tucson, although it's certainly more obvious up against the Canadian border.

Day-length changes affect flower production, whether in citrus trees or bolting vegetables. Most old-time vegetable varieties were developed for northern regions where the growing season has long days. Long days in the desert are the hottest, meanest days of the year and not good for most vegetables. The best desert growing seasons have short days, getting longer in the spring and shorter in the fall. Unfortunately, there aren't many short-day vegetable varieties. Only recently have plant breeders given them much attention.

A management piece of the desert puzzle becomes interesting when we try to grow onions. Most varieties are long-day types requiring at least 16 hours of daylight. There are only 14 hours of daylight at midsummer in southern Arizona and much less in springtime when onions should be bulbing up. We simply have to grow short-day varieties if we want bulbs.

Management Means Gardening

Our management capabilities call for a number of skills. In the area of soil im-

provement, you need to learn how to maintain soil fertility through careful use of chemical and organic fertilizers.

We need to irrigate heavily enough to wash harmful salts away from the roots, yet we mustn't drown them.

Use pruning techniques that will stimulate new fruiting growth without allowing the tree to be sunburned.

Pest management is vital and can be achieved through integrated approaches that maintain ecological balances.

A key to good gardening is careful selection of plant varieties suited to the desert's unique conditions.

Misconceptions About Varieties

Most gardeners, both beginners and old-timers, place a great deal of faith and hope in favorite varieties of fruit trees and vegetables. However, their selection is usually based on experience gained in other parts of the country where conditions are quite different. Mostly, those old favorites don't do well in the desert and for a very good reason.

—And About Seasons

The reason becomes obvious when we examine a year of gardening in the desert. Gardening "back-East" meant summer activity and winter rest, two simple seasons. If we think in these terms for our desert gardens, we miss the subtleties of several short seasons.

If you look upon gardening as an activity for the frost-free days you'll be pleased with desert statistics. In the

Southwestern desert of Arizona, for example, 242 frost-free days are recorded for Tucson and 353 for Yuma! However, right in the middle of that frost-free period comes an intensive hot spell. It's so severe that peppers, tomatoes, beans and corn stop producing. Some plants die from the heat.

Though we lose some growing days for certain vegetables, we manage by switching gears and recover the time by growing melons, squash and black-eyed peas during those hot days.

These short seasons are powerful and determine the varieties we need to select to be successful gardeners.

We could call the examination *Let us count the days.*

Warming Winter Season (Mid-January to Mid-March), 60 Days

Days get longer and the sun gets warmer. But there's still the danger of frost at night. It's not a busy time for vegetables until the end of the period when older, established plants begin to grow again. They—and a new sowing of bush beans—have to wait for the soil to warm up. If the days are unseasonably warm, many of the overwintering beets, carrots and cabbage-family plants waste their stored energy. Instead of developing more root or leaves, they produce a flower stalk. This season is a "leftover" time for winter vegetables in the garden.

Those vegetables that grow more slowly because they are long-term varieties are less inclined to bolt or flower. It's wiser to use such varieties at this time of year. This is the exception to the rule so bear it in mind when you sow turnip, carrot and beet seed directly in the warming ground near the end of this little season. They will grow without bolting until the end of May. At the same time, it's a preparation period for summer vegetables if you grow your own plants from seed. A greenhouse is needed to grow eggplant, tomato and pepper plants. These will be set out at the end of this little season.

Need to Hurry

Management practices have to be completed in a hurry before warm weather stimulates plant growth. This short season is quickly used up with digging planting holes, pruning grapevines

By selecting short-day varieties to match the short daylight hours in the Southwest, you can successfully grow bulb onions. This one is 'Crystal Wax'.

Winter cold is no longer a concern when plants are grown in a tunnel of plastic film. Sunshine enters to warm the soil against nighttime cold. Frost-tender plants are protected and temperate plants, such as these strawberries, grow vigorously and give an early crop.

and fruit trees and preparing vegetable beds.

This little season sometimes starts with a surprising burst of warm weather when we don't expect it. We delayed our pruning because we wanted our trees to get as much cold as possible. A warm spell can cause

the tree to "wake-up" and prematurely start its growth cycle. If the soil is moist from winter rains, the tree's sap begins to flow. Any pruning now means a dripping of sap at the ends where we cut. This adds to the risk of infection by bacteria that results in slime flux, and fungi which cause sooty canker. Prune as late as you can to avoid disturbing dormant trees but do it before the weather warms up. It's not an easy decision to make. If it has been a dry winter, we can offset the effects of this warm spell by keeping the soil dry. In other words, don't irrigate until after pruning and you see the buds swelling.

You're very busy at this time simply because it is a short season. Don't waste time and money by spraying your dormant fruit trees with Winter Oil. Firstly, there is little need because there are fewer insects than you're used to "back- East" and secondly, a bright, sunshiny, warm spell activates the oil, making it corrosive to the branches and buds.

Warming Summer Season (Mid-March to Mid-June), 90 Days

Statistical evidence says it's not going to freeze after March 15th, but in April 1976 a blanket of snow covered recently planted tomatoes in Tucson. Gardeners need target dates to structure their programs, but every year is different from the others. Use this date anyway and keep your fingers crossed.

This is the time to set out tomato plants and sow corn and squash seed. After a little while, set out peppers and eggplant and sow seed for cantaloupe and watermelon—plants that like heat and require a warm soil for good germination.

Toward the end of this little season the heat becomes too much for the corn, bush beans, tomatoes, peppers and eggplant. Plants continue to grow but they are under stress and their flowers fail to produce viable pollen. With the exception of cherry tomatoes, no fruit is set until the weather cools in September. It's most important to select varieties that mature quickly before the heat arrives in early July.

There is a management problem, though. If the weather stays cool in March, you have to delay planting and if hot weather starts in June instead of July, the good growing period has been shortened at both ends.

On the other hand, the heat favors watermelons, cantaloupe and squash. These plants can be joined by Chinese pole beans, okra and black-eyed peas.

Warming temperatures bring out voracious insect pests—whitefly, leaf hopper, squash-vine borer, hornworms, grape-leaf skeletonizer and the green fruit beetle.

Hot Summer Season (July and August), 60 Days

This is a climax of the year. Many plants are devastated by the heat even if you protect them with shade cloth and irrigate them generously.

It's too hot for most plants but there is an opportunity for second and even third sowings of squash, watermelon and cantaloupe seed. It's certainly too hot for fruit on the trees. Any late-producing variety is going to have damaged fruit, either skin-scorched or heat-damaged from the pit out into the flesh. The green fruit beetle appears. This event should determine as much as anything else, which fruit-tree varieties you plant. You get to eat the fruit from the early varieties—the beetles get to eat the fruit from the late varieties. It's hard to stop them.

Cooling Summer Season (September and October), 60 Days

This is the end of the season for heat-loving summertime plants such as squash, sweet potatoes, black-eyed peas, Chinese pole beans and melons. Anything planted during the previous months continues to grow and produce fruit, but now the plants are old and declining in vigor.

But tomato plants, and to a lesser extent the peppers and eggplant, start to flower again and their pollen survives to set fruit. It's a beautiful time for these plants. They often do much better than they did in the warming summer season before summer heat stopped their production.

You can sow corn and bean seed at the beginning of this period or even in August before it starts. They will grow quickly in the warm soil. By the time plants reach maturity, nights will have begun to cool and pollen will be effective in setting a harvest. There's little point in starting any new plantings of summertime vegetables in October.

It's a great time for planting fruit trees: citrus during September and deciduous kinds as late as October. Even though the days are cooling and the

Winter rains can cause sap to start running in dormant plants. This sap droplet (arrow) is sugary and if any fungus spores light on it, they will "feed" their way into the branch and destroy it. Slime flux and sooty canker start in this way.

Fruit produced under a canopy of foliage is protected from summer's bright sunshine and frost in the fall. This is a prime consideration when selecting suitable varieties for desert gardening.

Hot weather causes pollination death in corn cobs and gives us only a partial harvest. On the left, the exposed ends became too hot. Center pair is only half-pollinated while the right pair is acceptable, though not of the best quality.

Instead of putting their energy into bulb production, most onion varieties run to flower or "bolt" in desert regions where days are short.

A pretty sight on a sunny winter's day in the desert. But cold air flowing down from the snow on the mountain could kill the peach blossom during the night. We prefer quick-maturing fruit-tree varieties whose fruit ripens before summer's heat begins. Unfortunately, such varieties often start their growth before the danger of frost has passed. It's a dilemma.

nights are chilly, the soil temperatures remain warm. The tops of the plants don't grow very much—we don't really want them to—but the roots put out a lot of new growth. This establishes the trees before winter sets in. In the spring they really take off with a lot of vigorous new growth.

It's the best time to plant strawberries if you can find a neighbor to give you plants. The nurseries are not likely to have them at this time of year. They grow well during the winter months, gathering strength to flower heavily in the spring. If you plant them in February when the nurseries have a supply, you'll find that summer heat overtakes them before they become established properly.

The Cooling Winter Season (September through November), 90 Days

This is the same time period as the last, but now we are thinking in terms of winter vegetables. It's a wonderful time for them. The soil is warm and hospitable, the days are warm and sunny and the nights are getting progressively cooler.

The end of the summer vegetable season overlaps the beginning of the winter vegetable season. We have a hard decision to make. Shall we stay with the recovering plants after their summer stress, or shall we start fresh with new plants and new optimism? Winter vegetables require the soil to be prepared in early September—just when the faded summer plants begin to recover. We really need two gardens at this time.

It's usual to set out plants, but seed can be sown too. In early September try cucumbers, either plants or seed, and you'll be pleasantly surprised at their performance compared with springtime growth. For one thing, the fruit won't be bitter and varieties other than Armenian will do well.

Unfortunately, the good weather stimulates harvester ants which carry away carrot, beet and turnip seed, small seedlings and the leaves of recently planted cabbage, broccoli and lettuce. The larger seed, such as peas and faba beans, are left alone.

At the end of October, the weather cools to the point where plants grow slowly. If they are large and well-established, they continue to increase in size. Newly set out plants generally stand still, or grow very little.

The weather is so pleasant that deciduous fruit trees continue to grow, putting out new leaves. Sometimes grapevines set a second crop which looks exciting but is invariably bitter and useless. Experienced gardeners know the

forthcoming winter might be brief and not provide enough winter chill for deciduous fruit trees. They add a few weeks' dormancy to their trees by deliberately withholding water at this time. This puts trees into an early dormancy. Growth stops because of lack of water rather than because of cold.

The first frost in November stops everything. It kills the beans, tomatoes, egg-plant and peppers, knocks the leaves off the fruit trees and nips any precocious citrus growth.

The Dead Winter Season (December to Mid-January), 45 Days

Hardly anything grows during this short season though plants are not necessarily dead. Nighttime freezes can destroy new growth of citrus and peas. But the lettuce, carrots, beet and turnips, although frosted, are safe. There's a danger in daytime temperatures being too warm and stimulating for plants in their dormancy. If they are stirred out of it, they become vulnerable to later night-time freezes. Soil isn't warmed if days are cloudy. Clear nights indicate freezes. But if sunny days are followed by cloudy nights that keep daytime heat from escaping, our plants are safe from cold.

Management during this season centers around keeping vegetable plants warm. Sheets of plastic laid on the ground beside the plants make the soil warm. This leads to continued root growth. Putting clear plastic on a frame of construction mesh over the bed gives us a greenhouse tunnel. Inside, the tender plants, such as beans, can be made to produce all winter.

Plants that survive cold, but are dormant, can be made to grow inside the warm tunnels. This includes all the winter vegetables and strawberries, which gather strength in preparation for a springtime production.

That's the desert gardening year. Note that there are many seasons—not just two—and they are *short* ones.

Be Alert to Seasonal Changes— React Quickly

We have to be on our toes for the changes; they are neither regular nor predictable. We must also complete gardening tasks quickly because there is no time to lose. Soil preparation must be timely, fruit-tree pruning must be timely and fertilizer applications must be timely. All through the year we must be alert to changes and react quickly.

One of the Secrets to Success

The most important piece of the management puzzle is to select quick-maturing varieties of vegetables and fruit trees. Seed catalogs tell us the number of days needed from sowing or setting out to the first harvest for each variety. Always look for this number before you buy seed or plants; it appears after the variety name.

It's interesting that one seed company, Vesey's, produces a catalog called *Seeds for Short Seasons*.

But it's not a company located in the desert. Where do you think Vesey's is? In Maine at a latitude of 46°, where the growing season short because of *cold*. Nevertheless, most of their varieties do well in the desert.

Bye-Bye Beefsteak

You probably like Beefsteak tomatoes and are used to growing them "back

Desert winters are mild and you have only a short time to do your pruning. Start too soon and the plants don't get enough dormancy. If the buds break out into leaf before you prune, you've waited too long.

there" with great successs without even thinking of their maturity period. It didn't matter then. There were plenty of days available and you didn't even know it. Try to grow them in the desert and you'll be disappointed in their performance.

You'll have greater success with 'Early Girl' or 'Better Boy' and many other quicker-maturing varieties. It's the same with beans, corn, eggplant, bell pepper, cabbage, cauliflower—in fact, just about everything.

Successful tomato growing calls for knowledge about the desert situation, followed by management skills to handle it. Short seasons cause this gardening predicament and short-term varieties provide the solution.

A By-Product of Short Seasons

Curly top or leaf curl is a tomato disease that spells disaster. It is a virus carried by the beet-leaf hopper, a small insect that feeds on native annual plants. In May or June the desert vegetation which is infected by the virus dries out and the starving beet-leaf hoppers are drawn to our green irrigated gardens where they infect our plants. Just when our tomatoes start to bear fruit, their leaves curl and the plants wither. No more fruit is set. There's no cure and plants often die.

Management pieces of the desert puzzle include planting tomatoes on the east side of a wall where they are shaded from the afternoon sun. The beet-leaf hopper is a desert sun lover. Covering the plant with cheesecloth keeps the insect off, but the best answer is to plant disease-resistant varie-

ties. Sprays are useless.

Disregard Seed-Catalog Pictures

Shading eggplant, tomato and pepper plants with cheesecloth is a management trick to overcome the power of the sun. Also, avoid those varieties that thrust their fruit up in the air. Don't be seduced by the catalog pictures showing fruit displayed above the foliage for all to admire. In the desert, such pride will have its fall.

Fruit Trees in a Bind Too

We don't want deciduous fruit trees to flower until frosts are over, but their fruit should ripen before the green fruit beetle arrives. Because of these considerations, selection becomes a squeezed-in choice of a short-period variety—but the varieties are there. We just have to study the catalogs.

Gardening is an art, but there's a science to it too. Part of the science is in recognizing the short seasons of the desert and counting the number of days in each one.

Then match the pieces together— they should all fit one another.

Your picture will be complete, perfect, and a joy.

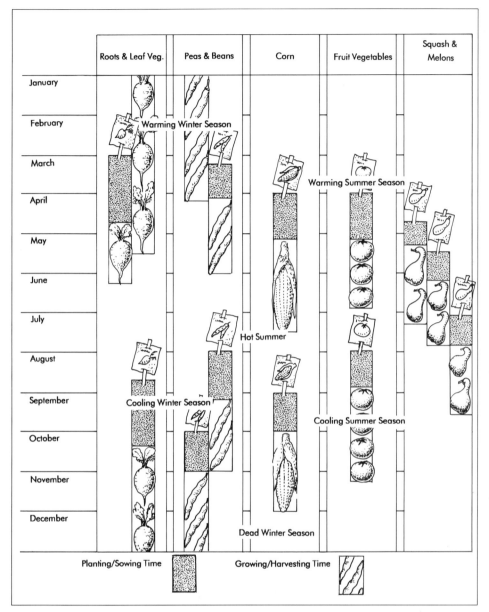

	Roots & Leaf Veg.	Peas & Beans	Corn	Fruit Vegetables	Squash & Melons
January					
February	Warming Winter Season				
March					
April			Warming Summer Season		
May					
June					
July		Hot Summer			
August					
September	Cooling Winter Season				
October			Cooling Summer Season		
November					
December					
			Dead Winter Season		

Planting/Sowing Time   Growing/Harvesting Time

Harvest eggplant while shine is on fruit. Smaller varieties do better in the desert.

Cucumbers should be grown up rather than on ground. This makes sure fruit are straight and in shade. String provides plenty of opportunity for tendrils to hang on and plant to climb.

If plant wilts for no apparent reason, suspect a borer in stem. Pull up ailing plant and split stem. If it looks like this, there is no remedy. You've saved yourself the trouble of growing a crop that won't develop.

New Year's Resolution: Keep A Gardening Diary

A fancy seed catalog arrived the other day. It had a majestic eye-catching statement. "Real Gardeners Don't Buy Transplants." The inference was that a true gardener buys seed packets, germinates the seeds and nurtures the seedlings until they are ready to set out in the garden—some seven or eight weeks later. No hasty trips at the last moment to the quick-serve nursery shelves. He plans his operations.

It's certainly true that a good gardener must be a good planner, one who becomes more methodical at the start of each new season's activities. One of his best helpers is a diary. They come in various degrees of thicknesses and spaces for writing in. And some commercial diaries are very ornamental. However, an ordinary school notebook works as well as a costly picture-book.

The best diary is filled in completely and systematically, regardless of its cover or cost. Try to keep a diary and try to keep it filled—with dates of things that happen, when you do things, varieties you sow, what the harvest tastes like and of course, the amount of food produced. If you are truly brave, write down the cost of everything, but don't necessarily total the amounts. You'll perhaps pay more for your home-grown food than you would at the supermarket.

Your reward is not measured in dollars and cents, but in the satisfaction of knowing your food was not sprayed with killer chemicals. It's fresh and tasty; growing it was a pleasure; and your gardening kept you away from the dogs or horses.

That reminds me! I remember a retired carpenter who turned his whole backyard into a melon patch one year, a squash patch the next, a tomato field the following year and so on. He worked diligently and was delighted with his work. Many of his practices reflected the Great American Ingenuity that made farming so successful in this country a generation or two ago. He sold his produce on the street-side to neighbors and took it to swap meets and to a Farmers' Market we had in downtown Tucson in those days. On weekends his old tobacco tin was full of money. Then he spent it all at once—at the racetrack.

Mac was a good gardener. He enjoyed gardening, but he never could be persuaded to keep a diary. But at least Mac had a cold frame and you can have one too.

Cold Frame—It's nothing more than a sunken, glass-covered, boxlike structure where you raise seedlings in warmth trapped from the sunshine. It lets you start your seeds in January, long before the usual planting time in mid-March.

The back of a cold frame is about 2 feet tall and the front about 8 inches tall, sloping to the south to let in the sun's rays. The cover should be transparent. And there are a number of materials you can use for this: an old window sash, a film of clear plastic stretched on a frame, a sheet of plate glass, and so on. Side walls—as well as the front and back—should be as airtight as you can make them.

Foam rubber placed on top of bricks, blocks or boards does a good job of keeping the "box" airtight and therefore warm on a sunny day. Many cold frames are temporary structures, taken down when spring arrives.

Gardeners often build their cold frames right over the place where their summer garden will be. A word of caution is appropriate here.

Although seeds in a cold frame can be sown directly in the soil, it's better not to. Your soil needs a rest from continuous cropping in order to reduce soil-borne diseases. Sow the seeds in styrofoam coffee cups and keep these in a tray resting on bricks.

What you have is a small greenhouse you must manage. This means watching the temperatures. When it gets too hot during the middle of the day—as it surely will—you must let in some cool air. Simply raise the sash and prop a brick under it. Before the sun goes down, put the sash back to make the cold frame airtight and keep the seedlings warm.

January—Here are a few observations about cold weather during January. Don't be alarmed about the red color appearing in leaves of many plants, from eucalyptus to cabbages—including weeds. Cold temperatures bring the color on; it will disappear when things warm up again.

The red color is sort of related to low phosphorus in the soil and the inability of plants to get what little is there. It could be an indication that you should add ammonium phosphate when you next dig your garden or landscaped area in preparation for planting a tree.

Remember: Phosphate fertilizer doesn't move through the soil very well, so it's normally a waste to throw it on top of the ground and water it in. You must dig it in. Remember, also, that it's a waste to throw fertilizer at plants that are dormant because of the cold weather.

On the other hand, growing plants—including ryegrass lawns and winter vegetables such as lettuce—will respond to an application of the right fertilizer. Use ammonium nitrate, which is soluble in cold water and carried down to the roots of plants by irrigation. Ammonium sulphate is not used by plants—even growing plants— when soil is cold.

Cold, wet soil is hard on plants. Don't leave your automatic irrigation system on a summer schedule during cold weather. If the soil stays too wet, your plants will be under stress. Pansies, petunias and geraniums can be attacked by *Rhizoctonia* organisms, and winter lawns by *Pythium* fungus.

Besides, you'll discover that a wet lawn can't be mowed easily. You tear out clumps of wet grass that stick together and rest in heaps on the lawn when you think you've finished the job. Use a catcher on your mower to pick up the wet clumps. Take them to your compost pile. You're going to need a lot of organic matter when you dig your garden in late Feburary.

Adapted from one of George's weekly columns in the *Tucson Citizen*. This one was dated January 8.

3

WINTER GARDENING IS MORE REWARDING WHEN YOU CLOSE THE GAP

The dead winter period can be eliminated. Combine good growing seasons of fall and spring. Use short-season varieties. Warm the soil. Warm the air around plants. Use clear and black plastic.

The "Gap"

If you just read the previous chapter, you know the "Gap" is that short mid-winter season of a few weeks that stops plants from growing.

Tomatoes, bell peppers and bush beans that begin to produce again in the lovely fall weather are usually killed by a November frost. Lettuce, cabbage, cauliflower or broccoli plants have their growth checked or stopped by the cold.

If this cold period is followed by a warm spell in February, resting winter vegetables go to seed. The crop is lost because all we get is open flowers when we want roots or tight leaves.

Most of our winter vegetables are biennials which means they grow flower stalks after their first winter. If the winter is mild—a mere three or four cool weeks between warm periods—short-season varieties tend to bolt.

Slow-maturing, long-season varieties are not affected as much. They need a greater impact, either lower temperatures or a longer period of cold, before their life-cycle is affected. Sandwiched as it is between the good growing periods of fall and spring, the "Gap" really messes things up.

If we can eliminate or reduce the influence of the "Gap," we can turn the two short disjointed periods of fall and spring into one long continuous growing season starting in late August and finishing in early June. That's more than half the year!

Comparing Summer & Winter Gardening

Let's make some comparisons between winter and summer gardening. The cool season is the time when you want to consider gardening because it's a lot easier and, as many gardeners are coming to realize, more productive.

In winter there are fewer insect pests—only grey aphids come to mind. You don't have to be so attentive to plants' water needs. Summer plants such as corn, cantaloupe and tomatoes are water hogs and require a long time to mature. Even the quick-growing zucchini needs a lot of water and suffers badly from the ubiquitous vine borer. Winter weeds are easy to control. Their single root is easily pulled out of moist soil. Creeping summer weeds such as nutgrass and Bermudagrass are difficult nuisances that greatly interfere with gardening.

On the human scale, gardening during the winter months is a much more pleasant outdoor activity. Summertime obligations of watering, pest control and weed pulling become a burden. If we fail to carry them out, the consequences are more severe than during winter. Neglect to water your garden in July and the next day all your labor of past weeks is immediately lost.

It's a lot easier to make the winter sun warm up a cold soil than to try to cool down plants on a summer's day.

We use this knowledge to close the "Gap." This is is how we do it but you can try some ideas of your own after you have read this part of the book. Much of the information will seem like common sense. You have probably done some of the operations already without realizing it.

You lose the crop when an unsuitable variety is planted. It can't take the short seasons and their quick changes. This too-temperamental variety bolted and flowered prematurely.

Plant Cool-Weather Vegetables

First, read through the seed catalogs and find summer vegetables that take cooler weather. For example, tomato varieties developed in Canada called *Coldset* and *Subarctic Maxi* are worth trying in the desert. Desert winters are, after all, more like summer days in Canada as regards temperature. The difference lies in the hours of sunshine. Desert winters have short days, whereas Canadian summers have long days. Your variety choices must therefore be unaffected by day-length considerations. Some varieties of vegetables fall into this category.

From the seed catalog, select winter-

Winter is relatively free of insect pests. However, grey aphids are common and do a lot of damage on cabbage-family plants. Don't let them get started on young cauliflower heads or in broccoli. Aphids are hard to control because they hide right inside the part you harvest.

Make a cookie cutter by sharpening the edges of a tin can. Press down firmly in the plastic and rotate. Young plants are easily set out through the holes. The plastic should lay on the ground for several days to warm the soil down to root depth before you set out any plants.

You can also make holes by marking a cross with a sharp knife and peeling back the plastic for planting. After setting out the plants, allow the plastic to fall back into place.

Black plastic warms the soil. The warmth encourages roots to grow during the winter when normally the soil is too cold for growth. Although the soil is warmed, the darkness under the plastic won't allow weeds to grow and this is a distinct advantage.

vegetable varieties that are quick-maturing. Earlier I mentioned that slow-growing kinds are preferred for late-winter growing. This is still true if you garden in a conventional manner, putting up with that dead-winter little season. This time, we'll surround our plants with warmer temperatures and because we want them to grow, we choose quick-maturing varieties.

Warming the Soil

We are also going to warm the soil. If you place a sheet of plastic on the ground, the sun will warm the soil much more than without it. Clear plastic encourages weeds to grow under it and they grow well too—enough to be a nuisance. Black plastic keeps everything in darkness and there will be no weeds under it.

You are merely warming the soil and your plants are set out through slits in the plastic. A cookie-cutter makes neat holes if you don't like slits. Plants flourish with their roots in warm soil, though their heads are in cool air. Cool air can turn into frost on a winter's night in the desert. Even so, you'll find this use of plastic keeps plants growing. In spite of the cold air, roots don't go dormant provided there's warmth in the root zone.

Anchor the edges of the plastic so the wind doesn't lift the sheet like a sail and tear out all your plants. Desert winds are cold in winter and slow down plants' growth so this method has limited, though still worthwhile, value. It is more effective in an enclosed sheltered garden than out in a farmer's field. Farmers do use the system when they grow high-value cash crops such as strawberries.

Trench Gardening

If you want to start seeds in your garden during the winter, try trench gardening. You must use clear plastic this time because the seedlings need light. You take your chances with weeds.

Use a hoe to scrape a long, flat-bottom ditch about 5-inches deep. When you spread the soil from out of the ditch you'll get a little extra height—or depth.

Sow your seed fairly thickly in the

Clear plastic also lets the sun warm up the soil, but light passing through it allows weeds to grow. These weeds are stimulated by the warm soil too. They push up the plastic and become a nuisance.

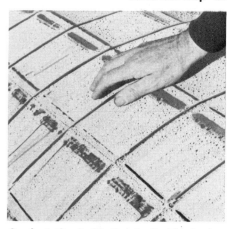

Condensation inside the plastic drips back to the soil. You don't have to be so attentive to watering and the plants grow well in the moist air. Be careful not to let humidity continue too long because there is the danger of fungus. Remember to open the ends of the tunnel once in a while.

An alternative for growing plants during cool weather is to give them room under an arch. This is inexpensive and easy to set up. Plastic and construction mesh are available in hardware stores. Plants can be set out in the soil or in 5-gallon buckets. Summer vegetables grow well in the heat generated in a moist tunnel. Containers raised on bricks absorb heat more readily than soil which exposes only its surface to the sun.

A south-facing wall is a good place to build a cold frame. Start your summer crop or young plants in pots as shown in this picture of corn in February. Keep the lid on. As the weather warms up, raise the lid a few hours each day until your crop can survive without the lid.

Trench gardening is a down-to-earth miniature greenhouse. Under the clear plastic, the soil and air around the seedlings is kept warm and sheltered from cold winter winds. As an added advantage, moisture leaving the soil condenses on the underside of the plastic and drips back to the plants.

bottom of the trench, scattering it rather than making thin rows. You can even mix lettuce, radish, carrot, beet and turnip seed because you are going to eat the young seedlings or transplant them before they begin to crowd one another. The radish seed is encouraging because it germinates more quickly than the others. Whenever you sow slow-germinating seed, such as beets, mix in a little radish seed. Their seedlings act as markers for what is to come later.

Now lay a sheet of clear plastic over the garden area where you made the trenches. Anchor the edges with bricks to stop the plastic being lifted by the wind.

Your seeds are now in a trench-cum-greenhouse. Sun warms both the soil and the air in the trench. Germination will be rapid. Cold winds may blow over the plastic, but they won't affect the protected seedlings after they have emerged. Soil moisture evaporates from the soil and condenses on the undersurface of the plastic to drip back into the garden.

As the seedlings grow taller, "lift" the plastic by placing a number of bricks under the sheet to give a further 4 inches of head room. You don't want warm leaves to hit a cold ceiling.

Trench gardening is a transition stage between merely warming the soil and warming the plants themselves and the air around them. That's what's done in a greeenhouse. But, we don't want the expense of building a greenhouse for just a short period of use. Tunnel gardening is a good compro-

mise: cheap, easy to put up—and take down when you are finished with it—and effective.

If you start your trench garden early in winter, thin out the seedlings and keep those remaining to grow into big plants. You'll find a tunnel the next step.

A Tunnel for Protection

You make a tunnel by bending woven mesh over the garden and covering it with clear plastic. The finished structure looks like a covered wagon.

Begin by making your garden 4-feet wide and as long as you like. Woven mesh comes from a hardware or builder's store in 100-foot-long rolls. Cut it into 10-foot-long pieces. Ten feet makes a nice arch, about 4-feet tall, over a 4-foot-wide bed. This is enough room for plants in containers, too. Cut as many pieces as you need to reach from one end of your garden to the other.

Buy clear plastic 12-feet wide. This enables you to lay 12 inches of plastic on the ground along both sides of the bed. Anchor it with bricks. Buy plastic 10 feet longer than your bed so it hangs down over the ends and lays on the ground. Hold the ends down with bricks.

You have just made a temporary greenhouse over your plants. Of course it has no fancy controls, so you have to watch it closely. Keep it closed most of the winter. The inside, which means both the soil and the air around the plants, warms up in the sunshine. Most of that heat will be retained during the night. The plastic keeps cold

winds off the plants. Insects and rabbits are kept out. Nothing gets in except warm sunshine.

And therein lies some danger. A few extra-warm days might develop too much heat inside. Be aware of this possibility. All you have to do is open one end and let the heat out. If you are in a hurry, open up both ends. Remember to close them *before* the sun goes down. You need an hour of direct sun to warm things up again inside before the cold of night descends.

Further, you won't have to irrigate so much. At night, when things cool down, the moisture condenses on the inside of the plastic and drips down to the soil again. You are recycling water. You save a lot of your labor.

More importantly, you are making your plants grow. You have modified or even eliminated the little season of Dead Winter. You have Closed the Gap.

Close the Gap at the beginning of cold weather in early October by setting up your tunnel over tomatoes, peppers and eggplant. These plants survived the summer's heat and, in the beautiful growing weather of the fall, are now beginning to fruit again. Unprotected, they will be killed by frost in late November. The tunnel will save them from that fate.

Early October is Tunnel Time

In early October, set up a tunnel over bush-bean plants that you sowed in late August. Make a second sowing under a new tunnel. Both will keep the plants growing and producing a harvest in spite of outside falling tem-

Plastic covers draped over a wooden frame keep out the cold wind and pests like early squash-vine-borer moths. Sunshine warms the soil and plants for an early harvest.

Fabrics are available to drape over your plants without a supporting structure. They breathe and no harm is done by their resting on the foliage.

Bag of soil mix wrapped with black plastic absorbs sun's heat. Plants are set into the bag, without even opening it, through holes made with a cookie cutter. Put it in a sunny place and you'll very quickly get a good growth of lettuce or any other out-of-season vegetable.

peratures. The plants will be saved from the first killing frost of November.

In October, cover your newly set out strawberry plants with a tunnel. Keep them covered all winter and they will grow. Your large vigorous plants will start flowering at the same time most of your neighbors are setting out their spring plants. You will get a good harvest—they won't. Yours will fruit during the cooler spring weather; theirs will begin as the summer heats up. Strawberries don't like summer's heat.

A second sowing of winter vegetables can be made in October. Without protection they will grow slowly, but with a trench system to start with and a tunnel system to follow, you will have continuous growth all through the winter.

You may want to make yet another sowing in November or December and again in January and February. A trench and tunnel system will allow it.

Close the Gap at the end of the cool weather or, if you prefer to call it, the beginning of the warm weather. Start warm-season vegetable seed under a trench or set out plants in a tunnel during February.

Include bush beans and corn too. The purpose is to get plants growing early in the season so they reach maturity and flower before the hot weather arrives and destroys their pollen. So often, if you wait until mid-March for the soil to warm up sufficiently for seed to germinate, you lose much of their season. That's when you dismantle your tunnel. The weather becomes too hot, too quickly.

All through the winter you can grow vegetable plants in 5-gallon buckets inside a tunnel.

It pays to Close the Gap.

Don't Rely on Calendar to Pick Best Time for Fertilizing Your Garden

June 1—A lot of calls coming into the Extension Garden Center this past week or two ask the same question: "Is it time to feed my citrus?" There's comfort in doing a lot of things on a calendar basis—like changing the oil in the car or having the carpet cleaned—but these things are governed by how many miles the car travelled and how many people tracked dirt into the house.

A citrus tree doesn't perform to a calendar, though it comes to life at the end of summer and grows furiously in the spring. During the summer heat it rests but recovers in the cooler fall weather and displays a lot of growth. During the winter months it goes dormant. But, the tree does not follow this cycle on the same date every year and it does not wait for a certain date to "do its thing." Calendar gardening almost always misses the opportune time to do things at the proper moment.

It's misleading for authors (and others) to declare categorically that certain things shall be done on certain dates. The Extension Service Garden Guide on Citrus suggests that trees receive fertilizer in February, May and August but that is not to say they must.

First, there may not be a need to apply fertilizer at all! A tree that has dense foliage with large dark-green leaves is well supplied with nutrients. There's no need to feed it.

There are two misconceptions about fertilizers. The first is that a stubborn tree can be made to grow by throwing fertilizer at it. A dormant tree, because of cool soil or hot summer air, won't respond to fertilizer applications in the same way it will during the growth-promoting cooler weather of spring and fall. Fertilizers *aid* growth, but they don't *cause* it.

The second erroneous belief is that fruit can be made sweeter and larger by more and more fertilizer. Not so. Trees that get too much fertilizer produce thick-skinned fruit. This is especially the case with grapefruit. So, if this has happened to your grapefruit, simply don't fertilize for a year.

Trees that get too much fertilizer grow soft, tender wood during their growth spurts. This is not too bad during the spring period but it can be devastating to the fall spurts of growth that are too close to winter's freezes. Soft new wood is frost-tender and has little resistance to fungus diseases and insect attacks.

So what's the rationale for the recommendation of applying fertilizers in February, May and August? The fertilizer you apply in February accommodates the first spring flush of growth that has a high demand on the nutrients stored in the tree from last year. Cold soil won't allow a release of nutrients stored there. The May application replenishes the soil that has, perhaps, lost nutrients to the spring flush of growth. The August application restores the tree for its fall flush of growth and replaces soil nutrients that were washed out by summer downpours and heavy irrigations.

Three times a year is, in itself, a compromise between one big application in the spring—conventional practice with farmers who usually can't afford more than one application—and fertilizing once a month during the growing season, which many horticulturalists regard as the best way to provide nutrients. Plants don't gulp their food in large mouthfuls, they absorb it in small amounts all the time they are growing. A little often is better than a lot infrequently.

If you want a good lawn follow this precept. Fertilize winter ryegrass all through the winter as it grows. Never mind the dormant Bermuda grass; it won't respond during cold weather. Fertilize summer Bermuda grass as it starts to grow in the warming spring weather. Keep up regular applications every two or three weeks during the growing season. Stop when the grass turns brown as temperatures drop.

Make each application a light one and even skip an application or two if the grass is dark green and growing well.

A pound of ammonium sulphate to each hundred square feet every two or three weeks is about right for grass that is well-watered—by rain or by irrigation—and growing strongly during the summer heat.

What is the right way to fertilize? Whether for trees or for grass, always apply dry fertilizer, such as ammonium sulphate, to wet soil. If you scatter it on dry soil there's a danger of a light irrigation merely dissolving it and taking it down a short inch or two, where it will be strong enough to burn plant roots. Pre-watering ensures adequate dilution, even if the post-watering is too light.

Scatter dry fertilizer over the moistened root zone of a tree, rather than piling a big heap of it in one place and trying to spread it by pouring water over it. The spread of the branches to indicate the spread of the tree's roots. That's how much a spread of watering you should give, too.

You read in other gardening books about eastern landscaping that you should calculate the fertilizer requirements of a tree according to its trunk diameter—so many pounds for each caliper inch. This is wrong and misleading advice because it suggests placing a heap of fertilizer at the tree's base. This advice has you place too much chemical over the nearby roots and no nutrients out at their ends, where the activity is. A tree's "well" is seldom big enough to cover the spread of the roots.

Fertilize during or immediately prior to growth spurts. It is pointless to apply fertilizers to dormant plants.

What should you feed your plants? For outdoor landscaping in the desert, make it simple and use ammonium sulphate every time. The complex and plant-specific "foods" are safe to use on *all* plants. You won't hurt your roses by giving them pecan food. You'll simply be spending more money than you need to.

Compare the cost of one pound of any fertilizer against the cost of another. Add up the three figures for the basic nutrients—such as 15-30-15, which comes to 60—and divide it by the cost of one pound of the fertilizer. That gives you the cost of one unit of nutrients. Compare the cost of one unit of nutrient of the other fertilizers you are thinking of buying. Which is the better buy?

Don't forget that the phosphate and potash are not going to give more rapid growth; only nitrogen does this. If your soil has already been provided with ammonium phosphate at the digging time, eliminate that ingredient in the calculations and consider it an unnecessary expense.

Adapted from one of George's weekly columns in the *Tucson Citizen*. This one was dated September 14.

4

SOIL DESCRIPTION: PHYSICAL, BIOLOGICAL, CHEMICAL

Soil is the very beginning of gardening. You need to know what you've got before you make the right changes to improve it. An experienced gardener understands his soil, empathizing and cooperating with it in a friendly way. It's hard to describe his feeling for it, but he helps it along patiently.

New gardeners tend to have a technological point of view. They like to measure things and do calculations. They ask questions like What's in it? Is it enough? How much needs to be added? Are the minimum requirements being met? And so on. Somewhere between these two extremes lies the best way to get the most from our soils.

Let's look at soil from three points of view: the physical, the biological and the chemical. They are so interrelated and interdependent that improvement practices must keep them all in mind. Don't make major changes to soil at one time, you'll upset a balance. Make your adjustments gradually.

Physically

From a physical point of view, we can generalize and say desert soils are sandy. Some soils are almost pure sand and others are mixed with silt or clay in varying amounts. Heavier soils are called *adobe soils* although adobe building blocks are best made of a particular sandy soil, relatively low in clay. This avoids excessive shrinkage as they dry.

Sandy soils are easy to work, whereas silts, and especially clay, are heavy and sticky. Sandy soils can be worked any time, but clay soils are structurally damaged if they are worked while they are wet. Sandy soils drain well and warm up quickly after winter.

Clay soils stay wet longer and are cold. They swell when they become wet and then shrink as they dry out, forming large cracks. Plant roots can be damaged during this alternate swelling and shrinking.

Silt particles are smaller than sand but larger than clay particles. They don't expand when wet or shrink when dry. Their water-holding capabilities are midway between sand and clay.

You can easily find out how much sand, silt and clay your soil has if you put a cupful of soil in a tall quart jar. Add 4 cups of distilled water and a teaspoon of Calgon® to act as a dispersing agent. Shake vigorously for five minutes and then put the jar on a shelf in good light and let everything settle.

After five minutes the sand will be resting on the bottom and in 30 minutes the silt will be lying on top of it. The clay particles may still be in suspension, but after a day they will have settled out to form a third layer. The water will be clear, but brownish-colored, depending on the amount of humus present in the soil. Bits of organic matter will be floating on the top. A lot of organic matter and a pale solution indicates a recent application of manure or compost that hasn't decayed. On the other hand, a dark-brown solution and very little material floating on top suggests the soil is from an old garden.

Measure the three layers and calculate the percentage of each. A good garden soil has roughly 70 percent sand, 15 percent silt and 10 percent clay, with some humus and some organic matter ready to decay into more humus. Carry out this mechanical analysis on some raw desert soil and soil from a good garden. Let them settle in

Clay soil cracks as it dries and feeder roots may be broken in the process. Adding organic matter reduces this tendency.

Shake up some soil in jar of distilled water and let mud settle. Sand falls out first, followed by silt and then clay. Relative thickness of layers tells you soil's composition.

You would hardly call this *soil*. There's so little vegetation to die and accumulate organic matter that only stones show on the surface. Overgrazing by cattle makes things worse. You could call this desert soil *rock bottom*. There's nothing below the surface either.

There's a bit more soil here and gardening is possible, provided you add plenty of organic matter and nutrients. However, it's not deep enough for fruit trees.

On the surface this soil looks presentable, but underlying are layers of hard material. Lower layer is a decided impediment to successful gardening. You might dig and never discover it, but water and drainage will be impeded and even your small plants will suffer. You'll find it if you dig a tree-planting hole 5-feet deep.

Four photos by Chris Cochran, Soil Scientist, Soil Conservation Service, Tucson.

a jar and look at the differences.

Sandy soils drain too rapidly; clay soils drain too slowly. You can improve a sandy soil by thoroughly mixing in a little clay. A clay soil can be improved by mixing a little sand into it. Both kinds of soil are improved by regularly adding organic matter.

Organic matter clusters the fine clay particles into aggregate lumps, leaving spaces for air, water and new roots. In sandy soils the effect is much the same, only the particles are cemented together by organic matter to form larger air spaces between them. The soil has been "opened up." Drainage is always good in a sandy soil and this

allows harmful chemicals to be washed out of range of the roots. Too good drainage means a soil dries out quickly and requires more frequent waterings. Although we want harmful salts to be washed out, we like to retain those chemicals that are plant nutrients. We can't have it both ways, but we can create the happy medium by digging in organic matter. In itself, organic matter is like a sponge—it absorbs moisture and holds it. Further, it is chemically attractive to plant nutrients. When we apply fertilizers to a soil, humus formed from organic matter "grabs" nutrients from the soil solution and saves them from being

leached out of the root zone.

Soils become fertile because any nutrients which are added to them are not lost in the drainage water. Organic matter breaks down into humus. Humus has colloidal properties and colloids act as magnets to attract and hold nutrients. A colloid is a substance dispersed in a surrounding medium. Clay particles contain colloids too and that's why clay soils are fertile.

Over hundreds of years our sandy desert soils have been subjected to intermittent rainy periods. These washed weak solutions of calcium carbonate, sulphate and chloride down through the soil. As the soil dried out, thin, but

Another shallow soil with solid caliche under it. You may be persuaded to garden in containers if your house is built over such soil. Raised beds won't be enough to give vegetable plants the drainage they need.

solid, layers began to form.

As time passed, the layers accumulated more deposits until a concrete-like barrier prevented further water passage. Now there was only evaporation and this accelerated solids collection on the layers. A thousand years later, we gardeners meet these solid layers when we dig planting holes for trees. We call it *caliche*. Sometimes it's quite close to the surface. Until we strike it, there's no knowing where it lies or how thick it is.

It pays to poke all over your yard with a 3-foot metal probe to see if you have caliche. First, irrigate to soften the soil and allow the probe to go though it easily. When it hits rock bottom, that's where the caliche is. The probe won't tell you the thickness—you'll find that out when you dig.

Rocks of varying sizes are found in some foothills yards. These are a nuisance when digging but they don't affect drainage very much. Roots grow around rocks so there's really no need to remove them, but many gardeners feel good about this hard work. After all there is satisfaction in replacing a useless boulder with a good soil mix and getting your trees off to a good start.

Soil texture, its sandiness or clay content, might change as you dig down. Close to a wash or river you may meet several layers of different texture.They were deposited as the river brought down different materials each flood time. Layers are bad because they hold water and nutrients in varying degrees.

Biologically

Biologically, our desert soils are poor in organic matter, either as dead-leaf litter or as live earthworms and beneficial microorganisms. The dryness, bright sunshine and high temperatures simply don't encourage accumulation of organic matter or the existence of organisms. You have to go to cool, damp, forests to see those sorts of things. It's only after a few years of irrigated gardening, which includes the addition of manures and compost, that earthworms and useful fungi and bacteria appear. There's a good side to this sterility, however. A garden soil generally starts by being free of harmful pests and diseases—no snails, no nematodes, no Fusarium wilt and no citrus foot rot. We add useful organisms to the soil when we dig in animal manures and composted materials. The soil benefits and so do the plants we set out in it.

Fir bark and forest products contribute life too, often in the shape of fancy little mushrooms that appear after a good watering.

Peat moss is a sterile material, both chemically and biologically. It is valuable only in improving the texture of our soils. Its sterility is particularly useful when we make up a soil mix for sowing seeds in boxes. We want to start with a clean, soil mix. Using soil

A 3-foot-long metal rod is useful when measuring soil depth. This soil probe has a round handle on top.

Answer to caliche near the soil surface—container gardening.

from an old garden may introduce Fusarium or Verticillium organisms.

Redwood soil amendment, besides being sterile, appears to contain growth inhibitors and is regarded by many gardeners as a poor material to include in our soils. If it is used in a soil mix for seed growing, germination is usually poor. This is not really surprising. Ranchers use redwood fence posts and people build houses with redwood lumber because the material is not attacked by termites or rot.

Microorganisms liven up a soil. They produce chemicals that actually enhance plant growth, suppress diseases and provide nutrients for larger soil organisms such as earthworms, pillbugs and grubs. A soil with life in it is a *productive* soil.

Some people think they can create a garden soil simply by throwing earthworms onto a desert soil. This doesn't work because a desert soil has nothing in it for earthworms. They starve to death. But as soon as a soil has some organic matter, it becomes attractive to earthworms and, though not so welcome, grubworms. They come all on their own—it's hard to say how. They tell you by their presence that your soil is now capable of producing good yields.

After you have built up your soil's organic population, don't spoil it by indiscriminate use of insecticides. Beetle grubs are large animals and require a lot of poison to kill them. In the process, you will overkill the earthworms and other beneficial life in the soil.

Pick out the grubs, throw them on the compost pile and let them chew on the big pieces for you.

Chemically

Chemically, our soils are low in plant nutrients, especially nitrogen and phosphorus. They contain an excess of calcium and sometimes sodium. Calcium, although a plant food, prevents the uptake of iron, zinc and other micronutrients when there is too much of it. Sodium is a plant poison. Both calcium and sodium are alkalies, high on the pH scale. They make your soil very basic.

Gardening books always mention the pH Scale, sometimes dwelling on it too long. The scale starts at 1, which is acid, and goes up to 14 which is alkaline. The midpoint of 7 is neutral and distilled water is a good example of something neutral. Everything else is either acid or alkaline to some degree. Some gardening books list every vegetable with its preference for a particular soil pH. There are extreme plants, such as azaleas, camellias and gardenias that must have an acid soil, but our vegetables and fruit trees are remarkably tolerant of the minor nuances of soil pH. Don't fret about soil pH. However, as a gardener, it's your job to make the soil as hospitable as possible. So you'll have to keep pH in mind. See illustration of pH/nutrient uptake on the next page.

You can get a rough idea of your soil's acid/alkali condition very quickly. Shake up a little soil in a test-tube. Use a stopper, not your salty

thumb, and distilled water, not from the faucet. Let the mud settle and then place a pH paper in the clear liquid. See what color the paper turns and match it against the color chart provided with the paper. If you can't get these pH papers at a nursery, look for them in swimming-pool-supply stores. You will find pH papers in the garden-accessories section of many seed catalogs, next to the soil-testing kits.

It would be surprising if you find an acid soil in the desert. Our soils are usually alkaline from an excess of calcium--or saline due to the presence of sodium. Sometimes both are present and if your test paper shows a very high figure, 8.5 and above, you might want to take a sample of your garden soil for analysis. Yes—even some soils should go into analysis. You can avoid this expense, however, by using a soil-test kit. These are available at some nurseries and through garden catalogs. The kits rely on color matchings. You add a chemical, the soil solution turns a color and you match it against a chart. Interpretations become difficult when you have to decide whether a particular color is greenish-blue or bluish-green. The difference might be a point of pH—not a pint of porter, as an Irish gardener might say. If you are colorblind, the differences are hard to detect and the recommendations become even more inaccurate.

Laboratory Analysis

A laboratory analysis sends you a sheet of figures to interpret. Some laboratories do the interpretation for you. The figures imply accuracy but it's better to use them just as a guide.

Study the whole sheet for its recommendations and look for anything out of average, particularly the calcium and sodium figures. There are lots of weaknesses to mathematical gardening and as far as soil analysis is concerned, the main weakness lies in the way you gathered the sample. It's pointless spending a lot of money on an analysis if you merely took a trowelful of soil from the exact center of your garden.

Take six samples from each 50 square feet of garden. Take three from the surface 4 inches and three from 14 inches down. Thoroughly mix the surface samples and select a half pound from the mix. Do the same for the lower-level samples. Samples from two levels will tell you if salts are moving up, or fertility is moving down. Remember that a soil analysis only tells you what chemicals are present in the soil. It doesn't tell you whether your plants can use them. However, a good chemist can give you some indication of that.

Unless you tell him how you garden, he can't tell you if poor drainage, and perhaps overwatering, is responsible for poor results. Perhaps you are using wrong varieties, or planting at the wrong time, or you have nematodes or soil-borne diseases. The chemist doesn't know. You'll have to help him. Nor can he discover whether residues of weed-killing chemicals are stunting your plants unless he carries out a specific test for their presence in your soil. If he is an alert gardener himself and interested in your soil beyond its chemical content, it's possible he will see weed seeds in the sample.

And, There's The Plant Pathologist

Another soil sampling is sometimes necessary. If you are satisfied about the chemical aspects but plants still aren't doing well, soil-borne diseases and nematodes may be attacking your plants. You'll want to know. Take soil samples together with sick-looking plants in a fresh condition to another wizard. This time it's the plant pathologist and he will look for disease organisms through his microscope. Don't just leave the samples on his doorstep but give him some information about what is happening. He will be in a better position to help if you give him some clues. He wants to see a complete plant, not just a little piece of it.

Larger soil organisms, earthworms, pillbugs and even beetle grubs, are useful in eating organic matter and reducing it to smaller pieces for smaller organisms to enjoy. Organic matter is spread through the soil as the animals move through it and excrete the digested material. Here, some old grass stalks have been covered with soil by termites. Photo by Chris Cochran.

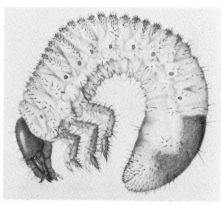

Beetle grubs in soil are useful. They break down large pieces of organic matter into smaller pieces. Of course, they eat plant roots, too.

Width of each bar is directly proportionate to that nutrient's availability. Potassium, for example, becomes decreasingly available at pH levels below 6.0. Chart's wide bands illustrate that the uptake of potassium, sulphur, calcium and magnesium is little affected by changes in pH for two points on either side of neutral (7). Nitrogen and phosphorus uptake is somewhat reduced as pH increases, whereas the uptake of iron, manganese, copper and zinc is decidedly affected as the pH rises. Between pH 6.0 and 6.5, most plant nutrients are in their most-available state. So, deficiency problems may actually be soil-pH problems. *Chart courtesy of William Knoop, Texas A & M University Extension Center at Dallas*.

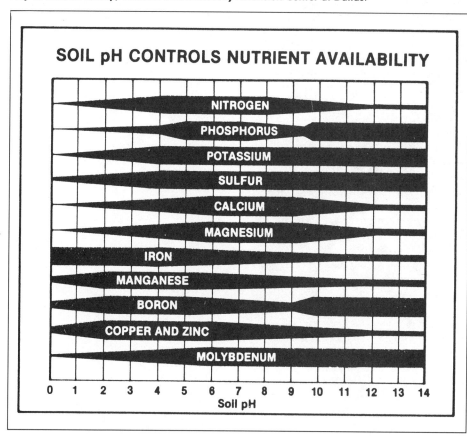

Don't dig in undecayed organic matter. This layer of corn stalk makes digging difficult and will take several weeks to rot down. Remove such remains from summer gardening and add them to the compost pile.

With heavy clay soil, a digging fork is better than a spade. Work is easier and you avoid smearing the wet soil. Smeared clay dries hard like a brick.

After a few years, your garden's topsoil will be improved by organic matter. It looks darker. The subsoil is redder because it is still lacking in organic matter. Each time you dig, go an inch or so deeper and mix in more organic matter.

Animal manure does more than recycle nutrients already in fields animals graze. When they are fed imported, concentrated food, their manure is enriched by peanuts. linseed, cotton seed and grains.

Sieve is useful to separate finely decomposed material. Use this as an ingredient when you make soild mixes for seedling and container plants. Material that didn't pass through the sieve may be used for covering the soil during hot summer months. Or it can be returned to the pile for further bacterial action.

5

THE IMPORTANCE OF CALICHE

There ought to be a law against caliche. It's death to our deeper-rooted plants and requires digging a hole 5-feet square and 5-feet deep whenever we want to plant a tree.

Where is it? It's almost everywhere and you don't know until you start to dig. In any event, it's under the soil. It may be hardly noticeable, a mere 1/4-inch layer felt as a slight resistance when you dig your vegetable garden. On the other hand, it may be a foot thick or even a yard thick. You won't know until you work your way through it. You may find it close to the surface or below 4 feet of good soil.

Check Before You Buy

If you are a keen gardener, it's a good idea to find out whether your soil is hiding caliche. Better not buy that dream house if caliche is present in the empty lot you want to call your yard. When you go house hunting take along your 3-foot soil probe and push it into the soil, making note of what you are buying. Caliche is a lot of hard work, expense and frustration.

What is caliche?

It's calcium carbonate, or chalk, mixed with various amounts of other chemicals, including iron that gives it a pinkish color. It's hard—very hard.

Why do we have caliche? Countless years of rain and floods carried chemicals down through the soil. There wasn't enough rain to wash them away completely. Nor was there a drainage system of streams and rivers to take them away to the ocean. They just rested where they lay. Now, you are finding them.

You find them at different depths because, over the years, the upper layers of some soils have been removed by wind and water. You find caliche in the foothills, on gentle slopes and

Crowbar, pickax and a lot of hard work are needed to remove caliche. Long crowbar is commonly called a *caliche bar*. Sometimes a jackhammer has to be used. Author George Brookbank and daughter Lesley Cordier are prepared to go to work on the tough stuff.

down in the valleys. It's generally in layers and sometimes you'll see the flood lines in different colors. But you also find it in lumps and nodules mixed with soil. Fortunately, it's not everywhere. There are acres of good soil in the desert.

What do you have to do about caliche?

To be brief—remove it. You have to dig it out. There aren't any chemicals that will make it go away— advertisements notwithstanding.

Where you have caliche and you want a vegetable garden or a flowerbed, give those plants at least 3 feet of root room. If you don't want to dig that far down, you may get away with digging 2 feet and then building up another foot of soil in a raised bed. But, you are hiding the dirt under the rug, not cleaning the house.

If you want to plant a tree, the work becomes even more formidable. You have to dig 5-feet down, or farther.

Although the standard hole is 5-feet square and 5-feet deep, that's not the end of the story!

If there's still caliche at the bottom of the hole, don't stop digging. You can lessen the work involved, if you dig in the center of the hole and make a chimney about a foot in diameter to take you through the concrete-like material. See illustration below.

When you think you have done an

You don't know where caliche is until you start to dig. Here a construction trench shows how thick the layer is. You have to dig through caliche to determine its thickness.

Thin soil overlaying several feet of solid caliche limits native vegetation to slow growth. Soil is only a foot deep. Gardening and especially fruit-tree planting, call for special measures in soil preparation to ensure success.

Your soil probe won't go through this solid layer of caliche, but a thin layer like this can be broken through and removed. It takes a long time to form caliche. Rainfall carried salts in solution to the same depth where it dried out and solidified. This sample was 3 feet under the surface. It shows the layers of different salts carried down by many years of rainfall.

When caliche layers are near the soil surface, tree roots cannot grow downward. If water rests on the caliche, there is a danger of the roots rotting.

adequate job, carry out a test. Half-fill the hole with water and go take a rest. Even sleep on it. When you come and look again there should be no water in the hole. It should have drained away. If water is still there, you have more digging to do. The water will have softened the caliche somewhat, and the work will be easier, but it has to be done.

Tools
The tools you need are a pickax and crowbar. There are chemicals advertised as being caliche-busters or dissolvers but they don't do much for you. It's the water in the bottle that's effective. When you come to caliche, chip away and then put 6 inches of water in the hole. Go and do something else for an hour or two. When you come back, you'll be able to work on the softer stuff for a little while. Take it easy. Don't try to get it all done in a day. If you need to dig several holes, get someone else to do the work or hire a man with a backhoe or a jackhammer.

Why go to all this trouble?
You must provide room for roots to grow. If they hit caliche a year or two after being planted, they will go no farther. You need unrestricted root room if you want a strong tree. Why? Trees planted over caliche have been blown right out of the ground in a storm several years later.

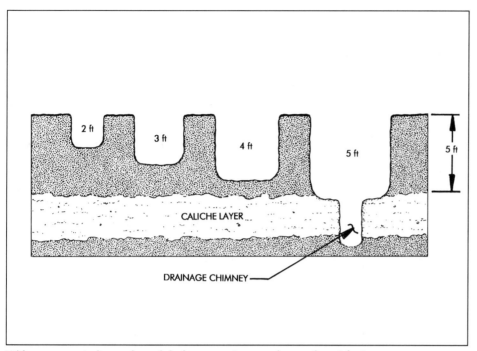

With proper watering and good drainage, roots grow deeper than 5 feet.

A 2-foot hole is all right for shrubs and bushes, but a 3-foot hole would be better.

A 4-foot hole is only 12 inches from the impenetrable caliche layer. Tree roots can't grow through it and water won't drain through it, either.

If you meet caliche at the bottom of a 5-foot-deep hole, you don't know how thick it is. But you must get through it. Otherwise your tree is sitting in a container. In the floor of the hole dig a small drainage chimney, rather than removing the whole floor. Roots will grow through this chimney and water will drain throught it.

Rock-like caliche must be removed if you want a tree to grow successfully. Dig down to 5 feet to make sure the roots can grow unhindered. Also make sure the water drains away from the bottom of the hole so it will take harmful salts with it.

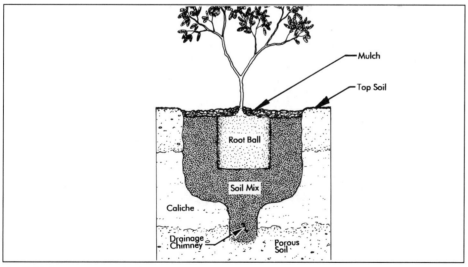

If caliche layers are too thick, you can save yourself some digging by excavating a central chimney in the center of the hole. This ensures good drainage.

Even more important, you must establish good drainage when you grow plants. If water collects at an impermeable layer in the soil, the roots in that area will be drowned. Don't confuse this death with Texas root rot, though in both instances the roots will be rotted. This time the rot will have been caused by a lack of oxygen.

Water that doesn't drain, doesn't carry salts from the root zone. It doesn't matter whether they are good salts, such as fertilizers, or harmful salts. Too much of them will stop your tree from growing and will eventually kill it.

Dig a big hole. Get through the caliche.

Screened garden room 12 X 20 X 8 feet brought peace of mind for this desert gardener. Now gardener gets to eat the produce instead of feeding local freeloaders of the Catalina Mountain foothills at the north edge of Tucson. Screened-out critters include pack rats, squirrels, mice, skunks, coatimundi, javelina, rabbits, ringtail cats, foxes, coyotes and birds. Grapes are grown on wires suspended from angle brackets along south edge of enclosure. Grapevine shade is augmented with shade cloth on top of room during hottest months.

The entire enclosure is covered with plastic during the winter months to give strawberries a head start. The big problem is keeping the interior temperature from getting too warm on sunny days! Plastic has to be removed from one end to keep the temperature below 100F.

6

SOIL IMPROVEMENT

You have a good idea of the potential of your soil because you carefully read Chapter 4 and are weighing the pros and cons of having a soil analysis made. If you decide to get one, be sure to take a representative sample to the laboratory. Don't just take a shovelful from some corner where there might have been a compost pile in days gone by.

Before You Start Digging Find Out What You Have

You've also read the previous chapter on caliche and you may be a little frightened by the prospect of digging out a lot of rocky material. Take heart and hope for the best. Not everyone is troubled by this nuisance. Nevertheless, get out your nice new soil probe and work systematically through the area you have set aside for your future garden.

Wet the ground first so the probe slides easily through the soil. Make a map using squared paper. Record how deep the soil is every 3 or 4 feet. If the soil probe goes down only 2 feet or less, you must remove the caliche. You don't want it to hold up water. If it's a thin layer, you may be able to smash a crowbar down and shatter it. If it's thicker than an inch, there's work ahead. You'll have to dig out the soil, physically remove the material and put the soil back again. If you are planting trees, the depth becomes 5 feet, not 2 feet.

In any event, deep digging is always good. There's a double benefit from chasing caliche.

There Are Good Alternatives to Gardening in Poor Soil

If the caliche layer is too thick to remove, you may be successful by gardening in raised beds. This means adding another 18 inches of good soil

Container gardening is sometimes the only answer to soil that is too poor or too shallow.

above the original soil level. A raised bed elevates the garden but it doesn't remove caliche below. This system works if the caliche has been smashed so water can drain through the cracks. Vegetable-plant roots need at least 2 feet of soil.

However, it's not just additional root room you are providing. Drainage of surplus water and removal of salts is your main concern. You need a total of 3 feet to ensure this.

A last resort is to garden in containers such as whiskey barrels.

You are more likely to find caliche in sandy soils, but clay soils have their own problems. They have to be handled with great care.

Handle Clay Soils Carefully

The structure of a clay soil is easily damaged. Instead of it being light and airy to allow water to drain and roots to grow in the air spaces, it quickly becomes compact and "tight." Clay soils call for careful handling to get the fine tilth necessary for small seeds to germinate.

This kind of soil is easily damaged if

it is worked while wet. The damage can last for many years! Don't even walk on it. It is very plastic and easily forms clods that are extremely hard when dry. Use a fork rather than a spade to knock large clumps into smaller pieces. A spade smears wet clay particles together and they stay solid chunks as they dry out. Leave the small lumps of soil to dry in the sun and then spray them down. Rake the wet lumps and leave them again until they break down into egg-size pieces. It's a slow process—be patient. Now you are ready to add organic matter and dig it in.

Everyone's Basic Formula for Soil Improvement

There's a standard recipe of ingredients for improving desert soils. For gardens, cover the ground with 2 to 3 inches of steer manure. Then spread 3 pounds of ammonium phosphate and 5 pounds of soil sulphur for every 100 square feet. Dig your soil 12 inches deep, mixing the materials very thoroughly.

In the case of tree-planting holes, you add the same materials at roughly the same proportions. This is how you work out the amounts. Calculate the cubic capacity of the hole you have dug. Divide by 5 to get the cubic feet of steer manure. Divide by 16 to get the pounds of ammonium phosphate, and by 4 to get the pounds of soil sulphur. Mix everything thoroughly and fill the hole again. Don't make layers.

Substitutions Are Allowed

Instead of steer manure or as partial substitution, you can use compost, peat moss, forest mulches, or other animal manures. Don't use chicken manure because it is stronger and likely to burn roots.

When planting a tree, it's a once-

A soil sampler brings up soil from various depths for your approval. Don't expect wonders in soil improvement to occur in a year or two. It's a long-term process.

A good crumb structure is the result of several years' soil improvement. The particles hold together in crumbs. Air spaces between the crumbs allow roots to breathe and water to drain away, carrying salts with it.

Dark garden soil is derived from desert soil by repeatedly digging in organic matter. Each time you dig your garden, go an inch deeper and eventually you will have a good deep soil. Don't try to get 12-inch-deep soil the first time you dig. Soil-building is a gradual process.

only opportunity, but with a garden you should repeat the operation each time the seasons change. You need to do this once in the spring and once in the fall for two or three years before you can say you have changed the desert into a garden.

Although they follow recommendations, beginning gardeners often become disappointed too quickly. They don't get bountiful yields the first time around and give up when success is just around the corner. Soil improve-ment is a gradual process that takes time.

Use This Shortcut to Success With New Gardens

If you are impatient and the first year's growth doesn't look exciting, there is a shortcut. When you irrigate your plants, use a hose proportioner at the faucet to draw nutrients out of a jug. Add a cupful of high-nitrogen house-plant food, such as MiracleGro®, to a gallon of water and insert the suction tube of the proportioner into it. You will be applying a tablespoon of liquid nutrients with each gallon of irrigation water. That's another universal recipe for fertilizing growing plants.

Progressively Increase Digging Depth

Every time you dig the soil, which should be at the end of each season, go an inch deeper into brighter color-ed subsoil. A deep soil absorbs more water, roots grow longer and you get stronger plants. If you start with a deep digging, you will bring up poor material that requires a large amount of manure to counterbalance the sterile soil. This will need a longer time to mellow and the manure will attract grubworms. Pick these out as you dig. Be patient.

Let the Manure Mellow for a While

The steer manure you put in the soil won't be strong enough to delay you very much. Wait a week before setting out plants and two to three weeks if you are going to sow small seeds. Keep the soil moist while you wait.

Flat Beds are Desert Favorites

Before you start planting, you have to shape the soil into flat beds. Make them about 4-feet wide to let you reach to the center without walking on the soil, especially if it's clay. The bed can be as long as you like. Make a lip 2-inches high around the edges. This

For a tree-planting hole you'll need 16 bags of manure, 8 pounds of ammonium phosphate and 30 pounds of sulphur. A $50 hole for a $5 tree.

enables you to flood the bed with an inch of water which is the best way to irrigate deeply and wash down salts.

In the Desert, Forget Hills & Ridges

You may be used to making hills or ridges for planting and sometimes you will hear advice to do the same in the desert. However, in the desert we want to keep a low profile as it were and reduce the evaporative surface of our gardens. Ridges may be a farmer's necessity—it's how he gets water to the ends of his fields—but home gardeners don't have to work in this way. If you insist on planting on ridges, you'll have to use a lot of water in the furrow to wet the seeds on top of the ridges. Further, the ridge tops will dry out first and gather salt from the rest of your garden. You'll soon see a salt line on them nearest your plants' roots. Ridges and hills are advisable in rainy country to give drainage that prevents seeds from rotting in wet soil. We don't have that problem in the desert.

Raised Beds are All Right

After a few years of adding bulky organic matter, you'll find you have a raised bed and a lowered walkway. To keep things tidy, you can surround your beds with railroad ties, or redwood two-by-sixes, or concrete blocks. Some gardening magazines stress the value of starting a garden with raised beds. Such articles are written largely for the rainy parts of the country where soils need to be drained. If you like the idea of raised beds, go ahead and make them to begin with, but they are not all that necessary. In the course of time, you'll have them anyway.

Mulches Have Drawbacks in the Desert

Here's another inappropriate idea from rainy places. Surround your plants with thick layers of mulch that naturally disintegrate with time and improve soil from the top down. It's a good idea and it works "back there," but in the desert it brings problems.

A heavy organic mulch acts as blotting paper when we irrigate. It draws and holds salts that are in the soil. The mulch itself has to be kept moist for bacteria to consume it and this means we have to sprinkle from above instead of soaking the soil down below.

Large clumps like these take several days to dry out before they crumble into smaller pieces.

Perhaps the greatest drawback to heavy mulching in the desert is its effectiveness. Certainly it shades the soil and keeps it cool in summer. Earthworms like to be there but so do the bad guys—pillbugs, grubworms, cutworms, cockroaches, crickets and millipedes. They prefer it to being out in the scorching sun.

Green Manures Have Doubtful Value

There's yet another idea, enthusiastically mentioned in garden magazines for the rainy states. Green manuring is praised as an operation to improve soil. It is a practice based on farming systems that used crop rotations. The land went into pasture for a number of years, livestock grazed and manured the fields and, when they were ploughed, the plants, roots and manure all went into the soil. Seed mixtures of grasses and clovers were used because different plants had varying ability to send roots down deep and extract nutrients from the soil. It's a nice system, though its success depended somewhat on feeding the animals with imported concentrates.

Some farmers, without the animal component—as we say these days— tried to keep the traditional system going just on bulky crops which were ploughed into the soil instead of being sold off the farm. If these were legumes, there was an increase in soil fertility because of their nitrogen-fixing roots. Otherwise the advantage lay in providing organic matter that improved soil structure and water-holding capacity, but not fertility itself.

A raised bed elevates the garden, but doesn't remove caliche below. This system works if the caliche has been smashed so water can drain through the cracks. Vegetable plant roots need at least 2 feet of soil.

With heavy clay soils, a digging fork is a better tool than a spade. Work is easier and you avoid smearing a wet soil. Smeared clay dries hard like a brick.

For a small garden measuring 50 square feet, you'll need 4 bags of steer manure, 2 pounds of ammonium phosphate and 3 pounds of soil sulphur. Spread the materials on the surface and then do your digging. Mix them thoroughly into the soil as you dig.

A hose attachment on the faucet siphons out nutrients from the gallon jug. You apply fertilizer to the soil as you irrigate.

Our sandy desert soils certainly need organic matter, but anyone who grows a green manure crop without the addition of fertilizers is merely recycling nutrients in the soil—and we know they are scarce. Moreover, such gardening requires a year's watering and caring with no harvest in sight. Most of us gardeners don't have enough extra ground for this operation or the money to pay for the necessary water.

Bypass Green Manuring With a Shortcut

It's more expedient to buy someone else's green manure, now called *brown steer manure*, and add ammonium phosphate and sulphur. You get going right away. However, don't discount the usefulness of crop residues. Put them together with weeds and grass clippings in the compost pile. If they are fibrous, add ammonium phosphate to hasten decay. Import farmers' residues—your kitchen scraps—into the compost pile, too. Farmers use a lot of fertilizer to grow their crops and it's a shame to waste it.

There's More to a Plant Than Meets the Eye

It's usually the top growth of plants that we eat. We leave a lot of vegetable material in the ground as roots when we harvest plants. Onions are a wonderful crop for soil improvement because they grow a massive root system and we fertilize the crop quite heavily. Although we eat the harvest, there's a residue of fertilizer treatment in the fibrous roots that are left in the soil. This increases fertility. There's also the value of organic material that improves soil structure and water-holding capacity.

You Must Bring in Things to Improve Desert Soils

Recycle as much as you can, but remember, you are starting with a small asset. You need an injection of working capital if you are to get a big return. This investment, necessarily from outside sources, is called *steer manure,* or *compost* and *ammonium phosphate.* To make the investment work, it's helpful to include soil sulphur. It makes the soil less basic which, in turn, releases nutrients from association with calcium so the plants can use them.

7

ORGANIC MATTER

Not many desert gardeners are lucky enough to have a naturally rich soil. Those who come from the Midwest or from garden states like New Jersey are both surprised and disgusted when they first dig into the ground. They soon come to the conclusion that Mother Nature was busy elsewhere when this desert country was put together.

Even those who don't garden realize our soils are sandy and light-colored. Desert soils lack humus—that material which gives a rich-looking dark color to garden soils. Humus comes from organic matter.

Where It Comes From
Organic matter comes from things living or once-living. Life in the desert is hard for man and beast—and for plants too. There's not a lot of life in the desert and not much humus either.

Sparse desert vegetation produces little leaf fall, broken branches or tree stumps. It's quickly consumed by hungry animals—and there aren't a lot of these. Short-lived annuals, the wildflowers and the weeds, and the animals, from termites up to deer, die with the dryness.

How It's Lost or
Why It Doesn't Accumulate
Everything dries out and blows away. There's no accumulation of organic matter, as there is in damp, shady forests or high-rainfall areas. There's no humus development. If you find any good soil it's almost certainly the result of continued efforts by a gardener. His results don't last long, either. Sunshine, high temperatures and dryness remorselessly burn up organic matter.

Sparse desert vegetation such as this accumulates little organic matter. Leaves not eaten by animals and insects blow away. If they stay on the ground they are consumed by the hot sunshine and dry atmosphere. Soil here is only about 18-inches deep.

Animal manure does more than recycle the nutrients already in the fields which the animals graze. When they are fed imported, concentrated food, their manure is enriched by peanuts, linseed, soybean, cotton seed and grains.

You can buy any number of soil amendments, mulches, potting soil, forest products, peat moss, steer manure and soil mixes at garden stores. The very profusion of names is confusing—and so are the insides of the bags. Don't buy anything that contains sand or other fillers.

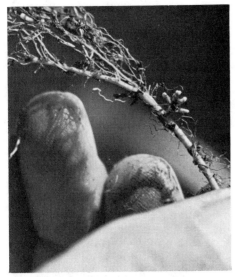

All legumes develop nodules on their roots. They are the result of an invasion by good soil organisms that use the soil air to make nitrogen compounds the plants can absorb. When the roots die or are dug under, the soil is enriched. Legumes make the best green manure because of this.

What It Does

Organic matter in the soil makes for a more productive garden for a number of reasons. The first is that it holds moisture in much the same way a sponge absorbs and holds water. Secondly, humus resulting from organic decay absorbs and holds plant nutrients. As plants' rootlets come into contact with a molecule of humus, an exchange takes place. It's as if the rootlets "breathe out" hydrogen and "breathe in" one or more of the soil's 13 plant nutrients.

This exchange capacity of the soil is a measure of its strength. A sandy soil doesn't hold nutrients. The fertilizers you apply to it are easily washed out. On the other hand, a soil high in organic matter absorbs and holds any fertilizer you apply, and releases it to plants' roots over a period of time.

Soils lacking organic matter and humus are usually light-colored, whereas those with organic matter are darker. However, some black soils are without humus and owe their color to iron, long-term moisture and lack of oxygen.

A third attribute of organic matter is that it feeds soil organisms. The more obvious creatures a gardeners sees after his soil has reached a certain stage of improvement are earthworms, snails and beetle grubs. They simply appear all on their own. The first is a good, friendly animal. The other two

are generally regarded as pests. But all are a good sign that your soil is becoming more productive.

The organisms we don't easily see include soil mites, springtails, protozoa, nematodes, bacteria, fungi, ants, termites, beetles and flies. It is said that if all were gathered from an acre, they would weigh as much as three horses. Organic matter is the food of these organisms and they break it down into chemicals that become available to plants' roots.

Although organic matter feeds the micro-organisms, it has very little value as a source of nutrients for our plants. It does provide some—not much— and its gardening value lies in its soil-building properties. Don't rely on organic matter by itself to give you big yields.

Because there's only a little organic matter in desert soil to start with, and hardly any accumulating, a gardener needs to add it. He has a wide choice of materials. Let's look at some of them.

How to Choose a Manure

Steer Manure — Steer manure is the cheapest and, some gardeners say, the best. They like its bacterial content that results from the bovine four-stomach digestive system. Bacteria liven up a soil. Some particles of manure are the right size for immediate breakdown, yet others are big enough to last a while. Some plant nutrients are present, though in small amounts, depending on what the animal has been eating. For example, dairy cows are better fed than steers in holding pens.

Bad stories once circulated about steer manure and with some truth. Many years ago, when big-scale cattle feeding was profitable, feed was placed before large numbers of animals in a pen and they were left to help themselves. Each animal's food intake was automatically regulated by mixing in 15 percent rock salt. An animal can ingest only so much salt each day. In those days, manure did contain salt. Gardeners who didn't know the feed-yard practice unwittingly added it to their soil. This management trick was all in the interest of stopping steers from making pigs of themselves.

Nowadays, most steer manure is really cow manure from dairies.

If you are concerned about salt in manure, try this test. Shake up a cupful of manure in a quart jar of distilled

In gardens and around our houses there is a bountiful annual supply of organic matter. Leaves from deciduous trees should be saved because they make excellent compost.

Make compost above the ground in a bin. This allows air to reach the bacteria that work for you. Keep the material moist by frequent watering and turning. Sprinkle manure in the pile to help it keep working.

A sieve is useful to separate the finely decomposed material. Use this as an ingredient when you make soil mixes for seedlings and container plants. Material that did not pass through the sieve may be used for covering the soil during hot summer months. Or return it to the pile for further bacterial action.

water. Let it settle, then dip a pH test paper into the solution. If the new color indicates a pH much higher than 7, there is salt in the manure.

Horse Manure—There's a lot of horse manure around, often for free. Because horses usually don't get the best feed, their manure is poorer quality than bovine manure. When father cuts back on expenses, Susie's horse gets poor-quality hay made from Bermudagrass rather than good-quality alfalfa hay. Horses have a different digestive system, one which doesn't destroy weed seeds so well. The seeds come out with the manure and to many gardeners, Bermudagrass in a garden is worse than salt in the soil. But, if you have friends who are lavishing the best-quality hay on their Arabians or thorobred horses, that manure will be worth using.

Bovine Manure—Bovines include sheep and goats. They give good manure—as do rabbits and guinea-pigs.

Pet Manure—Dogs and cats are fed rich food so their manure is rich. Medical authorities recommend you don't use these pet manures because animal diseases can be transmitted to man through their manure.

Chicken Manure—Chickens get good rations, so their manure is rich. It's so concentrated that you should use only a little at a time, otherwise you burn plant roots. Potassium permanganate is added to chickens' drinking water to keep it clean and pure, so

their manure contains some potash and manganese, both plant nutrients. Chickens—being silly creatures—are fed tranquilizers and sedatives. There are a lot of minor plant-food elements, such as manganese, iron, copper and magnesium in chicken manure. But it's strong stuff. Be careful.

The chemicals in chicken manure make it more of a fertilizer than a soil amendment. It doesn't last long in the soil because it's so well ground down by the stones in the chicken's gizzard.

How To Choose a Soil Amendment

Peat Moss—Peat moss is a nurseryman's favorite. It's clean and doesn't smell. The common kind is brown and comes from Canada but there's a better material, black and further decayed, from Michigan.

Canadian peat moss is dry and floats on water until it has soaked up some moisture. So it's a good idea to dampen it down a day or two before you start using it. It sometimes stays in chunks so you have to rub it through a sieve to get an even product, especially if you need it to make a mix for sowing seeds.

Peat moss is sterile, both chemically and biologically, so it's useful for seedling mixes where good, clean soil is a requirement. But remember, it contributes nothing to a garden—except its organic quality—and this doesn't last long.

Forest Mulches—Forest products, which include a miscellaneous group of ground-up tree bark and sawdust in various particle sizes, are useful soil amendments. They are not as "clean" as peat moss, indeed fancy mushrooms sometimes appear in your garden after using them. The mushrooms are not harmful and there's no record of forest diseases reaching our gardens through these materials. Sometimes the label on the bag tells you they have been composted and fortified with a nitrogen fertilizer. That's a sort of bonus that allows a more rapid breakdown of the materials after they have been dug into the soil.

These products are often called *mulch* but that is not really the appropriate term. A more accurate definition of mulch is any material placed on top of the ground to keep sun off the soil and moisture in.

Redwood Soil Amendment—Before leaving forest products, some mention should be made of Redwood Soil Amendment. A few years ago, a lot of people bought this material after strong advertising campaigns touted its use in the garden. Redwood, deservedly, has a great reputation for not decaying. Ranchers use it for fence posts, builders use it for constructing houses and patio decks. However, gardeners want a soil amendment to break down and provide humus to their soil: *redwood does not do this.*

In fact, redwood, even redwood

dust, retains its condition because of chemicals that have antibiotic qualities. Include it in a soil mix for seedlings and you'll discover poor germination and growth is the result.

Now we come to the best material of all—and not just because it's free. You can't "go and get it" so you'll have to make it yourself, although it may be a little bit of trouble.

Compost—Compost is easily made from any organic material. And it's not a smelly process when it's done properly. A compost pile in a corner of the garden is not an offensive thing. Obvious materials include kitchen scraps—leafy vegetables, citrus peels, potato parings, tea leaves and coffee grounds. All of these grew as plants and removed nutrients from their soil. Closer to home are grass mowings, hedge clippings, weeds (without seeds, please), and all your crop residues, like cabbage stalks, corn stalks, cobs and husks. Don't use meat or fish scraps or anything greasy. They attract vermin to your compost pile and they smell.

Not-so-obvious materials include sawdust from a woodshop. Once upon a time that sawdust was a tree. Hair from a barbershop grew on someone's head. Newspaper was also a tree. Straw bales grew in a farmer's field, and so on.

You can even occasionally compost woolen socks and cotton shirts, provided there is no synthetic mixed in the fibers. Don't use eggshells, as you did in the East. They are made of calcium carbonate and we have too much of this material in our soils already. They are useful in acid soils to bring them closer to neutrality

Soft, lush material such as green grass clippings decompose very quickly. Woody material such as hedge clippings and old tomato vines break down very slowly. Materials that are naturally waxy, like corn stalks and palm fronds, take even longer. They might resist decay—in even a well-managed pile—for two years or more.

There are ways to hasten the decay of woody materials and they rely on getting them into close contact with the bacteria in the pile. First, chop up, or grind up, all the larger pieces into smaller pieces—the smaller the better. Power-driven grinders are available for this purpose. Some will even grind

In summer, crop residues may be laid on top of the soil to keep in moisture. They also keep the soil cool. Eventually the material decays to enrich the soil. Don't dig in undecayed organic matter. This layer of corn stalks will make digging difficult and will take several weeks to rot down. Remove such remains from summer gardening and add them to the compost pile.

branches up to 2-inches thick .

If you don't want to buy a grinder, you can make a chopping block of thick wood and use a machete or a hatchet to turn long stalks into small pieces. Secondly, mix the ingredients of your pile as you build it to surround the small woody pieces with plenty of soft materials, that are full of bacteria.

The more air your bacteria get, the faster they consume the crop residues. Avid organic gardeners turn their pile frequently. If you are making compost from green-grass clippings, a weekly turning is in order—and you'll get useable compost in six or seven weeks. More woody material might be turned every two or three weeks to get a plentiful amount of air to the bacteria.

All this tells you not to try and make compost in a pit or in a trash can. People try to do this and usually they are quickly disappointed.

Others start their composting process by grinding all their kitchen scraps in a blender and pour the resultant slurry into holes in their garden. It's a quick way to get rid of garbage but it's not the best way to make compost—in a hole in the ground. Further, their soil is spottily treated, when they should be spreading a soil amendment evenly. If they spread the slurry evenly over the surface a lot of flies are attracted to the garden. The neighbors can rightly complain!

Treat the Micro-organisms Well

Build your compost pile above ground and keep it moist, but not too wet. Bacteria that carry out the decomposition prefer fresh air, moisture and food—just like people. The harder they work, the hotter the pile gets—also just like people on the dance floor. Turn the pile frequently to give the the bacteria the air they need to keep going. The more you turn the pile, the quicker you'll get a good product. Keep a compost pile tidy by surrounding it with sturdy netting or snow fence.

A good product means well-decomposed material ready to dig into the soil, just as you use steer manure. It also means half-rotted material, still with shape and substance to it that you can lay on top of the soil during the summer months as a mulch. This will shade the soil and keep it cool. If it is kept moist by irrigations, it will continue to disintegrate and add humus to the soil. You do have to keep it from blowing away, of course!

Old-Time Organic Amendments Are Expensive & Hard to Find

Other organic materials for gardeners include hoof and horn, leather wastes, fur and feather, dried blood, guano, tankage, bone meal and fish wastes. They decompose slowly. In other words, they last a long time. They have fertilizer value because they contain plant nutrients. In olden days, they were common by-products but now they cost a lot because they are no longer thrown away but used in other manufacturing processes.

Whenever you use organic matter, it's important to mix it well into your soil. Whatever you use must become closely integrated with the sand and clay particles to start chemical and biological reactions.

True Mulches Have Limited Usefulness

Organic material used as a mulch, placed on top of the soil to shade it from the sun's heat, is another story. In the desert, it tends to dry out and blow away between irrigations. It doesn't supply the soil with humus. In wetter climates, thick mulches save the soil from battering rain that causes erosion. They constantly decay and provide the soil with humus.

A serious drawback to mulches in

the desert is that insect pests are attracted to them. Mulches are moist, cool and contain plenty of food—the very opposite of the inhospitable, hot, bare ground. Insects soon find a mulch and hide in it.

Sawdust Has Its Drawbacks

Don't use fresh sawdust for a mulch. Sawdust is carbohydrate, pure and simple. Organisms need nitrogenous materials to balance their diet. If they are not given it, they find it in the soil, taking it away from our plants.

If you dig fresh sawdust into the soil, double the usual amount of ammonium phosphate to provide the balanced diet organisms need. Otherwise your plants will grow pale and poor through being very nitrogen-deficient.

It's far better to compost sawdust, along with ammonium phosphate, to feed the organisms. Leave it in the compost pile for a year and then dig in the matured material. It won't be thoroughly decomposed, but it will be balanced and will continue to improve your soil as it further decays.

Soil improvement doesn't stop with one application of your choice of organic material. You must repeat it at each opportunity you get to dig the soil. For vegetables, this means each January and August. There's no second time for fruit trees and that's why we dig such a big hole. Remember how big? A fifth of the volume becomes organic matter; 16 bags of steer manure for a hole 5-feet square and 5-feet deep!

You don't have to stay with one kind of material. It's all right to mix whatever you have. In the case of vegetables, you can use one kind now and another kind next time.

Organic Matter Disappears— You Have to Renew It

The point is, organic matter is used up as it feeds organisms, as it's burned by the sunshine, and as it's changed into humus.

You will develop a better garden if you progressively dig a little deeper each year. There is a noticeable difference between the cultivated darker topsoil and the brighter-colored soil lying under it. Push your spade an inch into the redder subsoil and mix it with the upper soil and the fresh organic matter. A deeper soil has more room for strong roots. The greater volume has more nutrients and holds water better.

Green Manuring Has Its Limitations

People who read organic-gardening magazines and come from the East are aware of green-manuring practices. They aren't common in desert regions but they can be used to improve soil *structure*. Don't rely on them to improve soil *fertility*.

If you dig the soil and sow seeds of a crop that produces a lot of bulk and dig it in before it gets woody, that's green manuring. You don't improve the fertility of a soil by this method because you are simply recycling the nutrients already there. A poor soil gives a poor green-manure crop with nothing in it—it's that simple. Under such conditions, green manuring becomes inefficient.

A way to overcome this situation is to fertilize the crop as it grows, before it reaches maximum bulk. Or, you apply fertilizer at digging and before you seed. Of course, you have to spend time and money irrigating a green-manure crop.

There's an extra hidden bonus to the green bulk that you dig in. If root development is strong, the soil is opened up deeper than the spading layer. The resultant rotting of those roots will improve the soil beyond the point where you and your spade can reach.

Legume Green Manures Add Nitrogen

Another way to add nutrients is to plant legume crops. They manufacture nitrogen from the soil air on their root nodules. Quite often you have to provide the necessary bacteria at sowing time, but this is not difficult. Suitable legume crops include vetches, cowpeas and especially sesbania. It's advisable to dig in this last plant before it sets seed, otherwise you will be plagued by it for years to come in places where you don't want it to grow.

Dig in Soft Green Material— Not Dry Stalks

The success of green-manure cropping lies in digging in soft lush material that easily rots, rather than producing a lot of mature, dry, woody stalks.

A drawback to green manuring is that you spend a season growing something that has little immediate use. You lose time and you spend money on water and fertilizer. There's a danger of introducing and nourishing weeds if your green-manure crop isn't thick enough to crowd them out.

Steer Manure—An Organic Shortcut

Desert gardeners usually add organic matter that has been someone else's green manure, namely alfalfa hay that has progressed through a steer's stomach. Steer manure has a quicker effect. It's readily available and it's less expensive than nursery "mulches."

Organic Matter— The Universal Remedy

Remember, organic materials improve soil structure. They bind sandy particles together, giving a poor soil some body. They improve water holding and provide humus that captures nutrients for later release to plant roots. Heavy soils benefit too. They become easy to work and the new crumb structure opens them up. They drain better and roots can breathe.

Soil organisms are encouraged because organic matter provides them with food. We don't fully understand soil organisms but we should all learn to love them.

After a few years, your garden's topsoil will be improved by organic matter. It looks darker. The subsoil is redder in color because it still lacks organic matter. Each time you dig, go an inch deeper and mix in more organic matter.

Chopped output from grinder will be composted with manure and kept moist. You must turn pile occasionally for aeration so bacteria will do their work. If center of pile doesn't stay hot, you are not keepng moist—or not turning it over—or both.

You can make compost without a grinder, but it takes a long time because large pieces may take a year or more to decay so they are useful. Lightweight electric grinder reduces garden and landscape residue to small bits and pieces that decay into usable compost in just a few weeks. Chopped-up material is collected in plastic trash bag. Heavier gasoline-powered grinders are also available, but they are difficult to maneuver on anything other than flat ground

Three or four weeks later, composted material is ready to be used as a soil amendment when you are planting your garden, trees or whatever. You won't believe how much better plants and trees can grow until you start using compost. Try it once and you'll become a believer.

Store your compost in neat piles in a holder made of redwood pieces 2" X 2" X 36", each with a hole drilled at its end. Stack the pieces as high as you want, using a dowel or rod at each corner to hold it all together. Spaces between the pieces let you poke in plants. Use the four sides as well as the top and you've considerably increased your planting space—without increasing your "acreage."

When you've harvested your vegetables, you"ve got a compost pile ready to dig into the conventional garden

8

WHICH FERTILIZER TO USE?

Garden stores offer a bewildering assortment of fertilizers and plant foods. The offerings suggest that each plant is on a diet and should not take any other kind of food designed for another plant. Supposedly it's good salesmanship—it is certainly superb confusion.

The very use of the term "food" helps us misunderstand the situation. We are deluded into thinking our plants must be frequently given a plate of goodies—in the same way we feed our cats, dogs and children.

It's not mere nit-picking to say that "feeding" plants is a misnomer. It's more accurate to call the chemicals *plant nutrients*. For the most part, the fertilizers don't go directly to the plants, but to the soil. There, they are held in storage and released to the plants as needed. Only half of the chemical is useful to the plant. The other half is called the *residue* and it helps build up salts in our soils.

It's worth getting rid of some other misconceptions at this stage.

What Fertilizers Won't Do

Fertilizers do not make plants grow. Once we understand this we will not waste time and money on applying them to dormant trees or vegetables.

Fertilizers don't make fruit taste sweeter.

Fertilizers don't make a tree produce more fruit—directly that is. And it's a mistake to think that the more you apply, the greater the return.

You can't cure a plant of a "sickness" by giving it fertilizers. In fact, it's usually better not to fertilize an ailing tree until it recovers from its discomfort and begins to put out new leaves.

Think About a Balanced Diet

To remain in a good state of health, plants need 16 chemical elements.

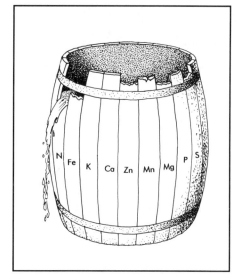

If any one particular stave of a barrel is shorter than the others, that one will determine the amount of water held by the container. Each stave represents a plant nutrient and the liquid in the barrel represents the plant. In other words, if only one nutrient is missing, it makes no difference that other nutrients are in adequate supply.

You can't fill the barrel (get good yields) if some of the staves are broken (some soil nutrients are missing). Mending just one stave (supplying only one nutrient) won't let you fill the barrel. You have to mend them all (supply all the missing nutrients) to keep the barrel filled (sustain good yields).

This law of limiting nutrients applies to desert soils which are low in nitrogen (N), phosphorus (P), sulphur (S), magnesium (Mg), iron (Fe), manganese (Mn) and zinc (Zn). The full-length staves of potassium (K) and calcium (Ca) don't have to be repaired.

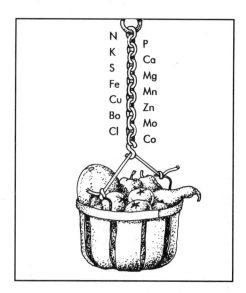

In a similar illustration, one weak link in an otherwise strong chain means the chain is useless. Each link represents a plant nutrient. The chain is the plant. No matter how strong most of the links (individual plant nutrients) are in this chain (soil fertility), the crop yield will fall (or fail) if only one link is weak (a single nutrient is missing).

For example: Your pecan tree will not produce good nuts even though there is enough nitrogen (N), phosphorus (P), potassium (K), calcium (Ca), sulphur (S), magnesium (Mg), Iron (Fe), manganese (Mn), Copper (Cu), boron (Bo), molybdenum (Mo), chlorine (Cl) and cobalt (Co), but insufficient zinc (Zn).

While the bottom four nutrients are needed in very small amounts, the links must be strong enough to maintain the strength of the complete chain.

Ammonium phosphate, the grey, pelleted fertilizer, works with a spade. Use it when preparing the soil for planting: put it down where the roots will find it.

Ammonium sulphate, the white, sugar-like crystals, works with a hose sprinkler. It is soluble and can be washed down through the soil until it reaches the roots of existing plants.

Iron Chlorosis

A shortage of iron is shown by the veins on leaves remaining dark green while the rest of the leaf is pale or even yellow. This occurs on old leaves, whereas yellow new leaves indicate a nitrogen deficiency. A similar discoloration indicates a shortage of manganese, and with some particular plants, a shortage of zinc. In the case of grapes and pecans, a shortage of zinc is shown by small, bunched-up leaves.

Visual diagnosis is confusing—even to the experts.

Lots of Fertilizers Are on The Shelves

After looking at pictures of plants showing deficiency symptoms, you hardly know where to begin. Most likely you go back to the nursery shelves and look over the fertilizers available to you. There's Rose Food, Tomato Food, Geranium Food, Tree Food, Shrub Food, Lawn Food, Vegetable Food, Flower Food, Citrus Food, Pecan Food, Magic Bloom, Ironite®, Miracid® and MiracleGro®. All are good chemicals. There's even weed-and-feed—a poison and a food all rolled into one.

Then there's the range of organic fertilizers: bone meal, going into blood meal, cottonseed meal, fish emulsions, seaweeds, hoof and horn, tankage, sewage and the animal manures. All of these are good, too.

Though their nutrient content is low, their slow release makes them safe for heavy-handed beginning gardeners.

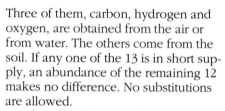

Three of them, carbon, hydrogen and oxygen, are obtained from the air or from water. The others come from the soil. If any one of the 13 is in short supply, an abundance of the remaining 12 makes no difference. No substitutions are allowed.

Soils textbooks invariably include illustrations similar to the barrel which holds water only up to the lowest stave. A chain is useless if one of its links is missing. Although 13 elements are necessary for the plant's health only three are needed in relatively large amounts. They are nitrogen, phosphorus and potash.

The trick to proper fertilizing is to supply those elements which are not available in the soil.

Soil Analysis By Itself Can Lead You Astray

Be careful because a soil-analysis result may read that the chemist found some iron or some zinc. Yet your plants aren't doing well and show deficiency symptoms of those elements. The reason is: Some soils don't readily release certain elements because of chemical combinations. This is particularly true of desert soils which are usually high in calcium. The condition called *lime-induced chlorosis* is caused by iron combining with excess calcium, making it unavailable to plants.

Soil analyses are useful when used in conjunction with other diagnostic tools. Alone, they can lead you astray!

Let's look at the three main elements and how they determine a plant's appearance.

What Nitrogen Does For Plants

A shortage of nitrogen stunts a plant's growth. Leaves are small and the older ones turn yellow and die prematurely even though new leaves may be a healthy green color. An excess of nitrogen—easily achieved by generous gardeners—is shown by large, dark-green leaves, an increased succulence that leads to frost-tenderness, and a reduction in flowering and fruiting.

What Phosphorus Does for Plants

Poor plant development, premature leaf drop, and spindly upright growth are the signs of phosphorus shortage. This can easily be confused with a shortage of nitrogen. The surest sign is a purple color to the older leaves of a plant, though this symptom also appears when the weather is frosty.

What Potash Does For Plants

Signs of a shortage are slow growth and weak stems. Also, poor flower and fruit production but these can be confused with a shortage of nitrogen or phosphorus. The sure sign is a dead brown edge to the leaves or the tips of leaves. Unfortunately, this symptom also appears when a soil is too salty.

Leaf symptoms by themselves can fool you.

Read the Label to Know What You are Buying

Any fertilizer label contains three important numbers. First is the percentage of nitrogen in the fertilizer. The second is phosphorus and the third is potash. Add them up to see how concentrated the fertilizer is. Divide the total into the price to get the cost per unit of plant nutrient.

If you read the fine print, especially on houseplant fertilizers, you may see how much of the nitrogen portion is made up of ammoniacal sources and how much of nitrate or urea. This useful information tells you how quickly the fertilizer is going to be used by the plant and whether it will be useful in cold weather.

If you want to simplify things, use this guideline when applying fertilizers to the calcareous (calcium-carbonate heavy) soils of your desert garden.

When to Use Ammonium Phosphate 16:20:0

Use ammonium phosphate whenever you prepare your patch for planting—plenty of P's.

When to Use Ammonium Sulphate 21:0:0

Ammonium sulphate speeds growth of plants' shoots—lots of S's. It's used on growing plants.

You can't go wrong by using these fertilizers in the following ways. Use the phosphate at the rate of 3 pounds to every 100 square feet. Thoroughly mix it into the soil as you dig deeply. Use the sulphate on wet ground and water it in. Putting it on dry ground and then watering it in means a strong solution hits the feeder roots and they can be burned easily.

Use ammonium sulphate on growing plants. It's a waste to apply it to dormant plants—it won't startle them into activity.

Ammonium sulphate, being soluble, is easily washed through the soil. For this reason it's better to apply a little at a time—say 1/2 pound per 100 square feet every two weeks—rather than a lot at once. A lot might burn the roots, besides being washed out and wasted.

Plant roots absorb nitrogen largely in the form of nitrate. Any ammonium fertilizer has to be changed into the nitrate form. This is done by bacteria. Bacteria are a kind of plant and they go dormant in cold weather too. This means ammonium sulphate is not effective in winter when the soil is cold.

For Cold Soils Change to Ammonium Nitrate 33:0:0

There is nutrient uptake during cold weather by growing plants such as lettuce, cabbage and strawberries when we use another fertilizer called *ammonium nitrate*.

Ammonium nitrate is a useful fertilizer for home gardens because half of the compound—the nitrate—becomes available immediately. The ammonium half is released to the soil where it is stored on the clay or humus particles. It is later used by plants after the soil warms up.

Many houseplant fertilizers contain ammonium nitrate. Their action is rapid and the customer is satisfied.

Use Urea 45:0:0 Carefully

Another quick-acting fertilizer—also requiring warm soil for bacterial conversion—is urea. It ends up as nitrate, without any residue. It's a concentrated chemical so use it sparingly.

Calcium Nitrate 16:0:0 Works in Cold Soils Too

You may be able to find calcium nitrate in nurseries. It's widely used by desert farmers who grow lettuce in winter and it's suitable for home gardens too. Its residue, calcium, is alkaline and not too desirable. Even less desirable and fortunately hardly ever available, is sodium nitrate, a common fertilizer in parts of the country where soils are acid. Its residue tends to neutralize the acid. In our desert soils you don't want sodium.

Ammonium Phosphate's Sulphur Residue is Useful

Looking at the name, *ammonium phosphate*, you wouldn't expect to find any residue. Ammonium is the nitrogen nutrient and phosphate is also a nutrient. However, there's some sulphur in the formula and it becomes a residue after the nutrients have been released. Sulphur has an acid reaction, which is what we want. Some manufacturers tell you of this bonus in their labeling.

Remember, phosphate is for digging in and sulphate for scattering on the surface. Both require soil moisture to activate them.

There are other ways to apply nutrients to growing plants.

Foliar Sprays Put Nutrients Where the Growth Is

If iron and zinc deficiencies occur in trees, a dilute solution of fertilizer can be sprayed directly onto the young leaves. You can use houseplant food if the instructions on the label indicate it is an appropriate fertilizer. There are also special foliar nutrients, usually formulated to meet a particular problem.

Commercial orchardists sometimes spray nutrient solutions containing anything from nitrogen and phosphorus to zinc, manganese, copper, iron and magnesium on their trees as the new leaves appear in spring. There's

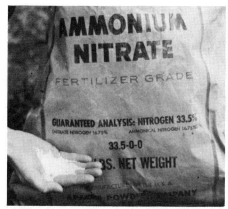

Ammonium nitrate, a pale whitish pellet, is very soluble in water. It is irrigated into the soil until it reaches plant roots. Furthermore, the nitrate part is immediately used by plants as long as they are actively growing—even in cold soil.

no point in spraying old corky leaves. Their tissue will not absorb the nutrients.

Soil applications of these nutrients are expensive and the dollars you spend are swallowed up by the abundance of calcium in the soil. The calcium grabs the zinc or iron and holds it from the plant's roots. Foliar sprays pay.

All Fertilizers are Good for All Plants—But Some are More Costly Than Others

If your neighbor gives you a bag of pecan food and you don't even have a pecan tree, go ahead and use it on peaches, oranges, grapes and anything else—including vegetables.

There's nothing wrong in buying the special fertilizer for each kind of tree you have, but it's not entirely necessary. It will be a lot less expensive if you stick to simple ammonium sulphate for growing plants and ammonium phosphate for digging into the soil at preparation time.

Apply Fertilizers to Match Plants' Growth

Fruit trees are usually fertilized just before they start their spring growth—late January for deciduous trees and in February for citrus.

Should you forget to "feed" your trees in the spring, don't worry. They get their "food" from the soil anyway and their roots will probably find enough for the next year without the tree being starved, provided you water adequately.

No matter which garden-supply center you patronize, there's sure to be a bewildering array of fertilizers to choose from. Surprisingly, some of these products are not so plant- or tree-specific as the labels seem to indicate. A leftover, partially used sack of Pecan Food doesn't necessarily have to be used on pecan trees.

If you over-fertilize a citrus tree, you'll get larger fruit, but the juicy part will not be any larger. The skin thickness will determine the size.

Don't play catch-up and give your trees an extra treat because you forgot. Too much fertilizer can burn the roots, shock the tree into dropping its young fruit, or produce ripe citrus fruit with extra-thick skins.

Vegetables are usually fertilized while they are still small and growing. Late applications tend to keep them growing at a time they should be maturing.

A New Idea About Fertilizer Timing

There's a new thought about fertilizing grapes and it comes from research conducted in California. It is that plants should be fertilized at the end of summer, after the crop is harvested, instead of the conventional springtime application. The researchers say that a springtime application doesn't get to the new shoots quickly enough to give a good yield of fruit.

This new idea is like "topping up" a plant with nitrogen in preparation for the springtime burst of growth. Forward-looking home gardeners may want to try this on their grapes—and maybe try it on their deciduous fruit trees, too.

Slow-Release Fertilizers

There are special "slow-release" fertilizers formulated to provide a balanced set of nutrients and they are concentrated. Osmocote® 18:18:18 is an example.

Osmocote-type pelleted fertilizers look like a heap of worm eggs, and their nutrients slowly pass through the "eggshells" by osmosis.

There are other slow-release fertilizers in various sizes of hard sticks that can be used around fruit trees. They are especially useful when you grow plants in containers because the nutrients are released slowly over a 16-week period— just about the life of a productive vegetable plant. They are usually added to an infertile soil mix as it goes into the container.

A disadvantage is that you may not need some part of the formulation, such as the expensive K, if you grow your plants in a desert soil that has adequate potash.

9

HOW TO WATER

If you live in the desert, the most obvious gardening necessity is irrigating your plants. The rain is unreliable and inadequate.

Water Makes Plants Grow More Than Anything Else

Vegetables must grow quickly if they are to be tender and tasty. If the soil dries out, they become woody, in the case of carrots and bitter-tasting if they are lettuce. And they will bolt and flower prematurely if they are beets, carrots, cabbages or turnips.

Fruit trees kept dry will drop their flowers without setting fruit. If they survive this ordeal and become dry later on, the fruit will be small. Young trees don't grow larger on short rations.

How Often Shall I Water?

Gardeners new to the desert want to know how often to water their plants. They like a set answer, such as once a week, or every month, but this is an inadequate reply. It takes no account of the changing seasons, the kind of soil, the age of the plant and the amount of water that was put on last time.

Here is the best answer to the question. Water often enough to keep the soil around the roots moist, but not soaking wet. But this reply invites other questions. Where are the roots? How far down will the water—should the water, go? How will I know when the soil is drying out?

Sometimes a new gardener will parry the statement with one of his own. "But I have the tree on a drip system." Or, "I give the tree a slow, deep soak." Or, "I have it on an automatic system." Or, "It's in a deep well." In a way, he's avoiding the issue.

How To Water a Tree

Let's counter all these statements of fact with instructions on how to water a tree. Its roots are spreading out as far

Roots do not grow into dry soil. Scrape dirt from outside the circle to make a little bank. This keeps water from running off. If you get dirt from inside the circle, you will expose the old roots. You might even cut them and allow disease organisms to enter. Quickly fill the saucer with water and keep it filled until you can effortlessly poke a soil probe 3 feet into the soil. With all this water you wash salts away from the roots. You fill a large volume of soil with moisture. You won't need to water again for a long time, maybe two weeks or more.

as the spread of the branches, so you water out that far. Its roots go down 3 feet or more, so you water as deeply.

Start by making a bank around the tree at the drip-line—that imaginary line made by rain falling off the ends of the branches. Scrape soil from outside the circle toward the tree. You don't want to dig out soil from under the branches and risk exposing roots.

You should have a shallow, wide basin or saucer, not the deep well that is the pride of novice gardeners. Open the faucet wide and fill that basin with water. When the total area is wet, turn the faucet down so water soaking into the soil is replaced just as quickly with water from the faucet. This is called *keeping a head of water*—and that's just what you do for as long as it takes to get water down to the root zone.

How Deep Should I Water?

How do you know that the water has reached as far as you want it to? Use a

A 3-foot-long soil probe is one of the most useful tools a gardener can have. It tells you where the water is—or isn't.

To make a suitable saucer around a tree, make a mark at the drip line at the ends of the branches. The ends of the roots are under the ends of the branches. That's where the action is. Each year, feeder roots grow outwards, provided the soil is moist.

The correct way to irrigate. Basin is out to the ends of the branches. Water as long as it takes the moisture to reach 3 feet down. Your soil probe easily goes into moist soil. You can't push it through dry soil.

Don't think you are deep-watering the roots of a tree by pushing a hollow tube into the soil and turning on the faucet. This disturbs the soil and the roots if the water pressure is too high. Good watering in the desert where the soils are salty, means watering from the top downwards and taking any salts with it.

1/2-inch-diameter, 3-foot-long metal rod. File marks on it to show the 1-foot and 2-feet depths. The handle is the 3-foot mark.

This metal rod easily slides through moist soil. You cannot poke it through hard, dry soil. Provided there are no rocks in your soil, you can tell exactly how well you water, whether for vegetables or trees.

You need to know how deep roots grow. You can assume that vegetables go down 18 inches to 2 feet. Trees' roots go down 3 feet or more.

As a tree grows, extend the watering circle. The active feeding roots of a tree are at the ends of the roots—just as new leaves are at the ends of the branches. Trees drink their food.

The Dangers of Wells— Avoid Them

People who create little concrete rings around their trees and call them *wells* are making a mistake. They get satisfaction from digging these holes rather deep and fool themselves into thinking they are watering properly by "filling up the well" three or four times. Such watering may get a good volume of soil moistened, but it will be directly under the trunk, and not very far out where it is needed.

A Deep Watering Leaches Salts

A good, deep watering does more than supply your tree with water, it washes salts out of, and beyond, the root zone.

Fertilize When You Water

A good, deep watering also carries nutrients down to the roots. Apply dry fertilizer, usually ammonium sulphate, in the watering circle halfway through the irrigation. You easily know when it's halfway because the soil probe reaches down 18 inches. Continue with the remaining half of the irrigation to send the fertilizer down to the roots.

Avoid Shallow Watering

If you give frequent shallow waterings, there will be a lot of evaporation which brings salts up to the surface. Salts damage tender growing roots. Sometimes you see these salts on the soil surface as white or grey deposits that disappear with the rains only to reappear when the soil surface dries again.

Analyze Signs of Wilting

When plants get short of water, their young shoots droop and the plant wilts. Unfortunately, a plant also wilts when the soil has too much water. The

A common mistake of beginning gardeners is to sprinkle daily instead of giving a deep soak. As a result, salts in the soil evaporate on the surface instead of being driven down. In this case, salts have concentrated at the edges where there is a raised lip. Although they are distant from the growing area, they are still too close and are a handicap to good growth.

Don't spray plants' foliage in the afternoon of a hot summer's day! If you do, the leaves will blister. Because the air is dry, salts left by rapid evaporation will accumulate on the leaves, Sprinkle, if you must, in the early morning and do it gently.

saturated soil has no oxygen and the roots are drowning. When you see a wilted plant—the young, tender, new growth is where you look—don't assume it is short of water. Check with the soil probe.

The Best Time to Water Is—

Here's a frequently asked question. "What's the best time of day to irrigate?"

With well-established plants it doesn't matter too much. After all, you are going to give a lot of water to the plant and it will last several days, even a few weeks for a tree during cooler times of year. With newly planted vegetables and trees, water in the mornings. The reason is that you want to prepare the plants for the stressful midday heat. If you irrigate in the evening, after the plants have wilted, a watering merely brings them back to normal. You want them to develop, and this can only be done by continuous growth. Plant growth should not be stunted by poor watering.

Water Before Winds

If you know it's going to be windy and desert winds are very drying, give your plants a prior irrigation. This will help them keep a good moisture balance, which may be critical in keeping flowers and immature fruit on your trees.

Watering During Summer Storms

It may seem strange, but it's a good idea to irrigate plants during the summer rain storms. These often come down in torrents and, instead of soaking into the ground, run off the soil's surface. *Gulley-washers* and *frog-stranglers*, they are called.

Summer rains are very localized. It can be raining hard a block or two away, and dry where you live. But the humidity is universal. Humidity stimulates plants to grow. But if the storms pass you by, your plants are starved of water in the midst of the plenty of humidity. Give them the water they want if your soil remains dry.

Don't Spray or Sprinkle Plants

Keep water off the leaves, especially during sunshine hours. Water in the desert is often salty. As plants transpire, a deposit accumulates on the leaves from the salty water passing through the plant from the soil. You don't want to add to this deposit by sprinkling more salt on the leaves. Lawns have to be sprinkled—there's no way to get water under the foliage—but trees and vegetables should be watered by flooding, by bubbling or by a drip-irrigation system.

Watering Systems with Bubblers

Bubblers require a well-laid-out pipe system that is permanently buried. Once installed, there's little flexibility if you wish to change the planting arrangement. Bubblers provide a fairly fast delivery of water. Keep it from running over the surface by earthen banks. Don't put bubblers into deep wells.

Drip Irrigation

A drip-irrigation system may be buried, or it can be laid on top of the soil in a less-permanent installation. If it's above ground, you can see what is happening and carry out repairs and changes quickly. A drip system provides water slowly—so slowly there is seldom the need for earthen banks. The water simply drips down and does not rush sideways.

Automatic Controls Don't Think

Both bubblers and drip systems can be controlled by time clocks and made to operate automatically. This is a great convenience to a forgetful or absent gardener but time clocks don't think. They come on at regular intervals whether the soil is wet or dry and whether the plants need water or not. They even come on when it is raining and can make the soil too wet.

Automatic systems are nothing more than gardening tools. Like any other tool they are productive when they are used properly. Don't imagine they will do your thinking for you. Also, you must keep tools in good condition so you can do the job well. The best gardening tool is your soil probe. Use it together with the irrigation system you favor.

A little well like this doesn't get moisture out to the feeder roots where the little girl is standing. Some gardeners try to make up for the lack of spread by making the well deep and filling it up several times. Even so, the water never gets out to the ends of the roots where it is most needed.

Large pecan trees should have wide-spreading roots and a wide irrigation saucer to match. You'll save water in the long run and you'll have healthy trees.

A Useful Watering Definition

The garden hose for flooding; the bubbler for quick delivery; the drip system for economy; all should be used with the universal truth of irrigation: *Water often enough to keep the soil around the roots moist, but not soaking wet.*

A Confusion About Deep Watering

There's a phrase used rather carelessly when we talk about irrigating—it's "deep watering."

To some people this means poking a metal tube attached to a garden hose, deep into dry soil. The water is turned on and a tree is supposedly irrigated. This is not a good practice because salts are not washed down from above. The roots near the surface are not moistened and a lot of hydraulic mining occurs in the sandy depths making air pockets. Further, the soil is moistened in a localized part of the root system. It's difficult to fertilize a tree with this kind of watering.

The Real Meaning of Deep Watering

If you think deep watering means getting water under the complete spread of the tree's branches down to 3 feet, you are quite right.

Suggested Watering Schedule for Southern Arizona Established Landscape Plants

Winter: Nov. to Mid-Feb. **Spring:** Mid-Feb. through Apr.
Summer: May to Mid-Aug. **Fall:** Mid-Aug. to Nov.

Type of vegetation	Season	Watering frequency		Major root zone/Minimum watering depth*
Citrus	Winter	20 to 30 days		18 to 24 inches
	Spring/Fall	15 to 20 days		
	Summer	10 days		
Summer lawns	Winter	20 to 30 days		12 inches
	Spring/Fall	5 to 10 days		
	Summer	3 to 5 days		
Winter lawns	Winter	5 to 10 days		12 inches
	Spring/Fall	3 to 5 days		
Cactus	May-Oct.	4 to 6 weeks		12 inches
Flowers, vegetables	Winter	7 to 14 days		12 to 18 inches
	Spring/Fall	5 to 10 days		
	Summer	2 to 5 days		
Indoor container plants	Winter	7 to 14 days		Until water drains out of container bottom
	Spring/Fall	5 to 10 days		
	Summer	3 to 7 days		
Outdoor container plants	Winter	10 to 20 days		Until water drains out of container bottom
	Summer	1 to 3 days**		
	Spring/Fall	5 to 10 days		
Trees		In grass lawns:	In desert landscaping	
	Winter	30 to 60 days	21 to 30 days	18 to 24 inches
	Spring/Fall	21 to 30 days	14 to 21 days	
	Summer	14 to 21 days	10 to 14 days	
Shrubs, hedges, vines	Winter	20 to 30 days	14 to 21 days	12 to 18 inches
	Spring/Fall	10 to 20 days	10 to 14 days	
	Summer	7 to 14 days	5 to 10 days	
Desert trees, shrubs	Apr.-Nov.	20 to 30 days	10 to 20 days	18 inches

Seeds should be watered often enough to keep soil surface moist.

Transplants should be watered often enough to minimize foliage wilt.

*Minimum depth water should penetrate. It's better to go 2 feet for shrubs and 3 feet for trees to wash salts down.

**May require water more than once per day.

The best plan is to use your soil probe and water only when needed. Proper plant irrigation is extremely important. After you have irrigated, poke a small-diameter steel rod into the soil to see if soil is damp to recommended depth: 12 to 18 inches for vegetables, 2 feet for shrubs and 3 feet for trees to wash salts down.

From *Desert Gardening* by George Brookbank. ©1991 FISHER BOOKS, Tucson, AZ

10

DRIP IRRIGATION

A few years ago, drip-irrigation systems were a hot topic of conversation in gardening circles. The concept of delivering water directly to a plant through plastic tubes instead of running it along an open furrow or flooding the whole garden, had a decided appeal to water conservationists.

As with many new inventions, the first models were not perfect and drip irrigation went through a development fraught with unreliability and breakdowns. This is all behind us now.

Installation Is Easy
Drip irrigation has become popular because handymen—and handywomen, too—can design their own systems, using inexpensive components. There's no hassle in putting them together. They simply fit into one another without messy glue. And they can easily be taken apart if you make a mistake. If you want to add on to your system, it's the easiest thing in the world. Just cut the plastic tube with a knife, install the proper fitting, and continue with a new delivery to the next part of your garden.

Buy as many different components as you need to set up your system. No glue is needed. Be sure to buy the special punch for making holes in the irrigation tubing.

Packaged Kits Seldom The Right Size for Your Garden Plot
Every garden is a different size and shape and this means packaged kits are not always appropriate. They seldom have the right number of pieces or the exact length of tubing.

Many gardeners think they are going to save a lot of water by installing a drip-irrigation system. And so they might if they have been wasteful in the past.

Don't Shortchange Plants' Water Needs
The point is that plants need a certain amount of water to survive, and a bit more to be productive. They must not be shortchanged. There is a danger of this happening when you change delivery systems. Be careful.

Any System Needs Your Management
No matter how complicated a system you put together—even with a time-clock and "computer" included—there isn't a gadget yet devised that will tell a system when a plant needs water.

Handy punch tool makes a neat hole in the tubing. Some tools are a simple punch with a plastic handle.

There probably will be one in the near future. People are working on it. In the meantime, you have to rely on your own judgment. Use the soil probe to help you reach a decision.

At this point it's worth repeating the basic concept of good watering. *Keep the soil around the roots moist, but not wet.* You can do this through any number of irrigation methods.

Simple Drip-System Expedients
Perhaps the prototype of a drip-irrigation system is the common garden hose. We sometimes water a tree by leaving the end of the hose resting on the ground near the trunk with the faucet barely open to provide a drip of water that runs all night. It's not the best way to water, but it works.

Another simple drip system can be made by filling a 5-gallon bucket with water and placing it in the center of a clump of vegetable plants. Bang a nail

When you make a hole in the wrong place, it's the easiest thing in the world to close it with a *goof plug*. Buy plenty of goof plugs. When you want to move an emitter farther out from a tree, pull it out, fill the hole with a goof plug, punch a new hole and insert the emitter. Lots of goof plugs in a system tell that trees are growing well and the gardener is paying attention.

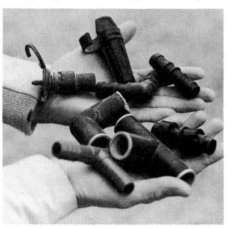

Irrigation tubing stands up to intense sunshine but sometimes a thirsty rabbit, gopher or javelina becomes impatient with the slow delivery of water at an emitter. Ungratefully, they chew into the soft plastic and mess up your system.

The next developmental stage: Fill the bucket quickly; let water drip out slowly. Set out your plants in the wetted areas around the bucket.

through the sides in four or five places near the bottom and your plants will get a slow and steady supply of water. You fill the bucket quickly and the plants are watered slowly. You save time.

Drip-System Savings— Water and Time

A drip-irrigation system, used carefully, will save water too. You put water near the plants and not all over. A bonus to this method is that weeds don't grow between the rows—unless it rains, of course. You save time because you don't have to pull so many weeds.

You also save time because the system irrigates any number of plants from one faucet. You no longer drag hoses around your garden, knocking over plants.

Confusion in Emitter Styles

An emitter is a controlling device that lets water come out at a steady flow, about a drip a second. It is inserted into the supply line, usually 1/2-inch-diameter soft-plastic tubing, after a hole has been punched with a special tool. Don't try to save a dollar by using a nail or an ice-pick. For one thing, you may go right through to the other side of the tubing. Also, the square-ended punch makes a clean hole that doesn't leak when you push an emitter into it. No glue is needed—it seals itself. If you make a mistake and punch a hole in the wrong place, there's another gadget called a *goof-plug*. No matter how smart you are, always buy a supply of goof-plugs. You'll find them very useful.

Don't forget your soil probe. It's an essential part of any watering system. Drip irrigation doesn't think, so you have to monitor its performance.

For this tree, one emitter will be enough for a couple of years. More than one will be needed when the tree is bigger.

There are many kinds of emitters and some are better than others. Select one with a large opening that gives a strong drip. Those with fancy orifices that give sprays or pulsating deliveries easily clog with salt or dust. Simplicity pays.

A particular model that has given good results under desert conditions is the Drip-Eze® Key Clip. Should it get plugged up, you merely turn the "key," pull it out of its housing, wash it in water and put it back. Key Clips

As roots spread, indicated by the branches, tree needs more water out where new roots are growing. Loop irrigation tubing around the tree and insert more emitters. Circles of moist soil should overlap.

There are many kinds of emitters, but the *Drip-Eze® Key Clip* performs best in desert conditions. Key Clip opens up for cleaning. Simply twist key and pull it out. Ribs may be crusted with salt deposits. Soak the key in a vinegar-and-water solution for a few hours, then scrub with a stiff brush.

Each of the near beds is watered by three Key Clips. Wetted areas show where to set out your plants or sow your seeds. And it also shows where added water is needed.

come in varying delivery rates. Avoid mixing them up. More of this, later.

A Key Clip drips away and makes a circle of moisture on the soil surface. It's smaller on a sandy soil because most of the water travels downwards. On a clay soil the circle is wider.

First Steps in Setting Up a System

You need to know what pattern your moist soil makes. When you set up a number of emitters on a line the circles of moist soil should slightly overlap. Your first step, then, is to put out a short test line with one emitter on it and leave it running all day and night. Measure the extent of the wet circle, and also determine how far down the water went. Use your friend, the soil probe.

You can grow vegetables in clusters around a single emitter. Leave a space in the line and install an emitter for the next cluster, and so on. This is a useful system for an irregularly shaped garden where you can't run long, straight lines.

Special Tubing For Vegetable Rows

If you plant in conventional long lines, you can use irrigation tubing called Bi-Wall®. It delivers water to the row of plants through very small holes spaced 12-inches apart. At first, these holes drip to make little circles. After a while they join up to produce a long row of moist soil about 18-inches wide on heavy soil—less on sandy soil.

Three rows of Bi-Wall® tubing adequately irrigate this raised bed. Continuous Bi-Wall® tubing leaks a drip every 12 inches. Wetted area tells you where to sow seeds, set out plants or add more water.

Sow seed or put out plants in the moist soil on either side of the Bi-Wall® to give a double-row system. Space the double rows far enough apart to allow a dry pathway between them. You won't have weeds between rows—no need for a mule and harrow.

Bury the Tubing Or Lay It on the Surface?

Gardeners setting up a drip-irrigation system often ask whether to bury the tubing or let it sit out in the sun.

Irrigation tubing is not damaged by ultra-violet rays, as many plastics are, so there is no need to bury it on that account. However, rabbits, rats, gophers and javelina have been

known to bite into it when they thought a drip of water was insufficient for their thirst.

If you leave the tubing on top of the soil, you can see what is happening and how effectively the drips are coming out. Surprisingly, the water will not be hot—even if the distance from the faucet is considerable. When you want to work the soil or replant, it's easy to lift up the tubing, lay it on one side, do your work and put it back. When the tubing lies on the surface, it's easy to make changes, either adding on a new part to the system or simply moving an emitter or two.

Proponents of burying the system say you have a cleaner garden with

Add liquid fertilizer through the opening at the top. A shut-off valve below the tank enables you to remove a full tank and take it to another location in the system. When you remove it, use a screw-in plug to keep the water within the system. As irrigation water flows past the tank, fertilizer is drawn into the flow at a steady rate. Don't use any fertilizer that doesn't completely dissolve. You don't want small emitter openings clogged with fertilizer residue.

Each time you add a section to a new garden, install a shut-off valve in your irrigation system. This allows you to work on each section without interfering with the others.

less weeds, because there's no surface moisture. However, it will be difficult to germinate seeds when you want to. Because moisture does not appear on the surface, there's less evaporation and, therefore, less salt residue.

On the other hand, it's awkward to direct water to different parts of your garden if the controlling in-line valves are buried.

Make a Map for Future Changes

Make a plan of your buried system. Otherwise you may find yourself chop-ping the tubing at a later date when you dig deep.

Keep your layout simple. It will be cheaper and easier to put together. It will also be easier to manage.

Use squared paper and make a scaled plan of the area to be irrigated. You may start either at the faucet and work towards the garden, or you can lay out the rows and tree sites and work back to the faucet.

Use Plenty of Controlling Valves

It's advisable to deliver water sepa-rately to areas that have different water needs, using different faucets. This gives you good management control, and it saves water. For example, fruit trees need more water at each irriga-tion but they don't need to be watered as frequently as vegetables, which have shallower roots.

Put in a shut-off valve each time you add a line to a different part of your garden. This lets you control water de-livery and it enables you to make repairs and adjustments without hav-ing to close down the entire system.

Here's How You Do It

Let's start at the garden and work back to the faucet. Lay out the Bi-Wall® where the vegetable rows will be. Allow enough space for a dry walk-way between them. Close the far ends by doubling over the tubing and pok-ing it into a short piece of the same kind of tubing. You may want to install an in-line valve at the beginning of each row in case you grow different plants with different water require-ments. Or, if you have transplants on one row and seeds in another, you will want control over the ways in which you water. Each row will have differ-ent needs.

Put tees on the faucet side of each of the in-line shut-off valves and join all the sides with 1/2-inch irrigation tub-ing. One end leads to the faucet. The distant end should have a screw-cap to let you flush out the system at a later date.

Irrigation tubing is flexible enough to make wide turns, but if you want a quick turn, install a 90° elbow to change direction.

Somewhere along this irrigation tub-ing you may want to branch toward your fruit trees. You can either cut into it, install a tee and a shut-off valve and lead off to the trees. Or, you can start a new line from the trees straight back to the faucet.

Follow Local Building Codes

When you get to the faucet you must follow local building codes and install an anti-siphon valve. This prevents water lying in a system from draining into your drinking water should it be turned off for repair at some time. Such valves are not expensive and often incorporate an adjustable flow valve—just what you want to provide the right amount of pressure in your system. You will need one for each faucet.

Optional refinements include a filter which would be necessary if you have an old house with rusty water pipes, or a well that keeps bringing up sand grains. You can also have a fertilizer tank in the line.

You can also install a solenoid valve activated by a time clock. This will turn the system on and off without you being there. This is an obvious advan-tage when you take vacations.

Automatic Controls Don't Think for You

But—a word of warning about auto-matic irrigation systems.

They only follow the clock, coming on and staying on without any regard to the plants' water needs. Indeed, they even come on during a thunder-storm. If you had set your clock to match mild weather conditions and it suddenly turned hot, your plants would soon dry out and suffer.

Also, remember that a drip-irrigation system only saves water if you had pre-viously been wasteful of it. After install-ing one you shouldn't think that your plants will thrive on less water than they need.

A drip system is just another method —albeit a very convenient one—of getting water to your plants.

You are still the manager—you are in charge. Your old friend, the soil probe, should not be set aside after you have installed a drip-irrigation system.

Don't Put Your Plants into a Mathematical Equation

Here's another warning about calcu-lating the amounts of water delivered through a system. Most emitters are de-signed to allow a particular amount of water each hour—a half gallon, 1 gal-lon or 2 gallons. Mathematically minded people like to multiply number of emitters by number of gallons and number of hours to reach a figure of a certain number of gallons delivered to each tree. This is nice—on paper.

Unfortunately, there's no simple way to determine how many gallons are needed by different kinds of trees, of different sizes, with different pruning systems, growing in different soils, with different exposures, during different times of the year, during changes of wind, cloud and sunshine.

You Be The Judge

Without doubt, there'll be the day when some ingenious person finds a way to measure the daily water needs of plants. Meanwhile, you have to make the judgement. Use a drip-irrigation system just like you use any other irrigation system. Don't expect too much from it.

Don't forget to use your soil probe. Feel the plants' leaves to see if they are hot. Watch for wilt. Keep your plants growing. Spend some time with your plants—talk to them and try to understand them.

Look Ahead to Bigger Trees

Design your system to water future root growth. Tree roots want to spread out. So it's a mistake to provide just one water outlet or emitter close to the trunk as is so often done. Once you have your system, leave it running long enough for water to get down to your plants' roots.

Once upon a time, a farm manager installed just one emitter close to the trunk of each of his newly planted pecan trees—several acres of them. They grew well but his delight was short-lived. Strong winds came in their due season, caught the luxuriant foliage, and blew the trees over. They hadn't developed an extensive root system because new roots don't grow out of moist soil into dry soil. Take warning!

As your trees grow, extend the system to encourage root spread. You know that if you flood irrigate, you enlarge the encircling basin as the tree grows. With a drip-irrigation system you do the same. Cut the plastic supply line, put in an extra length to give a larger circle, and add more emitters.

Single line takes water to several trees. Look! No weeds!

Constant dripping from emitter encouraged a mass of fibrous roots. Now it is perched on a mound. Such roots can invade an emitter and plug it. If it were underground, you wouldn't know this happened. On the other hand salts in the water accumulate on high, dry areas.

Building codes require you to install an anti-siphon valve. This inexpensive plastic one also has a controlling shut-off valve so you can adjust water flow.

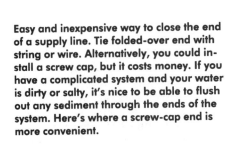

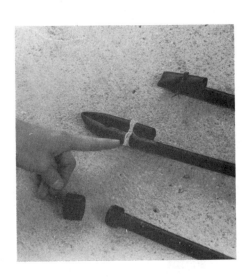

Easy and inexpensive way to close the end of a supply line. Tie folded-over end with string or wire. Alternatively, you could install a screw cap, but it costs money. If you have a complicated system and your water is dirty or salty, it's nice to be able to flush out any sediment through the ends of the system. Here's where a screw-cap end is more convenient.

11

VEGETABLE-BED SHAPING

People coming from the East are advised to change many of their gardening methods to suit new desert conditions. One particular practice that needs to be changed is shaping hills and ridges. They just don't do well in hot, dry, desert regions.

Making a radical change such as this doesn't mean you don't dig thoroughly. It's always important to aerate the soil as deeply as you can. In the desert, it is even more important to add organic matter and nutrients that are missing from our soils.

Ridges & Hills are a Legacy from Another Experience

Ridges and hills are fine for regions with heavy rainfall. They provide drainage around seeds and seedlings and thereby prevent rots. Most gardening books are written for the wetter parts of the country where ridges and hills are standard practice. Drier soil at the top of a ridge warms up faster than wet soil in the furrows. During a cold wet spring this is helpful when keeping up with a planting schedule, often determined by a calendar-based program. In the rainy eastern states ridges have value. When we move to the desert we can forget them. Excess water is not a desert problem.

Another residue of thought that keeps us doing the same old ridge routine without thinking about it, is from farming. Not so long ago, when we were all farmers, the home garden was a little farm on its own, managed by the farmer's wife. It was extensive because it had to be. There were no supermarkets or fast-food shops. Plenty of space was available and the farmer's wife was strong.

These large gardens were ploughed, ridged, planted and weeded with farm equipment. That was the man's contribution: he did the initial heavy work—the wife did the rest.

Until quite recently, Cooperative Extension Service bulletins and pamphlets proffered advice based on this traditional system. Even when country folk left the farms for the cities, the bulletins retained the farming concepts. The older, larger booklets were chopped into new one-page leaflets which continued to recommend ridges and hills.

What's Wrong With Ridges & Hills?

First, in the desert they dry out very quickly. We need to keep moisture in the soil for as long as we can. Second, as they evaporate they draw salts to their peaks. It's at the peaks where we sow seed and set out plants. On salty soils neither stands a chance. And on most desert soils the plants don't achieve their potential. Third, when heavy summer rains thunder out of the skies, soil is washed off the ridge tops to expose roots and sometimes wash out plants. Fourth, hoeing out weeds reduces the ridges and exposes roots of our vegetables.

Urban gardening has the same objectives as larger-scale gardening of olden days. In addition, we have to garden more intensively because there isn't free ground available. And, we have to be conservation-minded—our irrigation water costs plenty.

Farmer-style ridges look neat and tidy but in the desert they dry out too quickly. North side of ridges are always in shade. This means they are always cold in winter. Plants don't grow well in cold soil.

Just like a ring around the bath tub, salts appear at the waterline between the ridges. It's unfortunate that most salt gathers where young roots grow, doing the most damage to young plants just getting established.

Flat vegetable beds allow you to plant closely and make maximum use of limited space.

Conventional ridges use only a fraction of the available space. They are space-wasters and you have to wait for the soil to dry out before you can get to your plants.

Each time you dig your bed, improve the soil. This 50-square-foot garden received 4 bags of steer manure, 1 pound of ammonium phosphate and 2 pounds of sulphur. Spread the materials on the surface and then dig in. Mix them thoroughly into the soil as you dig. If your garden is new, do this twice a year for 3 years to get a beautiful soil.

When weeds are hoed off the sides of ridges, a lot of soil around the crop plants is disturbed. Their roots are either damaged or exposed. The north side of a ridge is always in shade and in winter this means it is always cold. Plants don't grow well in cold soil.

Flat Surfaces Better

Flat surfaces don't evaporate water as quickly as ridges. With flat ground you can plant closer and get more yield, especially with the newer, smaller varieties. You don't need as much water.

After you have added organic matter, ammonium phosphate and sulphur, and dug your ground, rake over the soil and level it. A bed 4-feet wide with a walkway round it, allows you to reach the middle. You can make the bed as long as you like.

Keep the Water in Place With a Berm

Rake to the outside edges making a lip about 3-inches high to contain the water you apply. Get it absolutely level and all the seeds you sow later will get the same amount of moisture. If you finish with low spots, some seeds will stay too wet. High spots will dry out too quickly. High spots also gather unwanted salts.

No More Salty Soil If You Use Flat Beds

On the other hand, the edges of a flat bed are deliberate high spots. Salt collecting there has been drawn away from your plants. Even if you irrigate vegetables with a drip system, make flat beds. There's always the need to wash your soil clean of salts with an occasional deep flooding.

Catch Spring Warmth With a Sloping Bed

Modifications of the flat-bed gardening system include sloping beds. They are particularly useful in spring when you want the soil to warm up for early melons and any other summertime vegetables. The lower edge of the 4-foot-wide bed is to the south, the upper edge is to the north and about 8 inches higher. By sloping the bed like this you get more direct sunlight on the soil and it warms up better.

Raised Beds are like Hills & Ridges

You read a lot about raised beds, and may wonder about them. They originate in the wetter parts of the country. Because they stick up in the air—even 3 or 4 inches—they expose more soil to dry air. We are back to the conventional ridges of olden days. Until, that is, we consider the handicaps of caliche. A raised bed gives you a greater soil depth but you should have more than 2 feet of good drainage over caliche for a raised bed to be succesful. After a few years of improving your desert soil with organic matter, you automatically make a raised bed. Although organic matter disintegrates, you add it at a faster rate.

Keep the soil moist and in place by surrounding the bed with thick redwood boards, concrete blocks, or railroad ties.

Allow enough room for a walkway. A bed 4-feet wide is easy to maintain. Most people can comfortably reach the middle without treading on the soil or plants.

When you think you have raked the bed absolutely flat, a water check will tell you whether you have done a good job. Here there's more work ahead because water flow is avoiding the high spots. Work the soil into flat beds with side borders that hold water. This enables you to water by flooding the soil so it is absolutely level, an important matter when you want seeds to germinate evenly. Flooding also drives down salts; light sprinkling draws salts to the soil surface.

Use a flow of water from the hose to trim the sides. This bed is a little low at one end. Take time to water-float the soil until the bed is absolutely level.

The highest parts of a flat bed are the edges—farthest away from the seedlings and young plants. Harmful salts will accumulate here, leaving the flat surfaces free of toxic materials. Note salt accumulation on edges.

Seeds will be sown in the bottom of these sunken beds where moisture is better retained than in hills or mounds. Cold winter winds will have no effect on tender seedlings if a layer of clear plastic is laid over the sunken garden.

During the winter months, sow seeds directly in trenches and cover them with clear plastic. You'll be surprised to see how quickly they grow.

Sunken Beds Protect Seedlings From Wind

A reverse method has been recommended. It's the sunken garden, and really there's nothing new about it. Ancient Egyptians found—as do modern ones—that a sunken garden made up of 3-foot-square plots, 6 inches below ground level, protects young plants from drying winds. Water stays put and lasts longer. But you need to start with good soil. It is bed shaping of a different kind.

Highest part of a flat bed should be the edges—farthest away from seedlings and young plants. Harmful salts will accumulate here, leaving flat surfaces free of toxic materials. Note salt accumulation on edges.

12

GARDENING A LITTLE DIFFERENTLY

Don't think you have to own a lot of acreage to grow food. You'll find a bit of a balcony or a patio corner is enough. You can grow vegetables and fruit trees in containers, in a bag, in a bale of straw, or hydroponically.

Advantages to Unconventional Gardening
You may be reluctant or even unable to dig and in that case you haven't even bought gardening tools. There's not much space available to you if you live in a townhouse or an apartment, or a mobile-home community. If you are a renter you may not want to invest time, energy and money in the long-term task of soil preparation.

If there is caliche in your garden, you won't be able to dig. If there are rabbits nearby, it's good to put your vegetables out of their reach. Gophers will not trouble plants in containers.

Early Start—Late Conclusions
In spring, before things have warmed up, you can get an early start on the season by planting vegetables and flowers in black-plastic buckets and setting them out in the sunshine. The sun's rays, aided by the black plastic, warm the soil and the roots grow vigorously. A strong plant is the result and you will harvest it earlier than those you planted out in the garden at the same time.

In a similar way, you can move a frost-tender plant into shelter as winter approaches. During the heat of summer, containers can be moved into the shadier parts of a patio, saving the plants from sunburn.

Mix 'Em Up
You can use containers to grow many vegetables mixed together. For example, try onions, lettuce and strawberries. There is no danger that the flavor

of one vegetable will affect the quality of another. You can have tall corn, straggling tomatoes cascading over the side, and even melons which scramble onto the ground and stretch away from the container.

More suitable plants are those which can be harvested over a period of time by either picking their fruit, or stripping the lower leaves without removing the entire plant. Lettuce and cabbage are examples. It's wasteful to grow a cabbage for 16 weeks to get a one-time harvest.

Unlimited Choice of Containers
Half whiskey barrels are periodically available at sale prices from lumber yards and home-supply stores. Place one near the kitchen door for a complete herb garden. You can also grow fruit trees in them with some small vegetables under the foliage.

Thoroughly cleaned 5-gallon paint buckets are good for a single plant of pepper, tomato, eggplant or a few lettuce, onions, strawberries and other smaller plants. Anything smaller than the 5-gallon size cannot satisfactorily hold a large plant that transpires a lot of water in summer. You'll have to water it several times a day. And that's a nuisance.

Other container choices include expensive clay pots and bowls, drainpipes on end, recycled trash cans, buckets, cans, boxes, plastic bags, styrofoam chests, bushel baskets, barrels, produce boxes and steel drums. All must have drainage holes and be free of toxic residues. Remember, the larger the container, the more difficult it will be to move.

Use a lightweight soil mix. These can be bought at nurseries, or you can make your own. Equal parts of coarse sand, peat moss or compost, perlite, and if you are certain there are no dis-

Grow a summer arbor using yard-long beans. This is a space-saver too. Plants grow up and not out.

ease organisms present, old garden soil. Some gardeners add a dash of steer manure if they are unable to get compost. This provides useful soil organisms. Thoroughly mix these ingredients before filling the container. Add a slow-release fertilizer, such as Osmocote® 14:14:14, at the rate of 2 ounces for each cubic foot of mix. Don't fill the container to the top, but allow a couple of inches to hold water when you irrigate.

Gardening in a Bag
Let's say you can't find any containers. Don't give up. Buy some bags of planter mix or potting soil. Lay them flat-side down and punch about six drainage holes in them. Now turn the bags over and pat them flat. Put them on the ground or raise them up at any

A half whiskey barrel serves as a garden to grow peppers and cucumbers on a wire trellis. They do double-duty by shading this western window.

A barrelful of herbs strategically placed near the kitchen door.

height from the ground to make your gardening convenient. For example, a wheelchair gardener would appreciate his bag garden at table-top height.

During the winter months when you want to capture the sun's warmth, put a layer of black plastic over the bag before punching the planting holes. Place the bag in a sunny location.

Use a cookie cutter to make six or eight holes in the top of the bag. Give the contents a good soaking with water by slowly pouring water into the

Fill a tray with sand. Make sure there's drainage. Sow sunflower seeds as thickly as you can. Put in a warm place and keep them moist. You'll have food in a week!

Sprouts will be pale if you keep a cover over them. Grow them in the sunshine if you want your sprouts full of chlorophyll. Seed hulls fall off as the sprouts lengthen.

Eat young plants by thinning out the masses of tender, green sprouts. The few plants remaining at the end can be grown to maturity and full size.

holes, or you can siphon water through a tube from a jug placed higher than the bag. Then plant your vegetables through these holes.

Water your plants by siphoning water through a tube from a gallon jug. From time to time, add a tablespoon of houseplant food when you fill the jug. Use the high-nitrogen formula if the plants are leafy and the more balanced formula if you are growing fruiting plants. Watch the color of the leaves to avoid overfeeding. Dark-green leaves are not wanted. When leaves turn dark green you know there is plenty of nitrogen in the solution and you can stop adding it.

This is a clean way to grow fruiting

plants because there's no mud to spoil strawberries or tomatoes. When the harvests are over, you remove the plastic bag and put the residue of roots and the growing medium into the compost pile. Nothing is wasted.

Some bags of planter mix are better than others. Avoid redwood soil amendments and don't use bags of steer manure—it is too rich.

Growing Sprouts on a Windowsill

Finally, here is an easy way to grow food without digging. Grow sprouts in a jar on the kitchen windowsill. Start a jar each week to get a succession of green food. Many kinds of seeds can be used, but for starters try alfalfa or mung beans.

Buy these in food stores. Don't use seed packets because such seeds are often treated with chemicals to reduce attacks by soil bacteria. Sometimes you can buy ready-mixed sprout seeds in gourmet food shops. These are fun to test because they give you new flavors to try.

Put a tablespoon of seed in a pint jar and add water to the halfway point. A mason jar makes a good container. Take off the screw cap and replace it with a circle of wire mesh. This lets you change the water without losing the small seeds. The water absorbs color from the seeds, so change it as often as necessary—perhaps once a day. After two or three days, rest the jar on its side to let the seeds get air and start their germination. Wash them once a day, but drain them too. When small white shoots appear, be careful with the washing or you'll break them.

You will have ready-to-eat sprouts in about a week. Before you start eating them, start a second jar. And as the second becomes ready, start a third. This ensures a continuous supply of nutritious green food, grown just from water.

To get pale gourmet shoots, keep the jar in the dark all the time or keep a cover over them. If you want green shoots, allow them good light. Grow them in the sunshine if you want your sprouts full of chlorophyll. Seed hulls fall off as the sprouts lengthen.

Above all, keep the water fresh. This is particularly important during the warmer months when high temperatures encourage bacterial growth.

Wrap an unopened bag of peat moss with black plastic. Make holes through the plastic and set out winter vegetables. Presto! A garden without digging!

Use the narrow space between neighbors to grow climbing beans, or cucumbers. Plants use space growing upwards rather than outwards.

Everlasting onions grow small bulbs instead of flowers. Put the bucket in a sunny part of the yard.

You won't get a great yield but while you are waiting for your house to be built, you can get your orchard started in half barrels. Wire support can be used for training or for holding covering for frost protection.

Don't completely harvest a lettuce plant and leave a vacant place in the garden. Remove a few lower leaves every time you want a salad and you'll always have plants.

And you can train a grape vine to be ornamental as well as useful.

Inside, on the kitchen windowsill, grow sprouts in glass jars. Change the water frequently to keep it sweet. You'll have gourmet sprouts in about 10 days.

Place an old tire or two in a sunny location. Fill with sawdust and water with a nutrient solution. As the sweet potatoes grow, add another tire and more sawdust.

As the sweet-potato vines grow longer, another tire is placed on top and filled with soil. Go as high as you like! The air is free, but there's work ahead when it comes to harvest time.

Straw Bales, Too!

Another inexpensive way to get started in a no-digging program is to buy straw bales. Wet them down and put in your plants and seeds. Straw bales become heavy when they are water-soaked, so determine where they will best suit your purpose because you will have to leave them there.

The bales will drain better if you raise them up off the ground. There will be less evaporation from the sides if you wrap plastic around the bales. If possible, set a number of bales together—rather than each one by itself—to reduce evaporation.

Because straw has no nutrient value, you have to add houseplant food to the water from time to time, just as with the bags of planter mix. Take care not to water too frequently, otherwise the center starts to smell because of undesirable fermentation.

When the crop has run its course, throw everything into the compost pile to complete the bale's disintegration.

Straw-bale gardening is a lot easier in the cooler months. Dampen straw bales and wrap them in plastic to hold in the moisture. After about a week you can plant in the bale. Plant closely and mix your crop plants. You don't have to dig and you shouldn't have to weed if the straw is clean. Here's a complete garden with onions, lettuce, radishes and turnips. When you are finished you can use the compost on your conventional garden.

Hydroponics—Growing in Sand

Vegetables can be grown hydroponically, as I describe in a chapter on hydroponics starting on page 265.

Month of the Bee

The Chinese name their years by the animals. If we could name the months by them, April would be the month of the Bee.

You have surely noticed the brilliant yellow flowers of the prickly-pear plants. If you get close to them you will see an interesting sight—a number of drunken bees. The common honey bee seems unaffected by the richness of the pollen or nectar, but the smaller grey-banded leaf-cutter bees can be seen rolling in the gutter, thrashing their legs in the powdery stuff.

If they haven't started already, leaf-cutter bees will soon be gathering material for their nests. They are solitary animals and find small holes—such as keyholes, stored copper tubing, air-conditioning drains and electrical outlets—wonderful places to make their homes. Into these holes they stuff small pieces of fresh green leaves. You know where these pieces come from if you have rose bushes, bougainvillea, wisteria or grapes.

The bee cuts a neat circular notch out of the leaf edge and flies home with it before you can pull yourself together. It's a fascinating thing to watch. Next time you see the damage and wonder what caused it, pause a little and hope that you can watch it happen. It's one of those wonders of nature. Don't get angry. Realize that you are contributing to the raising of little ones.

Leaf-cutter bees are industrious workers. In parts of Southern California they are raised—actually in boxes of drinking straws with their ends exposed—for the purpose of pollinating fields of alfalfa being grown for seed.

Next we have the biggest bee—the carpenter bee—to watch. It's that big black, slow-flying creature that sometimes comes into the house. Watching is all you need to do, because it won't sting unless you irritate it. If it comes into your house, just open a window and out it goes—all by itself. There's no need to panic, get excited or spray it.

Carpenter bees also pollinate flowers, so they have value in the scheme of things. Normally they live in holes of their own making in trees and woody shrubs. They find dead wood and tunnel into it, laying their eggs at the end of the tunnel. Often there's more than one bee, so you'll find a number of openings to several tunnels.

For some people, spraying is their knee-jerk reaction to any "bug" that flies near them. Or perhaps it is swatting it. You're allowed—even encouraged—to swat flies. It develops the reflexes and it's good exercise. But leave bees alone.

Now to the middle-size bees—the honeybees. They don't come singly. They are very busy, too, gathering nectar from our flowers and carrying pollen from one flower to another on their way home with a load for their babies. If their nest is too full of babies because there's been a population explosion, part of the family leaves with their own queen to start a new home. That's when you experience a swarm. Don't panic!

Swarming bees are not after you. Admittedly, they appear a little frightening the first time you see them. If they are hanging in a cluster they look menacing. If they are dancing in the air, they seem poised to come in your direction.

Neither of these possibilities is likely. This is the truth now.

The swarm that left the hive is made up of bees carrying a lot of luggage for their new home. They are gorged with honey from the old hive, so they are physically encumbered and find it hard to sting. Second, all they want is a new home and are anxiously waiting for news about it. As soon as the scouts come back with the good news, the swarm will fly off. So, there's no need to panic when you see a swarm. You should not disturb it by spraying it with the garden hose or with insecticides. Simply look the other way and it will go away.

There's an unfortunate complication to the swarm's disappearing act. They might find a vacancy in the roof of your house or in a nearby hollow tree.

Once bees get between the walls of your house they can be called a *nuisance* and have to be removed. Have them removed—or at least get someone to try it—before you get mad and resort to chemicals.

Bees are useful and, to some people, valuable. These people like to hear from you if you find a swarm in your garden. Their telephone number is in the yellow pages under—what else?—**B**. Such people are glad to get a swarm and shouldn't charge you. They usually gather it after dark, when all the bees are in a cluster. They need to work quickly because the swarm won't stay in your yard too long. Give them a call as soon as you see it. In a day or two—or sooner—the scouts will have found their permanent new home and the swarm will be gone.

If you are not frightened by bees there's an interesting hobby waiting for you. Catch a swarm, put it in a beehive box with wax foundation frames and let the bees build a new house—under your supervision. They will reward you with their industry and organization. You'll have a new perspective on life—and about bees—after getting to know them. And, there's the bonus of honey!

This information originally appeared in one of George's regular newspaper columns in the *Tucson Citizen*.

Raise Your Own Best Friends—
Grow Worms at Home for Your Garden

Every gardener should love earthworms. They are our best friends. In the desert they are not very obvious inhabitants of our soil—for good reasons—and we miss them.

When we were newcomers, we tried to tame this wilderness. We did our best to improve it. A lot of us bought a bucket of worms and threw them on the ground—expecting them to produce a Garden of Eden overnight. Well, the poor worms died.

Worms, by themselves, will not make your newly-purchased awful red sandy dirt into a garden soil. You can't make bricks without straw. You can't make a silk purse out of a sow's ear. And so on. But worms are still the gardener's best friend and you can grow them yourself if you want to take the trouble.

Find a wooden box and put drainage holes in the bottom. The size should be similar to a citrus box. You'll need a lid for it.

Place alternating layers of old garden soil—you get this from an old neighbor—and organic matter, each about 3-inches thick, until you've filled the box. Organic matter means manure from animals such as horses, cows, sheep, rabbits and guinea pigs. Don't use chicken manure—it's too chemically strong. Don't use pig manure—it's too "wet." You can use straw or hay to dry out any manure that is too fresh or wet.

Some worm farmers use kitchen vegetable scraps. They put them through a blender to grind them into small, soft, mushy pieces. Worms don't have teeth—they have to swallow their food.

Now you need to get some worms to start your farm. Some seed companies offer worms in their catalogs. Companies which specialize in organic gardening products sell them. Bait shops sell worms. And, there are worm growers whose business is selling worms. When you get the worms, add them to your worm farm.

After a few weeks the layers in your box will be mixed up because the worms will have traveled up and down through the layers, eating whatever organic matter they fancied. There's an interesting variation of this box that you can make for school children. Put a sheet of glass on the front of the box in place of the wooden side to make an observation worm farm.

At the beginning you'll clearly see the bands of sand, soil and organic matter of different kinds—like a layer cake. You'll soon see the tunnels made by the worms. And, before long, the layers become hazy stripes. Eventually the profile of stripes goes and all you see is a homogenous soil with tunnels through it.

Sprinkle some water on the top of your soil and watch it travel down through the worm tunnels. See how the air in those tunnels is driven upward as bubbles. If you never thought of the usefulness of worms before, you'll realize it after keeping an observation worm farm. But, back to the real thing.

Keep your worm box moist all the time, but not too wet, or you will drown the worms. You'll remember in your youth when the lawn became a mass of worm castings after a prolonged period of rain. Worms moved up out of the waterlogged soil to get some air.

As your worms use up the layers of organic matter you need to add more fresh stuff. That's where the kitchen vegetable scraps come in. "Feed" your worms a little blended mush at a time—just enough so they can clear it up in a couple of days—by spreading a thin layer on top of the soil. You don't want to develop a smelly product, particularly because you are keeping your worm farm in the garage or a storage room where the temperature stays around 60—70F.

What's the purpose of your worm farm? First, you will—if you are a good farmer—get more worms. You can put the extras in your garden to continue their good work there. The good work? Worms devour organic matter and mix it with the soil. They don't make organic matter, you have to feed them. They make tunnels that aerate the soil and allow good drainage—taking moisture down deep.

Second, the rich material you have in your worm box can be taken out—little by little, and as you need it—and mixed with soil to make a beautiful planting mix. Equal parts of the worm stuff and old garden soil mixed together gives us a very good potting soil for houseplants, for seed boxes and for young transplants. Plants grow well in such a mix.

If you can't be bothered with all this farming there's good news. You can buy worms from the sources I've already mentioned. Put them in your garden—provided there is plenty of organic matter in it already.

There's little point in a shortcut of putting worms in your compost pile to help the decaying process. First, a well-cared-for compost pile simply gets too hot from its bacterial activity. The worms are killed by the heat. Secondly, the fresh organic matter is too tough for the toothless worms. Third, unless you frequently and carefully turn the compost pile you'll find the worms don't like the wet middle or the dry outer edges, either.

The real good news is that you can buy worm manure or, as it is correctly called, *worm castings,* at some nurseries. Worm castings come in small bags—it's powerful stuff. Worm castings have more nutrients than steer manure . . . without any salt. It's more costly, so you use it for houseplants, container planting of flowers or vegetables, for raising seedlings—it doesn't burn delicate roots—rather than using it in a large garden. But you can use it on a large garden if you have lots of money.

This information originally appeared in one of George's weekly columns in the *Tucson Citizen.*

13

PRUNING FOR FRUIT PRODUCTION

There's a neat definition of fruit-tree pruning that most horticultural students have to learn in college. It goes like this: "Pruning means removing certain parts of the tree in order to modify and utilize its natural habits so more and better fruit will be obtained over a longer period."

It's a nice and tidy bundle of words. But before we expound on it for the home gardener, let's see what happens if you don't ever prune a tree. A lot of gardeners are initially reluctant to try their hand. In despair, they often hire the first person who knocks on their door asking for yard work. Such people don't always know how to prune properly.

It's sometimes better to leave the tree alone—especially if you are more interested in shade than fruit.

Don't worry, a tree that is not pruned won't die. It will continue to grow in its own way. This may even be to your liking if all you are interested in is a colorful mass of cheery spring blossoms and summer shade for an outdoor living area.

Reasons to Prune

This brings us to item number one. One reason to prune a fruit tree hard is to make it small, small enough so we can put a net over it as the fruit begins to ripen. If it's not pruned, it will grow in all directions and soon be too big for a bird net. Your bird-watching will not be enjoyable.

You won't enjoy the tree as a shade tree unless you remove the lower branches. Left to themselves, branches will grow long and droopy, touching the ground and walls, and going on the roof. Branches will grow against one another, rubbing and scarring themselves.

- An unpruned tree develops a dense shade in its center, usually followed by localized dieback. Fruit will not be produced in this "hollow" center.
- Long, drooping branches easily break, either from their own weight or by being thrown about by strong winds.
- Broken branches invite diseases which can progress down the limbs to kill the tree.
- Although an unpruned tree flowers nicely and most of the flowers set, there will be a lot of small fruit with large pits and little flesh.
- An unpruned tree tends to exhaust itself with a heavy flowering and small fruit one year—followed by a rest the next year—with hardly any crop.

- An unpruned tree produces a lot of wild growth, long straight shoots with no branches called *sucker growth*. This is usually unproductive and should be cut out as soon as you see it, especially if it originates close to the ground and below the bud union or graft.

If you recognize any of these conditions, your tree may not have been cared for properly. But it's not too late to do something about it. Don't worry! Corrective pruning needs to be done over a period of time. Don't try to do it all at once. Abruptly changing a set of conditions may have worse consequences that you can't foresee.

When fruit ripens, birds appear so we need to cover our trees with netting. Because of this we like to keep our trees small. Besides, many of us live in small spaces and there's no room for large trees.

63

A tremendously thick growth of wood occurred in this six-year-old apple tree during one year. This was stimulated by last year's pruning. Most of the growth has to be pruned out to let air and sunshine into the tree.

Most of the wood on one side of the same tree has been removed, but the other side still needs to be done. Note how the height of the tree has been brought down.

The Time for Pruning

Finger-and-thumb pruning on both deciduous and citrus trees can be done on a weekly basis, or whenever you walk by your tree. Do this during spurts of growth—usually in spring and fall. It's soft tender growth you can pinch early before it hardens.

Citrus trees seldom have their branches pruned, but lemon trees often produce strong straight growth on their main branches. These shoot through the tree to reach the sunshine. Such suckers should be removed as soon as you see them and before they steal strength from the tree. They are usually unproductive.

Deciduous trees are customarily pruned before spring growth—when the branches are bare and you can see what you are doing. January is the usual month because, in a normal year, the tree is as dormant as ever it will be. Try to get the job done before the buds start to swell. The movement of sap in the tree causes the swelling. You don't want the cut ends to drip. However, leaf buds and flower buds really show their differences as they swell. So, for one year you may want to delay pruning a few days in order to get a good look.

Summer pruning of deciduous trees can be done soon after harvest. Take out a few central shoots, maybe as thick as a pencil, that are shading the larger branches. Next year's fruit buds form on spurs during summer and they need sunshine. Cut out about 15—20% of this shady growth, but do it gradually over a three-week period so as not to cause a sudden exposure of inside wood to strong sunshine.

The Pruning Response

A tree is seldom killed by pruning—though a lot of damage is done by thoughtless butchering. It's surprising how resilient a tree's life force is. Even after being cut down close to the ground there's often a dramatic recovery. Strong and vigorous shoots appear from the sides of the trunk where latent buds were hiding. This is because the roots were not affected by the pruning and now greatly exceed the top growth.

We use this response when we prune fruit trees. Cut a lot off the top and the roots' energy makes new shoots grow where we cut. By being selective and knowing where to cut, we develop future growth and production. And we determine the tree's shape.

Tools Include Pruning Paint

Always use sharp tools. Hand pruners are appropriate for small twigs not much bigger than a pencil. Loppers should be used for larger stuff. Anytime you have to strain when using loppers it's time to use a pruning saw.

Whenever you cut, use pruning paint to seal the ends of the branches. This stops the cut end from drying out — remember how dry the desert is, even in January! And it prevents disease organisms getting into the tree. It avoids the consequence of careless pruning—dieback caused by bacteria and fungi. Always paint the ends of cuts you make. Protect your tree!

Pruning paint from a spray can soaks into the cut ends. Some horticulturalists say the black color attracts too much heat which damages the twigs, but experience suggests otherwise. An alternative, Stockholm Tar material, is thick and rigid. It requires both hands and a daubing stick. It goes on as a blob at the end of a cut. In the dry desert air, it dries out and falls off. Pruning paint from a spray can is the best material to use. Use it every time you cut and just after making the cut. If you

Six-year-old peach tree has been kept low by pruning. Annual pruning stimulated plenty of growth and it's too thick for next year.

Close-up shows what happens when you make a cut on a branch. You automatically get more growth which is often congested. It certainly has to be thinned out the following year.

Same tree as above left, pruned on one side with the other side still to go. See how height has been controlled and tree has been opened up.

Remember pruning makes a tree send out more shoots. These have to be reduced in number to keep good size fruit. Because this tree has had minimum pruning (and was not cut correctly when planted) it is now too large for a home yard.

This tree was pruned back but never thinned out. Congested top growth will provide too much summer shade. We prune in winter because the trees are dormant. Their bare branches also let you see what you have to work on.

Small branches can easily be cut with a sharp pair of hand pruners. It's a finishing tool for the final trimming. This anvil-type pruner tends to crush the bark if the blade is dull. Many gardeners prefer the scissor type at right.

Scissor-type pruner also needs to be sharp to help it do a good job of slicing the cut instead of pressing against the wood and bruising it.

We water a lot and summer growth is luxuriant because of good growing weather. Make sure new growth does not come from below the bud union as shown here.

Don't let the rootstock sucker growth get this big. Cut it out early so the young tree's energy goes into fruit-wood production.

Loppers give you leverage for cutting a branch thicker than your thumb without tearing up the bark. Buy one with compound leverage, not the simple scissors kind shown here.

Large cuts call for a pruning saw with a narrow blade to let you cut close. Also its teeth bite on the *pull* stroke. This is more effective than the woodsman's saw when you are dealing with a wobbling branch. This is a close cut to remove diseased wood—one of the reasons for pruning fruit trees.

Spray can of pruning paint is the best tool of all. Use it as you prune. Don't wait for tomorrow because the cut ends dry out quickly in the desert air.

wait until after lunch, the desert air may have dried out the ends of the branches and bacteria may have entered the tree.

Citrus Pruning Specifics

I've been talking about deciduous fruit trees, of course, but for citrus—one kind of pruning requires no more equipment than your finger and thumb. It's quick to carry out, which is fortunate because it's an operation you should carry out frequently—especially on lemons.

Young citrus trees often grow rather rangy. Their long branches reach out without any side shoots. Correct this by walking round the young tree, pinching the ends of the branches with your finger and thumb nails as you go. The tissue is soft and you easily make a clean cut if you have long, sharp nails.

The result of this gentle pruning is to stop the forward growth and stimulate side buds to break out. The long, empty shoots now become dense with foliage, and the tree's appearance thickens up. More important, you have stimulated lots of side shoots on which flowers and, later, fruits appear.

Side-Growth Stimulation

This little trick we use on citrus readily shows the effect of pruning on any tree. Everyone needs to understand it. *Cuts made on a live part of a tree stimulate side growth.* Home gardeners are interested in that new growth because it's usually fruit-bearing, not just foliage growth. It's actually the basis of pruning for production. Your concern for a tree less than four-years old centers on developing a strong system of branches. These, in due course, become the limb framework. Early flowers should not distract you from this goal—just ignore them and look into the future with nothing on your mind but the shape of the tree.

You can make a newly planted, deciduous (not citrus!) tree begin its branches very close to the ground by courageously cutting the trunk 9 inches above the bud union. This removes two years of growth, young branches 3 feet up. Emotionally, it's not easy to do—because all you have left is a stump. See the photos on the following page.

Never mind—do this just after you plant your newly bought tree. The re-sult looks awful and destructive, but very soon numerous side shoots break out just below the cut, some 10 or 12 inches from the ground. So many, in fact, that you have to thin out the weaker ones. Keep three strong shoots, evenly spaced around the tree and also spaced up and down. It's better they don't all grow out from the same place. They will be weak if they do, and will tear off from their own weight.

Let these branches grow uninterrupted for the first year. Next spring cut them back, leaving about 18 inches of growth. They are thin now, but they are the tree's framework branches for the rest of its life. They thicken up and grow branches of their own—secondary branches. These also remain with the tree for the rest of its life.

Second-year branches become fruit-bearing and you prune them every January to develop more fruiting wood.

Judiciously removing some three- and four-year branches doesn't hurt the tree. It merely stops it from getting too big. Pruning cuts make for more growth but the tree stays shorter and more compact. More growth usually means thicker growth. And, if it gets too thick, the inner branches don't get enough light. This means fruit is not developed inside the tree. We want fruit on the inside because there it finds protection from the fierce summer sun. Outside fruit burns.

Light summer pruning therefore becomes a necessity. It checks exuberant growth that came from January's pruning. It's important to get light onto next year's fruiting wood. Don't overdo it—be careful not to expose inner wood to sunburn.

Recognizing Fruit & Leaf Buds

Learn to recognize fruit buds. On a peach tree in January, you'll find them on twigs that developed two summers ago. The outside 10 or 12 inches of the twigs are greenish and have single thin buds. That's last summer's growth. Behind this the branch turns a pinkish color and buds are in threes—a fat one with a thin one on either side. More toward the center of the tree, pink wood turns to brown. This is three-year-old wood—too old to bear fruit. However, it bears two-year-old pink side branches with triple buds and farther out the green one-year wood with single buds.

Removing a diseased branch revealed this deeper infection. Further cutting will be necessary until no signs are evident. Infection probably started with an end that was not sealed with pruning paint.

Perhaps you've never thought of your finger and thumb nails as pruning tools. They do a good job on tender growth such as wild shoots of lemon trees in the spring.

When you plant a new tree you usually cut off a lot of the top growth to get three or four strong branches. These are called *scaffold branches* on which the rest of the tree grows in years to come.

If you want a tree with a lower scaffold system then you must cut even lower. New growth will start just below the cut.

This is what your tree looks like a year later. Now you have to select the strongest three or four branches for the scaffold and remove all others from the jungle.

Thin buds are leaf buds. Fat buds are flower or fruit buds. You can "eyeball" the year's fruit potential by "measuring" the pink growth and "counting" the fruit buds all round the tree. If there are many triple buds, you prune more severely than if you find only a few. If you leave a lot of flower buds and they all get pollinated and set, you'll get a lot of small fruit. If the tree didn't yield or grow much last year, don't let it bear heavily and exhaust itself this year. Prune out a lot of those triple buds on pink wood to control the harvest.

The amount of green wood indicates the vigor of last year's growth. If you have a few long shoots, cut them back halfway to start side shoots during the coming summer. If there are too many green shoots, remove some entirely.

Apples and pears produce fruit on the ends of new growth in the early years of the tree. You don't want long shoots, so you cut most of them back to keep the tree small. While you lose some production in the process, the side shoots resulting from this pruning also produce flowers at their ends. Meanwhile, as the twig matures into a branch, short sturdy side shoots called *spurs* begin to grow. These are strictly flower shoots and should not be cut off. Spurs last four or five years.

Apricots follow the same sequence of single buds and triple buds, but there's no color change as the twigs get older. There's another difference. Short side shoots called *spurs* begin to develop on second-year wood and remain as the twigs grow into branches. It's a mistake to cut off apricot spurs because they are fruit-bearing twigs, growing some 3-inches long and lasting for three years.

Apple and pear trees also produce fruit-bearing spurs. You can encourage their development by pruning the ends of vigorous, two-year-old, upright shoots. Remember, an end cut makes side growth.

Pruning Different Fruit Trees

Here's a brief summary of where different fruit trees grow their flowers and how they are pruned.

Apple— Apple trees grow their fruit at the ends of long upright branches, but also on spurs that develop on their sides as the tree matures. Some varieties tend toward end fruit and others toward spur production. It's hard to tell which are which until you observe one season's flowering. Some apples don't flower at the ends of new shoots. You'll have to be patient for four or five years until spurs appear.

In any event, you don't want a tall tree, so cut back the long, straight upright shoots and open up the center. If you cut off too much growth you will lose spur development on the sides, as well as flowers at the end. Don't worry, the cut will stimulate side branches and these will, in due course, grow their own spurs.

Don't let a young tree produce heavily during its first years. As soon as spurs appear you will know how far to cut back next year. Spurs stay productive for several years—treasure them!

The Anna variety, for example, may produce as many as 10 or 12 fruit in a cluster. They have to be thinned to one or two, otherwise the fruit will be small.

Mature trees are pruned to remove a percentage of the spurs—more are pruned after a heavy crop—less after a light crop. Cutting one tall branch might remove 10 or 12 spurs as well as reducing a tree's height. Try to keep most of the spurs on the inside of the tree where the fruit will be shaded by the foliage of spring growth.

Apricot—Flowers and fruit are borne on the sides of one-year-old twigs and also in clusters on short spurs on two- and three-year-old wood.

Fig—Flowers and fruit are borne on the ends of this year's growth. Prune back long shoots in January to develop side shoots. You'll lose fruit in the short run—the July crop—but you'll get more ends—and more fruit later in the fall or next year. The later crop may occur so late that it doesn't ripen. Figs are rapid growers and can be pruned severely without hurting.

Grapefruit, Orange and Tangerine —There is no need to prune except to remove suckers and wild growth. Although a tall tree can be "topped" to reduce its height, don't do this during the summer months. Strong sunshine coming into the center where it was shaded will kill unprotected branches.

Lemon—These vigorous growers need to be checked by pinching the terminal growth during spring and fall growth spurts. Lemons also develop a lot of wild suckers from older parts of the tree. Prune these out early.

Peach—Prune these vigorous growers hard. Remove about half of the pink wood where you find buds in threes. Severity of pruning depends on the amount of growth made last year. Don't be afraid to remove whole branches if the tree becomes too tall or too rangy.

Pear—Pear trees are very much like apple trees in their growth habits, except that they are slender and angular. Young trees produce terminal flowers

Single, narrow buds at the upper end of this peach twig will produce leaves. This is last-summer's growth. Farther back there are triple buds. These produce fruit from the fat buds between the two narrow ones. Even farther back, the wood is too old to produce buds unless a pruning cut brings them out.

As the buds begin to swell, they show their differences, but it is too late for pruning. The fat buds will be flowers, and these will give the fruit. The narrow buds will be leaves.

Apricot trees develop little twigs full of flower potential. Don't prune out these spurs—that's where your fruit will be borne.

Apple trees show even better spurs.

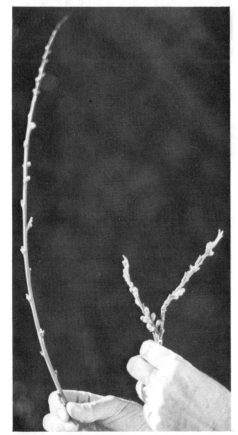

Dwarf trees have their branches telescoped. Because there are more buds per inch than on standard trees, you must count the buds, not measure the length of cuts you make. On the left is a standard tree's branch, compared with a branch from a dwarf peach tree on the right.

Pruning skills require you to judge a tree's capability to flower abundantly. Cut lightly if you don't see a lot of flower buds. Cut more heavily if there are too many.

and older ones flower more on spurs.

Cut back the tall growth as soon as you know where the spurs are. Too severe a cut means you lose some spurs. The compensation is that you get stronger side shoots—which will grow their own spurs in due course.

Follow the same pruning procedures as for apples. However, most pear varieties are tall trees and are usually trained to be tall by allowing a central shoot to lead the way upwards. After seven or eight years the leader develops side branches—each with its own spurs—and after a few years the central leader can be removed completely, to be replaced with a lower leader. This is how you keep a pear tree small.

Pears are usually harvested as hard fruit and birds should not be interested in them. We said this about apples when they first arrived in the desert,

but time has proved us wrong. Birds do like apples, and they'll probably like pears too when they find out what they are.

Keep pear trees small by hard pruning, but keep enough spurs on the tree each spring to give you a harvest.

Pecan—Don't cut back the tree. Let it grow as large and as naturally as possible. You don't climb the tree to get the harvest. You pick the nuts off the ground, so the tree's height is not a problem. On a young tree, encourage side shoots which bear flowers, by nipping back soft growth about 6 inches each spring.

Plum—In its early years, a plum tree is narrow and tall. Let it grow this way because it will widen out on its own later. You may cut out the top half after three or four years by going into the center and sawing off the trunk, keeping side shoots growing at their upward angles.

Pomegranate—The natural form of this small tree is weeping and somewhat untidy because of its multiple stems. Fruit is borne on the ends of branches so if you do any pruning, you also remove fruit potential. Let pomegranates grow the way they want to. They look more attractive.

Grape—Prune severely, as much as 90 percent of last year's growth. Read the grape chapter, page 139, for details.

Repair Pruning

There's another kind of pruning, done particularly on older trees that are weak and whose limbs easily break. It's called *repair pruning* and you simply remove any broken and storm-damaged limbs as they occur. This usually requires a bit of saw work. It leaves great gaps in the structure of your tree. These will fill in with new growth as time goes by. If a branch gets twisted in a storm and splits without breaking off, don't try to patch it up. Take the saw and make a clean cut where it comes off the limb without leaving a stub. Don't forget the spray can of pruning paint.

It's not only storm damage that requires attention. Watch for slime flux and sooty canker. Prune out infected wood to prevent a disease spreading within the tree.

There is little need to prune a pecan tree if you want to enjoy it as a shade tree on your patio. The nuts fall off when they are ready and you pick them up off the ground.

Pruning Dwarf Fruit Trees

The story is the same with dwarf fruit trees. But, because the spaces between the buds are much closer, you cut much less length than on standard trees.

Measure the green terminal twigs and the pink, three-bud wood on a dwarf peach tree. Count the buds and compare the number with those on a similar part of a standard peach tree. There will be roughly the same number of buds. However, the dwarf tree's buds will be spaced more closely on about 6 inches of twig, whereas the standard tree's buds are spread over about 16 or 24 inches.

Generally, you don't prune dwarf fruit trees for the purpose of stimulating new fruit-bearing wood. Pruning is necessary where branches are rubbing against one another or where you have any branches growing toward the center of the tree instead of outward.

A Properly Pruned Tree May Not Look Pretty

Don't be frightened about pruning deciduous fruit trees. Remember that the main purpose of pruning is to develop new wood that will bear fruit. That will happen, even if you make severe cuts. But it might take a year or two.

Remember, too, that a properly pruned tree doesn't always look pretty —or even attractive.

It's fruit that you're after—the tree's appearance is secondary.

Rain Is Good for Gardeners

Rain is a kind of stimulant. Don't you feel good when it rains? Rain gives us lots of gardening opportunities. A soft soil lets us pull weeds. A lot of black mustard, shepherds purse, mallow and foxtail plants set seed in the April rains. We should take care of them immediately. Apart from the foxtail that has shallow insignificant roots, they are deep-rooted nuisances that often break when we try to pull them up out of dry soil. On the other hand, when the soil is soft after a rain it's easy to get the whole plant. Pull your weeds now while the soil is still moist.

Rain washes the dusty plants clean. This makes them look nice, but there's an added benefit. Plants such as oleanders have their dusty poison washed off of the leaves. It's more pleasant to go trimming the oleander hedges. You don't get the dust up your nose to make you sneeze and on your lips to give you that long-lasting bitter taste that only a cold beer can dispel. The new growth on oleanders is ready for a trim.

Rain allows us to transplant shrubs and flowers, though perhaps not the bigger trees. If it rains again, use the opportunity to roll the lawn. Rain makes the soil soft and plastic enough so a roller will work effectively. A new lawn is usually rough because any levelling we did has settled unevenly. A roller is a useful tool after a good rain. Slowly roll it this way—and that. Then go diagonally, using it as a good cook uses a rolling pin—to get a level flatness. You can rent rollers.

Rain keeps the wildflowers growing, which at this time of their life means flowering. If it doesn't rain, give them a watering. Make the most of the rain if we get another blessing!

This information originally appeared in one of George's weekly columns in the *Tucson Citizen*. This was dated April 13.

Bend shoots down and hold them down with a weight on the end. A mass of new buds will appear on the branches. You'll get fruit quicker this way.

Young trees send out vigorous shoots that some gardeners call *suckers*. Actual suckers originate close to the ground and below the bud union or graft (see page 131). Top growth shown here (arrow) is a natural growth pattern that can be used to quickly develop a fruiting tree, as shown in the photo at right.

Don't chop off all the branches at the same height. That way the tree loses its natural shape and you get a bushy growth at the top—which makes matters worse.

Remove the taller parts of the tree by cutting branches where they leave the limb. Finish with an irregular profile like you had before. You have opened up   the tree to let wind blow through the foliage—thereby reducing the chance for damage.

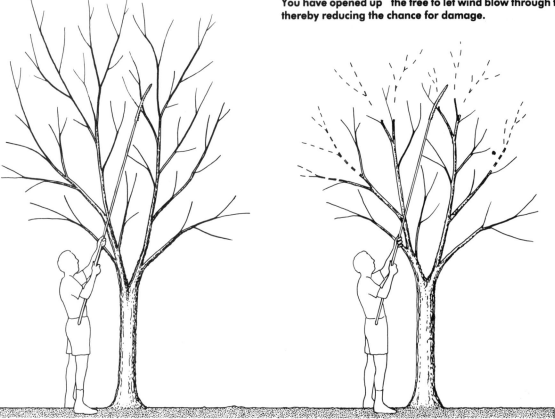

14

SOWING SEEDS

Many of us like to grow our own plants from seed. It seems the proper thing to do if we are gardeners. However, it's not easy to do unless you have some advanced gardener's equipment. More of that later. The choices are to sow seed directly in the ground, to grow them for a short time in little containers in a soil mix, or forget the whole idea and buy plants at a nursery when you need them.

Disadvantages of Sowing in the Ground

If you sow seeds directly in the ground, you risk having the seedlings stolen by ants or eaten by birds. They might be eaten by cutworms, too. If the soil is too cold, say in February, the seeds won't germinate. It's the same if you sow seeds in August. They might suffer from heat. There may be soil-borne diseases that will catch tender new plants. Seeds you start in the ground require care and attention. They can dry out easily, be damaged by wind, or be sunburned.

Our short growing seasons give us the greatest disadvantage to sowing in

Larger seeds, such as corn, beans and squash, can be sown by the younger set. Because these seeds germinate quickly, it's a good way to get children started in gardening.

Press a rake into the ground to make holes of the right depth, twice the diameter of the seed. Sow one seed in each hole.

the ground. We need to have large plants available when conditions are right for planting. There isn't time to start with seed. It will take too long to germinate in the cold soil and the growing season will be half over.

Advantages of Sowing in Containers

By sowing seeds in containers, we gain time. While we are growing seedlings and applying controls on the temperature—keeping them warm in winter and growing them in the shade during summer—the soil is warming up in the spring and cooling down in late summer. So we usually set out vegetable plants that were grown in

containers.

Most gardeners buy them at a nursery where there is usually a good assortment of suitable varieties. But not always. Perhaps they sold out and can't or won't re-order. Perhaps they couldn't get the latest recommended varieties. Perhaps the season started early and their main consignments haven't been delivered yet.

No matter what the reason, it's disappointing not to find the varieties you want at planting time when all is hurry and bustle. In the spring, it's especially important to plant the right varieties. It's not so critical in the fall.

Growing seeds on a kitchen windowsill often means the plants are weak from the day they start. They exhaust themselves stretching towards the light and never recover.

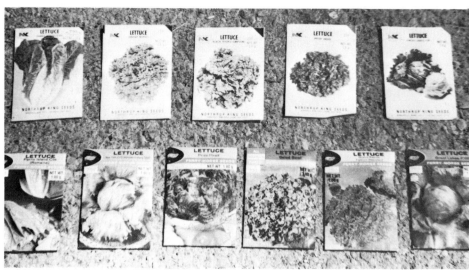

Seed packets are plentiful at nurseries and there's a wider range in the catalogs—even more than the few kinds of lettuce shown here. If you wait to buy plants at a nursery, they may not have the kinds you want. Sow seeds to make sure.

Styrofoam coffee cups make good containers. Sow only one seed or if you are a pessimist, two. Quickly thin to one plant so there is no competition. You want seeds to grow quickly. All containers, no matter their size, must have drainage holes.

Plastic trays taking many seeds let you organize your program in a small space. Part of that organizing is prompt labeling.

The best way to raise seedlings in the spring—if you don't have a greenhouse—is to put them in a cold frame to catch the sun's heat. Installing an electric cable beneath the containers makes sure they germinate quickly and grow strongly.

A good soil mix for seedlings is made of equal parts of peat moss, Perlite, clean sand, and vermiculite. This is a sterile mix and free of soil organisms that would harm tender seedlings.

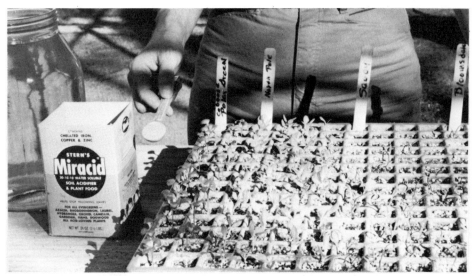

Seedlings at this stage have used up their food reserves and begin to pale. Encourage continued growth in the sterile medium by including a teaspoon of balanced fertilizer in a gallon of water every second watering. Don't keep the seedlings too dark green in color by overfertilizing.

Varieties Suitable for the Desert

Ask your local Extension Service office for the list of suitable varieties and show it to your nurseryman. If he doesn't sound convincing about getting those you want for the coming season, grow your own. You will need six or seven weeks to do it.

There are many mail-order seed companies. The big three—Burpees, Parks and Stokes, sell suitable seeds for the desert. They are very prompt in filling orders when most gardeners in the country are not even thinking of growing plants.

Stokes, a Canadian company, also offers suitable varieties for the desert. This seems surprising, but Canada has short seasons like we do. Snow is their reason—sun is ours. You always have a wider choice of seeds in a seed catalog, but don't get carried away by the pretty pictures. Use the list of locally recommended varieties as your guide.

What Will You Need?

You now have a stack of reasons to grow your own plants from seed. Understand you are committing yourself to six or more weeks of care and attention. One day's goofing off ruins the whole exercise.

You'll need plenty of space with good light and protection from wind. It's not feasible to grow seedlings on a kitchen windowsill. It's too dark and the seedlings stretch toward the light. They remain weak whatever you do to try to correct it.

Make a cold frame out of old sash windows and some bricks for the sides or use corrugated fiberglass. It doesn't have to be elaborate because you are going to use it only for a short time and then dismantle it. Let it face south so it catches the sunlight. Even better, turn your cold frame into a hot bed by adding a soil-heating cable. Place it on the ground and cover it with hardware cloth to protect it from sharp garden tools. Then cover everything with an inch of sterilized soil to help spread the heat from the cable. The seeds will be kept at 70F. This is the best way to stimulate germination and maintain seedling growth.

Which Containers to Use?

You will read in some gardening magazines that egg cartons—and even eggshells—can be used to grow seedlings. Don't believe it. They are too small. Don't use old plant containers either. They can be contaminated and one of the purposes of growing your own plants is to avoid soil-borne diseases.

Two suitable containers are available from your kitchen—milk cartons and styrofoam coffee cups. Both are about 4-inches deep, which means they have room for strong root development. Staple the opening of a milk carton and cut open one side which now becomes the top. All containers must have drainage holes punched in their bottoms.

Styrofoam coffee cups in 6- or 8-ounce sizes, are especially suitable. Put two seeds in a cup and remove the weaker of the two seedlings after a week or so. Write the name of the variety on the rim of the cup with a ballpoint pen. This is a reliable way to identify your plants. It can stay as a collar around a plant after it has been set out in the garden. Read the names of successful varieties at the end of the season! Moveable labels easily get lost or misplaced—even in commercial operations.

Whichever kind of container you use, don't fill it completely with soil. Leave about 1/2 inch of space that you fill with water when you sprinkle the plants. Don't let the seedlings soak up water from a pan below because they will be drawing up salts that will evaporate at the soil surface. Seedlings have little resistance to salts, even at low concentrations. Always sprinkle from above.

Commercial seedling trays made of plastic and holding more than 100 compartments can be purchased from seed catalogs. Sow only one seed in each box. If the roots become crowded, the seedlings may have to be transplanted into coffee cups for another week's growth to get some size on them.

Such seedling trays allow you to grow a lot of seedlings without taking up a lot of space. They are low-priced and a real bargain.

Soil-Mix Requirements

Make a soil mix of equal parts coarse sand, peat moss, perlite and vermiculite. Dampen it as you mix to get a more even consistency. Bang the container down when you think it is full of soil mix. This settles it *before* you sow the seed, which is better than afterwards.

Don't add any fertilizer or manures, though you can substitute compost for peat moss. Some gardeners like to add an amount of soil from their garden to bring the mix closer to the plants' future environment. However, there's a risk of introducing soil-borne diseases.

Your soil mix is designed to give a balance of drainage. This leads to good air space and water-holding capacity. This means strong roots!

A perfect plant for setting out in a day or two. The label tells you the variety and its date of sowing. Expose this plant in the open for a day or two to harden it off before planting. Watch out for frost at night.

Don't be afraid to pull up a seedling to see how the roots are developing. It's better to lift by the leaves, but this stout stem can be carefully handled. If you are heavy-handed, grasp the plant by the leaves and you won't bruise the stem.

How Many Seeds?

Sow one seed—or two at the most—in each space and lightly cover it with soil mix at about two or three seeds' depth. Water, and keep the containers moist all the time. If they dry out for even a day, the seeds will die just as they start to grow. Today's seeds are of high quality and if they don't come up, it's usually nobody's fault but your own.

Heat, Light & Ventilation

Seedlings need good light. It's best to keep the containers outside during the day to get warmth and light from the sun. Bring them inside for the night to keep them warm and then put them out again the next morning. This gets tiresome and you'll quickly see the advantages of a cold frame or a hot bed.

Bottom heat from a soil-heating cable is the best thing for seedlings during the spring season when conditions are cold. You don't need one in late summer—waiting for the weather to cool. You don't need a cold frame or hot bed either.

Beware of *damping-off*. This fungus disease thrives in still air when there is a lot of moisture. You'll find these conditions if you overwater crowded seedlings in soil used once before. The fungus invades the tender stem and weakens it. Plants fall over and don't recover. If you get this problem, throw everything out and start again. It usually happens early in the process.

Next time, sow thinly. Put the seedlings in the sun and keep them better ventilated. Sterile soil mixes are absolutely essential!

Use good-quality tap water when you sprinkle the seedlings. You don't want to put salts on their tender leaves. Use a gentle delivery—not a heavy blast of water. There are watering cans with fine sprinklers on them and these are worth buying for your seedling operations.

Fertilizing the Seedlings

When your plants have four or six leaves, they will have used up the supply of food stored in the seeds. No nutrients were put in the soil mix so now you have to supply them to keep your plants growing. Use a teaspoon of houseplant food to each gallon of water at alternate irrigations. Don't worry about putting salts on the

A watering can with a fine sprinkling rose on it makes sure seedlings are not washed out or knocked over.

Before the seedlings begin to crowd their soil, carefully, but firmly, pull them out and plant them in the ground in your garden. However, if they grew too quickly and the soil is still cold you will have to "warehouse" them in coffee cups until spring arrives.

leaves. You will be unable to avoid this, but the chemicals are plant foods—not plant poisons. There will be some useful nutrient absorption through the leaves. To play it safe, keep the concentrations on the low side, a teaspoon per gallon is enough to start with. You can increase this to a tablespoon per gallon at every irrigation just before the plants are ready to set out.

Preparing for the Real World

Finally, when your plants are big enough and the time has come to set them out, toughen them up a little. Move the containers into the open air close to the garden site. Let them experience reality for a day or two. Even let them wilt a little in the sunshine—but be careful not to overdo it.

Transplanting the Seedlings

When you transplant seedlings into a larger container or set them out, be careful not to grab them by the stem. You could pinch or bruise them that

way. Pull them out of their container by their strongest leaf. Evenings are preferred over midday for setting out plants because they go through the night without stress. A hot, sunny afternoon weakens newly planted seedlings. Make sure your garden soil, or your additional planting mix if you are "moving-up" seedlings, is moist. Work quickly so the tender roots don't dry out. Settle in the seedlings with a starter solution high in phosphate. Shade them if the days are hot and sunny. Shelter them from wind.

Where to Buy Seeds

Seed-packet displays at garden centers are often the most neglected part of the store. Consequently, gardeners prefer to order fresh seeds from catalogs.

Desert-gardening seasons are "out of step" with mainstream gardening, so many companies seem unable to respond to an order that is, to them at the time, an unusual and difficult request.

At the Extension Garden Center we have found the following seed companies to be prompt in filling orders. Their catalogs list a wide range of suitable varieties, and they are clearly described. They don't make extravagant claims for gimmicky novelties, recently discovered and untested.

There are sure to be other companies that sell good seeds. It's just that we have stayed with those that have given us good service:

- **W. Atlee Burpee & Co.**, 300 Park Avenue, Warminster, Pennsylvania 18974.
- **Horticultural Enterprises**, P.O. Box 810082, Dallas, Texas 75381-0082 (specializes in "authentic Mexican seeds"— peppers of all kinds).
- **Nichol's Garden Nursery**, 1190 North Pacific Highway, Albany, Oregon 97321.
- **Park Seed Company**, P.O. Box 31, Cokesbury Road, Greenwood, South Carolina 29647.
- **Roswell Seed Company**, P.O. Box 725, Roswell, New Mexico 88202-0725.
- **Stokes Seeds Inc.**, P.O. Box 548, Buffalo, New York 14240.
- **Sunrise Enterprises**, P.O. Box 330058, West Hartford, Connecticut 06133-0058 (supplier of oriental seeds).
- **Vesey's Seeds Ltd.**, P.O. Box 9000, Calais, Maine 04619-6102. Their *Seeds for Short Seasons* catalog is particularly appropriate to desert gardening.

Plant Chinese Pole Beans Now; Buy Tomato Seeds for Fall Harvest

There's one plant that does well in the summer heat. It has no pests or diseases. It loves the sunshine and the heat. It can be used for landscaping to screen or give overhead shade—and there's the bonus of an abundant and reliable harvest until the frosts of November kill the plant.

The plant is the Chinese pole bean, or asparagus bean (because it tastes like asparagus), or yard-long bean (because it has a long thin pod without strings).

If you've grown this summertime bean you know what a productive plant it is. If you never have, then it's time you did. June is the month to sow a few seeds. They come up in three or four days and, provided you give them a trellis of some sort, you can expect six feet of growth in six or seven weeks. Sow the seed and stand back! It's a Jack-in-the-beanstalk sort of plant. You need only five or six seeds because the plants are so productive.

You can buy the seeds through the seed catalogs and maybe at some of the nurseries. We have been growing the plant at the Extension Garden Center for the past 10 years or more, saving the very, very best for next year's planting at the center, giving the very best to interested gardeners and eating the best.

Over the years we have improved the strain and have shortened the maturity period to 56 days from the original 80. We started by selecting for pod length but realized that a bean measuring 36 inches long has no merit over two that measure 18 inches, so we switched gears to concentrate on quick production.

Several times in this column I've mentioned that summertime gardening is less rewarding than a fall planting. Chinese pole beans are the exception to this statement, but my advice to go easy on the acreage during summer is still good. We are due for shocking weather before too long. That will be followed by much better times and we should be prepared for them. The better days will start in early September—just three months away!

A number of Master Gardener volunteers at the center have said that fall tomatoes do very well. In order to get a good harvest in October and November you have to set out plants in August. And in order to do that you need to sow seed about six weeks beforehand. This means you'll be sowing tomato seed—in coffee cups in a sheltered place—sometime in late June and buying your seed in mid-June. Not far away on the calendar. Think about it!

Fall tomatoes don't get curly-top disease (which you can't treat), they don't get blossom-end rot and they set more fruit to the flower bunch because of the cooling weather. You'll save on water, too, because the plants don't have such a high demand as they do through the summer.

The garden strategy is to pull up the spring-planted tomatoes as soon as the harvest from spring flowering is gathered. There won't be any flowers or young fruit in July or August so the plant doesn't earn its keep in watering.

Another gardening strategy—for those who insist on eating lots of squash all through the summer—is to sow three seeds whenever the earlier-planted squash falls over with age. A fallen plant is believed to be more susceptible to squash-vine borer than a young erect plant.

As soon as the three new seeds begin to flower and produce, pull out the older plants. Older plants infested with the borer are not worth fooling with, though many people slice the stem and dig the grub out with a pin in an effort to save the plant. Usually, they're not successful.

Here's something to do for your desert-landscape trees. Warm weather causes them to grow and the irrigation you give them means a lot of new foliage is produced. If that foliage is congested and close to the center of the tree you can expect it to be blown over in the forthcoming summer storms. So, before it's too late, get out your pruning snippers and thin out the thick foliage so the wind can blow through. Don't cut back the branches—that simply encourages more side shoots just behind the cut. Such new shoots simply provide more wind resistance. Take care of the top growth to avoid having the tree blow over.

Take care of the bottom growth, too. That means the roots, which are dependent on the supply of moisture you give the tree through the irrigation system.

If you water with a flood basin—by far the best method—you should extend it to accommodate the new roots at the end of last year's growth. Roots grow where there's water. They won't leave moist soil to go into dry soil, so if you are watering the same old area for years and years there's little expansion of roots. Roots hold the tree in the ground and prevent it from being blown away.

To get more roots, especially wider roots, you've got to give wider watering. It's that simple.

If your trees are being irrigated with a drip system, you should consider moving the emitters out a couple of feet, and you might need to add three or four emitters on the widened circle you've made. Always water deeply. You want deep roots as well as wide roots. Trees with adequate roots don't blow over.

Later this summer when you see a tree that's been pushed over by a storm, go and take a look at it. More than likely it's been watered by a single emitter close to the trunk. And quite likely the maintenance person increased the flow of water to accommodate the hot weather. That additional watering created a mudpie close around the trunk and the soft soil had no strength.

Adapted from one of George's weekly articles in the *Tucson Citizen*. This one was dated June 15.

15

PLANTING OUT

It's exciting to sow seeds. There's heady expectation in getting them to grow for you that's only surpassed by going to a nursery and picking out young plants. Buying new plants is fun.

Pot or Sixpak?

First, there's the question whether to buy a good-sized plant in a 4-inch pot—at a higher price—or a sixpak of smaller plants for less money.

If you are an early gardener and always have everything ready on time, it's probably better to go the economical route and buy the smaller plants. Once in the warm ground they will establish quickly and start to grow. They will soon be the size of those more expensive nursery plants in the bigger containers.

If you are always late and have to hurry to catch up, there may be a point in getting the larger plants. But don't be fooled into buying a plant that already has small fruit—or even flowers. Such plants are already old before their time. Foliage appearance is important. It should be dark green and well-leafed down to the bottom of the stem. This is an indicator of the age of the merchandise. Pale, washed-out foliage tells you the small amount of soil the plant is growing in has run out of nitrogen. The plant has been in the nursery a long time and is no longer fresh and vigorous. As it ages, the bottom leaves turn brown and dry and then drop off. A plant with small bronze-colored leaves and a little bunch of tiny fruit borne on a skinny stem should have been consigned to the discard heap.

Look at the Roots

The best plant-freshness indicator is the root system. Even with a small container, the roots should be white and just coming to the edge of the soil ball.

A good plant in a 4-inch pot at a nursery.

Sixpak at a nursery.

Too many seeds produced crowded plants that are weakened from competing with one another for light, water and nutrients.

Good roots on a plant in a 4-inch pot.

They hold the soil together when you turn the sixpak upside down and tap out the plants for inspection. If the roots are brown and circling the bottom of the container, you are looking at an old plant.

Don't be afraid to take a look at the roots. A good nurseryman will respect your inspection of his plants and will be pleased when you make a good choice. After all, you don't buy a pair of shoes without trying them on—maybe several pairs go through your inspection-and-approval system. Why not do the same with plants?

Common Sense

Buy the plants on the last stop of your shopping trip. Don't put plants under the back window or in the trunk of a car and leave them while you saunter through a mall for an hour or two.

Don't unload your plants on the garage floor, or leave them there until the weekend. Plant them right away.

Sixpaks come in two kinds. The first

Use a starter solution made up of a table-spoon of a phosphate fertilizer in a gallon of water. It helps a new plant to establish itself quickly.

Cut off the bottom of a glass gallon jar to make an individual greenhouse over a newly planted plant. Cold winds are kept out and some mild frost protection is afforded. And, soil-living cutworms cannot get to the stem to chew on it. A plastic jar does not work as well.

Starter Solution Helps

Dig the planting hole to the full depth of the trowel, then fill the hole with a starter solution. This can be bought at a nursery ready-made as a vitamin-B solution. Or make your own by shaking a tablespoon of triple superphosphate in a gallon of water. Phosphate is a plant food and vitamin B is a stimulant, so take your choice. Both work well, but use only one.

Drop your plant into the hole and then pull it up to the level at which it was growing in the sixpak. Hold the top leaf rather than grabbing the stem. You don't want to bruise it. If you are naturally rough and tear a leaf, it doesn't matter so much.

Avoid pushing the plant down to the bottom of a shallow hole where the roots might be bent upwards. Make sure the roots stay down by giving the plant a little upwards tug. Then move the muddy soil sideways towards the roots. Invariably, the plant will sink a little the next day or two, so it's a good idea to finish a little on the high side.

Keep the soil moist by watering every day, even twice a day in summer. Water according to the soil moisture. It must not dry out but you don't want it too wet all the time, either. Watch the plant, too. Don't let it wilt while it is struggling to get established. Bottom leaves may wilt and even die, but top growth should remain fresh and vigorous.

If the plant immediately begins to put out new leaves, you have done a good transplanting job.

Help the New Plants to a Good Start

If the weather is cold or windy, it's a good idea to help the plant along for a few days with a glass-jar cover. Place a gallon pickle jar upside down over the plant. Each plant now has its own greenhouse but you have to watch greenhouses. They easily get too hot if there's no ventilation.

If the afternoons get hot, simply take off the jars until things cool down again. You can also use glass gallon jugs if you have a glass-cutting device to remove the bottoms. The open top prevents the plant from getting steamed up with too much moisture from the soil. Jar cutters are usually available at hobby stores.

Cold spring soil can be warmed by surrounding the new plant with clear plastic. This also saves water by preventing evaporation from the soil. Anchor the light material with bricks or the wind witll gather up the plastic with the recently planted tomato.

has separate compartments. Each plant has its own cube of soil and comes out of the plastic with a push from underneath. The other kind holds six plants in one volume of soil and that presents problems.

Do you tear the plants out of this volume, untidily breaking roots as you go? Or do you cut through the soil—and roots—to give yourself regular, sharp-edged cubes?

Either way is good, so don't agonize over this issue. The roots intertwine with one another and you're going to do some damage either way. There's a slight preference for gently tearing out the roots because you generally get more of them intact this way.

Don't try and keep every root by putting the sixpak under a faucet and washing all the soil away. Too much disturbance occurs when you do this.

Watch Temperature & Moisture

Always work in moist soil when setting out plants. Best of all is when it is raining, but we can't rely on rains in the desert. We have to provide our own moisture.

In the spring, it's better to set out plants in the evening because they get a whole night to settle in before the next day's heat. During the fall, a morning planting is better because a day's warmth follows.

Protect each plant from cold winds with clear plastic held on construction mesh with clothespins. If winds come from all directions, close the circle. Abundant foliage will completely fill this cage and its squares will hold the branches out of the dirt. In summer, drape a sheet over the top of the cage to give shade.

Strong fertilizer in a storage jar is taken out in a diluted form by the siphon every time the faucet is turned on. It's a labor-saving device if you have a large garden to care for.

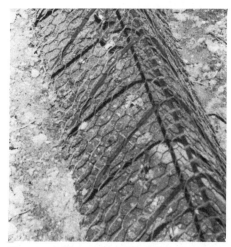

Young seedlings, especially lettuce, are attractive to birds. A portable and reusable chicken-wire tent will protect them.

Push the jar an inch into the soil around the plant to make a barrier to cutworms and surface grubs. Another way to protect your transplants—seemingly a favorite food of these insects—is to wrap a piece of aluminum foil around the stem. Don't forget to go below the soil level for complete protection. Cutworms spend most of their days in the soil and come up to feed at night.

Summertime planting, on the other hand, calls for a few days' shading from the sun. Place an upright board near each plant so it casts a shadow over it during the afternoon. Put the board upwind of desert gusts blowing sand at high speed and you'll give your plants added protection.

Fertilizing New Plants

Because you have prepared your garden soil properly, page 29, there should be no need to add fertilizer to young transplants. The soil itself will be sufficient to get them growing

nicely. Unless, that is, you are just starting your garden and good soil hasn't had time to develop. In that case, there will be no harm in occasionally adding fertilizer to the water as you irrigate. Every second or third irrigation might be sufficient.

Add a tablespoon of Miracid® to a gallon of water and irrigate your plants with the solution. For a large garden, it pays to use a hose proportioner on the faucet where it draws the same strength solution out of a container of

Cut top off coffee cup and keep it as a label for the rest of the season. It also acts as a barrier against cutworms.

Good roots down to the bottom of the container are a sign the plant is ready to set out. Brown and more numerous roots indicate plant stayed in its container too long

Tall tomato seedling can be planted on its side in a trench. Leafless stem will quickly grow roots in the warm surface soil. If you set the plant out in an upright position, its roots will be in cold soil and it will not establish itself quickly.

When you backfill a planting hole, do a rain dance on the soil to help settle it. Leave it for a day or two and then make the small planting hole in the center just big enough for the new plant.

A bare-root tree should have its roots spread out over a cone of soil.

Don't delay in covering the roots. They mustn't be allowed to dry out for a moment. Use plenty of water when planting a tree. It helps settle the soil besides keeping the roots moist.

Example of what happens if you don't stomp the soil and don't use a lot of water to help settle it before planting. A tree planted here would have sunk with the soil. Bud union will be buried when you fill in the cavity. In this case, it's better to delay planting and fill up the cavity with a mound.

concentrated plant food.

Planting Fruit Trees

If you are planting a fruit tree, the same principles apply. Work in moist or wet soil, use vitamin B, don't plant too deep, and shade the tree if you plant during the hot months. Follow up with frequent irrigations.

If you plant a bare-root tree, it's especially important to have the hole backfilled, moist and ready. Don't delay a moment between buying the tree and getting it into the ground.

A bare-root tree in a nursery often has its branches trimmed before you take it home. Have the same done with a tree in a container—even if it is in full leaf—to develop its future framework branches. Cutting back also helps the tree overcome transplanting shock. Remember it was pampered by shading and daily watering in the nursery and protected from drying winds. A tree, after trimming, has a more favorable balance of roots to leaves and this means it is likely to establish itself more easily.

Planting Citrus

On the other hand, don't trim back a young citrus tree unless there is some wild one-sided growth and it's the only tree left in the nursery. It's better to wait for an evenly branched one.

Bud union shows where rootstock meets the top-worked fruiting wood. Keep it well above soil level, otherwise roots may form on the fruiting part and the value of the rootstock will be lost.

Golden Rule for Planting

Whenever you plant vegetables or trees, there's a golden rule to follow. Always plant at the same depth as the plant was growing before. Not too high, because the roots will be too near the hot soil surface, and not too low because the stem will be drowned in soil. The bud union of fruit trees should always be above the soil level. If the soil settles too much after planting, the bud union is dragged down. Watch for this possibility because you don't want it covered with soil a year or two later.

The Exception to the Rule

There's just a little exception to the rule about setting out at the same level as the plant was growing in its container. Tomatoes can be planted with a lot of their stem in the ground. We even remove some of the lower leaves to let us do this.

In the spring, the soil stays colder down so we don't set out tomatoes in a vertical position. Their roots won't grow in the colder soil. Instead, we make a gently sloping trench and lay the plant with its roots at the deeper end and its leaves at ground level at the other end. New roots grow out of the nearly horizontal stem and give the plant an extra turn of speed. Although the leaves start by pointing along the ground, they grow upright in a day or two. See photo on previous page.

16

WHEN THINGS GO WRONG

Garden plants are like people—they come with their own personalities. Beginning gardeners find this hard to accept because they generally buy plants in half-dozens. When they are small they all look alike.

The nursery industry does a good job of mass-producing plants like Henry Ford's automobiles: standardized and uniform. Look in any large nursery and you'll see rows and rows of look-alike plants. On the nursery shelves we can't see the plants' capability to meet local conditions, their ability to handle stress, their resistance to disease, or their adaptability to soil conditions.

It would be almost silly to tell you that banana plants will not thrive in the desert. You understand this well enough, but you may not be so sure if someone said the same thing about rhubarb, blackberries, Brussels sprouts or nectarines.

Not Natural to the Desert

The point is that most of our garden plants—trees as well as vegetables, and many ornamentals for that matter—don't normally or naturally grow in the desert. We have to take special measures to help them survive and a bit more to get them productive. Most of the time they are under stress.

A stressed plant is a weak plant and susceptible to further attack and invasion. There is a school of thought that believes insects and diseases invade only weak plants. "Keep your plants strong and vigorous," they say. To most gardeners this means selecting adapted plants, enriching the soil, attending to irrigation, and removing pests and diseases as they appear.

Chemicals, Yes or No?

There's a spectrum of garden-care philosophers. Those at one end be-

This poor tree never had a chance. In its early life at a growing nursery it was left in its container too long. This might have been repeated each time it was "moved up" into a bigger container. When it finally reached the open ground, it was planted in a hole too small and the roots were not spread. The tree never did well, but the real cause could only be discovered after it was removed from its dreadful situation.

Another underground problem mystifies the gardener until he digs the plant. Nematodes start by handicapping the plant. It never responds to changed irrigations, fertilizer applications or chemical sprays.

lieve nature's balance will take care of everything. It should not be upset. They say today's plant troubles have been caused by undue reliance on chemical fertilizers that have "poisoned" the soil. It is true that many of us, gardeners or not, worry about large amounts of chemicals in the environment. These have been put there in the belief that all nasty things deserve poisoning—never mind the consequences to anything else. At the other end of the spectrum, the agro-business community says that today's high productivity has only come about through the use of chemicals. Without them we'd all be eating wormy apples.

Commercial growers have to make money. Chemicals, costly as they are, save money on labor. The home gardener doesn't charge for his labor. He

Nematodes—those microscopic worms that invade plants' roots—are killers and hard to get rid of. There are hundreds of species, some specific to particular plants; some infest many kinds of plants. All are a burden on an infested plant. Some plants linger, others die quickly. Bumps like these show how much the plant is irritated by nematodes. There's no quick-fix chemical to help the gardener. Those that kill the nematodes are too risky to human health.

Grubworms are the larvae of flying June bugs or scarab beetles. They are attracted to gardens where manure has been spread recently. They lay their eggs in the soil and the resulting grubs spend a year eating organic matter, both dead and alive. Pick them out as you dig. As as you continue to improve your soil with applications of organic matter, expect a fresh crop each year.

Herbicide damage to trees is expressed through the leaves, often several months after the application. Don't confuse this symptom with nutrient-deficiency symptoms that are less stark and defined. Weedkiller chemical damage such as this often appears only on the side of a tree where the chemical was put on the ground. By contrast, nutrient deficiencies are seen all over the tree.

Above-ground damage is seen more easily, but this damage is obscured by the terminal death of leaves on a branch. Female cicadas make these slits on a twig and lay their eggs in them. Sap flow is interrupted and the terminal leaves starve to death. That's what you see first—then the slits.

has plenty of time and it's his hobby. He likes to spend that time improving his plants' environment and health. A lot of the home gardener's time can be spent profitably in observing his plants and making adjustments to his management system. A change might be something as simple as watering less often after he discovers the soil is wet. Insect pests and sick plants can be picked out before troubles spread.

Plants Under Fire

Plant destruction comes from all sides. It's frequently cumulative and caused by several things at once.

For example, we know Texas root rot kills trees and the organism is a fungus living in the soil. A peach tree in the desert is under stress most of the time because it's not a native plant. It's particularly stressed during the hot summer when humidity is high and if the soil is too wet, from overirrigation or summer storms, or because of poor drainage due to caliche. A tree whose growth is forced by too much fertilizer has no stamina to withstand stress.

What conditions favor the fungus to make it so obnoxious? These could be first, an alkali soil; second, soil temperatures around 90F; third, a supply of suitable food—your peach tree's roots; fourth, an absence of predators on the fungus.

Another example would be fireblight

of apples and pears (as well as the common ornamental, pyracantha). At the ends of branches a bunch of leaves, *together* with flowers, suddenly dry out and die. It looks as if that part of the plant had been burned. The rest of the twig's leaves remain green and healthy—for awhile at least. It's not a heat or a water problem because the symptoms usually occur in the spring when the weather is mild. No insect damage can be seen, so you have a mystery on your hands. In this case the circumstances that favor the disease—natural flowering, insects attracted to the flowers and the initial presence of the bacteria— are beyond your control.

Of course, once you know what the problem is, you have to do something about it. Spraying won't make it go away. You have to prune out the infected parts, sterilizing your pruning equipment after every cut. Dispose of the infected parts. Then you have to spray the entire tree several times with an antibiotic solution.

If you know the disease is in your neighborhood, it is worth while spraying the flowers with the antibiotic solution as a preventive. But that's the only time in the year a control can be effected.

If the ends of the twigs continue to die back, you have to prune severely to control its spread through the plant.

Prune promptly wherever you notice the problem, then continue with the antibiotic spraying.

If you have a plant that gradually declines or simply doesn't grow well, try to realize it is doing its best, but something, or maybe everything, is wrong for it. The problem may be the soil is too alkaline; there's too much salt in the water; the temperatures are too high; there's too much sunshine; the drainage is poor; and so on. Maybe it's an unadapted plant or an unsuitable variety. It really pays to plant varieties that trial plantings have proved will thrive in *your* locality. Check with good gardeners of long standing, the serious garden clubs, knowledgeable nurserymen and the university experimental station annual reports.

Desert conditions are severe and when you make a garden you invite insects to trouble you. In early summer, as the desert vegetation dries out, there's only one good place for a large insect population to go and find green plants to eat: your garden. And, again, if you enrich a poor soil with fertilizer and give frequent irrigations to get plants growing quickly, you encourage soil fungi such as Texas root rot.

How Quickly Did It Happen?

Plants that look weary and decline gradually are showing us a long-term

Flat, bent leaves were damaged several weeks ago by tiny insects called *thrips*. Emerging leaves were tender and easily rasped for their juices. As the leaves grew, so did the deformity. There's nothing you can do at this point. When the damage was being done you probably weren't aware of it. Leaves are still working for the plant, but they don't look very nice.

Don't confuse these twisted and cupped leaves with thrips damage. It's the result of applications of weed-killer chemicals either as a spray such as 2,4-D, or uptake from a soil application like Banvel® or something similar. Effects are seen several weeks after application. The home gardener often does not connect them.

Another case of cause and effect being misunderstood. Small leaf cutter bee cut these notches out of the edge of pepper-plant leaf. She uses the material to build her nest in tubular cavities. She flies in and cuts the leaf so quickly that most gardeners don't know what happened. When you see it for the first time you are fascinated by the bee's dexterity. Spraying is a waste of time and the plant, though it looks devastated, doesn't suffer much.

Often you see leaves like this and wonder what happened. It's not a deficiency, or insect damage, or a disease. It's caused by wind rubbing parts of the plant against something—often another part of the plant.

Slime flux is generally caused by not spray-painting after pruning. A bacteria enters the tissue, feeds on it and generates gases. Toxic waste products are forced out through a weakness in the tree and corrode the bark where it drips out. The damage you see now started several weeks ago.

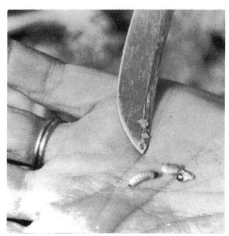

A squash suddenly wilts and it doesn't respond to corrective treatment. A borer is eating the insides of the plant. An egg was laid on the outside of the vine and hatched into a grub that worked its way inside. If you are prompt, you can slit the vine and extract the grubs before they do too much damage.

stress, usually caused by their surroundings. On the other hand, a quick death is usually the result of some particular happening. Maybe it was caused by a mistimed gardening activity, or a pest or disease attack. It's unkind to place a beginning gardener in the pest-and-disease category, but he *can* do a lot of damage before he realizes the error of his ways.

One error he easily falls into is to apply chemicals to all and any problem that comes his way. This is particularly true of that nervous person who sees a new insect for the first time.

"What is it called?" "What shall I spray it with?"

It seems we are firmly tuned in to medications and magic powders to alleviate our troubles and woes—real or imagined. Most insects we see are inoccuous, some are even on our side, and a few are undesirable. So it's not always the best thing to rush for the spray gun and a bottle of poison. Mind you, there is a place for chemical control as a last resort when hand picking simply can't keep up with a pest invasion.

Beginning gardeners are always asking the question—"What shall I spray my tree with?" The answer "You don't spray trees, you spray insect pests." is a bit more than pedagogical exactness. It's a truism that tells you to wait until you have a problem before you start spraying. Few preventive spray programs can anticipate an insect problem. Nor is there a treatment that protects a tree for all time.

Don't spray your plants when you see something is wrong, and don't know what it is. There's no universal elixir for gardening problems, no magic powder to make them disappear.

Sorting Out the Problems

It takes a few years of experience to sort out all the distress signs. If you have an inquiring mind and are not just full of blind hate for pests and diseases, it's fun working them out.

When something goes wrong the first thing to do is to take a good look at what you've got. You'll find a magnifying glass very helpful. Buy one with a magnification of 10 and no distortion at the edges.

Don't look just at the obvious symptom. Dig up the plant and look at the roots. An answer often lies in the roots. They can be bent, twisted, dry,

Summer sun burns fruit tissue and leaves a scar.

Rock squirrels love your garden. They live in the ground and disturb the soil to build their runs and nests. Unless you trap them quickly, they start a colony which is difficult to get rid of.

Common sign of early summer confuses beginning gardeners. They think disintegration of the end of the young fruit is a disease or a nutrient deficiency. It is caused by a lack of pollination. The first flowers of the year don't have a balance of male and female and the young fruit is aborted.

Red spider mites are tiny creatures but they make up for their small size by large populations. They envelop plant tissue with webs that enable them to multiply rapidly. The mites move to tender parts where they suck out the plant's vital juices.

chewed, rotted, dead or inadequate. Then, cast your mind back a few days. What was done to that plant? What happened nearby? Whatever you did, was it the right thing? Was too much of something—good or bad—applied? Sometimes a beginning gardener does belong in the pest category.

A checklist of past events in your garden will help you pinpoint what went wrong. One called *20 Questions* at the end of this chapter is an overall review of the plant's environment. It should provide you with enough clues to give an answer to the questions, "Why is my plant sick?" "Or dying?" "Or dead?"

Don't jump to conclusions. Don't forget that a plant may be suffering from more than one problem. One symptom may call out in an obvious way but the cause of the trouble is something else. For example, in the heat of summer a lot of plants develop light-green mottled leaves that "tell" us they are short of iron. "They have chlorosis," say the experts. They do indeed. But the salesperson's recommendation to apply iron doesn't effect a cure. The problem is centered on the high temperatures which cause the gardener to water heavily, which drives the air out of the soil, which prevents the roots from absorbing iron from the soil, which causes the leaves to show an iron deficiency.

Often, this chlorotic condition can be remedied by letting the soil dry out somewhat. It's that simple.

Try the key on the next page to help you identify common plant problems.

Desert birds, such as thrashers, cactus wrens and sapsuckers, look for moisture in ripening citrus fruit. The hole they make allows an entry of bacteria and soon the fruit is spoiled.

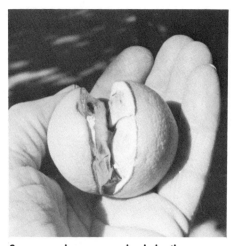

Summer rains or excessive irrigations cause developing fruit to split. Leaf-footed plant bugs enter the fruit, attracted by the smell, and bring bacteria on their feet to further spoil the fruit.

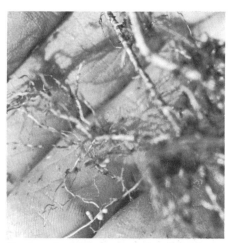

Don't confuse these spherical and regular nodules on legume roots with the bumps caused by nematodes. Bacterial nodules are beneficial invasions of the plant's tissue—converting soil nitrogen into plant nutrients. Nematode bumps are more numerous and crowded.

Crown gall is a harmful invasion by bacteria. They enter through a wound caused by an animal, or a careless gardener digging too close to a tree's roots. Sometimes you buy an already infested tree at a nursery and when you plant it you contaminate your soil.

If you use a single drip emitter, a tree's roots won't spread outward to give a good supporting structure. The tree will produce normal foliage that catches the wind. Result? The tree blows over. Water out to the drip line—and then some.

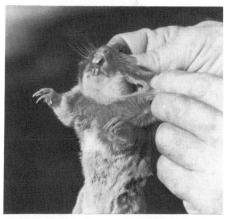

Gophers live underground and eat plants' roots. They make tunnels and heaps just like moles. Moles are insect eaters and, apart from their disturbance of the soil in your garden, are considered useful animals. There aren't many moles in the desert. You have to trap gophers. It's a waste of time to gas them, to flood them out, to throw poisoned grain around in the hope they will eat it.

GUIDE TO DIAGNOSING PLANT PROBLEMS

by George Brookbank and Master Gardeners

Plant Part	Overall Condition	Particular Condition	Possible Causes
LEAVES	A. normal-shape	1. green, small	a. nitrogen deficiency b. zinc deficiency c. nematodes on roots d. dry soil
	A. normal-shape	1. green, wilting	a. soil wet from poor drainage b. soil moist; grubs; chemical spill; excess fertilizer; Texas root rot; other root rots; nematodes c. soil dry from lack of rain—faulty irrigation system
	A. normal-shape	2. all yellow	a. old age b. nitrogen deficiency
	A. normal-shape, pale	3. green veins on new leaves 3. green veins on old leaves 3. green veins on all leaves	iron deficiency herbicides wet soil
	A. normal-shape	4. brown in center only 4. brown at edges only 4. all brown 4. brown on lower leaves only	sunburn a. excess salts b. herbicide residue c. wind-dried a. frost b. wind-dried c. terminal twig borer d. cicada damage e. Texas root rot f. lack of water g. fire-blight on pears, apples h. normal aging process
	A. normal-shape	5. mottled old leaves 5. mottled new leaves	herbicides virus disease
	A. normal-shape	6. silvery appearance	leaf-hopper damage
	A. normal-shape	7. bronze-color	red spider mite
	A. normal-shape	8. purple-color	frost, phosphorus deficiency
	A. normal-shape	9. grey, powdery appearance	mildew on peas, grapes
	B. abnormal-shape	1. twisted, puckered	a. aphids b. thrips c. leaf roller d. mites e. 2,4-D-type herbicides f. virus diseases
	B. abnormal-shape	2. bunched, small rosette	a. zinc deficiency b. mites
	B. abnormal-shape	3. chewed edges, holes	a. snails b. tomato hornworm c. crickets d. cabbage loopers e. cornstalk borer f. tortoise beetle g. grasshoppers h. birds
	B. abnormal-shape	4. neat-edged holes	leaf-cutter bee
	B. abnormal-shape	5. ragged edges, tears	wind damage
	B. abnormal-shape	6. wandering brown lines	leaf miner
	C. leaves gone or chewed	1. stalks remain	a. ants b. rabbits c. birds

Plant Part	Overall Condition	Particular Condition	Possible Causes
LEAVES (continued)	D. leaves on ground		a. frost
			b. drought
			c. fertilizer burn
			d. ants
			e. rabbits
			f. birds
			g. individual leaf drop, not widespread, is normal
			h. seasonal leaf fall
	E. lower leaves lost		normal aging process
	F. all leaves gone		a. ants
			b. tomato horn worm
			c. birds
			d. rabbits
			e. squirrels
			f. pack rats
STEM		1. soft rot (brown, mushy) on seedling	soil organisms
		2. soft rot (brown, mushy) on stem	damping-off fungus
		3. streaky under bark	bacterial wilts
		4. dark, dry spots	powdery mildew on grape
		5. flaky, black, dusty	sooty canker
		6. weeping brown fluid	slime flux
		7. weeping clear gum	a. heat stress
			b. citrus-foot rot
			c. bacterial gummosis (fruit trees)
		8. chewed, wet	squash-vine borer
		9. chewed, clean, dry	a. crickets
			b. cutworm
			c. gophers
			d. rabbits
			e. squirrels
FRUIT		1. dropping off	a. heat stress
			b. lack of water (see wilt, above)
			c. overbearing
		2. drying out	overbearing
		3. dry spot on side	sunburn
		4. soft rot	a. heat destruction of peach, apple
			b. poor squash pollination
			c. tomato blossom end rot
			d. stone fruits brown rot
		5. mottled spots	heat rash on tomato
		6. small black spots	leaf-footed plant bug
		7. holes	a. birds on citrus, tomato
			b. caterpillars on tomato
			c. BB shot in ripe grapefruit
		8. half-eaten, on the tree	birds, squirrels
		9. half-eaten on the ground	little boys
		10. split fruit	rapid fruit growth
ROOTS		1. knobby, bump galls— small and long lumps	nematodes
		2. knobby, bumpy galls— small and round lumps	legume nodules
		3. knobby, bumpy galls— large and rough lumps	crown gall
		4. soft, brown galls	wet soil
		5. soft flesh, central thread	a. wet soil
			b. chemical
		6. chewed wood	a. borer beetles
			b. gophers

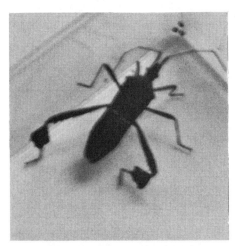

Leaf-footed plant bug is appropriately named. It is a juice-sucker and damages ripening fruit.

Green fruit beetle is notorious for the damage it does to figs, peaches and other fruit. It also attacks tree bark and sucks the juices out of a tree. Because they come in dozens, they can destroy a tree by girdling the bark.

Grey aphid is practically the only wintertime pest. The first ones are well-hidden in the heart of a plant, but they soon multiply and spread all over and then to the next plant. Catch them early. Pinch them out, taking the whole leaf if necessary.

If a young plant wilts for no apparent reason, suspect a borer in the stem. Pull up an ailing plant and split the stem to find it. There is no remedy. However, you have saved yourself the trouble of growing a crop that won't develop.

Citrus trees showing leaves like this are telling you that they are suffering from a deficiency of magnesium. Spread Epsom salts, magnesium sulphate, on the soil under the tree and water it in well.

Strawberries need a lot of water as the fruit begins to ripen. However, frequent heavy waterings keep the soil surface moist all the time and encourage pillbugs and snails. Both can be controlled by letting the soil surface dry out. This is achieved by infrequent deep watering instead of daily light sprinklings.

These carrots were planted too thickly in hard soil.

Extension Garden Center—Plant Ailment Form

20 Questions—or how to solve a puzzle

1. What is the plant?_____Planting Date_____

2. Describe the extent of the damage_____

_____

_____

_____

_____

3. How long has it gone on for? _____

4. What other plants nearby are affected?_____

5. How many hours of direct sunshine a day does the plant get?_____

6. Is the soil: sandy _____clay _____ loam _____ gravel _____ salty _____

7. How deep is it? _____

8. Is caliche present? _____ How far down?_____

9. Is there good drainage? _____10. How often do you water?_____

11. Do you fill the well:_____or water to the drip line? _____

12. How deep does the water go? _____(feet) How big is the well? _____(diameter in feet)

13. How often do you fertilize?_____What fertilizer?_____

14. When did you last fertilize? _____How much?_____

15. With what has the plant been sprayed?_____

16. Has the area nearby been treated? _____With what chemicals?_____

17. What insects are present? _____

18. What other pests are present?_____

19. Is the damage the result of sun(burn) or frost(bite)?_____

20. After all these questions, what do you think the problem is? _____

_____

_____

Date_____

If you have a leaf full of small insects and they start jumping around or flying a short distance, you have a problem called *leaf hopper* or perhaps *whitefly*. If you can't call in predators such as lacewings or ladybugs, you'll have to spray with Malathion 50 or diazinon.

This mess is called *wooly aphid*. They chew on leaves and suck their juices, thus weakening the plant. Chemicals don't reach pest because of the "wool." Although there are predators, it's better to pinch off the colony before it spreads.

This is not a garden pest, but a garden danger. Be careful when moving containers that have been in one place for a long time. Black widow spiders bite humans.

No one likes a tomato hornworm. It leads an undisturbed life most of the time. A small one is seldom seen.

Small eggs on leaf are "good guys." They hatch into lacewings. The babies are hungry and eat up mites and aphids.

17

TEXAS ROOT ROT

Texas root rot is a bane of desert gardening. It has been in the soil for a long time and has proliferated in land previously farmed for cotton. There, heavy summertime irrigations gave it encouragement. Those fields are now planted to houses and we inherit the problem in our yards. Its other name is *cotton root rot* and if you want to get scientific, you can use its Latin name, *Phymotochrichum omnivorum.*

It's not such a bad name either, the *omnivorum* part, that is. Texas root rot fungus is found in soil all over the place and it attacks and eventually kills practically all woody plants. Death is usually sudden and dramatic. Although some plants may linger in a steady decline for several years, there is seldom a complete recovery.

Geographic Distribution

The fungus is omnipresent over a wide range of territory where conditions include the following:
1. An alkaline soil.
2. A soil low in organic matter.
3. A warm climate with mild winters.

In other words, the southwest desert regions. The fungus is indigenous to the lower elevations of Arizona, California, Nevada, New Mexico and Texas. It is also found throughout northern Mexico.

On the eastern edge of this area the soils change from strongly calcareous black soils of East Texas to the acid soils of the Mississippi delta which are also more organic.

To the north, Phymotochrichum omnivorum is limited by cold winter temperatures, partly caused by mountain elevations. It has been discovered that the organism exists at higher elevations that were previously thought to be free of the fungus. But, at 5,000 feet, an infected plant stands a better

This peach tree repeatedly dies back because its roots are damaged. During cool spring weather the tree leafs out all over. During the stress of summer, leaves on the upper branches die because they do not get enough water. Lower branches, or suckers, grow during summer because moisture doesn't have far to go.

Flat ribbons of Texas root rot run lengthwise along roots. They are lightly attached. If you pull the roots through the soil for inspection, you often strip off the ribbon and lose the evidence. Because ribbons are often consumed by other soil fungi and bacterias, old samples are worthless.

93

In the hope that it could be saved, this apricot tree was severely cut back. When a tree loses a lot of roots, you have to balance the loss by severe trimming. After trimming, apply 2 inches of steer manure, plus ammonium sulphate and sulphur each at the rate of a pound to 10 square feet under the spread of the old root area. Heavy watering carries the chemicals down to the root zone. Manure encourages another fungus that devours Phymotochrichum. Sulphur alters the soil pH to accommodate it and discomforts the Texas root rot at the same time.

chance of survival—or at least a longer life while infected—than a similar plant at 1,000 feet or lower.

To the west, the sand hills and mountains of southeastern California once presented a barrier. However, man accidentally carried the fungus over this barrier and it became destructive in the Imperial and Coachella Valleys. There, alkaline soils low in organic matter and mild winters are the rule.

Summer Activity

The fungus is especially active in warm, moist soil. These conditions occur during the summer months when our plants are already under stress from high temperatures, bright sunshine and dry air. Rainstorms should bring relief but they seem to favor the fungus more than the infected plant.

During the summer rains we notice the fungus' spore mats. They cover a patch of soil sometimes the size of a dinner plate, but sometimes several square feet of soil. They look like

spilled pancake batter. At first they are light-tan colored and then, in a day or two, darker and powdery. This powder blows about when you disturb the mat by walking over it or splashing it with water. The ground appears to be steaming.

The powder is a mass of spores like mushroom spores. But the experts say that, unlike mushroom spores, they do not start new infections. The fungus spreads by moving along the roots of host plants and, where they intertwine, it "jumps" to the next plant and so colonizes an area.

Symptoms Demand Fast Action

Quick-growing trees, such as apricots, peaches and plums, have little resistance to the fungus and show their distress by a sudden wilt. They could have been in fine condition last week, but today their leaves, perhaps on one side of the tree but sometimes all over, are drooping. The first thought is that you forgot to water the tree, or didn't water enough, or that the last hot spell

distressed the tree. An emergency irrigation doesn't help. The leaves remain wilted and brown, yet don't fall off the tree. Watering actually makes things worse at this point.

By now you know something is wrong. Very wrong. You must act quickly; delay is fatal. Don't wait for the weekend, do it now.

The standard treatment is expensive and troublesome to apply. But if it's the first attack, and if you catch the disease early enough, it's worth it. Usually, the first few years of a tree's life are free of the disease. After the tree has become established and is giving its first harvests, the trouble begins. Having once tasted the success of a harvest you want it to continue, so you are usually prepared to spend money on the treatment.

First, trim off all those branches with wilted leaves. They are no good anymore. Even if your tree is reduced to a few branches, don't worry—they will become the tree's future framework. Then, throw 2 inches of steer manure on the soil all under the spread of the tree, and even a little farther out. Follow this with ammonium sulphate at the rate of 1 pound to every 10 square feet, and 1 pound of soil sulphur at the same rate.

Now dig these materials into the soil without damaging the tree's roots too much. Give the treated area a deep irrigation. Either flood in a basin or gently sprinkle for a long time. You want the water to carry the materials down to the roots which may be 3 feet down. After 10 days, irrigate again.

This treatment provides nutrients to the tree which encourage new root growth. The sulphur makes the soil less alkaline, thereby making the fungus miserable because it likes an alkaline soil. Ammonium sulphate also has an acidic reaction.

Research findings indicate that another, useful, parasitic fungus is encouraged by the acid-forming nature of this treatment. The good guy eats up the bad guy.

Don't overdo the amounts for "good measure." These are strong chemicals and they are already at the kill-or-cure level. The authoritative book on the subject recommends carrying out the treatment every year. Not everyone does this, in the interest of economy, and their trees seem to be all right.

On the other hand, don't underapply. Don't merely carry out part of the treatment or skip one of the ingredients. Further, you will do more harm than good by not watering sufficiently. Inadequately diluted chemicals are damaging to new roots.

Infestation Limits Your Choices

Should the tree die in spite of the treatment, or nearby trees become infected, you must realize it's going to be risky to plant similar trees in that spot. The soil may be so heavily infested that your choices are extremely limited. Only those trees that have a decided resistance to the disease can be planted. Use the following list from an Extension Service Garden Guide to help you decide what to plant.

***Immune species*—Can be planted without preparing tree holes as previously described:**

Trees:
True bamboos
Banana, Ornamental
Palms, all species

Shrubs:
Agaves
Bird of Paradise
Draecena
Pampas Grass
Giant Reed
Yuccas

***Resistant species*—Recommended for planting in treated soil, or near locations where root rot is known to occur:**

Trees:
Aleppo Pine
Cedar Elm
Citrus, on Sour Orange rootstocks
Cypress, Arizona, Italian and Monterey
Eucalyptus
Evergreen Tamarisk
Fruitless Mulberry, especially Stribling or Sycamore-Leaved
Mesquite
Palo Verde
Sycamore, American and Arizona
Walnut, native black

Shrubs:
Cacti
Crepe Myrtle

When you plant a deciduous fruit tree, anticipate Texas root rot and take precautions. If the hole measures 5 feet by 5 feet and is 5 feet deep, you will need 16 bags of steer manure, 30 pounds of sulphur and 8 pounds of ammonium phosphate. It's work and expense, but it's worth it.

Elderberry, Arizona
Honeysuckle, Japanese
Jasmines
Junipers
Oleander
Pomegranate
Pyrancanthas
Rosemary
Russian Olive
Siberian Pea Shrub

Cassias
Castor Bean
Cotoneaster, Silverleaf
Lilacs
Photinia, Chinese
Quince, Flowering
Roses
Silverberry
Spirea

***Very susceptible species*—Do not plant in treated holes or near any location where root rot has occurred:**

Trees:
Bottle Tree
Carob
Cottonwoods
Elms
Fig
Ginko
Pepper Tree
Poplars
Stone Fruits: Peach; Plum; Apricot; Almond
Umbrella Tree
Willows

Shrubs:
Buddleias

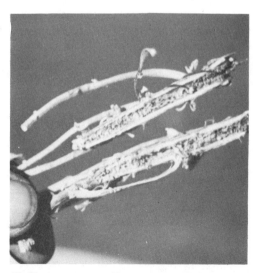

Similar symptoms to Texas root rot appear when a branch is infested with borers. Check out this possibility before you go to the trouble and expense of the standard Texas-root-rot treatment.

Not the Only Killer!

At this point you need some good news about this whole miserable situation. The name, the thought, the concept of Texas root rot is greatly overplayed by people who delight in frightening you. Be aware that trees, during a hot stressful summer, can suddenly die from causes other than Texas root rot.

Take comfort from this truth and find out what killed your tree. It could have been overwatering combined with poor drainage. The roots were simply drowning. Think back to the time you dug the hole. Did you dig through the caliche? Perhaps a borer was at work in a branch, causing its leaves to wilt. Maybe a root borer caused the whole tree to wilt. Someone might have spread too much fertilizer in a heap close to the trunk instead of scattering it all around and watering it in properly. Weed-control chemicals could have been applied too close to the tree. Gophers could be eating the roots. A leaking gas pipe can kill a tree while causing the same symptoms. And there are other possibilities—one being plain heat exhaustion.

Get An Expert Opinion

The only way to be sure *Phymotochrichum omnivorum* killed your tree is to have an expert look through a microscope at root samples from your tree. The fungus has a recognizable form and structure.

A less-reliable but often sufficient sign is found on fresh roots as shown in the photo on page 93. It is the flat-branched fungus ribbon running along the outside of the root. Its color varies between tan and dark brown.

Take care when getting a root sample not to rub off the fungus because it is lightly attached. Dig at the outer edge of the tree and cut a 9-inch length of root, about as thick as a pencil. Gently lift it out rather than trying to pull it through the soil.

If you are not sure what to look for, wrap fresh roots in damp newspaper with the mud still attached. Quickly take them to an Extension Office. If they dry out, you lose the evidence. If you dig up old roots, the fungus may have been consumed by other fungi and bacteria in nature's decay cycle. Half a dozen root samples are better than a single specimen.

Tree-Planting Precautions

Whenever you plant a tree, you should dig a big hole. It's a lot of work. The standard recommendation calls for a hole measuring 5-feet square and 5-feet deep. It's essential to dig through any caliche or layers of hard, compacted soil—more hard work.

As long as you are going to all this trouble, you might as well finish the job properly by taking precautions against Texas root rot. Here's a formula to help you determine how much of three materials to mix with the soil as you put it back.

First, calculate how many cubic feet there are in the hole. For example, if it measures 5-feet square and is 5-feet deep there will be 125 cubic feet (5 x 5 x 5).

Divide by 5 to get the amount of organic matter you need. It comes to 25. Steer manure comes in bags of 1.5 cubic feet, so you'll be buying 16 bags. Divide the cubic content by 4 to tell you how many pounds of sulphur to buy, in this case 31. To get the pounds of ammonium phosphate to buy, divide by 16 which will give you 8.

Mix these materials with the soil as you return it; don't make layers as you fill the hole. Firm the mix by standing on it and watering as you go. There will be a little more soil mix than you started with, unless you threw out a lot of rocks or caliche. This slight mound will disappear as the mix settles over a couple of weeks. If it doesn't rain, help it settle with a thorough watering.

Why Ammonium Phosphate?

Did you notice the sneaky substitution? Instead of ammonium sulphate used to treat an ailing tree we are using ammonium phosphate. Why the switch?

Our desert soils are short of phosphate—an essential plant food. It's not very soluble, so it doesn't move through the soil but stays where it is put. It is best placed in the root zone which for trees means 3 or 4 feet down. Always dig in phosphate; it's a preparation fertilizer.

Ammonium phosphate has an acid reaction, just as ammonium sulphate has, so it is just as useful for our purpose of reducing Texas-root-rot attacks. If we were to spread ammonium phosphate on the soil surface it would have little effect because it is

not soluble and would not be carried down by waterings. We have to put it where it needs to be.

Ammonium sulphate, on the other hand, is soluble and is carried through the soil by waterings. It's appropriate to use it on a suffering tree when we first notice the disease symptoms.

Soil Sterilant Will Clear the Way for a Safe Planting

If you have lost a tree to Texas root rot and are determined to replace it, the soil treatment using steer manure, ammonium phosphate and sulphur will not be enough—strong measure that it is. You must also sterilize the soil.

The chemical to use is Vapam®. The first thing to do is to read the label on the bottle. Follow directions carefully because it is powerful stuff—you need to know its dangers. Dilute it with water and apply it to the planting area. And, for good measure, a little bit beyond. Wash it down to three feet or more.

As the soil, (which should be neither too cold nor too hot) dries out, the chemical turns to a vapor and floats upward to the surface, killing everything in its way. Make it last longer by covering the soil with a plastic sheet for a week so the vapor is not blown away too quickly.

It kills all organisms, good and bad—so it's goodbye to earthworms and beneficial bacteria and fungi as well as the disease organisms. It kills the roots of nearby plants as well as weed seeds.

Vapam is something that you should use only after a great deal of soul-searching.

If you do use it, don't plant straightaway. Wait as long as you can before putting in a valuable plant.

Being Realistic

Texas root rot is here to stay, and it severely limits the choices we have when we want to plant fruit trees. The problem has been recognized for many years but research has not yet found a way to control it. Some chemicals that suppress the fungus are either too severe on the environment or are too costly. However, some plants are more resistant than others and these can be used as rootstocks. As an example, for citrus trees, Sour Orange is a more resistant rootstock than Rough Lemon. Dogridge Grape shows promise as a rootstock for grapes.

If you don't treat the soil, this happens. A few years after planting, just after the first two harvests, this grape vine died of Texas root rot.

Meanwhile, we have to live with the problem and be sensible about our gardening. Don't bring in topsoil from old cotton fields. It's probably infested with the fungus. Avoid buying container trees grown in suspect soil when other trees are available that have been grown in clean mixes. Don't scrape up leaf mold from under native mesquite trees. They are often carriers of the disease, though they don't show the symptoms.

Don't take sand from washes because flood waters often carry the fungus downstream. Be careful about accepting "free" gifts of other peoples' plants. Investigate the reasons they have for not wanting them any more. Dig a big planting hole and be sure to get through hard pan or caliche—your trees deserve good drainage.

Don't overwater your trees.

Especially, keep an eye on your trees for the very first signs of attack. If you suspect Texas root rot, take immediate corrective action. Don't stress them by under- or over-watering. Don't fertilize them excessively so they grow quickly with soft susceptible wood. Be thorough in your treatment.

Finally, good luck! It may not be your fault anyway. The Texas root rot organism—remember, *Phyomotochrichum omnivorum*—was here before you were. Maybe you bought some when you bought your house.

Should disaster strike—and you insist on remaining a keen gardener—you will have to sell your house and find a clean patch of country somewhere else.

In Mid-May Get Your Lawn in Shape

We all enjoy a grassed area and now that the weather is warming we find our Bermuda grass growing well. We should do all we can to get our lawns in tip-top shape before the stressful heat of July hits us. It's also a good time to start a Bermuda grass lawn or to repair a patchy one.

If your lawn took a turn for the worst and there are dead patches here and there, fill in the dead areas with plugs of new grass. First determine why the areas are dead. Dig a little into the soil and see whether the reason is a patch of poor soil in an otherwise good area.

Rubbish may have been buried in the site during construction. Or, moth larvae may be eating the roots. A third possibility is oil or fuel spills from your lawnmower. Remember how temperamental the darned thing was the first time you used it this season? It's not likely that the bare patch was caused by fungus—in spite of what some people say and encourage you to think. Fungus appears after several days of muggy weather and after you sprinkle at night—keeping the leaf surfaces wet enough for the fungus to creep over the blades and into the leaf tissues. We haven't had that kind of weather yet.

The bare patch is most likely the result of varying water absorption caused by varying soil characteristics. Wet the patch down with a hand watering. Cover it with two or three inches of steer manure and ammonium phosohate at the rate of three pounds to a hundred square feet. Dig deeply, mixing thoroughly.

Now be careful. Take plugs from the better parts of your lawn. A plug is two-inches square and two-inches deep. You can rent a little gadget to ensure uniformity in the pieces you extract and in the holes you make to plant them in. If you were to buy new sod to provide planting material, it's possible that it will be a different kind. In that case, you'll finish with a spotty variegated lawn. Better to be sure and use the same kind you already have.

If you want to make a new lawn, follow the same procedure. Space plugs about 12 inches apart if you have a median salary. If you are in the upper class you can place them even closer—or avoid plugging altogether and use complete pieces of sod to get an instant lawn. In which case, here's another caution.

Sometimes the sod farms grow grass in areas of heavy clay soils. Take a look at the thin layer of soil under the green grass and wipe it with a wet finger. It will smear if it is clay. Our garden soils are sandy and their absorptive properties are very different from this clay.

Don't buy such pieces of sod if you want to avoid trouble in getting your lawn established. Water will penetrate the sod only after a period of sprinkling—and then very slowly. Much of it will run off. The sandy soil underneath might stay dry instead of getting enough water to make new roots grow deeply. If you space the pieces of sod a little apart instead of close up tight, the water can get in between the cracks and penetrate the sandier soil below.

Keep your new lawn moist. A daily irrigation is necessary during hot weather with temperatures in the hundreds.

This information originally appeared in one of George's weekly columns in the *Tucson Citizen* dated May 7.

18

ALTERNATIVES TO POISONOUS CHEMICALS

A lot of people grow a garden because they don't want to eat the poisonous chemicals commercial growers spray on their crops. It's hard to know which supermarket or produce-stand food has been sprayed—for what reason and with which chemical. Avoid such doubt by raising your own vegetables and fruit. Only then can you be sure it is *not* contaminated.

Then there are those who don't use chemical poisons because they care for their bit of the environment, including their children, their pets and the birds that share their yards.

On the other hand, there's a third group of people determined to eliminate any flying, walking, crawling thing they don't like the look of—without considering whether it is harmful or helpful. It's made a hole in a leaf, it's something they've never seen before, and they have to kill it. Such people are unaware of the long-term effect their actions have on the environment. They're content only with the immediate kill—without counting the cost.

On balance, there's growing public sentiment against indiscriminate use of chemical poisons. The trend is to find other ways to reduce pest and disease problems. I'd like this chapter to aid that trend.

Philosophical Thoughts about Pests and Diseases

God put them on the earth, but man enables them to thrive. It's quite true. The fruits and vegetables we grow for ourselves are also food for pests and diseases. Pests lead a hard life in an inhospitable environment—the desert that surrounds us—and they find our gardens very inviting, especially when the desert dries out and offers even less than a starvation wage.

Grubworms, in this case the larva of the green fruit beetle, and pillbugs live in compost piles and break down larger pieces of organic matter into smaller pieces. Provided they stay in the compost, they are considered beneficial insects.

Adult green fruit beetle can only be classified as a pest—or perhaps a super-pest.

Adult moth that lays the eggs that turn into caterpillars called the *grape-leaf skeletonizer*. Note the egg cluster. Look for the moth flying around your grapes and her egg clusters on the underside of leaves. Don't let the pest develop any further than this. Catch the moth and squash the eggs.

After hatching, the caterpillars line up and advance—eating as they go. The bigger they get, the more they eat, leaving the leaf midribs as a skeleton.

First sign of forthcoming leaf damage on citrus is this small egg—usually laid singly.

Lady who left the egg. Be ready when the swallowtail butterfly hovers over your citrus trees in the summer.

Egg hatches into a nasty-looking caterpillar camouflaged as a bird dropping. It sends out orange horns and puts out a bad smell when pecked or squeezed. It eats a lot of leaves too.

Javelina, skunks, rabbits, squirrels, packrats, gophers, birds, grasshoppers, beetles, leafhoppers, and whiteflies all move to where there's food and water—our gardens. Weed seeds and diseases get blown in from the dry desert and thrive where there's food and water—our irrigated soils. A lot of our troubles are unavoidable.

Some people believe Mother Nature keeps a balance, and in that balance

It's easy to encounter the flying adult on a summer's evening but you don't often see the palo-verde borer beetle grub until your trees begin to die. They spend a year or two eating the roots.

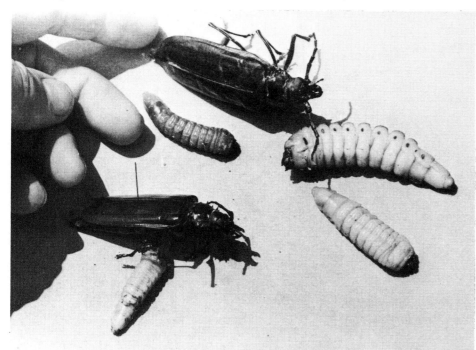

she keeps a check on things for us. Wrong! Birds don't eat the caterpillars that destroy grape leaves—they eat the ripening grapes. Rabbits don't eat up the weeds, they prefer your lettuce. Furthermore, Mother Nature shows little restraint. Grasshoppers and caterpillars don't come in ones and twos—they come in hundreds. Weeds multiply faster than rabbits and have few natural enemies.

Nevertheless, there is an interacting relationship between animals that eat one another which, much of the time, effects a degree of control. "So naturalists observe, a flea has smaller fleas that on him prey; and these have

smaller still to bite 'em, and so proceed *ad infinitum*." Poet Jonathan Swift wrote this in 1735.

Eliminate Misconceptions

Let's get rid of some misconceptions early in this story about insect management.

Bees are not willfully dangerous. They are far too busy attending to their daily tasks of gathering food and water to bother with silly humans. What's a beeline? It's the path bees fly—straight to work and straight home again. Of course, if you get in their flight path, that's another story. However, it's safe to go about your gardening while bees pollinate nearby flowers and collect water from drip-irrigation emitters.

Insects have been with us a long time and our memories are short. There's really nothing new about them. They do have their cycles of activity and resurgence—we call them *plagues*—but they follow some natural occurrence. For example, good winter rains mean abundant plant growth in the desert. This is food for insects and they thrive on it. When the desert dries, they travel to the next feeding ground which is invariably our green garden.

Insects are not picking on you. They are in your garden for a reason—because you have offered them something to eat. Here's a good example. Grubworms appear in the soil in large numbers after you dig in a generous amount of organic matter. And here's another. Green fruit beetles fly in from

A praying mantis is considered a "good guy" by practically everyone.

But how many people recognize this bump on a twig as the egg case of a praying mantis? Keep these on your property; don't destroy them. It's another example of good guys looking threatening. When you see an egg cluster like this—and they are all over the trees—you should feel pleased. Inside are a 100 or more preying-mantis eggs which hatch out, not all at once, but over a short period. They blow away to devour aphids, spider mites and bigger things as they grow older. If they all hatched at once they would eat each other—they are voracious!

Familiar ladybug beetle seen here eating aphids, a favorite food.

Not-so-familiar larval stage of the ladybug beetle. This wingless lady will not fly home but will stay to eat hundreds of aphids in order to grow up.

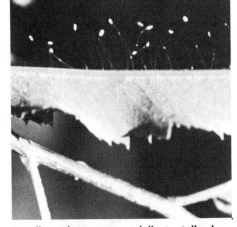

You'll see these eggs on delicate stalks during cooler times in spring and fall. It's a survival tactic. Lacewing that hatches from each egg is hungry and eats whatever is closest. If the eggs were in a cluster, side by side, hatchlings would eat each other and gardeners would lose a useful predator. Be thankful for these good guys.

"nowhere" to destroy your ripening fruit. You attract beetles if you allow spoiled fruit to stay on the tree or on the ground under it.

Don't get alarmed when you see one insect on your plants. Most insects are innocuous—neither good nor bad—and some are even beneficial. A few species are pests. Unfortunately, those seem to work overtime.

Alternative Pest Control Calls for Overall View— Not a Narrow One

When you see something on the cabbages, don't reach for the spray gun so you can saturate the area with chemical poisons that will kill everything within sight. Find out what the strange new creature is. What is it doing? Where did it come from? Is it indeed a pest? Is it food for something else, and is that "something else" here and about?

It's not a question of being more tolerant towards other creatures, but becoming more aware of the total situation and the implications of what you do. There's little wisdom in saying you'll share the peaches with the birds when their share is 10% of *every* fruit.

The overall view means taking several coordinated steps to see what is happening and to prevent things getting out of hand. And so we bring in a new term—Integrated Pest Management (I.P.M.).

Integrated Pest Management Replaces Poisons with Purpose and Perseverence

It's a total process that pays dividends in the long run. It's not a quick fix.

It begins with recognizing the first indications of a problem. Secondly, you measure its development. Then you arrange the environment around your plants to minimize an attack. Steps include erecting barriers to keep the pests away from your vegetables. Getting rid of weeds. Trapping the pests. Enlisting the support of other creatures. Confusing the pests with natural chemicals and interrupting their life cycles. Applying materials that are specific to the pest—not destroying everything in sight. You can use your finger and thumb to remove the larger pests from your plants once and for all.

You *can* effectively reduce pests without using chemicals.

Integrated Pest Management is very appropriate for home gardens because gardeners spend a lot of time with their plants and they see what's going on. Their time is valuable, but it's not counted in dollars. The commercial producer, with his hundreds of acres and loans with the banks, isn't nearly as fortunate.

Recognize the First Signs of a Possible Problem

Know the life cycles of insect pests. Here's a good example: The beginning

Cicada's larval stage lives underground and eats plant roots. Its powerful front legs are well-adapted to making the insect a pest.

Adult cicada flies around making a noise during humid summer days. They are ventriloquists so they're not easy to find.

Cicadas do noticeable damage to young twigs. Leaves at the ends of the twigs die, turn brown and hang on the ends of the twigs like flags. These slits are made to hold the eggs.

A natural enemy of cicadas is the cicada killer wasp.

It catches cicadas on the wing and drags them into its nest in the soil.

gardener doesn't recognize the adult blue-black moth flying around the grape vines in the spring as a potential problem.

But it's not long before he sees the result of that visit when the leaves are skeletonized by the caterpillars hatching from the eggs that she laid. When you see her flying around your grape vines in the spring, you should know she is bringing eggs—and trouble! Catch and squash her.

Our beginner also doesn't equate the damage done to citrus leaves by that nasty-looking caterpillar, the Orange Dog, with the beautiful black-and-yellow Swallowtail butterfly flip-flopping around his trees several days before. The Green Fruit Beetle, attacking ripening fruit in summer, started as a big white grub in a compost pile where it was usefully chewing large chunks into small pieces. On the other

hand, those damaging white grub-worms he finds when he digs his garden are the result of a visit from the little brown June beetle (June bug) attracted to the smell of the organic matter he added to the soil.

Learn to associate one with the other and attack any pest at its weakest point. For example, you can easily pick up grubs as you dig, whereas it's difficult to kill the flying beetle. Know the pests in all stages of their life cycle. Egg-laying adults don't do damage, but they bring it. Hand-picking the adult moth before she lays eggs means eliminating thousands of destructive caterpillars before they start. And it means not using chemicals.

On the other hand, the grub of the palo verde borer beetle that also kills fruit trees is difficult to control because it lives so deep underground. The large adult beetle can easily be hit with

a stick. If everyone did this to every palo verde borer beetle they saw flying around in July, we would have the pest under control in no time.

Learn to Recognize The Natural Predators of a Pest

Green lacewings gobble up aphids, wasps eat spider mites, and immature ladybugs look really threatening. If you don't know these friends and get frightened enough to spray them, you protect the enemy and build up problems for yourself.

Learn to recognize beneficial insects. Wide-spectrum chemicals kill everything no matter how careful you are in spraying. Even your finger and thumb can make mistakes if the controllng brain isn't functioning properly.

Cats eat gophers, coyotes eat rabbits, owls eat rats, and snakes eat squirrels. Know your friends! Be friendly towards them.

Introduce Predators to Eat Up The Pests

When most people see an eggcase of the praying mantis for the first time, they want to destroy it. The egg cases are inch-long brown bumps on the twigs of trees in winter. It's worth knowing their value because you can bring them into your garden from the desert and when the eggs hatch you've got a hundred hungry little creatures anxious to gobble up aphids and spider mites. It's even helpful to bring one into your house and let him catch flies in the windows and clean up your houseplants.

Corn cob with plenty of extended leaves at its end protects the sugary kernels inside.

Corn open at the ends allows entry of pests such as corn earworm and, in this alarming case, the green fruit beetle.

These beetles, attracted by the smell of decaying fruit, are caught in homemade trap made of a gallon glass jug and a window-screen cone.

Almost everyone knows the value of ladybug adults and they, too, can be brought in from the wild. But if you collect ladybugs in a cool forest and bring them down to a hot desert garden, they'll fly away, as the rhyme says. If they don't fly away they'll die of starvation after they've eaten up all the aphids. This suicidal event happens with all predators, so you need a steady supply to bring in repeatedly.

Importing predators is more effective in an enclosed greenhouse than it is out in the open garden, simply because the predators and their victims can't get away. By themselves, predators won't completely rid your garden of pests, but they should be an integral part of your control program.

Fortunately, predators have become a marketable commodity—you buy

them by the pint if they are big, or by the thousand if they are small.

Ladybugs and lacewings and Amblyceius and predatory mites and Trichogramma wasps, and Apidoletes, and Encarsia all gobble up aphids, mealybugs, leafhoppers, thrips, beetle larvae, moth eggs, spider mites, and dozens of other pests. Simply call your nearest Predator Farm, explain your problem, and they will deliver a package of what you need—together with instructions! You can even order by mail from catalogs!

Other Useful Predators

Wasps are most useful predators. They vary in size from tiny parasites laying eggs on caterpillars, to large cicada-killers and spider stingers. Their prey is drugged and dragged into a nest in the ground where the wasp young are

nourished. Black-widow spiders are a favorite food of mud-dauber wasps. During the summer months it's quite common to see dozens of tiny cone-shaped holes in the ground. People want to know what they are and what to spray them with. Surely they are something bad because they don't have permission to be there! If you patiently sit down and watch for a while, you'll see nothing happen until a wandering ant or other insect falls into the hole. Then, quick as a wink, the ant has gone. It's become another meal of an ant lion—the underground larval stage of a large clear-winged insect with a completely different adult appearance.

There are lots of other useful insects—ground beetles, dragon flies, syrphid flies, lightning bugs and our old friends, the spiders.

Your garden's insect management program needs to recognize these natural assets.

Proper Timing of Predator Introductions is Important

There's a dilemma with pest control using predators. If you bring them in before you have a problem there's the likelihood that they will die of starvation—after they have eaten one another! If you wait until after your problem has become a nightmare, they will take a bite out of it, but they won't consume it entirely. They'll seem to be ineffective.

Try to introduce the predators just before the pest finds a footing and begins to multiply.

A successful introduction is bound to end in starvation—or departure—of the predators as their food supply dwindles. As the hungry feeders disappear, the pest multiplies and starts again. At that point you need to bring in a fresh supply of predators—at the *exact moment*. It's not easy!

Management of your predators has become a little easier recently, through the use of "Bug Chow." This is specially formulated sugars and yeasts that are spread or sprayed on plants when the predators' natural food supply (the pests) has diminished to the point of starvation. It tides over that period when the pests are almost eaten up and the predators are starving—and inclined to move off, or die—and pest resurgence in the absence of

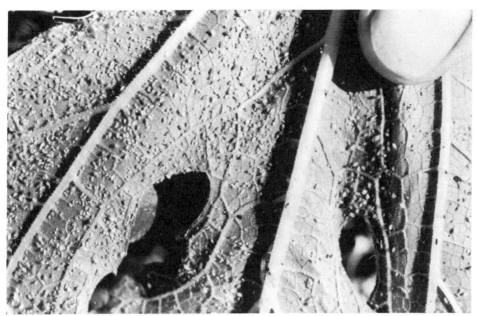

Mass of young aphids are lacewing's dinner—and ladybug's dinner, too.

Small bugs such as these aphids can be squirted off plant with strong jet of water. Soapy water is better. Pests lose their toe-hold, and wax covering their body dissolves, leaving them unprotected against the dry desert air.

predators.

This brings us to an important part of I.P.M.—monitoring insect populations in your garden.

You Need to Know What's Going on in Your Garden

First, you need to know whether there are any "bad guys" in the garden and how quickly they are increasing—by natural increase or by new arrivals. Don't get excited about just a few—especially if you can rub them out with finger and thumb.

You also want to know whether there are any "good guys," and how their numbers are changing.

Spend some time looking. If you don't have time, set out some sticky traps and count the dead bodies when you get home from work. Make a chart if you like—you need to know what's happening. Are there more than yesterday? How many more?

Monitoring is important and it should be done on a daily basis—don't do it just on the weekend—because insects develop very quickly when conditions are right.

Buy sticky traps or make your own from yellow plastic lids of coffee cans smeared with vaseline. Insects seem to like yellow, though recent advertisements said some pests prefer blue. Then you have to buy the certain blue plastic from the catalog. Try yellow—it's usually sufficient. Put the sticky

traps on sticks around the vegetables and hang them in the fruit trees, but don't get your hair caught on them.

Make Use of Insect Scents to Trap and Confuse

Scientists know insects operate by using their keen sense of smell. And it didn't take the scientists too long to find out that, after satisfying their hunger, they like to satisfy their sexual urges. In comes a new word that describes insect scents—*pheromone*.

Romantically-inclined insects find one another by sniffing the phero-mones. You can fool them with syn-thetic pheromones, attracting thousands of them to a bottle of the right stuff placed in a cage allowing them in—but not out. No need for poisonous chemicals!

Another, more subtle, approach is to saturate the air with the right phero-mone so the Saturday night rovers, looking for a playmate, buzz con-fusedly around in an abundance of attractive "come-hither" perfumes, can't see the trees for the wood, and never find what they are looking for. As a result, no mating and no egg pro-duction—and no pests for that year!

You can actually buy these perfumes! You only need to read the right garden-ing magazines.

Pheromones are specific, in other words there's one for each kind of insect and it works only for that partic-

ular insect. There's no universal Chanel No. 5 that lures all and sundry to their destiny. A number of lures have been developed to catch pests common in the eastern states, but very little is available for desert-region pests. Our market is only a fraction of that back east, so we are neglected!

Insects Are Supposed To Be Repelled By "Smelly" Plants

Insects are attracted to one another and also to their food—our fruits and vegetables—by smell. A large corn patch sends a strong invitation to corn stalk borer and corn earworm; cab-bages attract butterflies, and so on. A lot of people say that the more you plant the greater the attraction.

They also say that if you plant a mixed garden you will blend the smells, so the invitation won't be quite so persuasive. If you completely "aver-age out" the smells with lots of differ-ent plants, there won't even be an invitation. It's a bit like mixing all the wonderful colors of a paint box and finishing with uninteresting brown. Mixing makes your garden safe.

Some people say you can hide the crop by mixing in certain plants with a nasty smell. And by planting even smellier ones you can keep insects away.

Unfortunately, there's no scientific evidence that this is the case. When it has happened, it's been coincidence tempered with wishful thinking.

Here's a personal experience. In an attempt to drive away grapeleaf skele-tonizers I heeded the advice of a respected nurseryman who said that

Leaf stems without any green are a "give-away" that caterpillars are present. You'll have to look carefully because they are the same color as the leaves they have eaten—a natural camouflage.

Sphinx moth that lays the eggs that turn into caterpillars that eat the leaves of your plants.

Neat notches on the edges of leaves mean a leaf cutter bee has been collecting material for her nest. Damage to the plant is slight, but looks bad.

Katydids are a kind of grasshopper and are common in the summer.

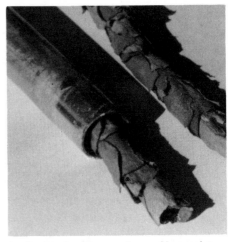

Leaf-cutter bee crams pieces of leaves into a small tube such as a keyhole or as here, a piece of plumbing tubing. This is the start of a nest.

Katydids are very neat about placing their eggs on the edges of leaves. Destroy these whenever you see them and reduce the next population explosion.

Grey aphids cluster on the tender growth, where they multiply quickly. Nip them out early in the game.

Tansy planted near the grapes would stop the moth from coming to the grapes. Tansy is smelly, but to us humans it's not all that bad. In fact we use it in cooking and flavoring breads. It didn't work. Perhaps it's not bad enough to the moth. The next suggestion was to plant Rue. Now Rue has an awful smell—to humans, that is. A Rue at every grape also failed to keep the moth away.

Another Smelly Myth That Didn't Work

A few years ago several gardening magazines advocated catching insect pests and grinding them up with water in a food blender. The "bug-juice" so developed would, if sprayed on the foliage of a susceptible plant, warn off the approaching enemy. After all, as children we were sure to stay away from the cemetery at night, so why wouldn't a similar approach work with bugs? Well, it *doesn't* work—nice idea that it is.

Minimize the Attractive Smells by Being Tidy

Insects quickly discover any rotting fruit that lies under a tree, or a ripening tomato that has been pecked by a bird. Their sense of smell is very keen. Become tidy as part of your Integrated Pest Management program and remove such fruit before it attracts insects.

Birds as Pests

Undoubtedly, birds eat insects. At least you hope that's what they are doing as they scramble over branches of fruit trees and vines. Unfortunately, they don't seem to be of much help when you get a plague of grasshoppers or grape-leaf skeletonizers or aphids. We notice birds more when they join in and spoil fruit.

The most effective way to reduce bird damage is to keep them out of your garden—or at least the fruit tree—by using a net. We use a similar control with insect pests by trying to physically exclude them from our crop plants. Unfortunately, bird nets do occasionally trap and kill birds and lizards between the times we pass by on our inspection trips.

Use Barriers to Protect Your Plants

A more mundane measure is to put a

In damp, cloudy weather the snails come out of the ground and wander over its surface. Now is the time to crush them underfoot. You can draw snails to a trap. They can't resist a drink of beer. They overindulge and drown in it. One kind of beer is as good as another for this purpose—until research proves otherwise.

fine-mesh net over your fruit trees to keep the birds out. You can cover the tree with an old bedsheet to keep the Green Fruit Beetle out. A sheet's whiteness reflects some of the sun's energy and saves fruit from being sunburned. Bunches of ripening grapes can be hidden in paper bags to avoid damage from birds and beetles.

Vegetables can be covered with a bedsheet or a manufactured material called Reemay® that breathes and "floats" over the plants. Don't use plastic for this kind of protection because it gets hot and sweaty.

If you are troubled by rabbits, then your best defense is a chicken-wire fence all round your garden. Bury it a few inches into the ground because rabbits can squeeze under a loosely stretched wire. Remember to wire the gate and keep it closed!

Packrats and squirrels can climb over chicken wire and birds can "drop in" so the ultimate protection is a complete cage around and above your garden. See the garden house on page 28. This is expensive, but the owner stretches plastic over it in winter and makes a temporary greenhouse. It also supports shade cloth during the summer.

Birds love vegetable seedlings as they come through the soil. Make a temporary framed "box" of chicken wire that you can move from new bed to new bed as the seedlings emerge. Birds appear to lose interest in the more-mature plants.

In gopher country you can make

chicken-wire "boxes" about two feet in all dimensions, in which you put your plants as you set them in the ground. The roots are safe until they begin to grow out of the cage. Sinking such cages in the ground calls for an extra amount of digging but it's more effective and more responsible than scattering poisoned grain all over your garden in the expectation that gophers will eat it.

Cutworms

You can prevent damage by cutworms —those miserable moth caterpillars that live in the soil during the day and come out at night to chew off plant stems. Simply encircle plant stems with aluminum foil, both above and below ground. Another way is to take a glass jar or a tin can that has had its ends removed and scrunch it into the soil around the plant.

Don't Overlook the Usefulness of Lizards in Pest Control

The common lizard spends a lot of time in your tomato patch. When you see him don't blame him for the holes in your ripening fruit. He didn't make them. Birds did! He's looking for insects when you see him darting here and there among your tomatoes.

You're less likely to see the horned lizard but if you do it's almost certain that you'll misjudge him—he does look frightening. He's mistakenly called the *Horny Toad*—and he's neither. The horned lizard is definitely a desert dweller and is protected because he is becoming uncommon.

Be thankful if a horned lizard takes up residence in your garden. He's a good insect-eater, especially of ants. And, he's protected by law. Don't use insecticides indiscriminately, especially when there are lizards around.

Pill bugs (wood lice) are also active in damp weather. They can be caught in a roll of damp newspaper. Actual size is about 1/4-inch long.

For one thing, cats eat him, and there are too many unsupervised cats in the desert suburbs. Horned lizards eat a tremendous number of ants and gardeners who know this bring them into their garden for that purpose. However, moving a horned lizard—even with good intentions—is an illegal act.

Lizards are seriously affected by poisonous sprays. Don't spray indiscriminately.

Finger-and-Thumb Treatments Effectively Replace Chemical Sprays

Insects are cold-blooded and are very sluggish in the cool of the morning. That's when you can easily catch them between your finger and thumb, or shake them off, or sweep them up with a butterfly net, and even use a vacuum cleaner to suck them up.

These positive measures are a surer means of removing a pest than indiscriminate sprayings, and they are less destructive to the general environment. You get among your plants and you see what is happening in the early stages, before things get too much out of control. Besides, large amounts of chemical are needed to kill big grasshoppers and tomato hornworms.

One Way to Avoid Pests and Diseases is to Adjust the Environment

Cottony cushion scale thrives in shady places. When you discover this static pest you can "clean up" the affected

citrus tree by doing a mild pruning to let in the light and the fresh air. A predator, the Vedalia beetle, will also help.

Aphids also prefer a still space and are encouraged by too close a planting. When aphids appear on the peppers, thin out every other plant and let the wind blow through those that remain.

Plant diseases are more easily controlled when you attend to their surroundings.

Foot rot of citrus is encouraged by keeping the soil against the trunk too wet. The remedy—other than using a lot of copper Bordeaux—is to make a bank around the trunk to keep it dry when you flood. Let the soil surface dry out between waterings. Let air and a bit of sunshine reach the trunk at ground level.

Powdery mildew on grapes comes—and stays—because the plant produces a mass of crowded shoots after each pruning that don't allow ventilation. The remedy—other than lots of fungicidal sprays—is to snap off the excess new shoots about a month after the initial pruning.

If you sow seed too thickly and keep the seedlings too wet, you're sure to get the "damping-off" fungus. Seedlings are delicate and can't stand chemicals. Avoid the disease by sowing thinly.

If you sow beans in too cold a soil—a February impatience to which we are all prone—they are almost sure to rot. Don't keep watering beans in cold soil to make them come up quicker!

If the Texas root rot fungus is in your

soil, your peach trees are more likely to be attacked if you keep them too heavily irrigated during the hot summer months. The same situation might arise with tomatoes and peppers if there's Fusarium or Verticillium in your soil. Watch the watering!

Soil-borne diseases—and nematodes too—build up over the years if you keep planting the same vegetables in the same place.

Traditional chemicals used to fight these situations are so strong and dangerous to man, bird and beast, that they have been taken out of general circulation by the Environmental Protection Agency. Avoid disasters caused by soil organisms by rotating your crops. Don't use the same piece of ground more than two years running. If you can, maintain an interval of three years free of the same crop.

Get Rid of Weeds

If you have a large gardening area, make a no-man's-land around your garden to make the dry, bare soil hot and inhospitable to pests. A 10-foot-wide strip will deter grasshoppers and caterpillars and other crawling pests. Just constantly removing weeds will be effective because you remove insects' natural habitat. We don't usually examine the weed patch and that's where insect infestations often begin.

An Important Part of I.P.M. is to Use Specific Materials

The old idea of pest control was to blast the garden with an all-encompassing insecticide. Saturate every plant. Don't let anything get away! Do it once a week—or even more often, just to make sure.

Spectracide®, by its very name, tells you that it will kill a wide spectrum of insects. But the label neglects to mention that it kills good ones as well the bad ones. That you have to work out for yourself—and most of us don't.

Thoughtless programs of heavy chemical use wiped out the good guys which allowed the pests free recovery. Insect pests developed a resistance to chemicals, but the predators did not!

The new concept is to use a material that affects only the pest, leaving the other insects in the garden unharmed. These "biologicals" are either diseases or specific parasites or materials extracted directly from plants.

The notable disease material is

Bacillus thuringiensis—sold as B.T. or Dipel®, or Javelin®. It kills caterpillars, not other insects, but they have to eat it. So, you spray it on leaves of plants where the caterpillars are a nuisance, they eat it and in a day or two they are dead.

Another is Milky Spore Disease; it controls Japanese beetle, and it's supposed to last a year or two in the soil. Because these materials are specific to only one pest, Milky Spore won't control desert pests such as green fruit beetle or white grubs. And, we don't have Japanese beetles in the desert!

There's an interesting way to treat nematode-infested soil. Instead of using the old chemicals, which also kill nearby shrubs and trees and are dangerous to people, you dig in Clandosan® which is made of broken shells of crabs and lobsters! The theory is that the *chitin* in these scraps from the ocean stimulates soil organisms to feed on the nematodes. It's like mustard giving you an appetite for more beef sandwiches!

Limit your expectations. Grasshopper disease spores can be mixed with sugar and bran—just as Arsenic of Lead was used in the bad old days! After eating, the grasshopper becomes sick enough to die. However, this strategy won't work in a small garden because grasshoppers are notorious for hopping in and out of an area. The bait might attract more than you had to start with and they'll eat up your plants before they die.

Insecticidal Soaps Not the Same as Bathroom Soaps

Some new products on the market are called *soaps*. However, they are not the familiar soaps of the bathroom and kitchen.

This is confusing because an old-time remedy for aphids on the roses was for Grandma to throw the wash water at them. This control measure worked because the soapy water dissolved the waxy covering of the soft-bodied insects and they died of evaporation.

New insecticidal soaps work in the same way but more effectively. Insect pests are "dried out" by a spray of wax-dissolving soaps, smaller ones more rapidly than the big ones. Of course, beneficial insects are also affected, but the plants are not contam-inated by the soaps, which are not harmful to humans. You can safely eat your vegetables soon after spraying with insecticidal soaps.

Read the Label—Some "Non-chemical" Materials Are *Not* Specific

When you discover that the contents of a bottle are described as being "broad-spectrum" or have "broad pest-killing properties" or are simply called "non-specific," you know that they kill all insects, good *and* bad.

This means that you will find it hard to manage your insect populations to the benefit of the natural predators. These chemicals are supposed to be non-harmful to the environment because they don't last a long time, and are mistakenly thought to be less devastating, simply because they are "natural."

Here are some examples. Pyrethrins have a rapid effect on insects. They "knock-down" almost instantaneously and the satisfaction you get from using fly spray containing pyrethrins is well known. A minute after you've pressed the button there's no chemical residue. Pyrethrins work well in enclosed spaces but they evaporate and dissipate very quickly outdoors.

Rotenone comes from a plant's roots and it degrades very quickly, leaving no residue to harm the environment.

Sabadilla, extracted from seeds, has been used as a dust for many years. Dusts, in general, find their way more easily into our bodies than do liquids and sabadilla is poisonous to pets and humans.

Diatomaceous Earth is finely-ground fossilized shells that scratch the tender parts of insects after it has been inhaled. You shouldn't inhale it either! Swimming pool filter material is too coarse for insect control.

Organic Materials Are Still Chemicals—Use Them With Caution

Uninformed debate about "natural" organic materials suggests they are safe because they are not manufactured "chemicals." Of course, they are chemicals and can be quite dangerous. Nicotine sulphate is perhaps the most deadly of all insecticides, and it is one-hundred percent organic—being derived from tobacco plants.

Don't be complacent about them because they are "naturally organic" or biodegradable. This last word has been misused a great deal. It does not mean safety—it means that a large, often synthetic, chemical is readily broken down into smaller harmless chemicals by bacteria and fungi.

Use care when applying any insecticide. Consider the environment and yourself before you use them. Try to measure the consequences of your actions.

Ugly Friends

We grew up knowing ladybugs are beneficial insects and we treat them with love and respect accordingly. However, the familiar red friend with the black spots is the adult and is not such a great eater of aphids, spider mites, and mealy bugs as at the creepy-looking larval stage. It is wingless and won't fly away when its house is on fire. Because it is a growing lad, it's hungry. Yet, a lot of people are horrified when they first see a larval lady-bug and spray it three times a week to get rid of it. It's not beautiful—so it must be bad, they reason.

Green lacewings are beautiful as adults. Their transparent wings, bright-green bodies and golden eyes are a delight. The larval stage is quite different. It's appropriately called *aphid lion* and it feeds hungrily on aphids, spider mites, thrips, leafhoppers and other larvae.

Deterrents & Traps

Some gardening magazines advocate laying aluminum foil on top of the soil and under the plants. Its purpose is to reflect sunlight up to the undersides of the leaves that are naturally shaded and where insects are hiding in the heat of the day. The brightness of the foil discomforts aphids, whiteflies and leaf hoppers. Unfortunately, it doesn't keep off the squash-vine borer. This double-dose of sunshine is also supposed to give your plants a boost of energy as does a suntan reflector.

Mothballs placed against a susceptible plant put out enough of a deterrent smell to keep insects away. In the dry desert air they evaporate quickly and have to be replaced frequently.

Sticky papers fastened to a stick, in a tomato patch, or in a grape vine will catch whiteflies and leaf hoppers. If wrapped around a fruit tree's trunk, they will catch insects moving up to the foliage or down to the ground for their resting period.

Trap insects arriving in large numbers to eat your ripening fruit. Make a funnel-shaped mouth of hardware cloth to fit a large can or jar into which you place overripe fruit as bait.

Place it a little distance from your tree and clean up all damaged fruit nearby. Let the smell from the jar draw the insects away from the tree. They easily crawl in after the fruit, but don't seem able to crawl out. It's the same principle as with larger bird traps—the entry hole points only one way.

If the green fruit beetle gets past your defenses, you can, as an innovative gardener discovered recently, use the vacuum cleaner to suck them off the fruit.

Slugs & Snails

You probably won't want to pinch out slugs and snails. They like moisture and appear after prolonged rains, generally at night and on cloudy days. For most of the year they hide deep in the soil. A heavy infestation is crunched by merely walking over them as they slide over the patio concrete.

Snails give us a good example of pest control involving traps. They can't resist beer! Place a beer can with a little beer still in it, on its side so the opening is near the ground. Next morning, pick up the can full of drunken pests and throw it in the garbage.

If you think it a waste of beer to trap snails, look for them under boards where moisture remains after a rainstorm. There might be earwigs and pillbugs there, too. Both are minor pests.

Earwigs, Pillbugs & Grasshoppers

If you want to reduce the earwig and pillbug population, tie a roll of damp newspaper with string and leave it in the garden overnight. They will crawl inside and you can dispose of them easily the next morning.

Even grasshoppers can be trapped in a sunken jar containing nine parts water and one part molasses.

Don't overlook the value of a strong jet of water on insect pests. Smaller ones, such as aphids and mealybugs, can be squirted off plants. If the water is a little soapy, the pests lose their toe-hold and the wax that covers their body is dissolved. This leaves them unprotected against the dry air.

With all the methods listed above, it's important to keep up the pressure on your pests. Don't stop at one attempt—it's usually insufficient. Try two or three methods at the same time. Be tireless in your efforts. Make insect management a regular part of your gardening practices.

Daily Vigilance

Your best management practice is to be vigilant. Some gardeners call this "talking to their plants," but what they are doing is spending time with them and looking them over. And looking under plants, too.

If leaf edges are ragged or have holes, there's usually something eating them. Birds fly away and so do grasshoppers and katydids, but caterpillars stay around. They may be hiding, but they won't be far away. Look all over, and very carefully—especially underneath the leaves. You find caterpillars exactly the same color as the plant, which isn't too remarkable because the caterpillars are made of that plant. Because they are lying along the leaf stalk it takes more than a casual glance to find them.

Egg clusters are laid on the underside of a leaf. There may be one or a dozen and they are usually a paler color. Once you know what to look for, they are obvious.

Use your finger and thumb to pinch out anything which should not be there. You've nipped the problem in the bud. This is particularly effective in controlling grey aphids on cabbage, broccoli and cauliflower. They start on the underside of the leaves and finish amongst the part you eat. When they get there, it's practically impossible to do anything about them. Grape-leaf skeletonizers are easily checked with the finger-and-thumb approach.

Control Without Poisons

Pat yourself on the back for reading this far without asking, "Yes, but what should I spray it with?" As you can see, there are other methods of insect control to be considered before you reach for the poison bottle and the spray gun. You don't need to be a *Rambo* in the garden.

Harvest timing is mentioned with the deciduous fruit trees, see page 131.

Select a fruit-tree variety that ripens its fruit before the arrival of the green fruit beetle in July.

Wait for soil to be warm enough for rapid germination and strong growth so corn won't be pestered by the stalk borer. Choose a corn variety that has extended leaves at the end of the cob so corn earworm won't get into the kernels.

Old-time farmers practiced crop rotation. For example, they sowed corn in a different field each year to avoid pest build-up in the soil. They plowed under all crop residues, thus burying any pests hiding in the stalks. They hoed out weeds that initially attracted insect pests, which then migrated to the crop plants.

Home gardeners find it easy to do these things, and it's still good farming practice.

Many vegetable varieties have a built-in resistance to diseases. These should be chosen over others, provided the quality of the produce is good and the variety is adapted to local conditions. There aren't as many varieties resistant to insect pests, though one day there will be. Start looking for them now, and test them.

Chemical Sprays

Here perhaps is what you've been waiting for—a list of spray chemicals. It's a short list. You don't need a shed full of insecticides.

There are many insecticide manufacturers and they use the same basic ingredients in their formulations. Don't just read the large print. It is designed to sell the product, not to inform you.

It's better you read the complete set of instructions on the label before you unscrew the cap. The name of the active ingredient will be printed in small letters under a heading that reads *contents* or something similar. You may have to hunt for it but it's interesting and important because it tells you whether the chemical is suitable for your purpose.

Those chemicals safe to humans, pets and your environment are those that don't last long. They quickly become harmless in the air and the sunshine. They're biodegradable.

Start with pyrethrum. This is the chief ingredient of aerosol cans of fly spray. Pyrethrum kills on contact with the enemy. In less than five minutes it's useless.

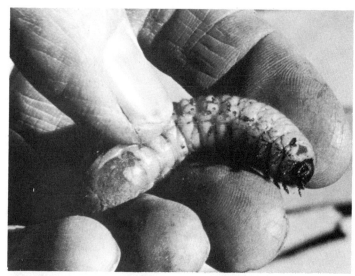

This stage of insect's life is not so damaging as the adult—when it is called the *green fruit beetle*. It then becomes a universal nuisance. Grub lives in heaps of organic matter, such as your compost pile. Sometimes it chews on roots of plants, too. Birds, as well as skunks, like them, but not nearly enough!

In damp, cloudy weather, snails come out of the ground and wander over its surface. Now is the time to crush them underfoot.

Malathion 50, Diazinon, and Spectracide® are good general-purpose insecticides for the home garden. They kill a wide range of insects and they degrade fairly quickly. Vegetables can be eaten a week after a spray application.

Carbaryl, Sevin®, is a wide-spectrum insecticide and is particularly effective on caterpillars. However, it is hazardous to bees and should not be used on fruit trees while they are flowering. If you don't care much about killing bees, go ahead with a couple of sprayings—or three, if you really don't care. The flowers do need to be pollinated but they won't be if you keep killing the insects. Serves you right if you don't get any fruit!

Just walk up and down the aisles in the stores to see the wide range of chemicals available to home gardeners. Although they are easily purchased, they should not be used indiscriminately. Always read the complete label to see if the chemical is suitable.

For example, there are systemic insecticides. These are either sprayed on the leaves or applied to the soil nearby. They are absorbed and carried through the plant's system to all parts, including the parts you eat. Please don't eat dimethoate, disulfoton or acephate. Put them on ornamental plants if you wish—but not on fruits and vegetables!

Chemical Dusts

You may be wondering about whether you should use insecticidal dusts or sprays.

The dusts are very finely ground and blow all over the place including into your eyes and lungs if you don't wear a mask. Their advantage is they may—in their blowing about—land on the undersurface of leaves which is where you want them to reach.

Sprays can be directed onto the target more accurately than dusts and they tend to stick to leaf surfaces longer.

Observe the Label Instructions

When using chemicals, don't get smart and double the recommended rates if you think you have a heavier- than-usual infestation. And don't spray more often than necessary because you think you can wipe out pests completely. Don't be a *Rambo* in your garden.

Where to Buy Predator Insects

One outlet for predator insects (biological controls) is :

  🌿 **Arbico**
    P.O. Box 4247 CRB
    Tucson, Arizona 85738
    602-791-2278 or 800-SOS-BUGS
    Their catalog is $2.75.

19

TOMATOES

Tomatoes are the most popular vegetable grown by home gardeners. This is the finding of several surveys and it's a creditable statement. It's also a reason you should know how to grow tomatoes in the desert.

Practically everyone has grown tomatoes at one time or another. Most of today's desert dwellers got their tomato-growing experience in another place and they remember. They remember too well. They repeat their experience without thinking of the differences between their old garden and their new home. Good practices there become mistakes in the desert. It's not your fault!

Forget the Past!
Initially, new desert gardeners are disappointed with tomatoes in the desert. They don't taste as good as before. They are not big like they used to be. They don't have the color of a good tomato. There's not the yield. The skins are too leathery. And so on.

So, the first thing to do is to forget almost everything you ever learned. Stop making comparisons and start from the beginning.

For instance, "back home" you probably set out plants on Memorial Day—the starting gun for the Midwest gardening season. In the desert we try to get plants in the ground on March 15th which is the official last day of killing frost and after the soil has warmed up a bit. Admittedly this is an arbitrary date. In some years planting is earlier and other years it's later, but it's the date we plan for. Soon after Memorial Day the desert temperatures get too high for reliable flower pollination, and this means no fruit is set. That's the first disappointment.

The second is that the sun is too strong to let you stake tomato plants and prune out the side shoots. This

Tomato plants take up a lot of room. This one was planted mid-March and grew to this size by mid-November when it was set back by a freeze. Although the tops are damaged, fruit underneath was protected from the damaging cold by the foliage. In the same way, fruit is protected from mid-summer heat by a canopy of leaves. Inside the jungle the atmosphere is moist and conducive to pollination and fruit set, even during the hottest months.

practice exposes stems, leaves and fruit for solar burning. It's much better to let plants grow into a jungle, even on the ground, where the shade of the leaves protects the fruit in a microclimate of trapped humidity. Carry this thought a step further and select varieties that develop their fruit under a leafy canopy instead of displaying them above it as some seed catalogs proudly advertise.

The desert sets limits on tomato growing and it's necessary to recognize them and to make arrangements to overcome these limits.

Our short little seasons (Chapter 2) there's not enough time for your "back-East" favorite kinds to grow properly. Select short-season varieties of 65-day maturity instead of the traditional Beefsteak that doesn't start producing for 85 days after setting out.

Get An Early Start
Short seasons demand that you make an early start. Sow seed in styrofoam coffee cups during mid-January to have plants ready for setting out in mid-March.

Where & When to Plant
Choose a sunny spot on the east side of a wall. It will warm up nicely in March and when temperatures rise in June and July, you can shade the plants with cheesecloth. Dig the ground in February. Let it set for weed seeds to germinate, and give a scuffling just before setting out 6-inch-tall tomato plants in mid-March.

Get your plants in the ground as soon as soil or air temperatures reach 65F. Every day you delay wastes valuable time. Good growing weather is going to stop when high temperatures

Soil thermometer is a useful tool for all planting situations. A soil temperature of 65F is warm enough for a good planting out. About 75F is shown here.

Good way to grow seedlings after transplanting from their first container. Plant at back is a little too mature; it has started to flower. Plant at left is also old as shown by thick stem.

If soil hasn't warmed sufficiently and your plants are growing fast, pot each temporarily into a larger cup. If stem loses its lower leaves, don't worry. Keep original rim of original cup as a label, giving the variety and date seed was sown.

arrive at the end of June.

Second Sowing

Take out an insurance policy in case the weather stays too cold for you to set out your plants. While you are waiting for things to warm up, the plants could become root-bound in their little containers. They may even grow flowers and small fruit. Such plants are not worth setting out because they will not give a sustained yield later. They are already old before their time.

Your insurance policy is a second sowing of seed at the end of January. If all goes well, and the first sowing is timely with weather conditions, you won't need the plants. If they are in good condition, a friend is sure to appreciate them.

You don't have to grow your own plants if you have a reliable nursery

that has the right varieties at the right time. But, if you visit your nursery on March 10th looking for plants and discover the right kinds won't be in for another three weeks, you are sure to be disappointed. Better be safe by growing your own and not be sorry.

A "Catch-Up" Trick

If the warm weather comes late and is uncertain in getting here, here's a trick to catch up a week or two. Instead of planting the tomato upright and putting the root ball in the deeper and colder soil, make a sloping trench for the plant. Lay the plant with its roots at the lower end and its leaves sticking out of the ground at the upper end of the trench. Cover the roots and stem with soil. The stem, especially if the lower leaves are removed, will grow roots along its length because the sur-

face soil is warm.

When setting out plants, always work in moist soil and help them get established by using a starter solution. Buy this at a nursery or make your own by shaking up a tablespoon of ammonium phosphate in a gallon of water. Use a pint of this solution for each plant as you set them out.

Warm the soil by laying a 2-foot-square piece of clear plastic on the ground around the plant. It will also hold in moisture. Remove this plastic when hot weather starts.

Protect young plants from cold winds by placing a gallon glass jar over them. It will provide a greenhouse effect and get the plants growing. Remove the jars during those sudden hot spells.

Use Extra Fertilizer

Good plants grow well if your soil is fertile. If your garden is a new one, it helps if you use Miracid® at every other watering until fruit is set. Use a tablespoon in a gallon of water to get some good color in your plants.

Beginning gardeners tend to fertilize too much. Strong, vigorous plants with a dark-green color flower less than plants with medium-green foliage. Dark-green leaves indicate there's too much nitrogen in the plants. If your plants are dark-green early in the game, lightly dig in an inch of sawdust around them to soak up the excess nitrogen. This may even trigger a new flowering sequence. Don't try to get more flowers from plants that are pale and weak from poor fertility.

Upper soil layers are warmer than those deeper down. Use this extra warmth by laying a tall seedling plant in a trench. Strip lower leaves off stem and it will send out additional roots to give you a strong plant.

Bumps on stem of old tomato seedling are new roots starting. If air is moist or if stem is buried in soil, these bumps quickly become roots.

Stem-side roots soon outnumber original seedling roots and contribute to strength of transplant. Originally laid on its side in warming soil, plant has straightened its stem.

You can buy starter solutions—or make your own. Use a tablespoon of ammonium phosphate—fertilizer you use when you dig a garden—in a gallon of water. Pour a pint of this around each plant when you set it out.

Cover young plants with glass jars to protect from wind and let in sun's warmth. Push edge of jars into soil and you'll also keep out cutworms that eat through stem on a dark night. If days get hot, temporarily remove each jar, but replace over plant before dark. Another way to capture sun's heat is to lay clear or black plastic on top of soil around plant. This won't keep out cold wind, but will quickly warm the soil.

The sudden change of temperature—spring ends on June 30th and summer begins—knocks the plants, and sometimes the gardener himself, "sideways." Neither recover their full productivity until the weather cools in September. The first flush of flowers in May is too important to neglect or mistreat by inadequate soil fertility or irregular watering. You depend very much on those first flower clusters.

Assist Pollination
Do all you can to ensure pollination of these early flowers. Shake them to dislodge the pollen from the anthers so it falls on the pistil close by. Gently tapping with a stick against the stem is all that's needed. If the nights turn cold or the days extra hot, there's another trick. In the morning, spray the fresh flowers with flower-set hormone. This chemical comes in an aerosol can and should be used sparingly. Read the label directions because it is absorbed into the plant's fruit. It stimulates fruit development without the benefit of pollination. As a result, the fruit is almost seedless.

Without a doubt, skins of tomatoes grown in the desert tend to be leathery. The sun and dry air cause it, so the remedy is to grow varieties that "hide" their fruit under a canopy of leaves. Don't expose the fruit by staking the plants and pruning out their side shoots like you did "back home." Instead, encourage plants to bush out and scramble over the ground,

keeping it moist and the inside of the bush humid. Unless growth is luxuriant, there's little point in providing the plant with a "tomato cage" because you are merely holding the branches up to the sunshine. Look inside the jungle to find the softest, sweetest, thinnest-skinned fruit. There'll be plenty of them all through summer.

Depend on the months of July and August to be searing hot. You'll find temporary relief in the shade of a nearby tree, but don't plant your tomatoes in shade because, for most of their time, they need sunshine.

Provide Shade in July & August
To give the plants relief during these two hot months, drape cheesecloth or an old curtain over them. You can erect a framework of wood or plastic pipe if you wish, but that will send up

the price of tomatoes. The drapery shade also maintains a higher humidity around the plants—a good thing.

Leaf Hoppers & Curly Top
The covering also wards off the wind and keeps out the beet-leaf hopper. Well—what's a beet-leaf hopper, and who cares? It's the downfall of every tomato grower in the desert because it feeds on native vegetation that is full of virus diseases.

In June, annual plants in the desert dry out and die just as our tomatoes begin to ripen their fruit and all is rosy in the garden. Then the leaf hoppers move onto your tomato plants to continue their feeding. They bring the

First flowers often don't set fruit because nights are too cold. But you can encourage them with a spray of hormone material. Instead of this . . .

. . . you get this.

Overhead shade during summer in the desert helps tomato plants. Fruit is shielded from fierce heat of the sun, humidity is maintained around the foliage, flowering continues and pests are kept out. If you grow plants inside a tower, you don't need so much garden space as if they grew over the ground. Don't prune tomatoes in the desert. Let 'em grow.

Leaves at left are permanently curled, a sure indication of the curly-top, or leaf-curl, disease. It starts just as you harvest the first fruit and can finish with the death of the plant. Once a plant gets this disease, there is little you can do except pull it up to reduce spreading of the disease to nearby healthy plants.

Wrapping of cheesecloth or similar material keeps out birds and bugs, particularly the beet-leaf hopper that carries the curly-top virus.

virus with them just like a jungle mosquito carries malaria from one human camp to another.

Leaf hoppers feed by rasping young leaves to get to the juices of the plant. They leave scars, but these are not important. The transfer of virus is. Your tomato plants begin to die and there is no cure.

Leaf hoppers prefer a sunny location, they are desert animals after all, so shading your plants during the summer months is a good idea. It's even better idea to select tomato varieties that are resistant to the virus disease called *curly top* or *leaf curl*—or something much worse when you find it in your garden. You'll be deeply disappointed when you first meet curly top. It's not Shirley Temple at all.

Red Spider Mites

Another affliction you'll feel you don't deserve is tomato rust mite, a microscopic creature related to the red spider mite. It causes the lower leaves to turn brown and die, weakening the plant so it stops producing. The mite spreads quickly from plant to plant. It's often transported into your garden on gift plants that should have been politely refused.

Blossom End Rot

Careless watering leads to problems. The first is called *blossom end rot*, but it's not a disease. No one really knows what it is. Some experts say it's related to *calcium imbalance*, whatever that means. Every desert gardener comes across it sooner or later. The end of the fruit farthest from the stalk—where the blossom was—shrivels and turns black. There's no cure, so don't think of spraying anything on it. One theory is if the plant is watered too much after a dry period, the fruit gets blossom-end rot. The fruit, or at least part of it, may be saved by cutting out the black part. Remove the damaged fruit so the plant won't waste its energy.

Split Fruit

The second problem is split fruit. It happens when summer rains or heavy irrigations follow a dry period and causes the inside of the fruit to swell rapidly. A leathery skin resulting from high temperatures, sunshine and dryness in the air doesn't stretch with the internal growth. Something has to give. That's why your tomatoes split and crack. Avoid this to some extent by keeping the plants adequately supplied with water all through the earlier growing period, but especially during those sudden bursts of hot days that are so typical of the change from spring into summer.

Spoiled fruit should be picked and thrown away. It's not going to get any better, it wastes the plant's energy and attracts nuisance insects.

Mulching Can Help

Mulching the soil around tomato plants with 3 inches of straw removes some of the effects of careless watering. Moisture is retained, so there's less extreme between being wet after one irrigation and being dry before the next. Soil is protected from the sun's heat and it stays cool. If you can't get straw, try old carpet underlay or *new* cooler pads. Never use old cooler pads—they are impregnated with salts that will harm your plants and the soil.

Be Deliberate When Harvesting

Beginning gardeners are hasty in harvesting their tomatoes—a natural failing because they've worked hard at the job of growing them. Any apparent success encourages premature picking. There's a secret to success, though, and it's as simple as waiting for the fruit to become really ripe, then waiting another day before you pick.

It seems that desert tomatoes don't taste very sweet until their last day. In several taste tests it has been shown that a particular variety may score poorly and then a couple of days later give very acceptable fruit with a flavor that takes you back to your childhood days when tomatoes were tomatoes.

Cut Back in Late July

All tomato varieties suffer from the heat during July and August, though the cherry kinds suffer least. Keep

Protection from the fierce summer sun reduces skin blemishes commonly seen in desert-grown tomatoes. Thick, leathery skins don't stretch, but crack as tomatoes grow in size. This can be reduced somewhat by increased watering during the early growing period and the hottest days.

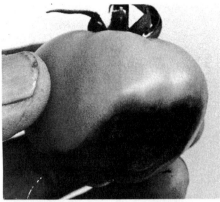

Expect blossom end rot if you grow tomatoes in the desert. It's common and, like the weather, everyone talks about it, but does nothing about it. Experts can't even agree on what causes it, except to say it's not a disease, but a "condition." Remove affected fruit to lighten load on plant and hope that the next fruit set will be free of the problem. It often is!

Watch for pellets on the ground around your plants—a sure sign that a tomato hornworm is busily eating the leaves. Look carefully and you'll find a number of them. Pick them off and squash them underfoot.

plants alive by shading, mulching and careful watering until cooler weather in September.

In late July, after it's obvious that no more flowers are forthcoming, cut the plants back by about a third or a half. New shoots grow from the stalks and will produce flowers in late August. In the cooler weather of September and October they will be pollinated successfully. You'll have lots of green tomatoes when the first severe frost kills off the vines. If the frost is late in coming, you'll have ripe tomatoes, though they ripen slowly in cool weather.

Plant Again in August
In addition to cutting back your spring-planted tomatoes in late July, set out fresh plants in August and grow them until the frost. The danger of curly top is negligible, the hot weather is over, and watering isn't so critical. In other words, it's easy to grow tomatoes.

This is true so long as the weather behaves itself by giving us a mild winter. Even if December turns cold, there's a way to keep the plants growing. Build a framework and cover it with clear plastic to give your tomatoes a temporary greenhouse. On a freezing night, cover your "greenhouse" with a light blanket and remove it in the morning. The plants will produce all winter.

Soil Problems
Old gardens that are continuously planted to one kind of vegetable often develop pests and diseases in the soil. With tomatoes expect nematodes.

These microscopic worms invade plant roots, swelling and distorting them enough to kill the plant. Two other killers are the fungi: *Verticillium* and *Fusarium*.

To avoid soil problems, become a rotational farmer. Protect your soil by planting different crops in it each year, thereby preventing the build-up of harmful organisms by not feeding them all the time. Don't grow tomatoes in the same part of your garden every year. Rotate your tomato patch.

Remember: If you keep tomato plants growing through a mild winter and into spring, you provide an opportunity for soil organisms to build up their populations. Your plants will suffer and, even worse, your garden's soil becomes contaminated. It's not easy to clean up contaminated soil.

Varieties to Choose?
The desert climate makes special demands on tomatoes. Many varieties are available. All look inviting in the seed catalogs, but only a few do well in the desert.

Cherry tomatoes are easily the best performers. Always grow one cherry plant to remind you that growing tomatoes in the desert is not impossible.

The results of Mark Burr's 1985 tomato trials in a desert locality (Tucson) showed that Celebrity, Lemon Boy, Sundrop, Betterbush and Cherry Grande were then the best catalog varieties available—in that order. Medium and small tomatoes do much better than large-fruited varieties,

especially in hot weather.

Although Superbeefsteak and Heavyweight had very large fruit, they yielded poorly in the summer. Both gave very large crops of green tomatoes *after* frost. This indicates that Beefsteak varieties could perhaps be planted in mid-summer for a successful fall crop, but you'll still have to pray for a late frost—or none at all.

A suitable variety yields well throughout the season, has good-tasting fruit, has fruit tucked under the foliage, resists curly top and produces early before hot weather arrives. It will also stand up to summer's stressful temperatures, recover to produce a fall crop and withstand the first light freezes.

A tall order you might say. One that's hard to fulfill so a continuous search has to be made.

There's no perfect tomato. An old reliable will let you down once in a while. Across town, a friend's favorite will do better than yours one year, but not in another. Improve your chances by growing three or four kinds, varying them each year, until you are entirely satisfied. But don't make a final decision after only one year's test.

If you don't want to garden during the summer, get varieties that fruit early and others that do well in the fall.

Don't overload yourself with a lot of plants. A family of four tomato eaters should eat quite well from six plants. The following "package" has done well for a few years at 3,000 feet. All were set out in mid-March and gave

You can get new plants from old ones if you take cuttings during July. Find strong axillary shoots and cut off 6-inch lengths.

Dip end of cutting in RooTone® powder to stimulate root development. Pot in a cup of lightweight soil mix.

In no time, because of warm weather, you will have a rooted cutting ready to plant out in late August.

Don't let roots get crowded at bottom of cup. Plant is just ready for planting out.

fruit at different times to provide an almost continuous harvest. Early Girl starts the season. Celebrity is mid-season, Flor America is a late variety and a cherry type provides a steady summer yield.

Growing good tomatoes in the desert is a decided challenge. You'll be successful if you are well-prepared, do everything right, and *if* Mother Nature smiles on you.

That's gardening in the desert, more so than anywhere else.

Summary of Important Points

Here's a summary to help you remember how to become a successful desert tomato grower:

- Get an early start. Plant as soon as soil or air temperature reaches 65F.
- Have strong plants, 6-inches tall, of suitable short-season varieties. This means less than 70 days.
- Encourage rapid growth through adequate soil preparation, starter solution and, if necessary, liquid feeding.
- Plant on the east side of a wall to get morning sun and afternoon shade. Warm the soil with a square of plastic.
- Encircle the plants with a framework and a plastic sheet to provide a greenhouse effect and to keep cold winds off.
- Keep the plants growing with adequate watering.
- Shake the flowers and spray with bloom set if temperatures stay below 55F.

- Cover the plants with cheesecloth as the first fruit sets.
- Let the plants sprawl over the ground; don't stake up or prune side shoots.
- Cut back straggly plants in early August.
- Set out new plants in early August. Don't plant tomatoes in the same soil every year.

Tomatillos for the Desert?

This fruit is becoming popular with gourmet cooks. And because serious cooks are often gardeners "who grow their own," it's worth mentioning *tomatillos* (little tomatoes).

The tomatillo plant sprawls over the ground like that of the tomato. And its fruit is the size of a cherry tomato. The similarity ends there. Flavor is tart and the flesh less juicy. Seeds are all through the flesh and the fruit is covered with a papery husk. Tomatillos more closely resemble the choke cherry, Cape gooseberry or Chinese Lantern. They are not truly tomatoes.

In the desert not many people grow tomatillos. But those who have tried them provide us with a little pioneering information. Tomatillos appear not to do as well at lower elevations as they do at 3,000 feet. It seems that they prefer, as do peppers, cooler nights that the uplands give.

You can find seeds in a few specialist catalogs and, of course, in the supermarket fruit you buy. Find the ripest yellowest fruit you can and make sweet pies or jam from them, but save the seeds. If you buy fruit to make hot sauces, it will be green and unripe—and the seeds may be immature.

Sow the seed in styrofoam coffee cups at the same time you get ready for tomato growing. Set the plants in the ground some six weeks later and treat them as if they were tomatoes for the rest of their life.

If you let them sprawl all over—which is their natural growth habit—you may lose fruit to pillbugs. This is because you must water the plants liberally; pillbugs like cool, damp shady places. They won't damage green fruit so much as the ripe yellow fruit. You can save some of the harvest for yourself by supporting sprawling branches off the ground on stiff wire trays.

20

PEPPERS

If you want to become an aficionado of the Southwest and adopt local ways, you'll have to grow your own hot peppers—or *chiles*.

There's a mystique involved, but you can penetrate it without a great deal of effort. Growing peppers is the gardener's equivalent of newcomers' affection for the cowboy hat, silver belt buckle and high-heeled boots.

At the same time you can learn to grow sweet peppers.

Both kinds are closely related so they easily cross-pollinate and produce seeds with a mixture of characteristics. It's easy to lose a favorite variety unless you are very careful of this fact. Keep your pepper plants away from one another. It's usually better to buy fresh seed of a particular kind than to save your own. However, old-timers are proud and possessive of their own seed strains.

The people of New Mexico have earned a well-deserved reputation for knowing the best ways to grow good crops, providing seed of good varieties and being creative with harvests. But, you, too, can make your own salsa and *jalapeños en Escabeche* or merely grind up your dried peppers for a hot surprise on your old gringo friends.

Hot or Sweet?

There are more than 300 kinds of chiles in the world and some of them are extremely pungent. It seems the smaller the fruit, the hotter they get. Whatever you get involved in, sort out your priorities to avoid confusion and hot surprises.

Study seed catalogs to find what you want from the varieties available to us in the Southwest. The following list will help you—as a newly arrived greenhorn—from being taken advantage of by a wicked old-timer looking for a laugh. Watch out! Hot peppers

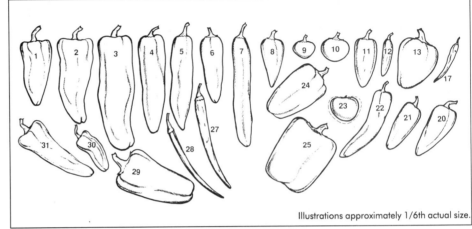

Illustrations approximately 1/6th actual size.

1. ANCHO: Mild/hot medium-size chile. Used dried, whole or powdered, or fresh, roasted and peeled. Also known as "Chile Poblano" in fresh state. Dark green/red/red-brown.

1. MULATO: Mild/hot medium-size chile. Used dried, whole or powdered. Dark green/red/brown-black. Imported from Mexico.

2. CUBANELLE: Sweet, medium-size "aconcagua" type chile. Used fresh or roasted and peeled. Yellow-green/red.

3. ACONCAGUA: Sweet, large chile, originally from Argentina. Used fresh in salads or roasted and peeled. Yellow-green.

4. COLORADO (mild & hot): Large pepper from New Mexico. Used fresh roasted and peeled, or dried and powdered. Excellent for chile rellenos. Green/dark red.

4. COLLEGE 64L: Mild, medium-size pepper. Used fresh roasted and peeled, or dried and powdered. Excellent for chile rellenos. Green/red.

5. ANAHEIM (mild & hot): Large pepper from California. Used fresh roasted and peeled, or dried and powdered. Excellent for chile rellenos. Green/red.

6. HUNGARIAN HOT WAX: Hot, medium-size pepper. Used fresh or pickled. Yellow/red.

7. PASILLA: Hot, long slender chile. Used dried and roasted in sauces. Dark green/red/chocolate brown-black. Imported from Mexico.

8. FRESNO CHILE GRANDE: Hot, small chile medium-thick fleshed. Used fresh in salads or sauces, or pickled. Bright green/red.

9. CHERRY: Sweet, round medium-size pepper. Used for pickling.

10. CHERRY: Hot, oblate pepper. Larger than "cherry sweet." Used for pickling. Medium-thick flesh.

11. JALAPEÑO: Hot, medium-size pepper. Used fresh in salads and sauces, or pickled Mexican style (in escabeche). Dark green/red. Also know as "Chile Chipotle" in red, ripe, smoked state. Tam Jalapeño is same as above, but milder.

12. SERRANO: Hot, small chiles.Green/red. Used fresh in sauces, etc., or pickled Mexican style (in escabeche). Fine flavor.

13. PIMENTO GRANDE: Sweet, medium-size pepper, thick fleshed. Used in cooking or picked red, roasted, peeled and canned. Fine flavor. Dark green/red.

17. TAKANOTSUME: Hot, small chile. Used fresh or dried. Green/red. Imported from Japan.

20. SANTE FE GRANDE: Hot, small chile. Medium-thick flesh. Used fresh in salads, sauces or pickled. Yellow/orange-red.

21. GOLDSPIKE: Hot, small hybrid chile. Heavy yields of uniform medium-thick fleshed fruit. Used fresh or pickled. Yellow/red.

22. YELLOW SWEET WAX: Long, medium-thin flesh sweet pepper. Used fresh or pickled. Yellow/red.

23. TOMATILLO: *Tomate verde* (green tomato of Mexico) walnut-size, husked tomato. Used for sauces and cooking. Cook without peeling. Used fresh in salads. Imported from Mexico.

24. ROUMANIAN (sweet & red): Medium-size pepper. Medium-thick flesh. Used fresh or canned. Yellow/red.

25. TITAN: Sweet, medium-size bell pepper. Thick-fleshed, blocky shape, good flavor. Green/red.

27. CAYENNE: Hot, long pepper. Used fresh or dried. Dark green/red. Imported from Taiwan.

28. YUNG KO: Hot, long, curved pepper. Used fresh or dried. Imported from Taiwan.

30. PEPERONCINI: Mild, small pepper; thin fleshed. Used mostly for pickling. Fine flavor. Green/red.

31. ITALIAN SWEET: Sweet, medium-long pepper. Used fresh, roasted or for frying. Superior flavor. Early yields.

Drawing and chart courtesy
Horticultural Enterprises
Dallas, Texas

116

Pepper plant produces well in a 5-gallon bucket, though it will do better in the ground. A container-grown plant can be moved to a warm, sunny place in early spring when the weather is still cold, then to a shady spot during the heat of summer.

In November, a container-grown pepper plant can be cut back and moved into a greenhouse or protected place. It will send out new shoots that will produce early fruit next spring—much quicker than a newly set out plant. Peppers can be kept alive for up to four years in this way.

Use a soil thermometer to let you know when to set out plants. Soil needs to be at least 75F as illustrated.

can blister your lips and make you cry when you rub your eyes after handling them.

Hot ones start with: Sandia; Serrano; Jalapeño; Rio Grande; Fresno Chile Grande; Santa Fe Grande; Cayenne; NuMex Big Jim; Colorado; Anaheim; Hungarian Hot Wax; Pasilla; and Hot Cherry.

Medium ones include: Ancho; Mulato; College 64; and Yellow Wax.

Sweeter peppers are: Aconcagua; Cubanelle; Sweet Cherry; Pimiento Grande; Sweet Roumanian; Titan; Bell Boy; Big Bertha; Yolo Wonder; California Wonder; Sweet Banana; and Yellow Bell.

Big ones that are threaded on string and sold as decorations for entryways at Christmastime are Sandia, Rio Grande and Big Jim. The big green bell peppers you find in grocery stores are usually California Wonder, Yolo Wonder or Bell Boy.

Three plants of hot and half a dozen of sweet peppers should be enough for most households. They are attractive plants and can be used in your summer landscaping, mixed with flowers in the borders, or planted in half barrels for patio display.

They will survive a mild winter, but hard freezes will kill them.

Peppers, both hot and sweet varieties, grow best in the upper desert regions where summer temperatures stay below 100F most of the time or the hot days are modified by cool nights. Peppers require a long period of warm weather, ideally around 80F, for continued flowering and development of large fruit.

In the low and medium desert regions, fruits are generally smaller because of the heat. Flowering slows during the hottest time of summer— just as tomatoes stop flowering. As with tomatoes, they flower vigorously again in the fall and it's a gamble whether frost destroys the late fruit in November.

Frost Damage

Bypass the possibility of frost damage by cutting back your pepper plants after fall harvest and before frost. Dig them up and grow them in 5-gallon buckets during the winter months in a greenhouse or a protected sunny part of your patio. Watch out for frosty nights and bring your pepper plants inside. The following spring, return them to the garden. Some gardeners keep their pepper plants for three or four years this way. Another way to keep a productive plant in your garden for two or three years is to cover it on cold winter nights with a large cardboard box.

Planting

If you are starting with seed, sow it six to eight weeks before the soil warms up. The seedlings grow more slowly than tomatoes, so require an earlier start at the beginning of January. A greenhouse where the temperature can be kept at 75F is needed.

Usually, you set out plants, your own or those from a nursery, a little later than tomatoes. Soil needs to be warmer for peppers—75F instead of 65F.

If night air temperatures stay below 60F after setting out, you might get some premature flowering. You don't want this to happen because it will produce small fruit.

Peppers need richer soil than tomatoes. The roots go down 2 feet, so it's best to dig and irrigate deeply.

Use a starter solution when you set out plants. Place a gallon glass jar over the plants to keep them warm and protected from cold winds. Warm the soil with a 2-foot square of clear plastic. Irrigate frequently to keep the plants growing.

It's especially important to keep the plants well supplied with water during flowering—just as it is with tomatoes, peaches and citrus, beans and berries. Usually, a pepper flower gives fruit 50 days later. There should be no water stress during flowering, otherwise flowers will drop off—an old gardening truth that relates to all fruit-bearing trees and vegetables.

Flowers appear at the ends of new branches, so it's also important to keep the plants growing. They need a fertile soil and *frequent*, but *light*, applications of ammonium sulphate or Miracid® or similar houseplant fertilizer. Frequent means every three or four weeks: light means 1/2 pound to every 100 square feet of garden.

As with tomatoes and all summer fruits, peppers burn and blister in the desert sunshine. Select varieties that produce their fruit under the canopy of their leaves.

If you grow peppers in half barrels or 5-gallon buckets, move them into a shady area during the hot summer months. During the winter they can be brought onto a sunny patio and used as an ornamental planting, particularly if you grow the yellow or golden bell peppers. If you become a hot-pepper grower, don't forget their pungency and hazard to small, inquisitive children.

Your garden site should be on the east side of a wall or house so your plants get afternoon shade after a morning of sunshine. If the plants unavoidably get afternoon sun, provide overhead shade during the hottest summer weeks. A 3-inch-thick straw mulch will save water and prevent the roots from getting too hot.

Bugs & Disease

Peppers suffer from whiteflies, leaf hoppers, hornworms and leaf cutter bees. They also suffer from curly top, the virus associated with tomatoes, which is carried by leaf hoppers. See the photographs in Chapter 18 , if you haven't already met these pests.

If pepper plants come into contact with old, contaminated garden soil, there is the danger of contracting

Square of clear plastic will warm soil and keep in moisture. Your pepper plant will establish itself more quickly with this help and you'll get an earlier harvest—before the weather gets too hot for pollination.

Verticillium and Fusarium wilt or their roots being invaded by nematodes. There is no cure, so pull up the plants. Until you can fumigate the area with Vapam, set out clean plants in another part of the garden where the soil is not infected.

Preparing & Eating

Peppers are good for you. They contain lots of vitamin C, especially when the fruit turns really ripe and red. They also contain a lot of carotene which turns into vitamin A.

Sweet peppers are best eaten straight from the plant, either slightly cooked or raw in salads. Hot peppers go into sauces and flavorings to liven up stews, soups and curries. A good curry containing plenty of pepper makes you sweat behind the ears one minute after the first mouthful. It's often said, "Peppers clear your sinuses!"

Hot peppers can be preserved by freezing, pickling or canning. They can also be dried which was the traditional method of preservation introduced by early settlers from Mexico. If you want to dry a harvest surplus, spread the ripe fruit on a piece of corrugated sheet metal or on a tin roof. Air movement up the corrugations of the hot metal ensures quick drying.

Productive plant such as this owes its vigor to being kept in shade during hot summer months. It will survive freezing nights if covered with a heavy sheet or light blanket during freezing hours. Fruit in the fall is usually larger than that produced in early summer.

This method gives a better product than threading the fruit on a string because bunched-up fruit has less air space and, thus, tends to mold. Don't trouble yourself with drying sweet peppers; they don't turn out very well.

Wear rubber gloves when handling a lot of hot peppers. Dried hot peppers can be ground into powder. Use it sparingly. Don't rub your eyes while working with peppers or pepper powder.

When you harvest, don't make the mistake of putting your peppers into plastic bags—unless you store them in the refrigerator. At normal temperatures the peppers in plastic bags are guaranteed to mold.

21

ORIENTAL VEGETABLES

Oriental vegetables are special for a number of reasons. They are easy to grow and they grow quickly. The wide range of different kinds allows you to grow them all through the year. You can eat roots, stems, leaves or flowers, and they have an interesting variety of flavors.

As if this weren't enough, they are good for you. Even though you've been told this about vegetables ever since you were a child, this time it's different. Because they are high in protein and vitamins, and low in calories, oriental vegetables are preferred by people who are watching their weight. A quick stir-fry preserves their food values without adding a lot of oil. But oriental vegetables are best eaten uncooked as salad ingredients. You can enjoy many different salads from the wide range of flavors provided by oriental vegetables.

Getting Acquainted

There's no need to be confused and mystified by oriental vegetables. Some of them—snow peas, Japanese radishes, yard-long beans and Chinese cabbage—are as familiar to the public in grocery stores as to gardeners through seed catalogs. There are winter or cool-season kinds and these are mostly interesting variations of our old friend, the cabbage. Some are loose-leaved, others tightly compact. They vary in leaf color, size, shape and flavor. You grow some for the sake of their flowers which are best eaten uncooked.

There are large radishes, sweet crispy turnips and mild bunching onions. These are also cool-season plants with slightly different flavors than the standard kinds.

You may not have met many of the summer varieties, apart from eggplants and yard-long beans, though they are

You can plant several kinds of oriental vegetables close to one another in nearby beds. Their different flavors give you variety in salads and stir-fry dishes. Variabilty between the numerous kinds of oriental vegetables makes for interesting gardening and cooking. Flavors are as varied as their appearance.

available in specialty food stores. Without knowing it, you may have eaten them in restaurants where they flavored a delicious dish.

You have to be a bit of an esoteric cook to grow any of the following. But once you're hooked on oriental cooking, you will need supplies from the garden all through the year.

If you insist on cooking throughout the hot desert summer, you'll find yourself growing bitter melon—a well-named plant—that grows just like an American melon. Small pieces of it are put into soups and stews or cooked with fermented beans.

Winter melon, like winter squash, is grown in summer, stored and eaten during the winter. It has a smooth, mellow taste. Mature fruit goes into soups with chicken stock and mushrooms. Young fruit, harvested as the plant

grows during summer, can be scooped out and filled with meat, mushrooms or water chestnuts. If you are on a budget, it can be simply steamed whole.

Water spinach is a graceful member of the sweet-potato family, grown for its tender leaf shoots.

Amaranth is a large, leafy, summertime vegetable that needs frequent picking to keep it in bounds and prevent it from producing seeds. The grain amaranth is another kind, similar in appearance to water spinach, that does not produce as good a quality leaf. Even so, amaranth leaves are best cooked as a summer spinach. Only the very smallest of tender leaves have appeal as fresh salad material. Older leaves quickly turn bitter.

There are fuzzy gourds, wax gourds, hot peppers, pickling melons, soy

Amaranth is another summertime leaf producer. Don't confuse it with its cousin, the grain amaranth. You must keep pinching out tender shoots to be sure of good flavor. Old leaves tend to be bitter.

Radishes grow longer than this, yet don't become hollow or pungent.

You'll also have many kinds of turnips from which to choose—often so mild and firm-textured you can eat them like apples.

beans and so on. It seems that many a familiar vegetable wants to get into the oriental-vegetable catalogs.

It's the same with winter or cool-season kinds. We discover that faba beans, sugar peas, chives, radishes, celery, asparagus and even Blue Lake bush beans have all joined the club. It's no longer exclusive.

Be a little adventuresome next cool season—for that's the easiest time to try something new. Try the cabbage-family varieties. Try radishes, turnips and onions, too. Get a special catalog, ignore the confusion of names and find three or four varieties to test. If you don't want to go to this trouble, you'll find a few easy-to-grow varieties listed in your usual seed catalog. Oriental vegetables are becoming more popular and more common.

If you are a little short on adventure in your gardening and cooking, start by taste-testing these vegetables in restaurants and supermarkets, remembering that freshly picked, home-grown vegetables always taste better.

Finding & Sowing Seeds
Many cities have oriental emporiums where the Chinese, Japanese or Korean owner—they all seem to be good gardeners who grow their own

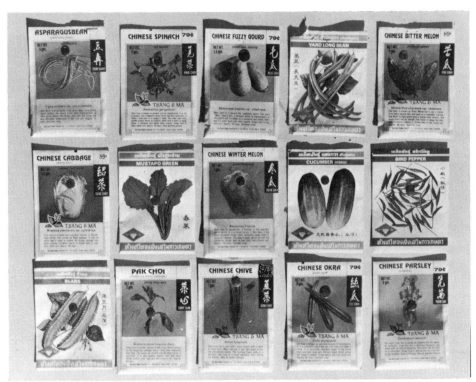

You'll also find the real thing at oriental stores in some centers of population. Store owners are often good gardeners who can give good advice.

In early summer, this variety of onion produces small tasty bulbs instead of the usual flower on top of the flower stalks. This is an out-of-season bonus to the usual "green onion" harvest of spring.

Many standard seed catalogs feature oriental vegetables, but you can get esoteric and go for the real thing. Fortunately, there are English sub-titles.

Celery-leaved cabbage: Remove a few leaves at a time. It doesn't have a celery flavor—it just reminds you of how celery looks. You can eat the stalks too, if they aren't old.

Chinese pole beans—also called *asparagus beans* and *yard-long beans*—love hot weather and are prolific producers. Give them a framework that will allow them to climb to 8 feet. Pick every other day. Don't let the pods get more than 3 days old. Eat them fresh or lightly cooked.

traditional vegetables—will recommend locally suitable varieties. Such stores often have seed packets of the real thing. You will need help with reading the labels written in a mysterious language. There's nothing mysterious in these wonderful vegetables, though.

Good soil is required for success. Use that part of your garden where you have applied a lot of organic matter over the years. If you haven't yet worked up your soil to a high state of fertility, go ahead. Dig deeply.

Sow seed in styrofoam coffee cups during August to get a steal on the cool weather. Set out plants in mid-September. Gardeners who prefer to wait for things to cool a little, say that *direct seeding*—seeding in the ground—gives plants a deeper tap root and, because of this, they are less subject to wilt during hot, dry spells. But don't forget that harvester ants are active at the end of summer—a good reason to sow seed in coffee cups.

If you prefer to set out plants, don't forget starter solution at planting time. Buy something at the nursery or make your own using a tablespoon of ammonium phosphate in a gallon of water. Pour on a pint per plant as you set them out.

Multiple Sowings

Make a succession of sowings every four or five weeks to ensure a steady harvest through the cool months until May. Go easy on the number of plants until your family has accepted these new vegetables. After that you'll be planting plenty, but remember, they are good yielders. If you plant three or four kinds for variety, you won't need more than a couple of dozen.

Keep the plants growing—don't allow any setbacks. Good growing weather usually lasts until October or November, so it's up to you to see that the plants don't dry out—even for a day.

Fertilizing

Apply ammonium sulphate every three or four weeks during warm periods; switch to ammonium nitrate during November, December and January. Scatter 1/2 pound of dry fertilizer over every 100 square feet of moist soil and water it in well. Keep fertilizer off the leaves, otherwise they may be burned. Oriental vegetables respond to plenty of nitrogen.

The Harvest

Leafy varieties may be harvested by removing a few lower leaves—just as much as you need for the next meal—and letting the plant continue to grow. This is an economical way to pick all leafy vegetables. You always have

Leafy vegetables can be kept growing for several weeks by harvesting the lower leaves before they get old. This way you always have fresh garden produce—and the original plant. It's a long harvest without the trouble of replanting and waiting for maturity.

Starter bed of oriental vegetables can be densely planted for a quick harvest of mixed flavors and colors. As you remove whole plants at a tender stage of their development, you leave space for remaining plants to grow larger. This is a winter garden bed.

Bok Choy, a very compact and tender kind of cabbage, is a rapid grower, even in winter.

Familiar Chinese Cabbage grows to 10 or 15 pounds in weight, yet its inside leaves are tender and crisp. It's a winter vegetable.

Flavorful as well a appealing to the eye, dark-green foliage adds interest to a mixed salad. Pick lower leaves before they get old and strongly flavored.

fresh material and no wilted leaves in the refrigerator. You get a quicker harvest and one that lasts longer. This is much better than cutting off the top and starting again with fresh transplants.

Some of the flowering kinds such as Tsai Shim, Hon Tsai Tai and White Flowering Kale should be harvested before the flowers are fully open. This is the same way you'd treat broccoli—but others are best picked after the

flowers have opened a little. Watch out for bees working the fragrant flowers.

Oriental vegetables are waiting for you! Surprise yourself! Usually the flowers are sweet and are best eaten uncooked. Taking them off doesn't stop the plant from producing more. In fact, the opposite is the case—the more you pick, the more you get.

Cold weather doesn't affect oriental vegetables, except to slow their growth. Some are frost-tender and, of

course, all flowers are tender. Manage the plantings of frost-tender varieties to avoid the coldest weather you might experience—or provide a plastic-covered shelter.

Insect Pests

Oriental vegetables suffer from the same sort of insects that attack the more usual vegetables. Watch for grey aphids on the leaves and growing points. Cabbage loopers might appear and make holes in the leaves. Spotted cucumber beetle can be a nuisance, too, if numbers get large. During the night, cutworms carry out their usual secretive stem-cutting on new plants and seedlings. Birds will go for the emerging seedlings. In other words—nothing new.

Bolting Usually Undesirable

Any warm spell—coinciding with neglectful watering—stimulates plants into flowering. That's all right if the plant is a flowering variety such as flowering kale or Tsai Shim, but it's undesirable in the case of Napa cabbage. When head vegetables *bolt*—the technical name for unreasonable flowering—they stop growing and usually develop a bitter taste.

22

CITRUS

Winter visitors to desert regions are impressed when they see golden fruit hanging on dark-foliaged citrus trees. Citrus trees are a beautiful part of our urban desert scene.

Visitors who become permanent residents invariably include citrus trees in their landscaping. A citrus tree does more than double-duty. It is ornamental in itself and defines a landscape area. It screens out noise from a patio and, without making us farmers, gives reliable crops of luscious fruit. Fortunately, they require very little attention throughout the year.

"What's the best kind of citrus to plant?" is the first question. The other how-to-grow questions follow quickly.

Many citrus varieties do well in the desert. Some don't do so well—just because of the desert conditions.

Winter Temperatures Are Important

The main condition to consider is winter temperatures. Mild freezes of short duration aren't much to worry about. But sharp freezes when the plant is not yet dormant do a lot of damage—even killing a tree down to the ground. When it recovers and sends out new shoots from below the bud union, you won't get good fruit any more. You see, citrus trees come in two halves—the fruit-bearing upper part, and the underground rootstock. More of this later.

If you are in an established neighborhood and there are no citrus trees in your neighbors' yards, there is a good reason why. Most likely it is a cold area. Other frost-tender plants that are indicators of warm areas are bougainvillea, hibiscus, ironwood, thevetia, figs, Queen palm, albizia and bauhinia.

Even though you may be in a cold part of town, there are localized warm spots, even around your house. A

You need room for citrus trees as with any other tree. Besides blocking view of street, tree offers temptation to children on their way to school. Concrete-block wall captures sun's heat during winter and creates a warm microclimate around tree.

patio on the west side of the house, especially one surrounded by brick walls and with a cement floor, will retain afternoon heat through much of a cold night. That's provided the sun has been shining during the day. There's the place to plant your citrus.

Sloping ground drains air just as it drains water. Moving air is warmer than still, trapped air. The coldest part of a landscape is along rivers and at low points of drainage areas. That's not the place to plant your citrus.

Citrus varieties vary in their freeze-resistance. The list, going from tender to resistant, is limes, lemons, oranges, tangerines, tangelos, grapefruit, kumquats and calamondin.

Root-Stock Considerations

There's another thing to bear in mind. Rootstocks, the lower, root part of the tree, also vary in their frost resistance. This list, going from tender to frost-resistant, is Citrus Macrophylla, Rough Lemon, Sweet Orange, Troyer Citrange, Sour Orange, and Trifoliate.

The right combination of fruit wood and rootstock will give strong freeze resistance. Then you will get fruit. For example, grapefruit grafted onto Sour Orange will give a much more frost-resistant tree than a lime grafted onto Citrus Macrophylla. Learn the value of rootstocks as you learn about the fruit.

Other rootstocks influences are tree

During the mild weather of spring and fall, take buds from branches of a tree you admire. This branch shows where buds are—at base of each leaf and thorn. Buds have already started to grow and are too old for using as budding material. Cut I-shaped opening in twig of one tree and insert bud from another.

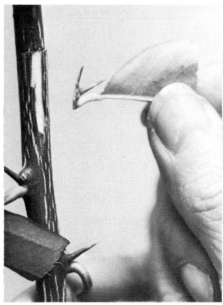

Push bud down under moist green bark as far as it takes to let top cross-cut join up again.

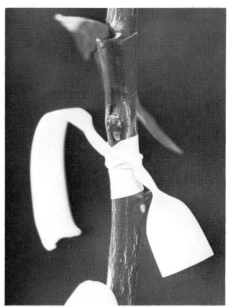

Wrap top and bottom of inserted bud with soft plastic budding tape. Don't use any other kind of plastic material, certainly not electrician's tape. Some gardeners cover bud completely to make sure it doesn't dry out in desert air. In this case, they have to be especially observant of its growth and cut away tape as soon as bud begins to swell. Tree needs to be well watered during this operation.

In a few weeks new bud will shoot out. A couple of years later it will produce fruit just like the tree you took it from—regardless of kind of citrus tree you have. Stay within the citrus family. It's a shame you can't bud on grapes, apricots and peaches. Don't try.

size, disease resistance and fruit flavor. While there are others, they are not important to a home gardener.

Used as a rootstock, Citrus Macrophylla makes a tree grow quickly to a large size. In a small home yard, that sort of performance is not desirable, especially because the fruit is watery and flavorless. And, the rootstock has poor resistance to a soil fungus disease called *citrus root rot*. It is more suited to sandy soils.

Rough Lemon as a rootstock is much the same.

Troyer Citrange rootstock makes a small tree suitable for small patios. It is rather slow growing, which is not so good for an impatient gardener.

Sweet Orange rootstocks are satisfactory, giving average-size trees with an average sort of flavor.

When used as a rootstock, Cleopatra Mandarin makes a small tree with good-flavored fruit, but yields are low. It's a good choice for heavier soils.

Sour Orange rootstock gives a small tree with good-flavored fruit. It is resistant to Texas root rot, as well as citrus foot rot.

Sour Orange had a bad name in California—and maybe still has—because it is susceptible to a devastating virus disease called *tristeza*. Tristeza is Spanish for sadness or sorrow. There is no cure once a tree is infected. In the 1940's and '50's, acres of diseased trees had to be uprooted because, up to that time, it was the favorite rootstock.

Away from the very sandy soils of Yuma, Arizona there is no doubt that Sour Orange is the most suitable

Yard enclosed by solid wall traps cold air during winter nights. Gardener deliberately provided ventilation holes to let out cold air. Vent holes would be more effective closer to the ground because cold air sinks.

rootstock for citrus in the home yard. It makes a small tree, yield is good and fruit quality is good, whether it be lemon, tangelo, grapefruit or orange. The rootstock is resistant to both citrus foot rot and Texas root rot. It does well in heavier soils. And, it has the best frost resistance.

Every citrus tree is really two trees—one on top of the other. Rootstock is chosen to meet soil conditions; top part delivers the fruit. As tree grows, this demarcation line fades, but rootstock's influence continues throughout tree's life. Tree is the right size for planting. Note high bud union, straight with trunk.

Other Planting Considerations

Although citrus trees can be seen planted close to a wall and in a confined townhouse patio, it's advisable to allow 9 or 10 feet from any wall, pathway, building, or other tree. Do you have enough room?

If you have caliche in your yard, is it easy to dig through it? Citrus needs good soil and drainage. Rocks and boulders are not really a problem because trees' roots grow around such obstacles, but they can't grow through caliche.

Which Citrus to Plant?

Well, back to the the first question: Which is the best citrus to plant?

The best kind is the one you most like to eat, bearing in mind the considerations just covered. For example,

Busy bee pollinating citrus blossom, reminds the good gardener that spraying thrips during flowering period can reduce fruit set. If the bees are killed along with the thrips—they are only minor pests— there will be a lighter fruit crop because of inadequate pollination.

if you like limes best of all—remembering Key Lime Pie—you should be living in a frost-free area.

What do you do if you can't make up your mind as to which fruit you prefer; or maybe you like them all? You can enjoy your own citrus every month of the year by planting different kinds so the harvest can be spread over several months.

You can pick Algerian tangerines and tangelos between November and January; sweet oranges between December and March; Navel oranges between November and February; Valencia oranges between March and May; grapefruit between December and June; lemons between September and April; Bearrs limes between August and December; and Mexican limes in September or October.

When's the Fruit Ripe?

You can't go by color. Ripe citrus fruit can be green. This comes as a surprise to most people, but if you go to the tropics, you seldom see brightly colored citrus. Even Florida growers have difficulty producing colored fruit that sells well. On the other hand, California weather conditions favor the natural development of good-colored oranges and tangerines.

California citrus growers decry the habit of dyeing fruit to meet customer acceptance. Dyed fruit is not allowed in California. You don't find Florida citrus in California stores.

The characteristic color of citrus ap-

If you pull fruit off tree, you make a hole in fruit that allows bacteria to enter and spoil it during storage. Fruit will dry out more quickly, too. Better to clip or cut it off, leaving a bit of stem with the fruit.

pears when temperatures cool in the fall. All of a sudden there's fruit on the trees—at least to the unobservant. Don't hurry to pick because the fruit is most likely not ripe yet.

The best way, indeed the only way, to tell if your citrus fruit is ripe is by a taste test. Cut a fruit and offer a piece to a neighbor. If his face puckers up, the fruit is not ripe. It's that simple. If he asks for another taste, you can start harvesting.

This does not mean you pull everything off the tree in one day. You'll be sorry if you do because picked citrus fruit doesn't keep well. The tree is the best place to store fruit. Pick just what you need—when you need it.

On some varieties, Valencia especially, the rind color changes back to a green tinge if the fruit remains on the trees during the warmer months.

When a Freeze Is Forecast

In an emergency—when freezing forecasts are all the rage—you have a hard time making up your mind whether to pick or not. Fruit is damaged by a severe freeze, so you should pick it. If you are nervous about doing this, pick the outer fruit that will be exposed to the cold night air; save the inner fruit that's protected by the foliage. Don't pick grapefruit as soon as you would lemons. Pick from exposed trees before you pick from sheltered trees. In short, when a freeze is forecast, use common sense rather than panic.

Tangerines are traditionally clipped with two leaves left attached because it makes the fruit more attractive and to show their freshness.

Lemons are clipped short. If you leave a long, sharp stalk, it will scratch other fruit in container. When your gift parcel arrives the fruit will be spoilt.

Minneola Tangelo tree provides you with delicious fruit during cooler time of year. It is a small tree and ornamental in any desert landscape.

How to Pick Citrus

Don't pull off fruit because you will tear a hole in its skin that will allow rotting to begin. Instead, cut the stalk with a pair of clippers.

It's customary to include two leaves with tangerines. This gives a pleasant appearance and, as the leaves wither, you can tell how fresh the fruit is. Lemons should have a clean-clipped button on the fruit. If you leave a sharp stub, there's the danger of fruit in the box being scratched by its neighbor every time the box is shaken. That's how molds start.

Keep harvested fruit at about 40F.

What's the best kind to plant? I haven't answered that question yet. Here's a list of the common kinds available from desert nurseries. There are many other kinds, but they have not been fully tested in the desert.

Oranges

Arizona Sweets—This name becomes a nursery buzzword from time to time and it's hard to know what it means—no one seems to know when you ask them. Cynics say the name was given to all the leftover trees without labels in the growing nurseries. Instead of the trees being thrown away, they were shipped to the cities and given a new name. There is no particular variety that is identified by this name because the term usually is a catchall for the following varieties: Marrs; Trovita; Pineapple; Diller; and Hamlin. Don't be seduced into buying any of these until you have tasted fruit from a tree in your

neighborhood and you are satisfied with it. It will be difficult to find such trees. That in itself should be enough of a message to you.

Blood Oranges—These small trees produce light crops of fruit whose insides are variously colored. Sometimes there are just a few pale spots of "blood." In other fruit all the segments are colored with an intense purple.

Taste also varies. For the most part, these varieties are conversation pieces, though in some countries people place a religious significance on the coloring.

Valencia—A medium-size tree that reliably produces good-quality eating fruit. Also good for juice.

Washington Navel—A nice, ornamental tree that flowers profusely. But most of the flowers drop off and fail to produce fruit. Older trees, growing in heavier soils, give good fruit and these are thought to be grafted onto Sour-Orange roots. Navels have few seeds and the peel comes off easily, making the fruit a good, fresh-eating orange. Younger trees grafted onto Citrus macrophylla or Rough Lemon and growing in sandy soils are very disappointing. It's not a good choice for the desert.

Tangerines

Algerian Tangerine—A reliable producer and the first citrus to be harvested—around Thanksgiving and Christmas. Its season is short and the fruit doesn't keep. But, ripening at the holiday season, it is a good variety to grow. Although the tree is relatively frost-hardy, early ripening fruit is subject to damage. If another variety is

nearby and it flowers at the same time, the resulting cross-pollination causes the fruit to be more seedy than if it self-pollinates.

Fairchild—A new variety developed for desert conditions that has not been fully tested. It ripens in November. It is a small tree and fruit quality is good, but has a lot of seeds. It does need another citrus tree nearby for pollination, otherwise yield is unreliable.

Fremont—Another recently produced variety for desert conditions has characteristics similar to Fairchild. It tends to produce fruit in alternate years.

Kinnow Mandarin—A large, yellow fruit with plenty of seeds. Fruit is borne in ornamental bunches and production is very erratic—heavy one year and nothing the next.

Tangelos

Hybrid fruit, resulting from crosses between tangerines and grapefruit. They are good as fresh fruit because of the tangerine's flavor and the grapefruit's juiciness. Flavor is excellent and the trees are small and ornamental.

Minneola—Small and open tree suitable for small-space gardening. Fruit is large, pear-shaped and is bright red tinged with orange. Growing on the ends of branches, the fruit makes a beautiful display during December and January. Fruit quality, which is excellent, stays good until March. Production is reliable, but improved by a nearby tangerine to cross-pollinate the flowers.

Orlando—This variety has yellowish

This is why this fruit is called a *grapefruit*. Twenty fruit in a bunch is not unusual.

Big tree in a big box doesn't have many feeder roots and will need extra attention for a year after planting out. Large as box is—a crane will be needed to move it—exposed roots are structural and should be covered by soil.

fruit, smaller than Minneola and with many more seeds. It is not so easy to peel and, therefore, suggests a juicing fruit rather than an eating fruit. A feature of Orlando that causes unwarranted concern to a number of gardeners is its leaf form. Leaves normally curl upward, suggesting a shortage of water or a virus disease. Usually, there's nothing wrong.

Other varieties of tangelo do well in humid Florida, but are untested in the desert. Let someone else try them out.

Grapefruit

These are interesting plants because they are constantly producing new kinds all on their own. They are called *grapefruit* because they produce their fruit in bunches—sometimes as many as 20 fruit together.

The first varieties were very seedy and so sour hardly anyone ate them. The first interesting mutation was a better-tasting fruit with very few seeds. Then a pink-fleshed variety appeared, followed by one with a decided red blush to the ripening skin and a deep flesh color inside. The public seems to like pink-colored fruit though it's hard for most of us, blindfolded, to tell which is sweeter.

Grapefruit trees continually mutate, and you could be a lucky winner yourself. Take note of any change in your tree. Usually one branch will be different in some way. If the leaves are bunched together on short twigs, you may have a dwarf characteristic expressing itself. Or you may find a different-color fruit or a better-tasting fruit, or who knows what?

Buds taken from that mutated branch will carry the new characteristic. If it's a good one, you should think of patenting it. You might make a lot of money, like Mr. Marsh.

Marsh's Seedless—Mr. Marsh noticed a mutation that gave fruit with few seeds. The good-quality, white-fleshed fruit appears to be ripe in the fall, but reaches a delightful maturity in April and May. The small tree is frost-hardy and produces reliably.

Red Blush, Ruby Red & Texas Red—Variously colored fruit produced on trees similar to Marsh's seedless. They do well in the desert.

Lemons

Fruit production in the desert tends to be more seasonal than on the California coast where a tree is always full of flowers, tiny fruit, immature fruit and ripe fruit.

Eureka—Yields a little less than Lisbon, but still gives you enough fruit. The smaller, more-open tree therefore has some landscape value because its branches are more visible. There are less thorns on a Eureka tree.

Improved Meyer, or Hardy—Excellent home-garden variety. Golden-color fruit has a first-rate quality, being seedless, thin-skinned, juicy and flavorful. Tree is small—it could be called *dwarf*—and can be grown in a whiskey barrel if need be. It's decidedly ornamental and, as if this weren't enough, it's also frost-hardy. Improved Meyer has been thoroughly tested and found to be free of the virus discussed below. It is sold commercially.

Lisbon—The common lemon variety, a very vigorous, dense, thorny tree. It's inclined to send out strong sucker growth. It needs plenty of room to grow, unless you are prepared to do a lot of cutting back. A mature Lisbon tree gives more lemons than you'll know what to do with.

Old Meyer—Because it carries the dreaded *tristeza* virus without showing symptoms, this variety is banned throughout commercial citrus-growing areas.

Although tree seems small, it is an appropriate size for planting. You'll get fruit in 3 or 4 years. Don't be led astray by advertisements that lure you to buy trees with fruit already on them.

Avoid trees in cardboard containers such as those at right. If cardboard is in good condition, tree was recently put in it. If tree was in container long enough to grow roots, cardboard will fall apart when tree is moved. When you plant, discard container. If you don't, cardboard will act like blotting paper and gather salts from the soil. Salts will be too close to the young roots for tree's health.

Villafranca—This variety is similar to Lisbon and Old Meyer lemon trees, particularly when they are small. There's little difference in the fruit, too.

Limes

Bearrs—Looks like a green lemon, but has a much better flavor. It does well in the desert, providing tree is grown in a frost-free area. Try it in a barrel and move it to a sheltered spot during freezing weather.

Mexican—A small fruit that ripens in August and September on a tree with wicked, sharp thorns, though they are small. Tree is very frost-tender. Because of this, not many Mexican limes are grown in the desert.

"Cocktail Trees"

If you want to have more than one variety of citrus, but don't have enough room for them all, there's a trick you might want to try. But don't—because it doesn't work!

You see "Cocktail Trees" advertised in the newspapers. These are composite trees made by adding several buds of different varieties to the trunk. Each bud gives a different fruit—an interesting novelty. However, what usually happens is vigorous lemon branches overide slower-growing tangerine, or grapefruit or tangelo

branches. The result is you will be left with a lop-sided lemon tree.

On the other hand, you can try another method of getting two or three different trees into a small space. Dig a big hole, the usual 5-feet square by 5-feet deep, and fill it with a good soil mix as explained in Chapter 17. Plant two or three—or even four—different citrus trees in the hole and take care of them as if they were one tree. Of course, they will be crowded and their inner branches will die of the competition, but their outer branches will produce fruit according to their kind.

What Size to Plant?

When you go to a nursery, what size tree should you buy?

Every now and again an advertisement draws your attention to a bargain. "Big, boxed, trees with fruit on them" are on sale at a good price. It's usually a good price for the seller, because such trees are too big for successful transplanting.

To get the tree into its box, the roots have been severely cut back and to balance the loss, so have the branches. The sight of fruit on the tree should not influence you to buy.

Trees such as this can stand the shock of being cut back only during cooler months. Plant in March and, as

soon as the weather gets hot in May and June, they will show signs of distress and often die. They may survive with a great deal of care. Even so, they will need a whole year to get enough new roots out to sustain new top growth. If new roots don't grow, the top growth will exhaust the tree. Big trees are a risky venture.

Fifteen-gallon trees are also risky. Again, the reason is that so much of their root system was cut back. Citrus trees have fine feeder roots that they depend on for survival. There's little point in buying a tree with structural roots only.

Look for a trunk that is 1 to 1-1/2 inches across at the bud union. Better still, look at the roots of any tree you think of buying. Roots should not crowd the container, which is usually a 5-gallon size. Roots coming out the bottom indicate the tree has outgrown its space. Nursery trees used to arrive with their soil wrapped in burlap bags, but this practice has stopped because it was not a good way to buy trees. They dried out too quickly and rough handling during transportation from the growing nursery often broke the soil away from the roots.

These days, citrus trees are usually sold in plastic 5-gallon nursery containers.

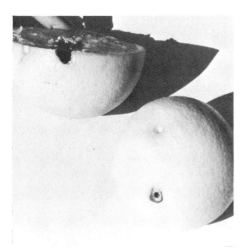

Grapefruit at right shows what bird searching for moisture can do. Rot is caused by bacteria brought in by small insects, as in fruit at left.

If you buy large fruit at the supermarket, you feel you've been cheated when you cut thick skin. If your own fruit looks like this, there's a message for you: You overfertilized with nitrogen. Don't fertilize next year. Let tree use up surplus in soil.

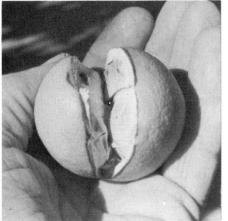

Temperate fall weather causes fruit to swell in a growth spurt. Skin hardened by strong summer sunshine is unable to stretch and it splits. Remove such fruit before smell attracts insects.

Watch out when you see this handsome butterfly hovering near your citrus trees. She is looking for a place to lay eggs.

If you don't find the eggs, you'll have this little creature to contend with. The orange dog is a hungry caterpillar that sends out a couple of orange horns and a nasty smell when you pinch it. Because of smell, birds leave it alone.

Avoid Cardboard Containers

Occasionally 5-gallon cardboard containers are used. Avoid these. They soak up salts exactly as blotting paper does and their bottoms fall out when you lift them. Further, there's a temptation to listen to poor advice about planting the tree in the cardboard. It seems a reasonable idea for the roots to be undisturbed by such an operation. Don't be tempted! Roots *do not grow through the cardboard* as claimed.

Cardboard acts as a barrier between the container soil and your prepared garden soil. They are often quite different, and watering becomes difficult because of these soil differences. Consequently, the tree will have a hard time establishing itself.

When To Plant Citrus?

It's usual to plant citrus trees in the spring—March is a good time—before the hot weather arrives. However, if summer comes early, the roots easily burn in hot, dry soil and new, tender leaves wither from hot, dry winds. Make sure you water generously. That is to say, deep down and far out to encourage root spread. Try to provide shelter from the wind, too.

Many experienced gardeners think a fall planting is better than spring. In September, the sun is losing its fierceness but the soil remains warm for another three months. This encourages new root growth, which is what you want. You are not interested in a lot of new leaf growth. It could easily be damaged by a freeze in November.

Bird Damage

Birds are learning to peck juicy citrus fruits because of the moisture in them. If you catch the damage early, it's all right to eat the fruit. Sour fruit beetles and gnats are attracted by the smell of damaged fruit. They bring in bacteria that cause decay.

Splits & Thick Skin

Fruit splits during late summer as a result of rainstorms and heavy irrigations. The insides swell with the increased moisture but the skins, hardened by the dry atmosphere and sunshine, fail to expand and the fruit splits open. Such fruit should be picked as soon as you see it. It won't get any better.

If your fruit has thick skins at harvest time, it's telling you something. You

Once you know what to look for, an egg is quite obvious. Remove it before it hatches; look for others, too.

Naturally grown tree has attractive shape and easy-to-pick fruit.

By cutting a tree to this shape, you lose a lot of the harvest—borne naturally on lower branches.

have been fertilizing too liberally.

A mature orange tree needs about 5 pounds of ammonium sulphate each year. It's best to split the 5 pounds into equal amounts in February, May and July. Do not fertilize citrus trees after the end of August. You will stimulate fall growth that will be tender and easily damaged by a winter freeze.

Potential Problems

Citrus trees are relatively problem-free. As far as insects are concerned, there are orange-dog caterpillars and grasshoppers that chew on leaves. There are also thrips that cause superficial scarring on fruit and some leaf twisting, but that's about it.

Root rot is not a problem, unless you are unlucky enough to have Rough Lemon roots under all your fruit trees. However, citrus foot rot gummosis, *Phytophthora citrophthora,* is a killer. With a name like that it should be! The fungus thrives under wet conditions, so its control is easy. Keep water away from the trunk. It's that simple.

To keep irrigation water under the tree, make a circular bank out as far as the drip line of the branches—or even farther. Draw soil from outside towards the tree. Don't pull it out from under the tree because this makes the trunk the lowest point in the circle and water will collect and stay there. Now, bring dirt from outside the watering circle to make a dry platform around the trunk. This will effectively keep

water away from it.

The fungus gets into the tree through a wound, caused by careless hoeing or an animal bite. It's a swimming organism and if the trunk is kept dry there's very little chance of an entry.

Gum seeps out of the point of entry, but the first sign of sickness is a general unthriftiness in the tree—the usual pale leaves, leaf-fall and poor production.

Inspect the trunk at ground level. If gum is there, let in the sunshine by cutting out branches on the southwest side of the tree. This will dry out the soil and give you an easy entrance to a workplace inside the tree.

With a sharp knife, cut out all the stained, affected bark and paint the area with copper-Bordeaux mixture. Trees usually respond to this treatment, especially if you catch the disease early. Remember, Sour Orange rootstock is resistant to this disease.

Pruning Generally Not Needed

Citrus trees are surprisingly easy to care for. For example, they do not need to be pruned. If you let a tree grow naturally, most of the fruit will be borne on the bottom half. You will destroy half the fruit-bearing potential if you prune a tree to look like a round shape on a stick. Further, you will have to whitewash the newly exposed trunk to keep it from being sunburned. It won't even look like a citrus tree any more.

A naturally shaped citrus tree has branches sweeping to the ground. Frequently, fruit is borne on these lower branches—especially grapefruit—but they can be protected from mud damage by being placed on a brick or board.

Young citrus trees send out a lot of long vigorous growth, sometimes called *sucker growth.*

In the case of lemons when it truly is sucker growth and undesirable, it should be cut out very close to the trunk to keep it from sprouting out again from a stub. In the case of tangerines, oranges and grapefruit, let it grow undisturbed. It will fall over when it gets too long and its side buds will break out to form a new jungle of greenery.

In no time, the tree is a mess of branches, but you can leave them alone unless they are rubbing against one another. The inside leaves will naturally fall off because they are shaded by the new outer growth, causing the tree to have an apparently dead inside. This worries new gardeners, but it's quite normal. Don't worry because fruit is borne on the ends of branches, on the outside of the tree.

Lemon trees can be very vigorous growers. Control this forward growth by pinching the ends of new shoots with your finger and thumb while the shoots are soft. Walk round the tree in the spring and the fall during growth spurts and pinch as much as you can.

Crinkling of leaves doesn't hurt a tree, but makes it look a little unsightly. When leaves were very small, tiny insect rasped on tender tissues and, as a result, leaf lost its symmetrical shape. Spraying should have been done several weeks earlier when insects were busy on trees. There's no point in spraying at this stage.

If fruit like this appears on your citrus tree, a sucker has come from the root and has grown through foliage of tree. Trace maverick fruit—Rough Lemon in this case—down through branches to where it comes off tree and remove it. If you leave it, resulting growth will overpower edible variety in a few years and you'll have no useful fruit.

You'll find every pinched shoot develops side shoots and the tree's foliage thickens. In addition to looking denser, the tree will be more productive early in its life because fruit is borne on side shoots, not on end growth.

Special Case Where Pruning is Necessary

Normally we don't prune citrus trees like we do deciduous fruit trees—every spring in order to get new fruit-bearing wood. Any cutting we make is usually a corrective measure that alleviates a bad situation.

If you have to remove so much dead wood that you cut below the bud union, the new shoots will not be the satisfactory fruit-bearing branches that you had before. You are probably in too cold a place for citrus if all you can grow is rootstock foliage.

If you are in a marginally cold area and have to repeatedly trim out frost-damaged branches, watch for the development of suckers below the bud union. Even a lightly-damaged tree will grow these as a sort of compensation for the loss of its upper foliage. They will have to be pruned out every year, and you may wonder whether you should be growing citrus at all.

Another kind of pruning may be necessary when your trees have the

disease Foot Rot—or *Phytophthora*. This is a waterborne fungus that thrives in shady damp places—such as the darkness of the canopy of an old tree. The treatment is described on page 130.

These "special" cases may seem commonplace to a lot of readers. If that's so it's because people impulsively plant citrus without considering the space a tree needs. Even a small corner of the yard appears big enough for a little tree in a five-gallon container—and so it is for a few years.

If a citrus tree becomes too tall and you can't pick the topmost fruit, cut off the top. If you do this during summer, the inside of the tree will be scorched by fierce sunshine and killed. September is the safest time to top a citrus tree. Even then, it might be best to keep a sheet over it for awhile.

In the same way, a tree that begins to "go over the wall"—into the neighbors, into the alley and so on, will have to be cut back before it gets lost.

Another tree, planted too close to a building and beginning to scratch the walls or the roof, needs to be cut back before it becomes a nuisance.

A frost-damaged tree eventually shows a lot of dead twigs, and even dead branches if the freeze was severe. New spring growth will tell you the extent of the damage. Cut into

Side shoots should have been cut out long ago when they were small. Their growth is wasteful and has reduced tree's vigor. Further, they come out so close to bud union that it's hard to know whether they are rootstock, suckers or fruitwood growth. Earlier, a sharp knife would have done the job. Now, a saw and pruning paint are needed.

green wood and include a couple of sprouting shoots. They will then be real pruning cuts that stimulate new growth—not merely a tidying-up removal of dead twigs.

Suggestion: You may be in an area where frost requires that you cover your citrus tree(s). If so, keep your trees small by pruning, Then you can handle covering them against frost damage. You'll also be able to reach the topmost fruit easier.

If you buy a house with poor trees in the yard you can improve things. Go out to the drip line—plus a little farther—and make holes as deep as you can as shown. Fill holes with organic matter, ammonium phosphate, sulphur and soil in the same proportions as you would for filling a planting hole.

Fruit trees should be kept relatively small so they can be easily covered to protect them from birds and frost damage.

Citrus Fertilization Schedule

Newly planted
Do not fertilize the first year unless using slow-release planting pills or diluted soluble fertilizer.

Second year
2 to 4 tablespoons of ammonium sulfate (21-0-0) monthly from February to May.

Third year
1 cup of ammonium sulfate 5 times from February through July.

Fourth year and older
5 cups of ammonium sulfate (1-pound coffee can) in early February before bloom and again in early May.

Note:
Halfway through an irrigation, scatter fertilizer out to the drip line and a bit beyond.

CAUTION:

No fertilizing after September so as to let tree go into dormancy.

It's a good rule to apply fertilizer when a plant grows, but in the case of citrus, we break this rule. Don't be tempted to apply fertilizer during the fall growth in September's mild weather. If you do, the new growth will be easily damaged by the frosts of November and December.

Irrigation Techniques

Use a soil probe! Proper plant irrigation is extremely important. After you have irrigated, poke a small-diameter steel rod into the soil to see if soil is damp to recommended depth.

Trees and shrubs: Water under entire spread of plant. Fill water basin as rapidly as possible and keep it filled—1-inch depth is sufficient—until you can easily push your soil probe down

beyond the root zone. It's 12 inches for vegetables, 2 feet for shrubs and and 3 feet for fruit trees.

23

DECIDUOUS FRUIT

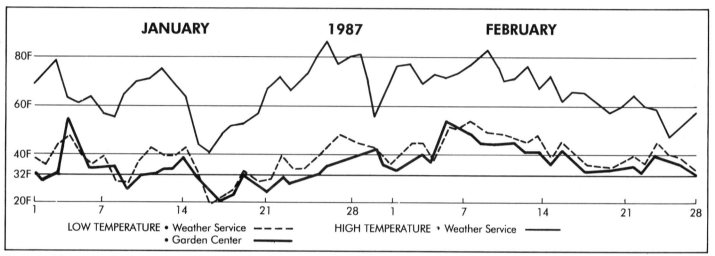

Horizontal line at 40F indicates temperature below which fruit trees gather chilling hours. They lose hours when temperature rises above 40F. Chart for January and February 1987 shows trees received very little chilling in desert during coldest months of the year. Two low-temperature curves generated from data gathered at two Tucson locations illustrate how temperatures can vary in two relatively close places.

When it comes to fruit production, it appears—on first glance, at least—that the desert gives us the best of both worlds. You find deciduous fruit trees growing in the same yard with citrus trees.

On the Ragged Edge
As you learn more about gardening, you realize both kinds of trees are living at their outer limits of temperature requirements. The deciduous trees may not get enough cold weather in the winter and, at the same time, the citrus trees are in danger of being damaged by freezes.

Various management tricks can help the gardener out of this difficulty. In the chapters on citrus, page 123, and on frost protection, page 153, there are suggestions on how to avoid serious damage to citrus trees caused by cold weather.

Deciduous fruit trees, by contrast, should be planted in the coldest part of your yard to make the most of winter's cold. A northern exposure is good and, if there is a tall wall to keep

the winter sun off a tree, so much the better. Low-lying locations where cold air accumulates at night are better than warm southern slopes.

This gathering of cold, which scientists call *cold units* or *chilling degrees*, is very important when choosing suitable varieties. Every variety has its own number of days or hours of chill that is necessary for fruit production. Many trees grow well enough in a warm area, but don't fruit properly. For example, if you get Siamese-twin peach fruits instead of a single fruit after flowering, it is because the last winter was too mild.

Varieties that are just on the brink of matching the local climate will fruit nicely after a cold winter, but produce little or nothing if the next winter is on the warm side. All cultural management aspects may have been properly attended to, but the weather made the difference.

A deciduous fruit tree benefits only if the weather stays cool all the time. The desert is an unreliable place because winters are sunny and mild with

several days of summer-like weather. Neither freezing nights or sunny days help the optimum chill-gathering temperature range of 36.5F to 48.4F.

Home gardeners need to recognize that fruit trees have hidden qualities and vary in their performance as much as they vary in their appearance.

How to Determine Chill Hours
Recent research carried out at the University of Florida where winters are also short and unreliable, is improving our understanding of how the cold hours are accumulated—and lost. We needn't trouble ourselves too much with the details—they can be left to the scientists—but the following outline explains the basics. It's an interesting concept.

When it is cold, a tree gathers chill units (hours). If it stays cold, chill units accumulate. However, if the weather warms up, the tree loses accumulated chill units. So, trees can gain chill units, but can also lose them just as quickly. And if it turns very cold, trees don't benefit.

Here is how it all works. You need to record the temperature *hour by hour* during winter months. A lot of accounting is required.

For any hour colder than 34.5F there is no chilling.

An hour between 34.6F and 36.4F gives a half hour of chill.

An hour between 36.5F and 48.4F gives an hour of chill.

An hour between 48.5F and 54.4F gives a half hour of chill.

An hour between 54.4F and 60.9F gives no gain and no loss.

An hour between 61.0F and 64.4F loses a half hour of chill.

Temperatures above 64.4F give a lost hour for every actual hour.

Following is a short cut to help you estimate the chilling hours produced in your locality. First, assume January is the coldest month. Call your local Weather Service to get the *monthly mean temperature* for the last 30 years. At the same time ask them for the monthly mean for the current month. Then you can tell whether it really was warmer than usual—or just how you felt.

Here's how the Weather Bureau gets its figures: The maximum temperatures of every day of the month are added together and then divided by the number of days in that month. This gives them the average maximum temperature. They do the same with the minimum temperatures to get the average monthly minimum temperature. Once they have the average monthly maximum and minimum, they add these two figures and divide by two to get the monthly mean. That's the number you're looking for.

Example: In January 1988, in Tucson, Arizona, the average maximum temperature was 67.3F and the average minimum was 38.7F. Added together and divided by two gives a monthly mean of 53.0F. Because the records over the past 30 years show the normal monthly mean to be 51.1F, we really did have a warm January. It's not just that we thought it was warmer. Mind you, it snowed on Christmas day, but that doesn't count for January. We just remember the snow clearly.

Now you need to know the personality of the fruit-tree variety. How many hours of chill units does it need before it will reliably produce fruit? The number often appears in catalogs

and, if available, is shown for each variety in the following lists.

Low winter chilling generally means a tree doesn't need much of a rest. Flower and leaf buds break out early in spring. In the desert this gives an early harvest before the heat of summer becomes destructive and before insects become a nuisance. However, if early flowering coincides with an unusual late frost, the crop is lost for that year. Also, there's the possibility that these new varieties may tire themselves out by continual growth without a dormant resting period. In other words, the trees may not live long.

The August harvest of older varieties is often spoiled by damp, hot weather and the green fruit beetle.

Here are the hours of chill for several *mean* temperatures:

Mean Temp (F)	Chill Hours
46	988
48	883
50	779
52	675
54	575
56	475
58	355
60	288
62	200
64	118
66	58
68	0

Late Frosts

Late frosts are always a hazard. They become more common as you approach 3500-foot elevations. There's not much you can do about late frosts except cover the flowering tree with a heavy sheet on a freezing night just as you would to protect citrus fruit in the winter. A light bulb or two under the cover may be needed to provide warmth.

All this means is there's a limited range of suitable varieties for the desert, although nationwide there are hundreds of varieties from which to choose. Fortunately, researchers are paying attention to this problem and have, to some degree, found some answers. Not much is being done in desert regions themselves, but we benefit from work done in California and Florida. Their success needs further testing under local conditions for verification.

For the time being, following is a list

of deciduous fruit-tree varieties you can plant with some optimism for success. Join the testing program!

Peaches

Desert Gold (300 hours)—A strongly growing tree that blooms early and whose clingstone fruits ripen at the end of May. This is long before the green fruit beetle arrives in July. The tree should not be planted where late frosts are usual. It's a heavy producer, so it's advisable to thin small fruit severely.

Mid Pride (350 hours)—One of the best low-chill peaches with a distinctive, pleasant flavor. Yellow-fleshed fruit is large and freestone.

Spring Gold (500 hours)—A semicling fruit of good quality that ripens in early June.

Gold Dust (550 hours)—A large, vigorous tree that bears orange-colored freestone fruit of good flavor in early July.

June Gold (650 hours)—Similar to Desert Gold. It produces large freestone peaches, provided a heavy fruit set is correctly thinned. Harvest is a week or two later than Desert Gold. Quality is the same.

Early Coronet (650 hours)—Ripens in mid-June.

Babcock (700 hours)—A white-fleshed, freestone peach which ripens in July. Most people think white-fleshed peaches are not as good as yellow-fleshed fruit because the flavor is not as rich.

Loring (800 hours)—Its large-size fruit ripens in late July or August when the green fruit beetle and summer heat reduce fruit quality. It is suitable for planting up to 3500 feet.

Early Elberta—A good-quality freestone peach that ripens in August and therefore is not truly an early variety.

Kim Elberta (850 hours)—An improved kind of Early Elberta that ripens in early August in the mid-desert areas. It is also suited to elevations up to 3500 feet.

Bonanza—A compact dwarf tree that can be grown in a half barrel. In the desert it's an unreliable variety because some trees bear good-quality fruit, but others produce disappointingly mushy fruit. Irregular bearing also seems to be very common.

Red Haven (950 hours)—A very productive tree that ripens in late July with a red-skinned fruit of good quality. It is suitable for planting at elevations up to 3,500 feet.

Nectarines

These are a kind of peach, without the fuzz on the skin. Unfortunately, there are no good varieties for the desert. Insects called *thrips* attack the fruit when it is small and cause deformities. But, more importantly, nectarines fail to give good-quality fruit of a decent size. They are definitely in the poor-relation category.

Cherries

There are no suitable varieties for the desert. Present varieties require more than 1,000 hours of chilling for successful fruit production.

Apricots

Most varieties ripen early and so avoid damage from green fruit beetle. Apricots, in general, do not need a lot of winter chilling.

Blenheim or Royal—Good-quality fruit, though on the small side, and an early ripening make this the favorite variety. The harvest is ready in late May and early June.

Gold Kist—Small tree with a heavy production of small, yellow fruit. Heavy thinning is recommended, otherwise the fruit remains small.

Katy—A new variety which has not been fully tested but shows promise. Ripens in early June with a dark-blush fruit color.

Castleton—A good-quality variety that ripens in June.

Reeves & Tilton (600 hours)—These good-quality kinds ripen later and are therefore suitable for cooler elevations.

Plums

Santa Rosa—Consistently yields well and has a purple plum that is harvested in late June or early July.

Beauty—Yellow-fleshed plum that ripens in early June. Requires cross-pollination using Santa Rosa but yields lighter than Santa Rosa.

Laroda—A high-quality plum that requires little chilling. It needs cross-pollinating by Santa Rosa. Harvest is in late August.

Pears

These are poor prospects because they need more chilling than the desert provides. Further, they are easily killed by fire blight, a bacterial disease car-

Apple tree pruned to small size to allow net to be put over it as fruit ripens. This is the most effective way to protect your fruit from birds. Until dwarf fruit trees have been thoroughly tested in the desert, this is the best way to keep tree within the space of a small backyard.

ried in the air and by pollinating insects.

Bartlett—Ripens in late September; Keifer ripens in late October. Both need more cold than they will get in the desert.

Figs

Black Mission—The best-adapted variety because it is self-pollinating and more reliable than the others. Furthermore, its fruit has a closed end which helps keep out the sour fruit beetle, a tiny pest that enters ripening fruit and causes it to ferment. Sometimes two crops are borne each year. Fruit quality is good when daytime temperatures exceed 95F. The green fruit beetle is very troublesome on figs.

Brown Turkey—Not such a good producer and more suited to higher elevations. Its open-ended fruit are often spoiled by the sour fruit beetle. Otherwise, fruit quality is good.

Conadria—A good-quality white fig with a closed end. Does well in the warmer parts of the desert.

Kadota—A white fig that does not do well in the lower desert areas. It is a good choice for higher elevations.

Apples

People are surprised to learn that apples can be grown successfully in the desert. This is due to the recent development of varieties needing less winter chilling than the common supermarket kinds. If you live in the lower

Don't buy large, old tree in a small container. Its roots will be crowded. Some might even be dead.

desert, it's best to plant apples in the coldest part of your yard.

Ein Scheimer (350 hours)—A reliable producer. Small fruit is a little too tart for fresh eating, but makes excellent pies and preserves. Boiling doesn't make the fruit mush down. It stays chunky and firm. Harvest starts in mid-July, but don't leave fruit on the tree too long because it will spoil in the heat.

Anna (350 hours)—Another reliable and heavy producer that gives excellent eating fruit, similar in size, taste and crispness to Golden Delicious. Fruit is shaded on the inside of the tree. It has a pink blush when ripe, usually in July. This variety does not keep well and exposed fruit easily sunburns. It is an excellent apple by any standards. It is self-pollinating.

Prima Red—A reliable producer of small, tart fruit that ripen in late July.

Dorsett Golden (350 hours)—This variety was discovered in the

Sometimes a nursery will let trees sit in one place for a long time. When containers are pulled up, a lot of roots are left behind in the soil. Trees without their full root system become shocked and don't tranplant well.

Large, old tree with a lot of air roots in small container: Container is only half-filled with soil. Bud union has crook in it. Don't buy one like this.

Look at branch system, too. Tree has only two main branches, which is a weak arrangement, even early on. Split was inevitable.

Tree with good framework low down to give dwarf-like tree to start with. You can continue to prune this tree hard to maintain small size.

Bahamas, of all places! It has not been fully tested in the desert, but looks promising in spite of its poor keeping qualities. Fruit ripens in July.

Granny Smith (600 hours)—A tart Green apple that, because of its high chilling hours, does not do well in lower elevations.

Other Fruit Varieties

Crab Apples—A variety called

Transcendent is mentioned in Extension Service literature as doing well in the desert. It's not common.

Persimmons (200 hours)—These are relatively drought-tolerant trees with few pest or disease problems. They are very ornamental with their bright-orange fruit, especially during the holiday season. Fruit needs to stay on the tree after leaf fall to lose its astringency. Nonpollinated fruit is seedless. Varieties are *Fuyu* and the supermarket one, *Hachiya*.

Pomegranates—*Wonderful* has the deep-red color, *Yellow Papershell* is the paler-colored fruit. Pomegranates split easily after the summer rains when they begin to ripen. They grow very easily in the desert and, if not pruned, are good-looking landscape trees because of their sweeping branches.

Fruit-Tree Rootstocks

Deciduous fruit trees are, for the most part, budded onto a particular rootstock. Unfortunately, we know little about rootstock performance in desert soils. At present we accept what is sold and hope for the best. Usually it's all right. Dwarfing rootstocks for apples have been developed extensively in England and are not suited to desert conditions. Dwarf rootstocks for other deciduous fruits are not tested. It's probably best to avoid them until they are. Rigorous pruning will keep your tree small and let you cover it with a net to stop birds from stealing the fruit.

Keep your tree small every spring when you prune.

When to Plant

Spring, which in the desert means January, is the traditional time to plant deciduous fruit trees. Plant as warm weather starts and hope roots get well established before the July sun makes the soil too hot. If you are late in planting, young roots will be scorched when they grow out into hot soil.

A few years ago there was no alternative to spring planting because nurseries obtained their trees from distant growing farms as bare-root trees in January.

The planting season was always a

Long trunk use as shade tree. Scaffold branches appear to be coming off trunk too close to one another for strength. Each should be cut back more than halfway to encourage more branching closer to trunk.

Two bare-root trees—actually packed in sawdust for shipment—with numerous branches up and down trunk. These give you good choices for initial training cuts. Both trees are young and vigorous.

Tree at left has been pruned to develop short tree. Hidden buds at trunk base will send out branches that will become scaffold branches. Tree at right has been pruned more conventionally, spacing scaffold branches up and down as well as around trunk. Roots are ready for unwrapping, spreading over mound of soil, planting, and watering well. Note pruning paint.

If you don't keep your tree small, birds will get the fruit. You'll find one net won't be sufficient. You must splice two or three together. There'll be a lot of naughty words when you try to cover a large tree with a lot of netting.

Four 10-foot pieces of plastic water pipe make framework for bird net. You can do this easily if you keep your tree small.

Here's how to fit the four pieces at top. Just slip them into a plastic cross without any glue and it will be easy to take framework apart and store it.

Fruit often comes in crowded bunches. These apples must be thinned or they won't develop to a proper size.

Reducing a dozen down to three makes for larger size fruit. New gardeners are reluctant to do this.

hurried one, but if frozen ground in the growing farms prevented tree digging, it might be the end of February before bare-root trees were available in the desert. Even if trees were planted immediately on arrival, the short period for root establishment before the summer heat arrived made success less likely. Part of the problem was, because the trees came from a cold part of the the country into the warm, sunny desert, they leafed out and flowered as soon as they were unloaded. The energy required for this growth came from stored food in the tree and left no reserves. Many plantings were failures because leafed-out trees were exhausted before they could be planted. Don't buy a flowering tree in a nursery. Your new tree should be completely dormant when you plant.

Which Size Tree to Buy?

Nowadays, trees are more commonly sold in 5-gallon containers. This is better for all concerned. Such trees are easier to plant and risks are less. Just be sure you don't buy a large tree in a small container. If you do, the roots might be too crowded. Ask the nurseryman to show you the roots of any tree you want to buy. They should fill the 5 gallons of soil, but should not be going round and round at the bottom as if looking for a place to get out. Also, if the container stood in hot sunshine, the roots that were lying against

the side may have been cooked. Dead roots are soft and dark colored; live roots are well filled and pale.

Container-grown trees are also available in the fall, which a lot of good gardeners consider a better time to plant anyway. At first, it seems illogical to plant a deciduous tree just before it drops its leaves and goes dormant. Cold air causes the leaves to turn color and drop, but desert soils stay warm enough to stimulate root growth while the upper part of the tree is dormant, leafless, and is not losing moisture. On second thought, this is the perfect set of conditions for establishing a tree.

Texas Root Rot

Always bear in mind that deciduous fruit trees are highly susceptible to Texas root rot. If your yard has a history of this disease, it may be a waste of time to plant fruit trees—even if you take the precautions of proper soil preparation. As soon as the first symptoms of the disease appear in an established tree, carry out the corrective treatment described on page 94. The longer you delay, the less chance of success in saving the tree.

Home gardeners are eagerly awaiting a rootstock that is resistant to Texas root rot.

The Planting Hole

Every tree should be planted in a backfilled hole measuring 5-feet square by 5-feet deep. It's a good idea to check the drainage before backfilling.

Half-fill the hole with water at the end of the day and look at it in the morning. If the water has gone, everything is all right and you can proceed. If the water remains, you need to dig through the caliche and test again for good drainage. Backfill the hole with soil, organic matter, soil sulphur and ammonium phosphate.

Digging large holes is hard work so it's nice to know that most deciduous fruit trees do not need a second tree to act as a pollinator. They are self-pollinating, or self-fruitful.

Prune Right After Planting

Prune trees immediately after you plant. The purpose is to develop a sturdy framework of three or four branches that will become the main limbs of the tree in a few years' time. Read Chapter 13, again to get the idea. At this point cut off all the thin shoots and keep three or four of the best that are closest to being evenly spaced around the tree. Cut these back to about 15 or 20 inches. Their side buds will form the secondary branches of the tree in due course.

After a year or two, start to think of fruit production and prune accordingly. Keep the tree small by hard pruning. You can't put a bird net over a large tree—and a net is the only way to keep birds away from your fruit.

When the first fruit appears—rejoice, but don't be greedy. The tree won't be able to carry all the fruit and you will do your tree a favor if you remove about half of it while it is still small.

Flowering Time is Critical

Flowers are delicate things that fall off if the wind blows hard, the weather suddenly turns hot, the winter was dry and the soil has no moisture reserve or a young tree is not well established.

This mean you can lose the harvest—and there won't be another flowering until next spring. Take care of your flowers.

- Keep a flowering tree well-watered.
- Don't fertilize a flowering tree—you may shock it.
- Don't spray a flowering tree to kill thrips or aphids—you will also kill pollinating insects.
- Cover a flowering tree with a sheet on a freezing night and, perhaps, provide warmth with a light bulb or two.

Thin the Crop

After a tree has become established, you will still need to remove a lot of developing fruit, otherwise it weakens the tree. Deciduous fruit trees flower profusely. They are very attractive doing this and set far more fruit than they can carry to a large size. You have to remove a lot of the small fruit a month after flowering is over. If you don't, you'll get a bumper crop of little fruit with large stones.

There will always be a little involuntary fruit drop. But there will be more if the tree comes under stress from too little water, or a sudden change to hot weather. Deciduous fruit trees are not like citrus trees that automatically thin their fruit after a heavy set. You must remove the excess fruit.

Don't hurry to thin fruit if the tree suffers from a late weather stress—but don't forget it either. Imagine big, ripe fruit on the branches and estimate how much space they need. Look forward to apricots, 3 to 4 inches across, or peaches 5 inches across. Remove all the little fruit that gets in the way of this dream. Where you see a cluster of fruit—four, five or six in a bunch—take them all off except two.

Thinning is an easy operation but it calls for hard decisions. You must make room for fruit to develop to a good size. If you find you can't do it, ask a neighbor to come and thin your tree while you go and do his.

Perhaps he lacks courage, too, but don't stand around watching him. You're sure to want to interfere—imagining he is taking off too much—and he won't like it.

Here's what happens if you don't thin out fruit. Tree is under stress and drops a lot of fruit—sometimes all of it if there is a sudden change in weather.

Get Your Flowers Growing In Mid-May!

While this may seem out of order, I wanted to include some information about flowers. The following is excerpted from one of my articles in the *Tucson Citizen*.

Now for something completely different: In May it's change-of-season time for annual flowers.

Winter flowers such as pansies, stock, snapdragons and poppies are finished and should be replaced. Many gardeners are looking ahead to the rigors of summer and a high water bill. Instead of replacing a large flower bed they are confining their new plantings to whiskey barrels and other containers. So the question arises: What's the best container size for flowers?

First, consider the chore of watering. Anything smaller than a 5-gallon size will need daily watering to keep the plants alive. Even so, they might suffer from heat. Everyone should know that damp heat is more damaging than dry heat. Daily watering and the heat can cook the roots of plants in a small container.

A large concrete bowl is heavy to move. A whiskey barrel is conveniently midway. It can be moved fairly easily if it is placed on metal pipes that act as rollers. Watch out for black-widow spiders under the barrel. Put a loop of rope around it when you move it with the rollers. Don't put your fingers underneath!

In any case, a barrel needs to be raised off the ground to make sure that water drains out and runs away. (Any container you use must have holes in its bottom.)

What are suitable flowers? For a sunny spot you might try *portulaca*. This plant looks like a succulent, but you'll find it needs frequent waterings to give its best performance. It will give you bright colors all through the summer. There are single flowers and double flowers, but all are colorful: white, pink, red, magenta, yellow and orange. Each flower lasts just a day, but there'll be constant flowering. Portulaca spreads out and overhangs a container very attractively.

Another summer flower for a sunny location is *purslane*. It's a bit like portulaca, but the flowers are not so bright and its leaves are broader. It's a good overhanging plant in a container or a good spreader in the ground.

Then there's the old standby, *petunia*. It's already so popular that there's little that need be said about petunia. If you have old plants surviving from a winter planting they will be long and rangy. Correct this by pinching them back. Checking their forward growth will encourage side shoots and that will make the plants more compact and bushy. It will also give you more flowers in due course. You'll only have to wait about two weeks.

It's not easy to get color in a shady location, but you can try with *coleus*. Actually, coleus flowers are insignificant—though attractive—it's the bright leaf colors that are interesting. Coleus is a useful houseplant, too, but it gets rangy and spindly in the house unless it's placed in a good light. The leaf colors brighten considerably if the plant gets an hour of morning sunshine every day. It won't take full sun for even part of a day.

Another shade-loving plant that flowers is *four-o'clock*, but they don't appear until late afternoon—hence the plant's name. Because of this the plant is a bit disappointing, though the foliage is attractive. Again, it can be a container plant or a ground plant.

A third shade-loving plant is *impatiens*. It comes in many bright colors and can be used in the house, providing things aren't too dark there.

For all container plantings, set out your plants in a crowded space. Let them jostle one another out to the edge of the container and over its sides. Get a full foliage effect. Keep pinching any long growth to encourage side shoots. Every second irrigation put a tablespoon of houseplant food in a gallon of water. You'll have success!

Try and get fruit alternating on either side of branch. Leave enough space so that ripe fruit won't be touching.

Deep hole like this doesn't allow water to spread—roots won't spread, either. Large, shallow basin is better than small, deep one.

In spring just before new growth starts, you can cut out buds from a peach in your neighbor's yard for implanting into your tree.

You can store buds like these for up to two weeks in a cool—not freezing—part of your refrigerator until your tree is ready for them. Bark of tree needs to be slipping, showing that sap is moving up to start spring growth.

24

GRAPES

Grapes grow well in the desert—they are a natural. Wild grapes grow along the canyons where there is a little more moisture than out in the open.

Good-Looking Shade Providers

Around our houses, where they can be irrigated, grapes are one of the best plants to put out in a sunny location. They enjoy it. Their large leaves provide wonderful shade that will cool house walls and patio floors. You can easily train grapes as an arbor to provide a green ceiling over an outdoor area and thereby provide an extra summer room. The shade is wonderful because it is open and it breathes—far different from wooden structures or artificial cloth.

Even more wonderful is the fact that this cool, green shade automatically adjusts to weather changes. Bare branches renew themselves as spring temperatures rise and threaten us with summer's misery. In the fall, leaves drop off and allow the winter sun to warm our house and patio.

As if this weren't enough, grape shade over strawberries or other plants, such as blackberries, that don't like summer's sun, keeps the high temperatures and bright sunshine from destroying sensitive plants. After giving us some landscaping benefits, the grape vine gives us food and drink.

Cookbook recipes call for grape leaves to add flavor and hold things together. Fresh grapes are delicious. Grapes go into jellies, jams and fruit salads. Grapes don't grow old. They naturally turn themselves into raisins. Raisins are rich in iron and sugars for athletes and add interest to puddings and pies for more sedentary folk.

For many people, the ultimate product from grapes is wine. Even desert-grown grapes are getting

Grapes make a pleasant arbor or overhead shade. They cool an area where you can sit and relax. They cool the surroundings to a house and save on summer utility bills.

In winter the sun comes through bare vines to warm up area underneath.

Pruning prepares plant for further vigorous growth during hot months. Grapes love sunshine and heat. Plant them in the hottest part of your yard.

If your neighbor has an outstanding plant, ask him for cuttings when he prunes in the spring. Each cutting will produce a plant exactly like his.

Dip lower end of cutting in root stimulant, then set it into sandy soil in a gallon container. Keep two buds above in air and two buds in soil mix.

With roots like this—a bunch from each of buried buds—expect a powerful growth of shoots from two buds above ground.

After a year's growth, your cutting should look like this.

Next spring, remove all of last summer's side growth, leaving two buds. Now you have made a plant with little top growth, but plenty of root power. Use these two buds to determine kind of growth you want from your grapevine.

recognition as suitable for wine-making. There's an increasing commercial acreage of wine grapes being planted in the desert. The home gardener does it, too.

Grapes Are Easy to Grow

Grapes are easy to grow and they grow rapidly. If you admire your neighbor's vine, ask him for a cutting when he prunes his plants in February. A cutting looks like a stick, a little thicker than a pencil, with three or four buds on it. Dip the lower end in RooTone® hormone powder and half bury it in a pot of sandy soil mix. Use a mix made of 1 part sand, 1 part compost and 1 part garden soil. Put it in a sunny place and keep it moist.

The following spring, cut back all the growth to two dormant buds. Your new plant is ready to set out. Find a sunny place for it—grapes don't do well in the shade.

Dig a big hole at least 2 feet square x 2 feet deep. Get through any caliche. Then backfill with soil mixed with compost or steer manure, ammonium phosphate and sulphur. Use the same proportions as if you expect Texas root rot, or 1-1/2 cubic feet of compost or steer manure, 2 pounds of sulphur and 1/2 pound of ammonium phosphate.

Prune Right Away

Both of the two buds will probably break out, but you need only one shoot to form the trunk of the future plant. After a few weeks, remove the weaker of the two.

As the remaining shoot grows, tie it upright to a stake. Be careful. The shoot is brittle and can break easily. If you don't tie it, a wind can snap it off. Make ties a little loose to accommodate future growth. It's best to use the soft green plastic tape that stretches. Put tape on every 4 or 5 inches.

Rub out any side shoots that develop. Later, cut off the top of this strong single shoot at a height that you determine according to how you want the plant to grow. It will send out side shoots just below the cut. These side shoots will be the side arms of your vine.

In a field system, the two side arms are at chest height, making it easy to prune the vine and harvest the bunches. For an arbor, it's best to stop upward growth at 8 feet. This will allow you to walk under the vine and look at the bunches hanging down freely. It's a pleasant sight.

Espaliering

A third way is when you want to grow a vine against a wall as an espaliered plant. Make the cut at about 18 inches and train the side arms parallel to the

One option is to let leading shoot grow up to 8 feet before you restrain its vigor by pinching out terminal bud. Removal of terminal bud will cause side shoots to begin. For an arbor, lead them horizontally to develop a canopy.

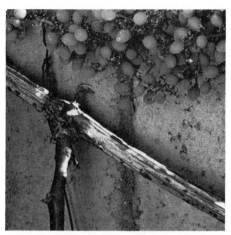

One disadvantage of growing grapes close to wall is poor ventilation which encourages mildew. Mildew invasion leaves blotches such as these. Prune them out in the spring.

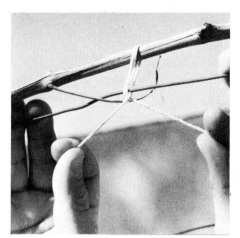

Always make loose ties so branch can thicken safely.

ground. In due course, upright shoots develop from these low arms and you can cover the wall with them.

Mildew Control

A disadvantage of espaliering is that the wall doesn't allow much ventilation around the foliage, and mildew is likely to set in. Mildew destroys leaves, twigs, and—if it is left untreated—the whole plant. It is caused by a fungus that hides in fallen leaves and in infected shoots. You should not use infected shoots as cuttings for starting new plants.

When spring growth begins, mildew invades tender new leaves. It's a good idea to assume your plants are going to be invaded because fungus is blown about by the wind. Start a preventive spraying program as soon as the leaves break out of the buds. Spray wettable sulphur—the same as you use for mildew control on roses—every week, making sure both sides of the leaves are covered. Stop spraying when the temperatures reach 95F because, at that temperature and above, sulphur becomes corrosive. Other chemicals are available for the hotter months, but the mildew fungus doesn't like the heat either. It's supposed to die.

Finding the Grape You Want

What if your friendly neighbor doesn't have the kinds of grapes you like? The choices at local nurseries, though good, are usually limited. Innumerable varieties of grapes exist, all with fascinating names that reflect years and years of world-wide interest in this wonderful plant.

You may want to order from an out-of-state catalog, but first read the list of recommended varieties prepared by your local Extension Service. As a reference, see the list for the Tucson area at the end of this chapter. For example, Concords don't do well in the desert. But, there are others besides the reliable Thompson's Seedless that you may not have heard of, and will want to try.

Give your grapes plenty of room to grow—at least 12 feet from one another. If you have space for three plants, try Beauty Seedless for a June harvest, Thompsons for an August

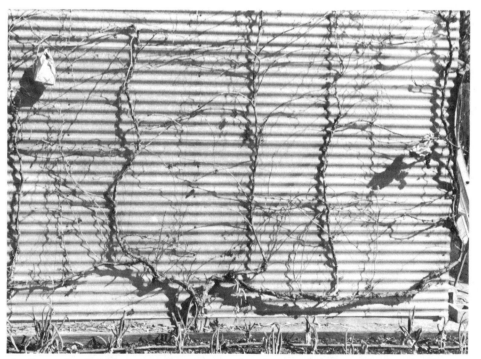

Another option is to stop upward growth very close to ground and use side shoots as the beginning of an espalier system.

Grape flowers are green and insignificant. They turn into berries if vine is well supplied with water.

If plant becomes short of water during flowering, there's usually a loss of berry set; bunches will be light. Don't let this happen.

crop and a Muscat for a September harvest. If you are planting only one kind, Thompson's Seedless should be your first choice. It grows vigorously and yields well. For these very reasons it is a mistake to plant three of the same variety. You would have too much fruit

in too limited a period.

Most people prefer seedless grapes. It's rather old-fashioned to spit out seeds at the dinner table—or even in the arbor. Wine grapes are usually thick-skinned and seedy, whereas table grapes are the opposite. But, you

can make wine out of table grapes.

Fertilizing

After grapes have become established, they don't need heavy fertilizing, unless you are interested in getting a lot of foliage for a shady arbor. Too much nitrogen reduces fruit production and produces soft canes that are susceptible to mildew.

Most growers—both commercial and home gardeners—follow a conventional program of fertilizing grapes in the spring, just before new growth starts. Recent research in California suggests that nitrogen applied at this time finds its way to the growing shoots too slowly. Now, it is suggested you apply nitrogen during the period between flowering and harvest. It appears to be better to "top up" the plant with nitrogen in late summer before it goes dormant. When growth starts in the spring, the stored nutrient immediately moves toward the new leaves.

Tying Up New shoots

As the new shoots grow—and they grow vigorously—separate them and guide them onto a trellis or wire system. Use soft, green, plastic ribbon and make the ties rather loose, to accommodate future growth. Air should circulate around the branches, so you may have to thin out extra shoots. Just snap them off while they are young.

Zinc Spray Can Be Helpful

Sometimes, because of our calcareous desert soils, grape leaves remain small. This is often due to a shortage of zinc or the inability of the plant to extract it from the soil. The treatment is to spray

Here's a useful sign. Plant produces strong tendrils while it is vigorously growing. If tendrils become short and small, plant is telling you it's short of water. Plant is in a good growth spurt.

Grapevine growing slowly because it's short of water will produce short tendrils and less vigorous new shoots.

the newly emerging leaves with a solution of zinc sulphate—one tablespoon in a gallon of water. Keep spraying every week until growth slows, or it gets hotter than 90F.

There's no point in spraying older, thick-skinned leaves—they don't absorb the nutrient. Soil applications aren't much good, either. Calcium in the soil will gobble up the zinc sulphate as quickly as you apply it.

Irrigation

When the flowers appear, give the plant good irrigation, otherwise fruit will not form. It's the same for all flowering plants, a good fruit set depends on there being plenty of moisture in the plant. If strong, dry winds come at flowering time, give your grapevines an extra irrigation—just to be sure. If the plants become short of water at flowering and fruit set, you might lose the entire crop overnight. It's a tricky time. Be attentive to Mother Nature and her whims

A useful sign concerning water needs is given by the grapevine itself. Watch the terminal tendrils—those at the end of new branches that are searching for a place to grasp. A plant with plenty of water grows strong lengthy tendrils. A plant short of water produces short, "lazy" tendrils. This sign is remarkably accurate and it's one you need to watch constantly.

Keep irrigating frequently and deeply while the berries are developing. They are, after all, 95% water. But as soon as harvest is over, you can economize on your water bill. There will most likely be enough residual moisture in the soil to carry the plant through with moderate growth until leaf fall.

Grape-Leaf Skeletonizers

Watch out for the grape-leaf skeletonizer. It will eat up all your grape-vine leaves in a short time, leaving the skeletons of midribs as evidence. You should know the appearance of the first sign of this problem—the adult moth. It's blue-black and about 1/2-inch long.

They are active during the day and you can easily catch them because they are slow fliers. Buy a butterfly net if there are a lot of them. When you squash them you'll see their yellow eggs. That proves they were up to no good.

Blue-black moth—only 1/2-inch long—is the beginning of trouble. They can be squashed in early morning when cold and sluggish. Moths can be caught with a butterfly net when on the wing—they are not quick fliers. Your assignment is to stop females from laying eggs.

Eggs hatch, eat, get bigger, eat more and turn into black-and-yellow caterpillars that are easily seen. By the time you see them the damage has been done.

Eggs always come in clusters on underside of leaves. Rub them out before they hatch.

While small hatchlings are still on one leaf, it's easy to prevent further damage by removing leaf entirely. Such leaves act as flags among the general foliage to tell you that something is threatening. Very soon these small caterpillars will separate and spread to every adjacent leaf and damage will be widespread.

Search undersides of leaves to see if eggs were laid when you weren't looking. They are pin-head size and clustered in groups of about 100. Rub them off with your finger and thumb.

If you don't find them, they will hatch into small, pale caterpillars that line up, side by side. In a day or two they start spreading out, eating as they go. Damage isn't very obvious at this stage. It is just a silvery, paper-like blotch on the leaf. This is just the beginning—but there's time to save your plant. Pinch off the damaged leaf and crush it, pests and all.

The next stage in the destruction of your vine is dramatic. Whole branches are skeletonized. The softer leaf tissue has all been gobbled up and only veins remain. The caterpillars are now evident and seemingly all over the plant. They are 1/2-inch long with black-and-yellow bands around them.

Sometimes you return from a vacation to discover half your plant devoured. Weeping is no good. Get out the spray gun and blast everything with Diazinon. You're mad at everything and you want to poison every caterpillar.

Birds and beetles can be kept away from ripening grape bunches if you bag them before they begin to ripen. If you wait too long, pests will tear open bags to get to the juicy fruit.

Beetles quickly devour a bunch of grapes.

Other Insect Pests

There's another caterpillar to watch for. It's a brown, 3-inch-long horn-worm with a voracious appetite. Pick him off. This is the larva of the sphinx moth—a night flier.

Caterpillar damage can be minimized by a preventive spray using Dipel® or Thuricide®. This biological control uses *Bacillus thuringiensis* which, when eaten by a caterpillar, damages its digestive system.

A nonchemical method is to shake the vines vigorously in the early morning. A cold caterpillar, it seems, has a poor foothold and will fall to the ground. It can't make the long journey back to the leaves—even if it knew where they were.

There don't seem to be any natural enemies of these pests and no grape varieties are resistant to them. Com-

panion plantings of smelly herbs, such as Tansy, Hyssop or Rue, don't keep caterpillars away. You're on your own.

Be vigilant. Visit your grape vine every morning while it's cool and shake the branches. Search and destroy. Don't wait for damage to be done.

Green Fruit Beetle

In late summer, there's another pest—the green fruit beetle. Paper bags take care of this, unless rain softens the glue and the bags open a little. Beetles work their way in through the smallest of holes. In fact, they chew right through the paper if it has been flavored by damaged, moist fruit inside.

You don't get just one fruit beetle. They come by the hundreds during a bad summer. We're talking about a

serious problem; fruit beetles are voracious eaters. One enterprising gardener gets even with them by sucking them up with his vacuum cleaner. Then he empties the beetles into a bucket of water—they don't swim very well.

They spend most of their lives as grubs, feeding on organic matter, but they appear—unmistakably shiny and green, with a whirr of wings—after the onset of the rains. Only late-maturing fruit is damaged. Bunches of Beauty Seedless and Black Monukka are usually harvested before the green fruit beetle arrives.

After harvest, grape plants need a rest, so reduce the frequency of irrigations. As soon as color changes appear in the leaves, hasten their fall and put the plant to rest by watering even less. There's not enough cold in desert winters to give many plants their needed rest. Dryness substitutes for cold. Don't keep grapes—and deciduous fruit trees—growing until the last minute for frost to knock off the leaves.

Harvest

Your reward will be numerous bunches of delicious fruit. The birds know this too and sense when the grapes are ready for harvest—usually a few days before you do. The best-tasting fruit ripens on the vine, so the bunches should stay there as long as possible. There's no point in picking fruit several days before it's ripe just to save it from the birds. You can buy lots of fruit like that in the supermarkets.

Long before the fruit ripens, place a paper sandwich bag under each bunch and staple it at the top. There's no need to punch breathing holes in the bags—in fact they'll act as open doors for the birds. If you wait until after a few grapes have been eaten, the birds, knowing where to go and, irritated by the bags, will tear them open. Don't use plastic bags. They will sweat and spoil the fruit.

One enterprising gardener sews beautiful bags in three sizes out of close-meshed nylon, complete with drawstrings. The whole bunch is harvested and washed in the bag before bringing to the table. The bags can be used again and again.

There's no alternative to bagging the bunches except, perhaps, putting a net over the whole vine. Plastic owls, rub-

Start your pruning by cutting all top growth down to 6 inches off main framework. Take it away to see what you've got left. You now have spurs all over and there are too many. Remove surplus to leave only those that are necessary as shown on facing page.

Grape vine before pruning: All branches came from one season's growth. They must be cut away to renew plant's fruiting potential.

Grapes after pruning to cane system.

ber snakes, stuffed cats, pie pans and whirligigs are not scary enough when there are juicy grapes to be had on a hot summer's day.

Pruning

Grapes need to be pruned severely. The first three years is a training period. Fruit is borne in the fourth year; thereafter prune for fruit production.

Fruit is produced on new canes every year that grow farther and farther from the trunk. They become more numerous, too. Limit this strong growth by pruning back severely every January or February. Don't be afraid to cut off 80 or 90% of last year's growth.

It's not easy to learn pruning from a book—you have to experience it with a master. Attend pruning demonstrations, look at video tapes, help a neighbor with his pruning—after determining that he knows what he's doing—and watch carefully.

Here are some basics: Fruit is produced on new growth that comes out of 1-year-old canes. These are usually light tan and 1/2-inch thick. Most varieties need to be pruned to short lengths of last-year's growth, each with only two buds. These are called *spurs*. After pruning, an average plant will have 40 buds. These are either on one long rod for an arbor or on two arms if you grow grapes on a field system. Space them evenly along arms about a hand's breadth apart. They should point up—no downward hooks. There should be a total of 10

Another example: Grape vine before pruning . . .

. . . and after pruning. Only a few short spurs remain, but they will produce as much new growth as was taken away in pruning.

If soil is wet, you'll get a lot of dripping at cut ends after pruning. Don't worry about this. It's not dangerous for the plant and it will stop in a day or two. Spraying with can of pruning paint won't stop dripping.

spurs to each arm.

Two varieties commonly grown in the desert are Thompson's Seedless and Black Monukka. Should you prune these kinds to a spur system, you won't get much fruit—if any—because the first six or seven buds on their canes are leaf buds. Fruit buds don't appear until farther along, so leave 10 buds on each of four canes to get a total of 40 buds per plant.

There's a slight complication to cane-system pruning. In addition, you prune one or two canes to two-bud spurs. They are called *renewal spurs* because each gives a new cane, close to the trunk, that will be cut back to 10 buds next year. If you don't do this, your canes will grow longer and

longer—and out of sight.

Expect drippings at the cuts when you prune, even in the cool of a desert winter. If it has been dry and you have held back on irrigating to keep the plants dormant, dripping will be minimal. On the other hand, if rains are plentiful, a great pressure within the plant forces buds to break out earlier than usual.

When you hurriedly prune under these conditions, a lot of sap will drip out the ends. Spraying the cut ends with pruning paint doesn't help. Even the heavier, tar-like stuff is pushed off. Don't worry. Simply let it drip. Go away and do something else. It stops in a day or two and the plant will seem none the worse.

GRAPE VARIETIES for TUCSON AREA
by
George Brookbank, Extension Agent
&
Michael W. Kilby, Fruit and Nut Crops Specialist

Cooperative Extension
University of Arizona

TABLE GRAPES

	Seedless Yes	Seedless No	Pruning Spur	Pruning Cane	Pounds Per Vine	Harvest
REDS						
Flame Seedless	X		X		20-30	Early
Ruby Seedless	X	X			20-30	E-M
Cardinal		X	X		25-35	E-M
Red Malaga		X	X		20-30	Medium
BLACKS						
Exotic		X	X		20-30	E
Ribier		X	X		30-40	M
Black Monukka	X			X	25-35	M
Beauty Seedless	X		X		30-35	E
WHITES						
Perlette	X		X		25-35	E
Thompson Seedless	X			X	39-40	M-L
Muscst of Alexandria		X	X		30-40	Late

WINE GRAPES

	Seedless Yes	Seedless No	Pruning Spur	Pruning Cane	Pounds Per Vine	Harvest
REDS						
Barbera		X	X		25-30	L
Petite Sirah		X	X		20-30	M
WHITES						
French Colombard		X	X		40-60	E-M
Emerald Riesling		X	X		40-60	E-M
Sauvignon Blanc		X	X		20-30	E

E = Early maturity, usually end of June
M = Mid season maturity, usually end of July
L = Late maturity, usually end of August

Reviewed March 1988

25

STRAWBERRIES

Strawberries grow well in lower and intermediate desert regions. But, if you want good yields, it's necessary to have strong, well-established plants in January. This is when natural conditions encourage flowering and fruit set.

Plant-Availability Problem

Plants don't reach maturity until four or five months of growth. To get lots of flowers in January, set out plants in September. They establish easily then because the weather is cooling and plants grow well during the mild winter months. Even if we experience a few nights of frost, there's usually no problem. Unfortunately, it's difficult to find plants at the nurseries in fall.

On the other hand, nurseries have lots of plants in the spring and, for a short time, the weather is favorable for planting and establishment. Spring is the traditional time to start the gardening year, anyway.

However, a spring planting is frequently disappointing because weather conditions determine flower production. Newly planted strawberries don't develop roots fast enough in cold soil during January and they don't have time or resources to produce lots of flowers. The harvest will be light and plants weak—so weak that, when summer heat arrives they will not be able to take it. Most spring-planted strawberries die of premature exhaustion. So, a January or February planting is often a waste of time and effort.

Keep Plants Alive In Summer

To overcome this problem, do all you can to keep your plants alive and well during summer. Above all—provide shade. Water deeply to 12 inches and let the soil surface dry out between irrigations. Mulch the plants with straw or coarse compost. You are now caring for your bed so the strongest survivors will give you a supply of new plants in

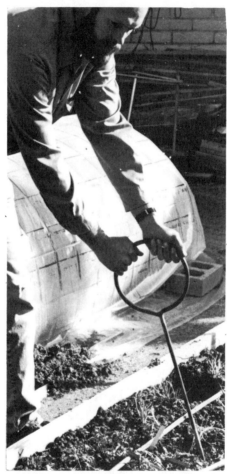

During the winter growing season, keep soil moist down to 12 inches. Check depth with a soil probe. In background, a cover of clear plastic over frame lets in sunshine to keep plants warm and growing.

the fall.

Strawberries produce runners in June and July. These are long stalks from the mother plant that develop a young set of leaves at their tips. Runners can be pegged into the soil or pots of soil buried in the ground close to where new roots grow. Use these new plants to stock up your bed or start a new bed in the month of September.

Use the tunnel wire of winter to put shade cloth over the bed in summer. Plus, use plenty of straw to hide the foliage from the intense sun. This is how you can help your plants survive through the summer.

Fall & Winter Strategy

Irrigate and fertilize fall and winter growth. If the weather cools unduly, erect a framework over the bed and lay clear plastic over for a greenhouse effect. Your goal is to grow strong plants that will start to flower in January and produce fruit abundantly until hot weather arrives in July. You can easily get good vigorous growth during a normal winter.

Covering of open-weave synthetic fiber breathes and makes adequate shade over strawberries in the summer months.

Bare-root plants, either from a nursery or friend, should be free from soil that carries disease organisms. It's more difficult to set out bare-root plants at the correct depth than to use potted plants rooted from runners.

Strawberries lying on wet soil are frequently damaged by pillbugs and snails.

Soil Preparation

Most of our desert soils are sandy, which is fine for strawberries because they prefer a well-drained soil. However, these soils lack organic matter—which strawberries like! The standard procedure for preparing garden soil for all small plants is as follows: For strawberries, start in August.

Water the new bed to soften the soil and stimulate any weed seeds to grow. Pull out the deep-rooted weeds and hoe out the small ones.

Find out if your soil has an underlying layer of caliche by poking your soil probe down as far as it will go. If it meets resistance at 2 feet or less, you must dig down and remove it. That's the minimum. Even if it's deeper than

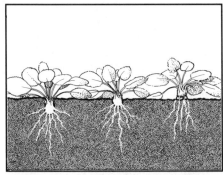

Center drawing shows right depth to plant strawberries. If plants are buried (at left), growing point (crown) will be in wet soil. If planted too high (right), roots will dry out and plants will not produce fruit.

2 feet, I recommend that you remove it to ensure good drainage.

Now, lay 2 or 3 inches of organic matter on the moist ground. Homemade compost is excellent, but composted steer manure is more readily available. Don't use horse manure. It often contains weed seeds, especially Bermudagrass. These don't germinate until your strawberry plants begin to send out runners. Bermudagrass and strawberries in the same bed don't make for a happy marriage. As you pull out the Bermudagrass, you disturb the freshly rooted runners and as the summer progresses, it's harder for them to reroot in the hot soil.

Avoid chicken manure, too. It is a strong material that is likely to burn young roots. Besides, it doesn't improve soil texture as well as compost and other animal manures.

Scatter ammonium phosphate over the organic matter at the rate of 3 pounds, and soil sulphur at the rate of 5 pounds to every 100 square feet. Dig all these into the soil, going 12-inches deep if you can. It's all right to bring up a little of the more brightly colored dirt from below, but be sure to mix everything very thoroughly. One or two waterings will settle the soil and let it mellow.

After a week or two, rake the area level and make a little bank around the bed to hold water when you flood irrigate. Don't make ridges or raised beds which dry out very quickly and draw salts from the soil to their peaks. Soil salts kill roots and stunt plants. We

need to wash them down through the soil and away from the root zone by flood irrigation. Strawberries are well known to be salt-tender.

Planting

As I said early in this chapter, the best time to plant is during fall. The days are cooling off, but the soil remains warm. Old plants recover, too.

If you don't have plants of your own, find them from a good gardening neighbor who is resetting his bed and has some to spare. At this time of year good strawberry growers always have a surplus of young plants recently developed from newly rooted runners. You can try your luck at the nurseries and, if they have plants, they will be more expensive than in the spring.

Set your plants in the ground at the same level they were growing before. This is critical. If you set them too high, they will dry out easily and the crown won't produce new leaves or flowers. If you set the plants too low, the growing point is buried and the plant rots. See the nearby illustration.

Inspect the bed after a few days and give a watering or two. Adjust any plants that moved if the soil settled.

Place plants about 12-inches apart in both directions, aiming for a solid planting rather than neat rows. Rows are all right for farmers, but they waste space in a home garden. Anyway, next year new runners will obliterate any rows you started with.

To repeat what I said earlier, nurseries will have lots of plants in

After flowering in spring, strawberry plants send out runners. They normally form roots and peg themselves into the soil. Make holddowns out of baling wire for securing runners in pots of soil. These anchor the new roots, keeping them in place until their roots grow into the soil.

Surround old plant that is sending out runners with clay pots sunk into soil. Capture runners in the soil in pots and anchor runners with holddowns (at left) to prevent wind from disturbing them.

In a couple of months, new plants will have vigorous roots. Runners have broken off and new plants are ready to set out in a new bed.

Let your garden go fallow in summer and cover it with flakes from a straw bale. The wind won't pick them up as it will with shredded straw. A scattering of ammonium sulphate allows the straw to decompose—without it, any nitrogen in the soil will be used by bacteria as they digest the straw.

February, but that's not the time to make your main planting. Buy a few to keep the bed filled. Bare-root plants are cheaper than those in 4-inch pots, but they are usually a bit more fragile.

Varieties

Nurseries do a good job of selecting suitable kinds for you. From the many dozens of varieties available throughout the country, only a few are worth planting in the desert. They include Sequoia, Shasta, Tioga and Ozark Beauty. New varieties are produced every year and are well advertised, but they should be tried with some caution. Try half a dozen to satisfy your curiosity, but beware of extravagant claims made by mail-order houses and in Sunday newspaper supplements. These wild advertisements merely reflect the public's great interest in fresh-grown fruit—and beginning-gardeners' cupidity.

There aren't any climbing strawberries. No varieties produce fruit as big as a silver dollar. None produce fruit all through the year. Court actions have already established these facts.

Management

Keep the soil around your newly planted strawberries moist, but not wet. Pale-green leaves with darker veins caused by iron chlorosis can often be cured by simply watering less frequently.

Avoid overhead sprinkling. It puts salts on the leaves if water quality is poor. A drip system is fine. Leave it running long enough for the water to reach 12 inches deep, then turn it off for a few days. Snails and pill-bugs, which eat fruit, thrive on the surface of constantly moist soil. Fruit resting on the ground will be eaten by snails and pill bugs. Minimize these pests by letting the soil surface dry out between irrigations.

Apply fertilizers when new growth starts, even during flower development in the spring.

Scatter ammonium nitrate during winter and ammonium sulphate in the warmer months, on the ground and between the plants at the rate of 1 pound to every 100 square feet every three weeks. Be sure to follow with a good sprinkling to wash off any crystals resting in the crowns of the plants.

For a more rapid result, dissolve houseplant fertilizer in water at the rate of 1 tablespoon to a gallon. For a large bed, it's easier to use a hose proportioner at the faucet, where it sucks a stronger solution from a gallon jug. Liquid feeding reduces leaf-burn risks and provides nutrients in soluble form that makes for quick uptake.

When the weather turns cold, cover the bed with a sheet of clear plastic spread over a frame. This makes a greenhouse that will need to be ventilated on hot days by opening the ends to let in fresh air. On freezing nights, an extra blanket can be placed over the plastic to keep in warmth.

Your main objective is to develop strong plants ready for the spring season of warming temperatures and lengthening days. That's when strawbery plants begin to flower and set fruit.

A light scuffling of the soil when it is dry will remove germinating weed seeds. Don't let Bermudagrass get established.

During early summer, runners grow on older plants and are rooted by fall. They are valuable when we want to increase our plantings, or to rejuvenate an old bed, or to fill in gaps left by the ravages of summer.

If you are confident you don't need new plants, pinch off these runners as they start. Your plants will be stronger for it. If you need new plants, bend

some baling wire into a kind of clothespin and fasten the ends of the runners into the soil. This can be the nearby soil, where there are no plants. Or, bury pots filled with soil and fasten the growing tips into them. The runners will in due course die on their own and the new plants will be independent.

Reduce stress on the plants during summer by providing shade for the bed. Sixty-five percent shade cloth is suitable, but a number of gardeners find an overhead grape arbor serves very well. It is shadiest at the hottest time of the year and leaf-fall in the autumn allows sunshine in to the plants during winter. It's nature's automated shade system. If you can't make an overhead shade, a thick layer of fresh straw on top keeps the soil cool and sun off the leaves.

Watering down to 12 inches washes salts down away from the roots. It also allows the soil surface to dry out between waterings—to the discomfort of snails and pillbugs. Frequent shallow waterings cause the leaves to become chlorotic, page 87.

Problems

Nematodes in the soil cause plants to be stunted. You can't see them without a microscope, so take a suspect plant and some soil to a plant-pathology laboratory for diagnosis. If nematodes are present, all plants must be destroyed and the soil fumigated. The same must be done if *Fusarium* or *Verticillium*—both soil organisms—are dis-

covered.

You may replant a few weeks after soil fumigation, but it's a good idea to put in a different kind of vegetable. Remember, this is crop rotation which is the least you can do to prevent a particular soil organism from building up by parasitizing one crop all the time. Play it safe and set out your new strawberries in another part of the garden.

It's too hot and dry in the desert to grow plants successfully in *strawberry jars*—clay pots with many planting holes in their sides. Tiered arrangements of layered beds called *strawberry pyramids*, are also unsuitable.

Strawberries can be grown in half whiskey barrels. Anything smaller calls for frequent watering and the consequent risk of keeping the soil too wet, which invites fungus and bacterial diseases. On the other hand, one day's forgetfulness will dry out the plants. Admittedly, containers can be moved to a shady place, but it's still hot in summer's shade.

It's not worth trying to grow strawberries from seed, though some reputable seed catalogs encourage you to try. You won't get fruit the first year, in spite of claims to the contrary.

It's easy to overwater the bed during summer months. Always use a soil probe to help you determine whether the soil needs irrigating before you turn on the faucet.

Plastic film on the soil is used during winter to warm the soil and get plants growing. In a new garden, lay a sheet over the whole bed and use a cookie cutter to punch holes through it. Plant through these holes. Hold the edges of the plastic down with bricks, otherwise winds may lift it along with your plants. Clear plastic warms the soil better than black, but allows weeds to grow under it which become a nuisance. You won't get weeds with black plastic.

Either kind of plastic prevents runners from establishing themselves, though they can be "caught" in pots resting on the material. Plastic sheets are also difficult to remove from an established bed. They must be removed before summer arrives, otherwise the soil gets too hot and the plants die. Cut the plastic between the plants and carefully pull out the pieces.

Strawberries can take a lot of cool weather, but must be kept growing during winter months. If weather becomes very cold, they must be protected.

Spring growth can be speeded up by warming soil with black plastic. "Cookie-cutter" made from tin can lets you make planting holes. Clear plastic does just as well, but light allows weeds to grow.

26

FROST PROTECTION

The first fall frost is unpredictable. It always seems to catch us by surprise. If it comes while trees are still growing, a lot of damage can be done to leaves, twigs and even branches. Vegetables such as eggplant, tomatoes and peppers—often showing a remarkable comeback from summer's heat—can be killed. On the other hand, winter vegetables such as lettuce, broccoli, cabbage, carrots, beets and cauliflower don't seem to suffer. They continue growing, particularly if they have some size to them.

Strawberries will survive cold temperatures, not only in the air surrounding the leaves, but in the soil where their roots are. While they stop growing new leaves and roots under these conditions—they don't die.

The first frost turns leaves on deciduous fruit trees and vines a fall color and they start to drop. Such signs are nothing to worry about. As a rule, these trees don't get enough cold.

Citrus trees and tender ornamentals, such as Bougainvillea, Hibiscus and palms, give us the greatest anxiety.

Are You In A Frost-Free Area?

Every part of a town has areas that are colder than others. These are usually low-lying places that gather cold night air. Cold air moves, just as water moves, to the lowest point. Washes and rivers are cold places on a winter's night. Some locations enjoy a warm reputation and are quickly labeled by real-estate developers as "thermal belts." You need to know whether you live in a cold area or a warm one.

The survival of mature Bougainvillea, citrus, Hibiscus or Passion Vine—all of which are frost-tender—indicates a warm area. In a new development without mature landscaping, the native vegetation will tell you something. Because Ironwood, Jojoba and

Snow storms come in quickly and get us all excited for a day or two. Snow doesn't stay long and doesn't do a lot of damage either. It acts as a blanket against more damaging freezes. Snow adds to the moisture reserves in the soil. As the snow melts, the moisture gradually soaks into the soil.

Western Coral Bean are killed by frost, their presence indicates a warm area.

Remember, it takes only one night of sharp frost to do a lot of damage, and such a frost may not recur for a number of years. Plants have a way of recovering from frost damage. For example, palm trees are frost-tender and look awful after a week of freezing nights, but in a year's time they look healthy again.

The most reliable way to find out whether you live in a cold or a warm area is to record the cold temperatures in your yard. You don't have to stay up all night to do this.

Buy a minimum-recording thermom-

eter in a hardware store. Put it near your valuable plants. Buy more than one if you want to know the temperatures in different parts of your property. For example, a northern aspect is colder than a western one. We change microclimates when we build concrete houses and driveways, and brick patios with enclosed walls. The inner city is generally warmer than open country.

Start keeping records in October and write three temperatures for each date. First, the forecast given on the radio or TV. Second, last night's low temperature recorded at the weather station. Third, last night's low temperature in

The way palm trees are affected by weather conditions tells us if it is warm or cold. These plants, though severely damaged by a night's frost, will recover during the summer. Their new growth will tend to hide evidence of last winter's freeze.

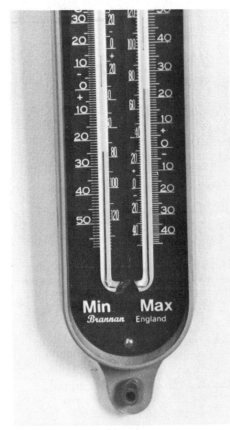

Recording thermometer is a most useful tool for the gardener. Each mercury column pushes a little bar. When the mercury starts to return with a change in temperature the bar stays where it was pushed to. You read the extremes of cold and of heat, then bring the bar back in contact with the mercury by using a magnet, for the next period of recording. There's no need to wait up until the coldest hour before dawn to find out how cold it got last night.

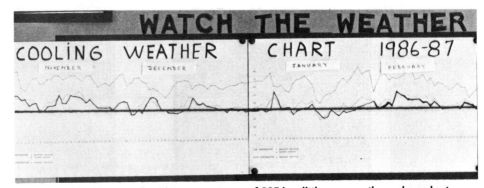

Chart's horizontal line at freezing temperature of 32F is a little warmer than when plant damage is done. Temperature jump for a few days is a danger sign that plants may respond by starting up their growth cycle before winter is over. This makes them more frost-tender. Winters seem to be getting milder and summers hotter, but it takes only a few hours below 28F to damage plants. If temperatures fall steadily during November and December, most plants are hardened enough to withstand the usual freezing nights. The most damage is done to plants that are unprepared for freezes.

your yard. After a week or two you will see how accurate the forecasts are. You will be able to compare the official temperatures with those in your yard. How close are they to one another? Are you in a warm or cold area?

Is Temperature Falling Steadily?

There's something even more interesting for you to observe through a daily —or nightly—temperature recording.

You should know whether temperatures are dropping regularly or not. If they're falling a few degrees each week, starting in October, you can be assured that your trees are naturally *hardening off* and preparing themselves for cold weather. On the other hand, if the temperatures bounce up and down with a few warm days interspersed between the overall cooling trend, your trees are not going to settle down, either. They might even put out new growth during an extended warm week in November. That will end up being trouble in December when the first killing frost arrives. If you put the figures onto a graph, the lines should slope steadily downwards as the days go by. Again, compare your location with the "official" location.

Citrus & Frost

Citrus trees are semitropical in origin, yet vary in their resistance to freezing temperatures. If you live in a cold part of town, don't plant limes—they are most tender. Lemons come next, followed by oranges, tangerines and grapefruit, in that order. Sour Orange is even more tolerant to cold and

many such trees in the cold parts of town have survived several freezes. Sour Orange is a common root stock of citrus trees. When a grafted tree is "killed" by a freeze, the top part is lost, but the root sends out shoots that eventually turn into a tree—a Sour Orange tree.

New shoots coming from the roots bear sour fruit, replacing the previous sweet fruit. This explains why fruit trees appear to change their characteristics. Disappointed beginning gardeners think the change is due to something they did—or did not do. The fact is: Jack Frost caused it!

If you live in a cold part of town, always buy citrus trees on Sour Orange roots. Trees on Sour Orange will be the survivors. Avoid Rough Lemon and macrophylla roots because they are frost-tender and their trees will be the victims of a cold winter.

Choose Warm Location For Your Tree

Plant frost-tender trees in the warmest part of your yard. A southern or western exposure with a masonry back-up wall and a paved patio in full winter sun will gather heat during the day. Sufficient heat will be released during the night to save a tree during a mild freeze. Wall-enclosed spaces on the north side of a house are likely to be cold because they don't get much sunshine. Still air trapped inside an enclosed wall is much colder than slightly turbulent air out in the open.

Surprisingly, we do get some mild, frost-free winters, but they cannot be relied on. It's wise to be prepared for some frosty nights. Your daily ther-

Subtropical plants such as citrus, can be damaged, especially if they are not fully dormant, so we have to be careful where we plant them. Even in a recognized cold part of town a tree can be "warmed" by a corner of two walls. A concrete patio also absorbs daytime sunshine and releases the heat on a cold night to make the difference between damage and safety.

An enclosed yard fills up with cold air until it spills over the top of the wall. To avoid this, let the cold air drain out through holes close to the ground.

mometer readings will tell you how quickly night temperatures are falling. If they fall steadily in October and November, your plants will be hardening off nicely.

Stop Fertilizing & Watering

Don't fertilize trees after the end of August or trim or prune after the end of September. You don't want to stimulate new growth by this sort of attention.

Help trees go into dormancy by reducing irrigations in October. Their ripening fruit will not be hurt by this, though the soil must not be allowed to dry out completely.

When Frost Time Comes

A few cloudy days prevent the earth being warmed. If they are followed by clear starry nights, watch out for a freeze. A cloudy night following a sunny day is usually warm.

The middle of November seems to give us the first hard freeze; the middle of December gives us another. In November, start paying attention to weather forecasts. They are very accurate in telling us about approaching cold storms from the north.

Do weather forecasts give you a real warning? If temperature records in your yard indicate your yard is usually 5F warmer than the official location, then you have little to fear when the forecast says the cold will reach 28F. Of course, we have no way of knowing how long that low temperature will last. At least two hours are necessary before damage is done.

If your plants are fully dormant, there's even less to worry about.

Here's an idea if you don't have a minimum-recording thermometer, or live in a place not listed in the forecasts. A gardener in Green Valley, which is colder than Tucson and doesn't get the specific forecasts that Tucson does, keeps an ordinary thermometer outside his window. If it reads less than 45F at 10 p.m., he protects his frost-tender plants before going to bed. He discovered that a freeze invariably follows such a temperature at that hour.

Frost Protection

An hour or two of temperatures just below freezing will not hurt a dormant tree. When they hover around 29F, try to conserve heat that is already in a tree from a day's sunshine. Cover it with a heavy sheet or a light blanket.

It's like putting a hat on a bald man's head. Don't use plastic because it has zero insulating value. Take off the covering in the morning to let the sun warm the tree again.

Don't build a frame around your tree and stretch clear plastic over it. This will give a greenhouse effect, warming-up the tree during a day of sunshine to stimulate growth. Plastic will not keep the plant warm during a cold night. It will be worse than if you had done nothing.

When temperatures fall below 27F, cover your tree and provide heat. The easiest way to do this is to place two 40-watt light bulbs in a metal bucket on the ground under the tree. Enough heat will flow up through the branches and will be held in by the sheet, keeping the twigs and fruit from being damaged. Strings of Christmas-tree lights also provide useful heat as long as they are inside the foliage and are not merely warming the vacant air.

Frozen plants dry out as does meat in a deep freeze. Citrus fruit shrivels after repeated frosts. A tree that is in good water balance withstands a freeze better than one that is on the dry side. Keep your plants well supplied with moisture, but don't overdo

Small trees can be covered easily but . . .

it with heavy irrigations such as commercial citrus growers use to warm the soil and their grove of trees. Liquid water is certainly warmer than frozen water or frozen soil, but your tree will suffer from too wet a root system if you try to use water as a warmer every night.

There seems to be little value in spraying down a frozen tree or a frozen vegetable garden. Let the plants thaw out on their own.

Wrap the trunks of young citrus trees with several layers of newspaper or cardboard, and wrap their foliage with loose bundles of palm fronds or corn stalks. Small trees are more vulnerable than mature ones.

During a threatened freeze there is always the agony of deciding whether to pick the fruit to avoid damage, or to let it take its chances. Leave fruit on the tree unless the temperature falls below 28F for 3 or 4 hours. Of course, if you covered the tree and put lights under it, you shouldn't worry until the outside temperature drops to 26F.

What To Do About Frost Damage

Don't worry if outside leaves and even small twigs get killed. Think of the damage as a natural pruning because the loss is slight and will be made up by spring growth. You will, however, lose some of next year's fruit production because citrus flowers are produced on new outer growth.

Wait until late spring when growth starts again to prune trees that have branches damaged by frost. You want to know where the damage was done and how far to cut back. New growth will tell you. Cut into live wood to

. . . a large tree is another story. However, a partial covering serves a good purpose. Covering acts as a hat on a bald man's head—keeping in the heat. If the daytime sunshine didn't provide heat because it was cloudy, two 40-watt light bulbs placed in a bucket under tree will develop enough heat to protect it.

stimulate side shoots that can be directed to fill in a gap created by winter injury.

If limbs and larger branches have been killed, cut them back cleanly to below any serious bark damage. In the spring, severely injured bark splits and peels back inviting invasion by *sooty canker*.

Treat all pruning cuts with pruning paint. If you have to cut away a lot of foliage that previously shaded inside limbs and trunk, additional protection from the coming summer sunshine is needed. Paint them with whitewash or latex paint. Don't use enamel paint because it will damage the bark.

Once in a while, a plant will be killed right down to the roots. New growth on a grafted plant will come from the rootstock. It will be quite dif-

ferent and usually undesirable. Your citrus tree will be just as ornamental as before, but its fruit will be unpalatable.

Any new growth will be thick and luxuriant because there's a powerhouse of roots forcing it out. If the tree is to be nursed back to a normal shape, take a couple of years to select and thin out the new shoots, even if you want a bushy shrub. If, on the other hand, you want a single-trunked tree as before, remove all the shoots except one. Let it grow to the height you wish, removing side shoots if they develop. Then, cut off the top and allow the few, remaining sideshoots to become branches of your future tree.

If growth starts both above and below the bud union, take away all the shoots from below and selectively thin out those above.

Winter sunshine prevents soil from becoming too cold. Cool-season plants may stop growing, but don't die.

It's air temperature that matters during winter months. Frost-tender plants suffer, but winter vegetables—though covered with frost—are not harmed.

These outside twigs will be lost, but the tree has only been given a light and even pruning.

As soon as the weather warms up in the spring following a severe freeze, there will be growth in the undamaged part of the twig. Cut off the dead part and 1 or 2 inches of live material. The live part will respond by sending out side branches. Had you merely cut into a dead end there might be further die-back.

Don't expect fruit for at least two years.

It's far better to err on the cautious side. Protect your frost-tender trees during a cold winter and avoid all this fussy repair work.

Spring Frosts

Although deciduous fruit trees need a cold period to give them rest, they can suffer from unexpected cold snaps that appear in spring. Unseasonably warm weather in late spring often starts a fruit tree's growth cycle. Leaf and flower buds open up and the tree is on its way to fruit production. Should a cold front move in, these buds can be killed by a freeze in one night. You will have lost the whole of next year's crop.

Spring freezes are a definite hazard to fruit growing. Both low-chill and standard varieties can be damaged if they start up too early in the spring.

If this happens to your flowering fruit trees, take the usual precautions of covering them with a sheet or blanket at night when frost threatens.

Snowstorms come in quickly and get us all excited for a day or two. Snow doesn't stay long or do much damage. It acts as a blanket against more damaging freezes.

Pretty sight, but dangerous for your plants. Late snow on mountain could send cold air down to flowering fruit trees in valley below. Next year's crop will be lost if flowers are killed.

Don't buy a flowering tree in a nursery. Your tree should be completely dormant until after you've planted it.

Look at roots of tree before you buy. If container stood in hot sun, roots lying against side may have been cooked. Dead roots are soft and dark; live ones are well filled and pale

27

CUCUMBERS, SQUASH & MELONS

Squash is formed with the female flower—not as a result of pollination. If the flower is not pollinated, fruit fails to develop. It turns yellow and drops off.

Male flower has no fruit behind it—yet it is attractive to bees. This is good for the melon grower.

The botanical family to which cucumbers, squash and melons belong is a large one and there is confusion over the names of individual members. For example, the words *cantaloupe* and *muskmelon* are interchangeable in some parts of the country. In the southwest the commonly used name for *Cucumis melo* is *cantaloupe*, whereas east of the Rockies the same vegetable is called *muskmelon*.

Melons are vegetables? Surely they're fruits!

It's easy to get round this particular nit-picking because they can be called *vegetables* when you find them in the vegetable section of supermarkets. You are botanically correct when you call them *fruits*, because they naturally develop from a flower. And it's this flower that has a great bearing on several discussions about these kinds of plants in your garden.

Flower Recognition
No matter what plant of this large family you are talking about you need to know that it has two kinds of flowers—a male and a female—on the same plant. Male flowers never develop into fruits—or vegetables—and they usually appear before the female flowers.

Sometimes it seems that a particular plant is never going to produce a female flower—it simply continues to produce apparently useless male flowers—which means no fruit. But the male flower has, of course, a purpose in life. Its pollen fertilizes the female flowers. So, if you don't get male flowers—only female flowers—you still don't get a crop.

Young Fruit Decay
Observant gardeners know that peaches or apples or citrus fruit appear after the flower has faded. This is not the case with cucumbers, squash and melons. The fruit is there before the flower opens. It's a long miniature cucumber, or a fatter miniature squash or, if it's a melon, a furry little ball sitting directly behind the female flower. That's how you know it's a female

flower. The male flower is on a long clean stalk without any fruit bulge.

An unpollinated female flower will not allow the fruit to develop. It turns brown at the end, withers and falls off.

It's hard for beginning gardeners to realize that a shrivelling cucumber, squash or melon fruit is not diseased.

Pollinating: Insects & You
Pollination is effected by insects, notably honey bees. If it is not done naturally, you, the gardener, must do it.

Take the male flower off the plant. Remove the yellow petals and you're left with a long stalk with a sticky orange knob on its end. Pollen grains are clustered on this knob, which you rub into the center of a female flower which is, of course, still on the plant. Use one male flower for four or five female flowers.

The operation is best done early in the morning just after the flowers have opened up and are at their strongest. A flower only lasts a few hours, so it's a daily job.

Even before first leaves develop, cucurbit seedling is searching for moisture. Finger and thumb show soil level. It is best to sow seed in moist soil that is drying out from a deep irrigation. Deep digging and deep irrigations are necessary—things that home gardeners sometimes forget.

Success, A Combination of Circumstances.

To be a successful cucumber, squash or melon grower, you need a combination of circumstances: a balance of male and female flowers, an abundance of active pollinating insects, and a continued production of both kinds of flowers.

Cucurbits

From now on we are going to call all the relatives in this large family of cucumbers, squash and melons, *cucurbits* to save space. This scientific name will give you an aura of mystique when you talk about them at the dinner table.

Cucurbit Family

This large family can be divided into its main botanical groups or genera. Each genus contains different species and each species has a number of garden varieties.

Regional names given by farmers, based on rough market comparisons, are not matched by botanists' classifications based on minute morphological

GARDEN VARIETY	GENUS	SPECIES
Acorn squashes	Cucurbita	pepo
Zucchini squashes		
Yellow Crookneck		
Scallop squashes		
'Jack o'Lantern pumpkin		
Connecticut Field pumpkin		
Garden marrows		
Vegetable spaghetti squash		
Garden marrows		
Sugar pumpkin		
Table Queen		
Cushaw pumpkin	Cucurbita	moschata
Butternut squashes		
Kentucky Field pumpkin		
Hubbard squashes	Cucurbita	maxima
Banana squashes		
Turk's Turban squash		
'Big Max' pumpkin		
Boston Marrows		
Buttercup squash		
Malabar gourd	Cucurbita	ficifolia
Bottle gourds	Lagenaria	siceraria
Dipper gourds		
Cucuzzi squashes		
Loofah	Luffa	cylindrica
Chayote	Sechium	edule
Cantaloupes	Cucumis	melo
Honeydew melons		
Casaba melons		
Muskmelons		
Crenshaw melons		
Mango melon		
Serpent melon		
Cucumbers	Cucumis	sativus
Watermelon	Citrullus	vulgaris

details. You may be interested to know that while the Kentucky Field pumpkin really is a pumpkin, the Connecticut Field pumpkin is botanically a squash, as is the Big Max pumpkin.

Here's what botanists say about crossing of cucurbits: Garden varieties within a particular species will cross-fertilize—and usually produce an off-type seed. However, garden varieties of one species will not cross-fertilize with varieties in another species group. To make things difficult for you, there are exceptions to these rules.

All garden varieties in the species *C.pepo*—for cucurbita pepo—cross with one another and with garden varieties in the species group *C.moschata*. Those in the species *C.moschata* will cross with those of *C.pepo* and *C.maxi-*ma. However, garden varieties in the species *C.pepo* will not cross with those that are of the species *C.maxima*.

Cross Pollination

Now, here's another thing: All cucurbit fruits and seeds they contain are the result of cross-pollination between two flowers—often, but not necessarily, from two different plants. There's no other way the seeds can be fertilized.

This means that any curcubit seed you collect is not likely to grow into a plant like the one it came from.

Cucurbit Seed

Never save seed of cucurbits from your garden—even if you have a most successful crop. Always buy fresh seed. Packet seed has been "brought up proper" by careful plant breeders who saw to it that only the best pedigrees were introduced to one another.

And here's yet another thing. Some gardeners swear that cucumbers, grown next to melons, have a melon taste. It can't be that the flavor physically rubbed off one to the other. But it could be that the cross-fertilized seed, as it developed, affected the development of its fleshy surroundings, fruit you harvest—or vegetable you buy.

The moral of that story: Don't allow the different social classes to rub shoulders with one another. Be sure they "play" only with their own kind.

Cultural Requirements

Cucurbits need a deep, rich soil if they are to yield abundantly. Use the best part of your garden and further build up its fertility by digging in organic matter and ammonium phosphate. Use the standard procedure outlined in Chapter 6 which includes an addition of sulphur to make the desert soil less alkaline. Digging down to 2 feet is advisable, though few gardeners do this—and that's a frequent reason for their crop not doing well.

Cucurbits develop a strong, deep root system if given the chance and they need a lot of water. Well-dug soil allows for both, whereas shallow new soil doesn't.

Although the desert sun is a bit fierce, cucurbits are warm-season plants . Their large, thin leaves quickly burn if they are allowed to get dry and the fruit is easily sunburned if it is not protected by luxuriant foliage. Squash seem to take the heat best and cucumbers the least. In fact, cucumbers do better in the cooling fall season, after a late August sowing, than they do from a March sowing after which the air and the soil quickly heat up.

A lot of space is needed. One watermelon seed will produce a plant that spreads over 100 square feet and more. We are used to accommodating cucumbers' need for space by growing them on a trellis. We can do the same for melons, too.

Cucurbits have large seeds that germinate in three or four days if conditions are right. The plants grow quickly. This makes them—particularly squash—suitable for childrens' gardening.

Cucurbits are relatively free of pests and diseases. However, one of the most irritating of pests is the squash vine borer, a grub that burrows into the stem and destroys it. Because the stem is so severely eaten up, it is unable to carry moisture from the roots to the leaves and the plant is killed. Cantaloupe suffer from powdery mildew, but you can sow seed of varieties that are resistant to this fungus.

This is a smooth-skinned melon, but foliage didn't shield it from the summer sun. Quality is spoiled by deep cracks and patch of sunburned dead rind. When fruit ripens, there will be a hard flavorless portion on one side.

How to Get A Good Crop

Dig the soil as deeply as you can and mix in organic matter with ammonium phosphate. Give the area a good deep soaking. This drives down salts away from the seed and new roots. Cucurbits don't like salts. As the soil surface starts to dry out, sow the seed. The soil under the seed needs to be moist in order to get initial deep rooting. If the soil is too wet at this point roots will be shallow.

Deep Roots Must be Developed by Deep Irrigations—Your plants should grow deep roots in readiness for later high temperatures when the leaves transpire a great deal of water. All your irrigations should be deep. This is why you dug deeply in the first place—to let the water travel down easily.

Side dress with nitrogen—Apply ammonium sulphate in small amounts —one tablespoon per plant, well watered in—as the plants grow in size.

Don't let the leaves turn pale because of rapid growth, but don't get them too dark, either. Large, dark green leaves are impressive, but too much nitrogen discourages flower for-

mation and the yield is reduced, though the plants look great.

Tip pruning—Cucurbits make long runners. It pays to keep these from spreading too far. It also pays to pinch out 4 or 5 inches of soft growth at the ends of strong runners. This causes side shoots to develop and the plant becomes more dense and compact.

Long runners produce a certain number of flowers on their mature vines, but they produce many more on the numerous side shoots that develop from tip pinching.

Insect Pests

The *squash vine borer* is mentioned as a major pest that is, fortunately, restricted to squash members of the curcubit family.

Aphids attack the young tender shoots of all curcubits. Heavy infestations stunt the growth of leaves and may even kill the plant. Leaves become sticky with honeydew and, when colonies become crowded, many winged aphids are produced, which fly off to infest nearby plants. A relatively low temperature of around 68F seems to favor aphid growth—and too low a temperature for predators to multiply. When this happens aphids

can be checked by spraying with Malathion® or diazinon.

Red Spider Mites are also to be found on tender shoots, particularly those of cucumbers.

Other insects are of minor importance, even the *Cucumber beetle* which, with a name like that, ought to be a major pest. The list also includes cutworms, crickets, grasshoppers, thrips, leafhoppers—that carry curly top disease—and leaf miners.

Don't Use Insecticides At Flowering Time.

First, sulphur and Toxaphene® are injurious to the foliage of curcubits. Secondly, there aren't any chemicals that kill the bad insects without killing the good ones.

Cucurbits—with their two kinds of flowers necessitating cross-pollination—depend on insect activity for their fruitfulness. It would be devastating to the crop to apply insecticides at flowering time.

What Can You Do?

Use soapy water to wash off small numbers of aphids and spider mites before you initiate a spray program that will also kill helpful insects. Also,

Plant is beyond repair—its stem has been completely devoured by grub at left. If you see your well-watered plants wilting, quickly slice stem lengthwise to remove grub—and there may be more than one. Dust with sulphur to reduce disease risks, wrap the two halves of stem together, cover with soil, and hope plant continues to grow. Squash vine borer seems to attack older plants—so overcome this problem by succession planting. Always have young squash around you.

Severe stunting of shoots at the ends of the runners tells you that aphids were busy earlier! They suck the juices of plants—and carry virus diseases too—and ruin the prospects of a good harvest. This shoot is useless. Early in the season it could be pinched off in the hope that the resultant side shoots will be normal.

there are natural enemies that help in keeping mites and aphids under control.

The encouragement of ladybird beetles, wasps, lacewings and predaceous mites should be part of every home gardener's strategy. Don't kill the good guys by spraying indiscriminately!

Nematodes

Repeated cropping of the same piece of ground invites parasitic nematodes. An infestation will destroy plant roots. A heavy infestation makes the soil useless for gardening—everything dies. Good cultural practices include resting the ground from such repeated cropping.

Poor sandy soils seem to favor nematode build-up so the addition of organic matter, the use of balanced fertilizers and adequate waterings to keep the plants from stress all help to minimize this danger.

There are no chemicals available to treat the soil or the damaged crop.

Notes On Cucumbers

Cucumbers are best trained up on a trellis. They climb and hang on with

their tendrils all by themselves. You may have to spread the shoots after a windy period to make sure growth is not all bunched up. This gets the foliage away from the hot soil and the plant does better for it.

However, cucumbers don't do well in mid-summer. It's too hot, even in the shade, and their fruit becomes bitter tasting. Often the flowers, if they are produced, abort because of the hot, dry air that kills the pollen. Misshapen fruit—narrow pointed fruit instead of rounded ends—is caused by inadequate or partial pollination.

One variety, Armenian, performs more reliably than the others in the desert dry heat. Other kinds give bitter fruit while it is hot, but quality improves during the cooler months. Cucumbers like a temperature of 75F during the day and 65F at night.

Loofah is a vigorous grower through summer's heat and, though not strictly a cucumber, its fruit can be eaten fresh or lightly cooked when small and tender. Of course, when it is allowed to mature, the fruit forms the vegetable sponge that we use in our baths.

Sow a cluster of two or three seeds directly in the ground about 12 inches apart after the soil has warmed to 60F in the spring. Wait in the fall until the soil has cooled to 95 F. Provide a trellis

Bees help you to get a crop, but other insects work flowers, too. Don't use insecticides on your cucurbits. Bees are single-minded creatures. They will fly right past your melons to gather pollen from weed flowers, or to get water. You can attract them to your garden with a drip-irrigation system or with water put out for the birds.

Get cucumber plants up on a slanted trellis where fruit hangs down straight in shade of foliage. Fruit on ground usually is misshaped and often sunburned.

Use string to get shoots climbing. Once you've guided their early growth, they will use their tendrils to climb.

String "teepee" is an easy way to get plants up into the air and off ground. Notice how fruit resting on ground are short and blunt when they could be longer and straighter.

so the young shoots start climbing right away.

Slope the trellis so fruits hang freely. This keeps them straight. Fruit tend to get tied up on a vertical trellis and are usually deformed or, at the best, severely curved.

In spring the soil takes a while to warm sufficiently. Thereafter there's not too many reliable days before the weather and the soil gets too hot. At best it's a short season.

A sowing in late August germinates and grows quickly in the warm soil. Days—at least nights—are cooling and a good crop can be expected before frost kills the plants. There are about 90 good growing days before frost, so chose short-term varieties.

Notes On Squash

There are many kinds of squash. All have large seeds that germinate in three or four days. They are easy to grow and they grow quickly in summer's heat. One year in Tucson, a second sowing of seeds was made on July 4th. Fruit were ready to eat within 30 days!

Succession Sowing Advisable

Because of the initial rapid growth and quick-fruiting habits of squash, it is better to make several sowings rather than keep an individual plant for as long as you can. Pull up an old plant. It takes up a lot of space, it easily tires and, furthermore, it's almost sure to get the vine borer.

Sow a second lot of seeds two weeks after you harvest the first fruit from the previous sowing. You may be able to get four sowings between the end of March and mid-September.

Winter Squash

Beginning gardeners are fooled by this name, enough so that they wait until the end of summer to sow seed of winter squash.

Winter squash is so named because it is a good keeper and it will last all through the winter if kept cool in storage. You sow the seed in summer; you eat the fruit in winter. Other

Squash fruit still has withered flower, telling us it is tender, though on the large size for perfect picking. Heat of midsummer has affected flower pollination and ultimate shape of fruit. Fruit should be evenly thick from one end to the other.

Don't worry about a metal trellis being too hot—even in summer heat. Plants don't suffer at all. Later, these young melons will be cradled in a sling.

If you grow melons on a trellis, fruit will fall off as they gain weight. Put them in a sling early on and keep them shaded.

Bird's eye view of a watermelon stood on end shows flat bottom that suggests ripeness. Weight of fruit presses soft flesh against soil. As it turned out, melon wasn't quite ripe.

squash don't keep; you eat them as they grow.

When to Harvest Squash

Most squash should be picked—by cutting the fruit off the plant with a sharp knife—a day or two after the flower has faded. In other words, remove them while they're in an immature stage of ripeness. While the fruit is small, it is tender and seedless and has gourmet value. Furthermore, as young fruit are removed, more flowers appear and you get a bigger harvest than if you allow only a few fruit to reach enormous size.

Winter squash and marrows are allowed to grow as big as they want. Their skin hardens as they ripen which helps them to store well.

Advantage of Yellow Varieties

It's easy to overlook a green-fruited zuchinni among jungly foliage. A week of fruit growth gives you a seed-filled monster that has lost its quality. Golden-fruited varieties stand out against the green foliage. You can harvest them in good time.

Don't Plant Too Many Seeds

Summer squash grow quickly and produce heavily. They take up a lot of space and need a lot of water. You don't need more than three producing plants at any one time. With this in mind, sow three or four seeds in clusters about 5 feet apart. Thin the weaker seedlings in each cluster to leave only one plant.

Wilt At Mid-day In Summer

Don't be alarmed when your plants wilt temporarily at mid-day. Their leaves are large and thin and the plant transpires a lot of water. It's quite normal to have the leaves droop for an hour or two—even if the soil is wet from an early morning irrigation.

If the wilt continues all afternoon and into the evening, start looking on the stem for vine-borer damage.

Expect Vine-borer Damage

If you escape this common pest two years in a row, you will be lucky. It usually strikes just after about two-weeks' harvest. There's no acceptable control. Remember, plants need insects to pollinate their flowers.

Inspect the stems daily and if you see a little pale-colored egg, simply rub it off. If you don't do this there'll soon be some wet sawdust coming out of a hole where the grub is chewing away.

Notes On Melons

There are many varieties of watermelons and even more of cantaloupe, Casaba, Persian, Cranshaw and Honeydew.

You have to find out for yourself which kinds you prefer, and which perform best under your conditions. Your Extension office should be able to help. Otherwise, read the seed catalogs and select the short-term growers—in other words, the quick-maturing kinds. Avoid the late-maturing kinds that need 90 days before you get the first fruit.

A new trend has shown itself, to the benefit of home gardeners. New varieties of watermelon have been developed that are small and quick-growing. A single fruit is enough for a family, so there's no need to fill the refrigerator with a giant remainder left over from a family picnic. Try these watermelon varieties: Sugar Baby, Yellow Baby, Sweet Baby, Yellow Doll, Sugar Doll—you get the idea.

Summers: Too Hot/Too Short

As in all desert gardening situations, there are too few reliable days that are suitable for successful vegetable growth. Spring starts late in some years and fall days arrive too early, so summer isn't long enough for melons.

Melons grow well in the heat, but they don't like too much of it.

August sun burns the leaves which can be saved by copious irrigations, but exposed fruit can't be saved from sunburn except by putting a paper bag or cardboard box over them.

Growing Melons Can Be Expensive.

If you have to pay a high price for water, consider buying your vegetables at the corner store instead of growing your own. Seventy days of summer watering can be very expensive.

Pick Fruit When It's Ripe

Store-bought melons are picked in the field before they are ripe. This has to be because a ripe melon won't stand

Cut small piece out of fruit and inspect inside. Put plug back for a day or two if it is not to your satisfaction. Method requires practice. There is a danger of bacteria spoiling plugged melon, especially if it rains.

Tendril at left is hard and dry; one at right is still green and supple. With a split decision in this case, it's better to wait.

Here's a hard, dry tendril, but look at two more, farther from fruit to be sure melon is ripe.

the handling and traveling to your table. However, it means you lose out on taste, flavor and juiciness.

If you grow your own, you can be sure of high-quality fruit—as long as you know when to pick. Most people—experienced gardeners as well as beginners—pick too soon.

How to tell when watermelon is ripe—Method One: Thump it, bang it or tap it and listen for the right sound. It should have a solid watery echo. This doesn't mean anything and the method is a highly subjective one, so it isn't worth much. Someone tried to organize this sound method by saying that if the fruit sounds like your head

being tapped it's not ready. If it sounds like your chest, it's ready. If it sounds like your stomach, it's over-ripe. Take it or leave it.

Method Two: A ripe watermelon is full of water and its weight causes the top to press on the bottom, which becomes flat against the ground. This is often hard to determine.

Method Three: A ripe watermelon is pale underneath where it touches the ground. This is another judgmental measure that varies with the different members of your family.

Method Four: Cut out a piece of the fruit and see what it's like. Put it back if you don't think it's ready to harvest.

This is a fair way to see if the fruit can be eaten, but your mind might already have been made up and you still pick before the fruit is at its best.

Method Five: The tendrils on the vine near the fruit should be brown, dry and hard. Look along the vine in the direction of the roots. If three such tendrils are brown, dry and hard, you can safely harvest a good ripe fruit.

Method Six: If you are too excited to carry the fruit inside without dropping it, there's a final test. As it hits the ground, a ripe fruit "explodes." An unripe fruit merely cracks.

The trouble with all these methods—except No. Five—is that you forget be-

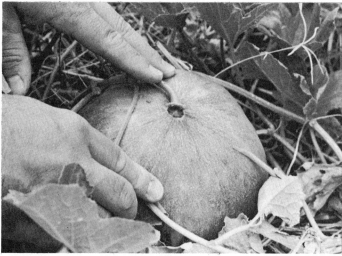

Stalk easily slips away from a ripe melon. This is the best way to tell whether it's ripe . . . and it's easy.

Ordinarily a strong netting of veins suggests ripeness, but it's deceiving in this case. Fruit is small—that's no bad thing by itself—but true test is how stalk is attached. This one's still firmly attached, indicating fruit is not yet ripe.

tween one year and the next. The lessons—poor as they are—have to be learned all over. And a committee of four or five means you'll never reach a decision that is worth anything.

How to tell when cantaloupe is ripe—Cantaloupe are the easiest to judge for ripeness. The stalk merely slips off a ripe fruit when you roll it lightly on the ground. Although there are signs of the golden color and the prominence of the veins on the skin, these are judgmental and vary be-

tween different varieties. Go for the "slip."

How to tell when casaba, crenshaw & persian melons are ripe—To begin with, it's not easy. The characteristic color of each kind is often masked by sunburn. There is no conspicuous netting of veins, and the stalk sticks tightly to a ripe fruit.

Some experts talk of a soft end where the flower was. Press it in and measure the resistance compared with the hard sides of the fruit. Some talk of

the soft white underneath of the fruit where it lays on the ground. Some tap and listen. Others smell, testing for a characteristic aroma.

All of these are very subjective—but add them up and make an average. *And then wait another week before you pick the fruit.*

These kinds of melons usually take longer to ripen. Don't be in a hurry to harvest them.

And Now While The Soil Is Still Warm . . .

Soil temperatures at the Extension Garden Center are falling (September 14). Last week at 2 inches depth they ranged between 80F in the morning to 94F at 1 pm. At 6 inches they ranged between 78F and 95F, while at 18 inches they were very close to 88F the whole time. The message is that the surface is still on the hot side for seeds, but temperatures are right for setting out plants and there are plenty of heat reserves at the lower depth. This tells us that it's good for tree planting.

During the next six weeks or so, it is a good time to plant fruit trees, even if they are deciduous fruit trees. Although the leaves fall off because of the colder nights, the soil will remain warm enough to encourage the growth of new roots. And the new roots will be well established by the time the soil heats up again in May and June.

Trees that are planted in February have to sit in cold soil for nine or 10 weeks while the air temperatures rapidly rise. This is a bad combination and many spring-planted trees won't start very well—or they die with the shock of hot air in June before their new roots have stretched out.

September and October are tree-planting months. Take advantage of this good weather!

September is time to set out the vegetable plants, and the sooner you do it, the better. The soil temperatures are just right.

In the warm soil of the fall there's not the difficulty of getting your plants to put out new roots, so there's no need to "start off" your little plants with a phosphate solution. The soil is warm enough for root growth to occur naturally. However, if you want to make a starter solution (as opposed to spending money on a bottle of the stuff) you can shake up a tablespoon of ammonium phosphate (which you may have left over from your initial soil preparation) in a gallon of water. After you have made the planting hole, you pour in a pint of the solution. Keep shaking the jug to keep the phosphate from settling out.

There's a starter trick that you should follow, however. Give your garden bed a deep irrigation a week before you set out your plants. This applies to flower plants as well as vegetable plants.

The idea behind this trick is to have a good deep reserve of moisture under the fresh plant. Help it develop deep roots. If you plant it in dry soil, and don't use a pint of starter solution, the roots don't have anywhere to go, and your plants get a poor beginning.

You should also use this trick later in the fall when you sow seeds. Give a good prior irrigation to your garden.

Better get your plants in the ground now before the temperatures fall too much.

The suitably warm weather of the next few weeks will start the bud into new growth, and if you are careful about protecting the new growth during any possibly frosty periods in November and December you'll have strong shoots in the spring.

You can bud any kind of citrus onto any kind of citrus. For example, lemons onto oranges, grapefruit onto tangerines, lemons onto grapefruit, tangelos onto sour orange and so on. If you have a large tree, you can bud a number of different citruses onto one tree and have a variety of fruit on that tree. It's especially useful if you have a small yard that won't allow the planting of many trees. Besides, the usual citrus tree provides us with plenty—perhaps too much—of one kind of fruit. Spread the production.

And now for something completely different. Squirrels and packrats.

These animals are also enjoying the cooler weather and are active. If they are doing too much damage to your plants and you don't like them, you'll want to get rid of them.

Please don't scatter poisoned grain around in the expectation that they'll eat it. They won't. But other animals, including domestic pets, might. Don't gas them. You'll never be sure that they were killed. Don't try to drown them out with a garden hose—it's seldom effective so you just waste a lot of water.

Keeping a cat is a good way to minimize gopher, rabbit, squirrel and packrat populations. Cats are natural hunters, but get lazy if you over-feed them.

One way to get rid of packrats is for you to become a prime nuisance. You do this by pulling their nests apart and scattering the pieces all over. They'll bring them back again, but you scatter them again and again.

You can also trap packrats and squirrels. Use peanut butter or a piece of apple as bait. The very large rat traps work, and so do the cage traps. But be careful of other animals—perhaps the fat cat—if you use the open rat traps. Place the trap in a piece of tubing that allows the curious rat in, but suggests to cats and children that it's better to keep out.

Good luck!

Adapted from one of George's weekly columns in the *Tucson Citizen*. This one was dated September 14.

28

DESERT GARDENERS' CALENDAR

Desert Seasons:
Not Just Winter & Summer

A desert gardener needs to know that our growing seasons are much more subtle than two simple seasons—winter and summer. To know this enlarges our gardening opportunities.

Most gardening books, with their charts and colored maps, base their recommendations for planting times on simple temperature changes, from cold to warm. The last-frost date in spring starts the gardening year. And the first frost in the fall signals the end of gardening in "single season" parts of the country. However, in most places in the desert, you can garden throughout the year.

In Chapter 2 you read that there are gardening sub-divisions of the two main seasons. They are all short-duration seasons. At first it's not easy to recognize them.

Each plant has its own season. At any time of the year you can grow many vegetables in a desert garden, provided you know when to take advantage of the appropriate conditions. You can't go by the calendar. Memorial Day, for example, has no gardening significance in the desert. For a safe gardening journey, you must learn new guideposts.

Weather Unreliability:
Time & Place

"Everybody talks about the weather, but nobody does anything about it." Weather is a topic of conversation because it's so unpredictable, changeable and untrustworthy. It's as true in the desert as anywhere else. At first the desert appears to be unrelieved monotony, but it's full of surprises—good and bad.

You can't rely on day-to-day weather, nor can you rely on seasonal changes. Each year is so different from

Winter rains in the desert, usually more widespread and gentle compared to localized summer storms, may turn to snow overnight, even reaching valley floors on rare occasions. Hurry outside before breakfast and you may find enough snow to make a snowball. To determine whether you have to protect your plants from freezing overnight, interpolate what will happen at your place from the local weather forecast.

the last that we lose that convenient yardstick—the "average year." We no longer experience average rainfall, a normal time of planting or the punctuality of the first fall frost. It even snowed in May one year at a 2,500-foot elevation. And that's just one location!

Another example: Tucson's Spring of 1988 gave us a week of scorching temperatures that broke five records in seven days. It went like this:

Date	Actual Temp (F)	Normal Temp (F)
March 20	89	72
March 21	89	73
March 22	84	73
March 23	89	73
March 24	90	73
March 25	93	74
March 26	99	74

And this was a dry period of no rain since March 2, when 0.35 inches fell.

March usually has 0.68 inches of rainfall—after a wet winter of 2-1/2 inches.

It was an unusual spring!

Trends in desert weather seem to be more erratic rainfall, hotter summers, and winter freezes later into the new year. This means that there can be no exactness to the timing of gardening operations. We have to be alert—ready to take advantage of opportunities offered us, and be prepared against a sudden arrival of bad things.

Even garden troubles appear unreliable. This is not too hard to understand when we stop to think that it's rainfall and temperature—directly and indirectly—that influence insect activity, support disease organisms and make weeds grow.

When one writes a book of this kind, the object is to try and help people in several places. That's when an author loses accuracy. A writer cannot be precise for everyone. The desert is a vast area—with its ups and downs. You,

One thing that can be counted on in the desert is intense sun. Netting shades plant from sun, keeps in humidy and, to some extent, keeps out insect pests.

Another thing you can depend on in the desert is frost. Winter vegetables are covered with frost, but they'll survive.

the reader, will have to do some interpretation for yourself.

As you gain experience, write things down as they happen. *Keep a diary.* Much of your gardening will consist of making timing adjustments to meet the vagaries of the weather and climate. When—not if—you are taken by surprise, you must make quick adjustments. But don't let Mother Nature's tricks make you mad. Match your intelligence against her. It's part of the fun.

Perhaps, in years to come, there'll be "precise" mathematical tables to tell us how to garden accurately—and the fun of the whole thing will have been taken away from us. An activity with no mystery to it loses its challenge and that nice feeling of achievement when you are successful.

An Excuse for Duplication

There's no great mathematical accuracy in the following weeks' and months' diary. For instance, you will find a suggestion to do or watch for the same thing in adjacent months. This is not forgetfulness—just the reverse. One year summer rains come in mid-June; in another they won't arrive until late July. You need to be ready for them and the things they bring— whatever date they might arrive.

It's better to mention it for you twice than not at all.

Resources Available to New Desert Gardeners

How do you know when to sow seed, set out plants, prune trees, expect pests, or protect plants from heat or frost? You can use a number of resources, but no single one is sufficient. It's better to use several.

The following paragraphs detail some of the more obvious resources available, with comments on their value.

Local Experience

If you are a recent arrival, experience that made you a successful gardener in another geographic area can easily lead you astray—it usually does. You must learn gardening all over.

You may think the neighbor down the street knows how to garden—and well he might. There are some good desert gardeners in all of our cities and towns. Discover the reasons for his successful transition to the desert. Ask questions. Unfortunately, there are also some pretty stubborn gardeners, especially with landscaping matters. Don't blindly follow a "leader" who is always harping back to what he did in another place.

Join a garden club. Typically members know a great deal and share that information freely. If one of them boasts too much without substance, he is quickly checked by those who do know. You can be an interested spectator to start with. Join in later.

The Cooperative Extension Service, a localized part of the U.S. Department of Agriculture, has offices in almost every county of every state in the nation.

In urban areas there are agents who are trained and knowledgeable in gardening matters. Sometimes you'll find agents in rural areas, too. Their offices often contain a wealth of literature written for the locality. You might even find videotapes that show you how to garden. Agents have back-up resources that include local gardener volunteers and technical people—horticulture specialists—on the university campus.

Local newspapers and radio stations often have regular gardening features, but beware of syndicated columns written by someone living in New York who "puts plants in sunny locations and waters sparingly."

Build on local experience by keeping a gardening diary as you launch out into desert gardening. You might use it later to help with writing a book!!

Climate-Zone Maps

Generalized gardening books that have colored maps to show different climate zones give the impression of being accurate. A map covering a large area of the country groups several places within the same climate. This can be deceptive because colors are based on long-time average air temperatures. Air temperatures can vary greatly from one year to another. Averages balance out extremes, but these extremes are important to us.

For example, you might be surprised to discover that Tucson, at a 2,500-foot elevation, is in the same colored zone as Sacramento—1,000 miles to the north, but at an elevation of only 17 feet. If you were to visit both places on the same day, you would find they are as alike as chalk and cheese. Besides, there's more to gardening than simple temperature.

Such maps suggest there are distinct lines on the ground. Across the line on the map there is a different color where, supposedly, things are different. Can you see the line on the ground and step over it? After you stepped over it, did you feel a climate change?

Further, if the map covers several

To protect from freezing plants are dug up from garden and placed in pots, then stored in sunny spot on patio next to westward-facing masonary wall. Plants are set back out after last freeze.

states, you'll never determine the climate zone for your vegetable garden using one of these maps.

Localized Variations—Microclimates

Suppose you have a gardening friend who lives across town in the same climate zone as indicated by a map. Your friend follows a different timetable because his house is built near a low-lying drainage wash. His garden takes longer to warm up in spring and freezes before yours because cold air from your location flows to the lowest place and pushes up his warm air. He has a shorter growing season than yours.

A northern slope is colder in winter because it gets more cold winds and less sunshine. You can see this on a hill whose northern slope doesn't grow any saguaros or ironwood trees. Half a mile away—around the corner on the southern slope—both kinds of plants grow well.

As a home gardener you have probably discovered that your front yard has a different microclimate than the back. The eastern side of a wall gets morn-

ing sun and afternoon shade—a useful combination during hot desert summers. During winter months the reverse is the case and the warmer western side of a wall is a better place for frost-tender plants.

A garden exposed to strong frequent winds won't produce in the same way as a sheltered garden.

All this is to say that there are many factors that determine when you can safely sow seeds or set out plants in the spring; how long your growing season will be; and when to expect growth to stop in winter.

You must get to know your own little plot of ground at first hand. Colored maps don't help much.

Weather Charts & Time-of-Planting Charts

Air temperatures give us useful, though limited information. With several hundred places being recorded daily and many years of records, there's a mass of data for us to use. However, what comes out of the calculations is an average for any particular place. Most are either to the left or right of it. Remarkably few are aver-

APPROXIMATE AMBIENT TEMPERATURES
FOR BEST GROWTH & QUALITY OF VEGETABLES

Approx. Temperature (F)

Optimum	Min	Max	Vegetable
55—75	45	85	Chicory, chives, garlic, leek, onion, salsify, scolymus, scorzoera, shallot
60—65	40	75	Beet, broad bean, broccoli, Brussels sprouts, cabbage, chard, collard, horseradish, kale, kohlrabi, parsnip, radish, rutabaga, sorrel, spinach, turnip
60—65	45	75	Artichoke, cardoon, carrot, cauliflower, celeriac, celery, Chinese cabbage, endive, Florence fennel, lettuce, mustard, parsley, pea, potato
60—65	50	80	Lima bean, snap bean
60—75	50	95	Sweet corn, Southern pea, New Zealand spinach
65—75	50	90	Chayote, pumpkin, squash
65—75	60	90	Cucumber, muskmelon
70—75	65	80	Sweet pepper, tomato
70—85	65	95	Eggplant, hot pepper, martynia, okra, roselle, sweet potato, watermelon

Chart from *Knott's Handbook for Vegetable Growers* copyright 1980
courtesy John Wiley & Sons, Inc.

age. You are not average. You must adjust from the average on the chart to your garden.

Daily temperature recording lets you immediately compare your garden temperatures with "official" readings at the local airport. This tells you whether you are in a relatively warm or cold part of town. This becomes especially useful in winter when you want to know when to protect your frost-tender plants.

The last-frost date in spring and first-frost date in fall are critical bits of information. The days in between are called *growing seasons*. Because plants don't start growing at just-above freezing or stop just at freezing, agronomists have gone a step further and determined growing days for particular crops. These are based on actual plant behavior.

The Desert Exception

Last-frost dates and first-frost dates in the desert give the impression that growing seasons are longer than other places. Chambers of Commerce are proud to claim more sunny days than anyone else. Unfortunately, the argument doesn't apply to gardening. Right in the middle of summer there's so much heat that most plants are under stress for six weeks or so. Many die.

The apparent long season indicated by charts and colored maps is chopped into three short seasons by this period of intense heat. Although our gardening choices are restricted in one way, they are expanded in another. You can grow additional heat-loving crops of short duration.

Last-Frost/First-Frost Charts

Air temperatures are determined by both time of year and altitude. Everyone knows that winter is early and spring is late in the mountains. Page 173 has a table to guide your planting dates. It is produced by the Extension Service in Arizona where there is a great range in elevation from 200 feet in Yuma to 8,000 feet in Alpine. Elevation and last frost/first frost are the criteria used.

Do you see any surprises?

Watch for Natural Events

New gardeners will find these guardedly useful—simply because they vary from year to year in accordance with the vagaries of weather changes. Only the swallows of Capistrano pay attention to the calendar. These are some natural events you might notice.

Birds start singing. They respond to warmth and changes in day length.

Mesquite trees flower as the air warms. Traditionally, there's no freezing after mesquite trees flower.

Spring starts when harvester ants come out of the ground and go foraging. They are responding to warming soil.

Cicadas "sing" just before summer rains start. They are stimulated by warming soil temperatures and humidity.

As tree leaves turn color in the fall because of falling temperatures, plant growth slows. Leaves drop at the first freeze.

There are other signs—your oldest local inhabitant will know them—but they will need checking, because Mother Nature is a fickle lady. You can't depend on her at all.

Become a more scientific gardener. Buy a maximum/minimum thermome-

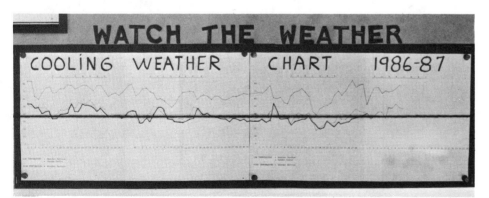

Daily lows for November through February are represented by bottom curves: dark one for local temperatures, light one from Weather Service. Freezing (32F) is indicated by horizontal line. If temperatures fall gradually during November and December, most plants will be hardened enough to survive below-freezing nights.

Use inexpensive soil thermometer to determine whether soil is warm enough to plant out.

Take advantage of warmth near soil surface by planting out tomato plant horizontally in shallow trench.

ter to monitor air temperatures and a soil thermometer to discover changes taking place in the soil. Keep records and compare your findings with the wider experience of the Weather Bureau people at the airport.

Use Local Weather Reports

During winter months you'll find radio and TV weather reports useful. The satellite system of weather watching is becoming more accurate. Notice how announcers get excited about coming freezes.

Temperature readings at your garden site will allow you to feel safe if it is several degrees warmer than the airport. You might become anxious if your place is a few degrees cooler by comparison.

Know Your Vegetables' Temperature Needs

The table on page 172 shows soil temperatures that "make" vegetables grow. Note that each has its *comfort zone,* as well as upper and lower limits. You already know peppers won't grow in winter because it's too cold. Build on this knowledge.

Figures come from *Knott's Handbook for Vegetable Growers.*

To obtain a copy of this book, write John Wiley & Sons, Inc., Distribution Center, 1 Wiley Drive, Somerset, NJ 08850, or call 201/469-4400.

Suggested Planting Dates Based on Freeze Dates

Gardening operations should be decided by the local last-freeze date, either the official average at the nearest weather station, which is often the airport, or the more exact records you have been keeping at your garden site. Official records, though distant, are accurate because of observations over a long period. But your own brief records on the spot are more important to you. If you like interpolating, here's your chance.

Planting Dates Based on Elevation

Page 173 has a table to guide your planting dates. It is produced by the Extension Service in Arizona where there is a great range in elevation from 200 feet in Yuma to 8,000 feet in Alpine. It's not surprising that elevation is the criterion used.

This table says the same thing in a different way because altitude helps to determine the last-frost date as well as the first-frost date in fall. It tries to relate your place up the mountain to air temperatures.

Many Extension offices produce their own tables based either on air temper-

atures or altitude. Ask at your local office for the one that will help you most.

Remember, they are guides and not absolute, rigid dates. If you go to the trouble of checking these two previous charts against one another you'll be frustrated. The dates should be close, but many are not. As with colored maps, planting charts have limitations.

Spring Air Temperatures Can Cause False Starts

Air temperatures are useful in telling us about approaching freezes in the fall, but are unreliable when it comes to the start of the gardening year in spring.

Often in the spring there are brief spells of warm—even hot—days before the soil warms sufficiently for successful sowing or planting. Beginning desert gardeners are often fooled by these into planting their summer vegetables too early. Plants set out because the air is warm simply don't grow if the soil is still cold.

Importance of Soil Temperature

Soil temperature directly affects root activity and seed germination. Plants don't grow in cold soil.

Skin of citrus hardens from intense rays of sun. As fruit tries to swell, it splits.

Soil-Temperature Conditions for Vegetable-Seed Germination

Vegetable	Minimum (F)	Optimum Range (F)	Optimum (F)	Maximum (F)
Asparagus	50	60—85	75	95
Bean	60	60—85	80	95
Bean, lima	60	65—85	85	85
Beet	40	50—85	85	95
Cabbage	40	45—95	85	100
Carrot	40	45—85	80	95
Cauliflower	40	45—85	80	100
Chard, Swiss	40	50—85	85	95
Corn	50	60—95	95	105
Cucumber	60	60—95	95	105
Eggplant	60	75—90	85	95
Lettuce	35	40—80	75	85
Muskmelon	60	75—95	90	100
Okra	60	70—95	95	105
Onion	35	50—95	75	95
Pea	40	40—75	75	85
Pepper	60	65—95	85	95
Pumpkin	60	70—90	95	100
Radish	40	45—90	85	95
Spinach	35	45—75	70	85
Squash	60	70—95	95	100
Tomato	50	60—85	85	95
Turnip	40	60–105	85	105
Watermelon	60	70—95	95	105

Chart from *Knott's Handbook for Vegetable Growers* copyright 1980 courtesy John Wiley & Sons, Inc. Compiled by J. F. Harrington, Department of Vegetable Crops, University of California, Davis.

Take Advantage of Warm Soil in the Fall

Soon after you start recording temperatures, you'll notice air temperatures—either rising or falling—precede soil temperatures by several days. I mention this in regard to false planting starts in the spring.

During fall, soil temperatures stay warmly conducive to root growth and seed germination long after air temperatures have cooled.

Beginning desert gardeners, using their past experience, wouldn't dream of planting deciduous fruit trees in September. But, in the desert, it's an excellent time. Cool air slows top growth and warm soil stimulates new root growth. Trees establish themselves quickly.

A Better Way to Determine Planting Dates

There aren't any colored maps to tell us when soil temperatures are sufficient for each crop in different places. However, it's easy to measure your own soil temperature. Even though

each year is different from the last, you will always be accurate no matter where you are on the mountain or in the valley, and no matter what vegetable you want to plant.

The microclimate of your garden will not change the accuracy of your findings. You'll be accurate because you are on the spot and don't need to make any adjustment from another place's average. You'll be on time with your plantings because the soil tells you when it's ready.

Every home gardener can accurately tell the best time to sow seed or set out plants. All you need is a soil thermometer, and it doesn't cost much. As soon as the soil is the right temperature don't delay planting or sowing.

Seasons are short and you don't have time to waste.

Above are some soil temperatures taken from *Knott's Handbook for Vegetable Growers,* to tell you when it's best to sow seeds or set out plants of different crops.

Plant or sow according to soil temperature, ignore the "official" calendar, and your impatient neighbor, and you'll always be successful.

Following on page 174 is a month-by-month Desert Gardeners' Calendar designed to help you get ready, to remind you of things to do and to introduce some possibilities you should know about to help with your desert gardening.

VEGETABLE PLANTING DATES BASED ON ELEVATION

Vegetable	Zone 1 - Elevation 10 - 1000 ft.	Zone 2 - Elevation 1000 - 2000 ft.	Zone 3 - Elevation 2000 - 3000 ft.	Vegetable	Zone 4 - Elevation 3000 - 4500 ft.
Asparagus	Oct. 1 - Feb. 1	Oct. 1 - Mar. 1	Oct. 1 - Mar. 1	Asparagus	Feb. 15 - Apr. 1
Bean, bush	Feb. 1 - Mar. 1	Feb. 1 - Mar. 15	Mar. 1 - Apr. 1	Bean, bush	Apr. 25 - July 15
	Aug. 1 - Sept. 1	July 25- Aug. 15	July 15 - Aug. 15	Bean, pole	Apr. 25 - July 15
Bean, pole	Aug. 1 - Sept. 1	July 15 - Aug. 15	July 15 - Aug. 10	Bean, lima	Apr. 25 - July 15
Bean, lima	Feb. 1 - Mar. 1	Feb. 15 - Mar. 15	Mar. 1- Apr. 1	Bean, edible soy	May 15 - July 1
Bean, edible soy	Mar. 1 - May 1	Mar. 15 - June 1	Apr. 1 - June 1	Beet	Mar. 1 - May 15
Beet	Sept. 15 - Mar. 1	Sept. 1 - Mar. 15	Aug. 25 - Apr. 1	Broccoli	Apr. 15 - July 15
Broccoli	Sept. 1- Jan. 1	Sept. 1 - Dec. 1	July 25 - Oct. 1	Brussels Sprouts	July 1 - Aug. 1
Brussels Sprouts	Sept. 1- Jan. 1	Sept. 1, - Dec. 1	Aug. 15 - Oct. 1	Cabbage (seed)	Feb. 15 - Apr. 15
Cabbage (seed)	Sept. 1 - Nov. 20	Aug. 15 - Dec. 1	Aug. 1 - Dec. 1	Cabbage (plants)	Mar. 15 - May 1
Cabbage (plants)	Oct. 1 - Dec. 1	Sept. 15 - Jan. 1	Sept. 1 - Feb. 1		July 10 - Aug. 20
Cantaloupe	Jan. 15 - Apr. 10	Feb. 15 - Apr. 1	Mar. 15 - June 1	Cantaloupe	May 1 - June 20
Carrot	July 15 - Aug. 15	Sept. 1 - Mar. 1	Aug. 25 - Mar. 15	Carrot	July 15 - Sept. 15
	Sept. 1 - Jan. 1				Mar. 1 - May 10
Cauliflower	*Same as Cabbage*	*Same as Cabbage*	*Same as Cabbage*	Cauliflower	*Same as Cabbage*
Celery	October 15	Aug. 15 - Oct. 15	Aug. 1 - Oct. 15	Celery (plants)	May 15 - June 20
Chard	Sept. 1 - Jan. 1	Sept. 1 -Mar. 1	Aug. 15 - Apr. 1	Chard	July 15 - Sept. 15
Chinese Cabbage	Sept. 15 - Dec. 1	Sept. 1 - Jan. 1	Aug. 15 - Jan. 15		Feb. 15 - Apr. 30
Collard	Sept. 15 - Dec. 1	Sept. 1 - Jan. 1	Sept. 1 - Jan. 15	Chinese Cabbage	July 1 - Sept. 15
Corn, sweet	Feb. 15- Mar. 1	Feb. 15 - Mar. 15	Mar. 15 - Apr. 1	Collard	June 15 - Aug. 1
	July 30 - Aug. 30	July 20 - Aug. 20	July 15 - Aug. 15	Corn, sweet	May 10 - July 15
Corn, Mexican June		June 20 - July 20	July 1 - July 5	Corn, Mexican June	May 10 - July 15
Cucumber	Jan 15 - Apr. 1	Mar. 1 - Apr. 1	Mar. 20 - May 15	Cucumber	May 10 - June 15
		Aug. 15 - Sept. 15	Aug. 1 - Sept. 1	Eggplant (plants)	May 1 - June 15
Eggplant	Jan. 15 - Apr. 1	Feb. 1 - Apr. 1	Apr. 1 - May 15	Endive	Feb. 1 - Apr. 1
Endive	Sept. 1 - Dec. 1	Sept. 1 - Jan. 1	Sept. 1 - Feb. 1	Garlic	Feb. 15 - Apr. 10
Garlic	Sept. 1 - Dec. 1	Sept. 1 - Dec. 1	Sept. 1 - Jan. 1	Horseradish	Feb. - Apr.
Horseradish	*Not adapted*	*Not adapted*	Nov. 1 - Feb. 1	Kale	Feb. 1 - Mar. 20
Kale	Sept. 1 - Dec. 1	Sept. 1 - Dec. 1	Aug. 15 - Feb. 15		Aug. 1 - Sept. 15
Kohlrabi	Sept. 1 - Dec. 1	Sept. 1 - Dec. 1	Sept. 1 - Feb. 1	Kohlrabi	Feb. 15 - Apr. 15
Leek	Sept. 15 - Dec. 15	Sept. 1 - Jan. 1	Sept. 1 - Jan. 15	Leek	Feb. 15 - Apr. 10
Lettuce, head	Sept. 20 - Nov. 20	Sept. 1 - Jan. 1	Sept. 1 - Feb. 15	Lettuce. head	Feb. 15 - Mar. 15
Lettuce, leaf	Sept. 20 - Jan. 1	Sept. 1 - Mar. 1	Aug. 20 - Apr. 1		July 15 - Aug. 15
Muskmelon	Jan. 15 - Apr. 10	Feb. 15 - Apr. 1	Apr. 1 - July 15	Lettuce, leaf	Mar. 1 - Apr. 15
		July 1 - Aug. 1			July 15 - Sept. 1
Mustard	Sept. 15 - Dec. 15	Sept. 1 - Jan. 1	Sept. 1 - Feb. 1	Muskmelon	May 10 - June 15
Okra	Mar. 1- Apr. 15	Mar. 1 - June 1	Apr. 1 - June 15	Mustard	Feb. 15 - July 15
Onion, green bunch	Sept. 15 - Jan. 15	Sept. 1 - Feb. 1	Aug. 15 - Feb. 1	Okra	May 10 - July 1
Onion, dry (seeds)	Nov. 1 - Dec. 15	Oct. 15 - Jan. 1	Oct. 15 - Jan. 1	Onion, green bunch	Feb. 15 - May 1
Onion, dry (sets)	Nov. 15 - Jan. 15	Nov. 1 - Feb. 1	Nov. 1 - Feb. 15	Onion, dry (seeds)	Nov. 1 - Dec. 15
Parsley	Oct. 1 - Jan. 15	Sept. 1 - Jan. 1	Sept. 1 - Jan. 15		Jan. 15 - Mar. 15
Parsnip	*Not adapted*	Sept. 1 - Jan. 1	Sept. 1 - Jan. 15	Onions, dry (sets)	Nov. 15 - Jan. 15
Pea, fall	Sept. 10 - Sept. 20	Aug. 15 - Sept. 15	Aug. 15 - Sept. 15		Feb. 15 - Apr. 15
Pea, spring	Jan. 20 - Feb. 15	Oct. 15 - Dec. 15	Feb. 1 - Mar. 15	Parsley	May 1 - June 15
Pepper (seed)	Nov. - Jan.	Feb. 1 - Mar. 1	Feb. 15 - Mar. 15	Parsnip	Mar. 1 - May 1
Pepper (plants)	Feb. 1 - Mar. 15	Mar. 1 - Apr. 1	Apr. 1 - June 1	Pea, fall	July 20 - Aug. 25
Potato, Irish	Sept. 1 - Feb. 15	Feb. 1 - Mar. 15	Feb. 15 - May 1	Pea, spring	Feb. 1 - Mar. 15
Potato, sweet	Mar. 1 - June 20	Mar. 1 - June 1	May 1 - June 15	Pepper (seed)	Feb. 15 - Mar. 30
Pumpkin	July 15 - Aug. 15	July 1 - Aug. 1	Apr. 1 - July 15	Pepper (plants)	May 10 - June 1
Radish	Sept. 1 - Apr. 1	Sept. 1 - Apr. 15	Aug. 5 - May 1	Potato, Irish	Mar. 20 - Apr. 20
Rhubarb	*Not adapted*	Not adapted	Oct. 1 - Mar. 1		July 25 - Aug. 15
Rutabaga	Sept. 15 - Jan. 15	Sept. 1 - Feb. 1	Aug. 20 - Mar. 1	Potato, sweet	May 10 - 25
Salsify	*Not adapted*	Not adapted	Oct. 1 - Dec. 1	Pumpkin	May 15 - July 1
Spinach	Sept. 15 - Feb. 1	Sept. 1 - Feb. 1	Aug. 20 - Mar. 1	Radish	Mar. 1 - May 15
Squash, summer	Dec. 15 - Apr. 10	Feb. 1 - May 1	Mar. 15 - July 15		July 15 - Sept. 15
Squash, winter	July 15 - Aug. 15	July 1 - 31	July 1 - 31	Rhubarb	Mar. 1 - Apr. 20
Tomato (seed)	Nov. - Jan.	Jan. 1 - Mar. 1	Jan. 10 - Feb. 15	Rutabaga	Mar. 1 - Apr. 1
Tomato (plants)	Jan. 15 - Mar. 15	Feb. 15 - Mar. 15	Mar. 15 - Apr. 15	Salsify	Mar. 15 - June 1
Turnip	Sept. 15 - Feb. 1	Sept. 1 - Feb. 1	Aug. 15 - Mar. 1	Spinach	Feb. 15 - Apr. 15
Watermelon	Jan. 15 - Apr. 1	Feb. 15 - Apr. 1	Mar. 15 - June 1		July 15 - Aug. 15
				Squash, summer	May 10 - July 15
				Squash, winter	May 10 - July 1
				Tomato (seed)	Mar. 1 - Apr. 1

From Arizona Extension Garden Guide: *Ten Steps to a Successful Vegetable Garden*

by Norman F. Oebker, Extension Vegetable Specialist

January
WEEK 1

Keep fruit trees small so you can easily put a bird net over them as fruit begins to ripen. Congested growth on right side has yet to be removed. Pruning on left opened up branches to let in air and sunshine.

Busy January!

The gardening pace suddenly speeds up after the Christmas holidays. Everything has to be done at once. Seed catalogs begin to arrive in the mail and we have to study them if we are serious about our gardening. Soil mixes have to be prepared. Containers must be saved and hidden to prevent someone throwing them away as garbage. Ears have to be tuned to the radio and TV for frost warnings. Covering materials have to be handy. Tree holes have to be dug. Wildflowers sown as seed in September will need watering to keep them growing if the rains don't materialize.

Winter Pruning

Above all, the important task of fruit-tree pruning cannot be avoided. If we put it off too long, the first sustained warm spell will force out new growth. Then it's too late for pruning.

This satisfying gardening operation—more than any other—brings out the farmer in the city man. There's a great enthusiasm for pruning, which may ac-

count for it often being done poorly. The work of cutting the branches is rewarding—as is the heap of unwanted branches when the job is finished. Go back and reread the pruning chapter.

The tree will bear abundant fruit as a result of our attention. Perhaps, subconsciously, there's a remnant of tree worship in our actions during mid-winter. If we prune correctly, we will get better production. This annual ritual goes beyond fruit production. We are guiding the tree's future growth and keeping it healthy.

Remember, there are two basic kinds of pruning. One is to improve the appearance of ornamental trees and shrubs. The other is to develop a fruit crop and to keep the tree productive for many years to come. Although the purposes are quite different, the plants' responses to the actual cutting are always the same. A cut makes for new growth.

Don't mix up corrective or shaping pruning with production pruning. Too many people have pruned their mulberry trees as if they were peaches and

have spoiled them. Don't join that misguided crowd.

Each January seems to be a little different from the last. A warm winter means our trees don't go dormant. The leaves hang on the branches because they are full of sap. You may have heard old gardeners talking of "the sap being down." What they mean is the tree has gone completely dormant. There is no action.

Even with the leaves off the tree, there might still be a little sap flow. Check this before you start any pruning by snipping off a twig or two. See whether any sap flows out. It's easily seen as the milky sap of mulberry trees and the clear copious juice of the grape. You need to look closer on the ends of apricot and peach twigs. There will always be a little moisture, but satisfy yourself that there is no great sap flow when you snip the branches.

You'll need a pole saw when pruning shade trees, but fruit trees are kept small and you should be able to do all the work standing on the ground. Stretch a little perhaps, but your long-handled loppers will get you to the upper branches. You may want to buy a pair of hand shears, too, but many gardeners find loppers are sufficient. But be sure to select the parrot-beak type rather than the anvil kind that squeezes the branch and often leaves

Here's one use for grape vines. Cut long canes to make wreaths for decorations. The canes will dry out and you can keep them to make decorations anytime.

Even a good clean saw cut opens up insides of tree to bacteria and fungi. Note there is no dripping of sap because tree is truly dormant.

Cut must be protected by spray of pruning paint to prevent bacteria and fungi from entering. Spray paint soaks into branch tissue, providing better protection than dab of solid tar.

Horrible example of infection could have easily been prevented by a spray of pruning paint. Last year's cut became contaminated when it gave entry to bacteria that worked their way backwards even though pruning cut caused forward growth. Disease will continue to spread.

a bruise. The narrow blades will allow you to cut off almost flush with the limb or trunk—you shouldn't leave stubs on a tree. Make sure the blades are sharp and the holding nut is tight, otherwise you will leave ragged cuts—another sign of poor pruning.

A small, curved, pruning saw is good to have when you find a thick, undesirable limb. Its teeth are set in reverse so you cut wood on the *pull* stroke, not the *push* stroke as with a carpenter's saw. Make sure the saw is sharp. To complete your set of tools you need a spray can of pruning paint. There's some academic controversy as to whether black paint is good for pruned trees in the sunny desert, but years of practical experience show it is safe to use.

Go easy when pruning shade trees. Try to thin out rather than cut back. But cut away to your heart's content on fruit trees, roses, and especially grapes. You can't do a lot of harm. The worst you can do is reduce the crop by cutting off too much fruiting wood. You won't kill the tree. Remember that a cut makes for more growth.

Open up the center. Cut back the long branches. Cut the top back to keep the fruit down low. Have a good time. Spray the cut ends before you go to lunch, otherwise you'll forget. It

takes only a day for a thick branch end to crack in the dry desert air. Cut close. A lot of stubs left on a pruned tree will result in a lot of extra and congested growth. Besides, stubs crack readily and die back.

Careless Pruning

If you don't protect the cut ends with a spray of pruning paint, the bark can peel back. Bacteria or fungus spores get under the bark and begin to travel down the conducting vessels that carry

the sugary sap. Spores are blowing in the wind and are everywhere around us. An infected branch soon shows more dead bark that easily peels to reveal a black sooty material—more spores for more infections. A tree with sooty canker may die in 3 or 4 years. If you have any signs of this disease, cut it out while doing your pruning.

Another tree disease encouraged by

Short stubs developed thicket of shoots. Remember: Each cut makes for more growth. Instead of using loppers, gardener could have got closer to limb or trunk with pruning saw.

careless pruning is *slime flux*. This time it's a bacteria that travels down the conducting vessels, which eventually become gummed up. Pressure forms inside the branch and brown, infected, sap is forced out. As it runs out of this weak spot on the branch, it corrodes and kills the bark.

It's so easy to avoid these diseases. Spray pruning paint on each cut at the ends of the branches as you prune.

Grape-vine ends "bleed" profusely, even in cooler winters. Pruning paint washes off and you can count the drips as you can with a leaking faucet. Try not to worry, though it's hard not to, when you see this happen. In a day or two the dripping stops—unless it has been raining or you have been irrigating unwisely. The vine is none the worse for this experience.

A properly pruned grape vine looks as if it has been worked over by a wild teenager. There's hardly anything left and it seems to have been ruined. Don't worry. Remember, pruning encourages growth. Your grape vine will come back.

Irrigating & Fertilizing

A part of pruning is irrigating and fertilizing. The three make a team for proper growth. Water out as far as the spread of the branches—before you

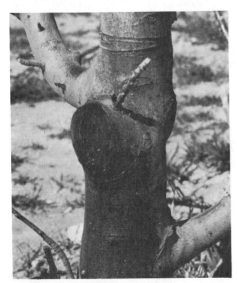

Unprotected large cut soon became contaminated. Infection spread under bark right down to ground and halfway round trunk.

prune. Halfway through the watering, spread 2 pounds of ammonium sulphate for each 100 square feet and continue watering until you can poke your soil probe 3 feet into the soil.

Feel good about what you have just done. Your trees are ready for another year. Now get on with the other January tasks.

More About Fertilizers

Don't be alarmed about the red color appearing in the leaves of many plants, from eucalyptus to cabbages—including weeds. Cold temperatures bring the color on and it will disappear when it warms up again. The red color is sort of related to low phosphorus in the soil and the inability of plants to get what little is there.

It could be an indication that you should add ammonium phosphate when you next dig your garden or landscaped area in preparation for planting a tree.

Remember: Phosphate fertilizer doesn't move through the soil very well, so it's normally a waste to throw it on top of the ground and water it in. You must dig it in! Remember, also, that it's a waste to throw fertilizer at plants that are dormant because of the cold weather.

On the other hand, growing plants—including ryegrass lawns and winter vegetables such as lettuce—will respond to an application of the right fertilizer. Use ammonium nitrate, which is soluble in cold soil, instead of the usual ammonium sulphate, which is not used by plants—even growing plants—when the soil is cold.

In addition to the main tasks of digging holes for planting, pruning fruit and shade trees, sowing seeds, and getting ready for digging the soil, there are lots of little things to attend to.

Asparagus

For example, the asparagus bed needs attention. Some plants may have stayed green through the winter, but most of them will have died back and turned brown and brittle. Now you must clean up the bed and cut down all the plants. Put them in the compost pile, together with the weeds you pull out. Try to pull out weeds by the roots. Don't cut or snap them off or they will grow again and you will be no further ahead.

Spread compost or steer manure a couple of inches thick all over the asparagus bed and lightly dig it in with a fork—without damaging any asparagus roots. Give the bed a good deep irrigation that will, along with the warming temperatures, start the plants growing again. Some gardeners like to apply a pound of ammonium sulphate, or ammonium nitrate if the weather is cold, halfway through the irrigation. This acts as a booster to the fertilizer value of the manure.

Asparagus shoots will soon start coming through the soil and you can begin to harvest the first crop of the year. Sharpen your snakes-tongue weeder and poke it down beside the growing shoot. Cut the shoot off cleanly before it grows too long and opens up its leaf buds.

Harvest as frequently as the shoots appear but don't take anything thinner than a quarter inch. You'll exhaust the plant if you do, and in any case you need to let some shoots develop into leaf for the summer.

Starting an Asparagus Bed

If you want to start a new asparagus bed, be prepared for some work. Choose a place that will get full sun. Dig a trench 18-inches deep, placing the upper soil on one side and the poorer deeper soil on the other. Put an inch or two of steer manure or compost at the bottom of the trench and work it in. First use the better soil and

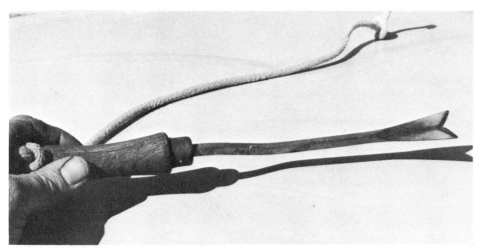

Snake's-tongue weeder becomes an asparagus-harvesting tool. Sharpen it to ensure clean cut of asparagus shoot under soil surface.

Thick-skinned grapefruit tell gardener too much nitrogenous fertilizer was used last year. Fruit at right is beginning to show extra thickness at top to make a *sheep's nose.*

Bring top of a tree down by removing tallest branch where it starts from limb lower down. In this way you preserve the shape of an ornamental tree by avoiding development of unsightly stubs. If stubs don't die back, they produce even denser growth than the original branch.

put it in the trench with a shovelful of manure to each four shovelfuls of soil. Firm down the soil as you go. Now return the poorer soil, mixing manure with it, too. Don't fill the trench. Leave about 6 inches, which you are going to fill in later.

Get asparagus roots from a friend or from the nursery. Plant them in the trench about a foot apart. Bury them with a light covering of soil taken from the side of the trench. Don't worry about it being poor soil, the shoots will grow up through it; the roots will grow downwards into the better soil.

As the green shoots grow, continue to add soil and maintain a light cover over the growth. It may take three or four weeks to fill the trench.

Water well and wait. Wait for a year before you think of harvesting anything. Let the plants gather strength.

During the summer, keep the asparagus well-watered with occasional applications of a pound of ammonium sulphate for every 100 square feet of bed. Asparagus is a good grower if you help it along. And it looks attractive too. Many gardeners grow a few plants among their flowers to act as ornamental background material.

Thick-Skinned Grapefruit

Do your grapefruit have thick skins? If so, overfertilizing last year is the cause.

Fruit quality is not affected. The grapefruit are still juicy and tasty, even though we are at the beginning of the harvesting period. If you save fruit on the tree until April or even May, you'll be more pleased—and perhaps surprised—at the superior taste.

If your fruit is thick-skinned, especially near the stem end, you can bring up a little trivia at the dinner table and ask your guests if they have any *sheepnosed* fruit this year. This is what the "trade" calls such fruit and they are considered undesirable. If your friends do have this condition, advise them to forego fertilizing completely this year. The next harvest will be quite normal.

Pruning

Remember, shade trees should not be cut back drastically. Thinning out congested branches may be in order, but it's better to let them grow as naturally as possible. Any ornamental tree or shrub that is getting too tall may be "brought down" by cutting the tallest branch where it originates from the plant—perhaps quite low down. Cut it cleanly and treat the cut with a spray of pruning paint.

The shoot that was the next lowest is now the tallest, but not such a nuisance or a threat. You have maintained the natural shape of the plant.

Carry this philosophy to tall eucalyptus trees. That's how you shorten a tall tree. The person who saws everything off at the same height is really asking for trouble. He gets a bushy new growth from each saw cut. The natural form is more appealing.

Drying Winds

A couple of days with strong winds quickly dry out a garden and its plants, especially those recently set out. Try to anticipate winds by listening to weather reports. Then give plants an extra watering so they don't suffer. Watch plants in containers too—they dry out a little quicker.

Tree Dormancy

A wet winter is usually cool, and that's all right. A sunny winter is a warm one and fruit trees don't get the dormancy they need.

If a tree does not get enough winter chill—and therefore a rest—it easily tires out and produces small leaves

Deciduous fruit trees require a certain amount of continuous chilling, but snow covering is too cold to be of much help. In any case, snow doesn't last very long in the desert.

and a light crop of fruit.

We can't change the weather, but we can hold back on irrigations during a warm, dry winter. This slows the tree's urge to break out into growth. Eventually, Mother Nature will have her way and the tree will leaf out even if we don't water it. But we can delay the event considerably.

Don't be in a hurry to irrigate fruit trees—let them rest. However, once they start to leaf out, you have to go with the growth and irrigate—even if happens much earlier than usual.

Before this happens, you should have completed pruning deciduous fruit trees. Don't go by the calendar—go by the trees' condition. Watch the weather.

Cold Soil Is Hard on Plants!

Cold, wet soil is hard on plants. Don't leave your automatic irrigation system to run on a summer schedule during cold weather. It the soil stays too wet, your plants will be under stress. Pansies, petunias and geraniums can be attacked by *Rhizoctonia* organisms—and winter lawns by *Pythium* fungus. Besides, you'll discover that a wet lawn can't be mowed easily.

Don't prune dwarf fruit trees. This peach tree is enjoying cold weather. But, because it is surrounded by concrete that is quickly warmed under winter sun, it might start growing prematurely. Delay this growth by holding back on irrigation until the last moment when the buds swell.

Get your planting holes ready. Enjoy the cool weather and work up an appetite.

The bare-root season is one of January's main events. It's not a long season so be prepared for it by having your planting holes dug and ready to receive the trees you buy.

All deciduous fruit trees are grown in cooler parts of the country and are shipped in. Some years, the weather at the growing nurseries is so severe the trees cannot be dug until the soil thaws—for us, time is running out. You also have to make up your mind what sort of tree to plant.

Selecting Fruit Trees

Many of our deciduous fruit trees are self-pollinating, so only one is needed for a harvest. If you have room for several trees, you can choose different kinds. Consider apple, apricot, fig, peach, plum or pomegranate. Another way is to concentrate on your favorite fruit and plant an early variety, a mid-season and a late kind. Spread the harvest. Plant only what you like to eat.

Don't overdo it. Trees cost money and so does the water to keep them growing. Your labor is important, too.

To help you choose a good tree at

Dwarf fruit tree is small because buds are "telescoped" together on twig. Your measure of pruning is not length of growth, but number of buds.

Twelve inches of twig on standard peach (long cutting) has equivalent of 20 buds on dwarf peach (smaller cutting). You can easily remove too much growth from dwarf trees, so prune very little—if at all.

Crown gall is caused by a soil bacteria that invades trunk just below soil level. Tree may carry disease for several years before you attribute its decline to this infection. There is no cure. Soil remains contaminated after you remove sick tree.

the nursery, study the Garden Guides prepared by the Cooperative Extension Service.

It's better not to order from far-away mail-order places. You can't see what you are buying and their trees may not be suitable for the desert. Our winters are unusually mild but deciduous fruit trees need a long period of cold. Our summers are dry, hot and sunny. Varieties with a low winter-chill requirement are a must.

An early ripening variety will avoid the damaging green fruit beetle as well as the heat. If you habitually go away for the summer, there's little point in choosing a variety that fruits during the months you are absent.

Although the idea of dwarf fruit trees is attractive—we all seem to be living in smaller spaces—those varieties have not been fully tested for desert conditions. Many of those which have been tested have proven to be disappointing. You can create a dwarf tree merely by pruning hard. For the time being, that's the way to go if you don't have much room.

Get the most out of your fruit trees—make them a part of your landscape. A tree, such as an apricot, with a good flower display should be planted where you will see it. Don't hide it in a distant corner. Many trees can be

espaliered against a wall to save on space, though this operation calls for more work and some skill. If you are planting for shade, use a fruit tree and let it grow tall enough for you to sit under. Because of its height, you will lose most of the fruit to the birds and the beetles.

Allow your trees plenty of room to grow if you have the space. A tree looks small when you buy it but give it at least 10 feet distance from a wall, a pathway or another tree. Twenty feet would be better, if you have the room. It's nice to be able to walk around your tree when you prune and pick fruit. Also look upwards. There may be overhead wires and these will require your tree to be cut back later in an unproductive manner.

Remember, the planting hole is 5 feet by 5 feet and 5 feet deep. It should be dug, caliche got through and removed, treated with manure, ammonium phosphate and sulphur then allowed to settle for at least a week before planting the tree. If you don't attend to this, the hole will settle after you plant the tree and its bud union will be buried. Read Chapter 5 for the full story. It's important.

At the nursery, you may find a choice between bare-root trees and container-grown trees. Both are good,

but you should be aware of the good and bad points of each.

Bare-Root Trees

Bare-root means just what it says. The roots are without soil and are exposed. You can take a good look at them—something you cannot do with a tree in a container. Good gardeners like to look at the roots to make sure they are not twisted or broken, and don't have cankers. Crown gall is a killer although

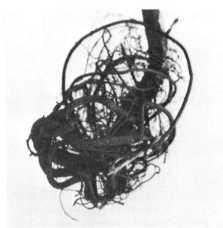

Twisted and knotted roots also remain hidden. Often you buy such roots from a nursery where tree has been kept too long in a small container. Tree may live several years in a slow decline until its unthriftiness causes you to pull it up in despair. Then you discover the problem.

Large-diameter trunk in small container means an old tree—too old for planting out. Look carefully and you'll notice roots coming out of drainage holes at container bottom. Don't buy a tree like this!

it takes a while. It shows as a knobbly, crusty bump on the side of the trunk just below ground level, or on the main root branches. Don't buy crown gall and infect your soil—and lose the tree. Roots should be longer than 18 inches. Don't buy an old tree that has had its roots cut back to short stubs so it can be planted in a 5-gallon container.

Bare-root trees should be less expensive than those in containers. They were shipped without soil and are sitting in the nursery waiting for a buyer. Overhead is low, but spoilage can be high.

Bare-root trees require good care while waiting for that buyer—you. The warmth of the desert air, the sunshine and low humidity combine to dry them out. Their roots should be covered in a bin of damp sawdust and they should be sprayed with water frequently. Trees should be in the shade to prevent the sunshine from stimulating bud break. Never buy a bare-root fruit tree in bloom or new leaf. It looks great, but it has no reserves to fall back on after it has expended its stored energy on this display.

If you buy a bare-root tree, get it home as quickly as you can. A good nurseryman will wrap the roots in

damp sawdust or sacking and tie a plastic bag around them. Don't go shopping, or visiting friends on the way home. The roots must not dry out!

When you get home, take the tree out of its bag and set it in a barrel of water to which you added vitamin B. Let it soak overnight.

Some nurseries side-step the difficulties of maintaining bare-root trees by planting them in containers, usually 5-gallon buckets. Other nurseries have simply decided not to sell bare-root trees.

Container-Grown Trees

Be careful about buying trees in containers. If they have just been put into the container, there's little advantage. In fact, the soil will fall off the roots when you try to plant the tree. Many good roots had to be cut off to get the tree into a 5-gallon container. Ask the nurseryman to split the sides of the can. Someone is going to have to do this anyway, and most nurserymen automatically do it as a courtesy after you have selected your tree. If the tree has grown in the container for some time, you should see fibrous roots that pushed against the insides of the container and are now holding the soil together. Check these small roots. If the container has been

sitting out in the hot sun, the roots may be scalded and look brown and soft instead of tan-colored and firm. Some trees may be in a container too long and become root-bound.

Roots have been known to grow out of a container's drainage holes and penetrate the soil below. When these are broken by pulling up the container, there's a great loss of roots. Those remaining in the container may not be enough for a large tree. Don't buy trees such as this.

In the spring, newly shipped trees often go into containers for fall sales. These are usually good buys because they are a good size and have survived the summer. Fall planting is easier on the tree and is preferred by many gardeners.

If you decide to buy a container-grown tree, think roots. Look at them. Don't buy curled-up roots that have been in the container too long. They can be unravelled at planting, but the tree will never be thrifty. Don't buy a tree with an abnormally thick trunk. It's a sign of old age and old age in a can isn't worth it.

The roots should be fresh-looking, pale brown, or whitish. Dark-brown, soft, roots mean something bad happened—perhaps overheating or overwatering, or fertilizer burn.

With a container-grown tree there isn't the hurry to get it planted. Set the tree aside in a shady place, but don't forget to water it. It can sit for a week without harm.

You should know what to do next if you read about planting, Chapter 15. If you skipped that part, go back and learn how to plant and care for a tree in its first year.

Take warning. It can become too hot for planting trees, especially bare-root trees, in March. Be an early bird and get it all finished during January. The soil will be warm enough to stimulate new root growth, but not hot enough to kill roots. Irrigating will not be so critical. The tree's new shoots will not be so vulnerable to hot drying winds.

Plant now—not later!

January
WEEK 4

If you intend to plant a deciduous fruit tree, don't be late in digging the planting hole. Because the hole needs to be 5-feet square by 5-feet deep, it's good to get started early and take it little by little. Don't overexert yourself by trying to do it all in a weekend. If you want to plant more than one tree, consider having the work done for you by someone with a backhoe. If your garden is surrounded by a wall that prevents machinery getting to the site, find someone with a strong back.

Tree Planting

The planting season will last until the middle of February, so there's plenty of time if you start now. However, before you start, be quite certain where you want the tree to grow. First, look up and make sure there are no overhead wires or cables to get in the way of future growth. Find out where the gas and water pipes and electric lines are laid. You don't want to be cutting into these, especially on a weekend. Keep at least 10 or 12 feet away from other trees, walls, buildings and pathways. Twenty feet would be better so you can walk around your tree. Try and imagine whether your tree will block a view, or the drive-way exit. On the other hand, you may want to use your tree to screen something unsightly.

Most varieties of deciduous fruit trees, even the new Anna apple, are self-pollinating, so you don't need two to ensure a crop. Study Garden Guides published by the Cooperative Extension Service to help you select the best kind of apple, apricot, peach, pear and plum.

Although it's too early to plant citrus trees, it's not too early to start digging holes for them. The weather is cool and you can work with enthusiasm. Backfill and let the soil settle until the end of February or the beginning of March.

Planting Hole

The worse your soil is, the greater the need to dig a large hole. There's false economy in skimping at this stage. It's helpful to remove the rocks as you dig, though you'll find tree roots grow

Better to have a back-filled hole settle like this before you plant tree. Give yourself plenty of time to dig hole. Fill it again with soil amendments and let it settle.

around them just as water drains around them. If you come to a caliche layer, you must dig through it. It may be as hard as concrete, and discouraging, but soften it up by letting a foot of water stand on it overnight. You'll be able to chisel away a few inches thickness the next morning. Keep going in this manner until you have worked your way through it. If you don't, you must expect poor drainage and waterlogged roots in the future. This will cause a decline in tree vigor and, sooner or later, the tree's death.

Enriching Soil

Now, when you've got all the dirt out of the hole, you put it back. Here's your opportunity to improve the soil by adding three materials: organic matter, sulphur and ammonium phosphate. If you dig a full-size hole, you will need 15 bags of steer manure, 30 pounds of sulphur and 8 pounds of ammonium phosphate.

This should be your standard treatment when you plant any fruit tree in the desert. It improves the soil from a textural and nutrient standpoint and helps suppress future attacks from Texas-root-rot fungus.

In case you want to dig smaller holes, say for shrubs, here's the formula for the amounts of materials to mix with the soil as you return it to the hole.

Multiply the dimensions of the hole in feet to get its cubic capacity. Divide this by 5 to get the cubic feet of organic matter. You can use peat moss, compost, or animal manures. Divide the cubic capacity by 4 to get the pounds of sulphur to add in, and by 16 to get the pounds of ammonium phosphate.

Mix these materials with the dirt you took out of the hole; don't make layers. As you backfill, stomp down the soil and water well to encourage it to settle. Plant the tree only after the soil has settled—it may take a couple of weeks. There's nothing so irritating as discovering after planting that the soil is sinking, taking the tree with it.

Setting Tree in Place

Before planting, take a look at the roots of the tree you have bought. It should have as much roots as possible to give the tree a good start. Don't buy a tree that has had its roots cut back severely so it will go into a 5-gallon container. If the ends are torn and jagged, prune them cleanly and dust with powdered sulphur to disinfect them. To plant the tree, dig enough soil out of the newly filled hole to accommodate the roots. As you plant, spread the roots in all directions. Plant a bit on the high side, anticipating a slight settling later. You should make sure the bud union is well above soil level. Work in damp, or even wet soil.

Trimming the Tree
(Not for Citrus)
The bud union is where the tree received its top growth in the nursery. The root is chosen for its vigor and disease resistance, not for its fruit quality. Suckers growing below the bud union should be removed because they are often of poor quality and take the strength from the upper part of the tree. You can see the bud union quite easily. There's a bend in the trunk and the two parts are often of a different color and bark texture.

The top of the tree should be pruned to leave three or four main branches. At the moment, these look like little straws but they will fatten up to produce the main framework limbs. Cut them to leave 10 or 12 inches and try to space them evenly around the tree—not all on one side. Remove all the remaining wispy little twigs. For the moment, forget all about fruit production. It will come in three or four years.

Aftercare
After planting, the soil should be kept moist by weekly irrigations. To prevent the water from running off the surface, it's helpful to make a bank around the tree, about 3 feet from the trunk. Scrape the dirt for the bank toward the watering basin from outside or use surplus soil from the planting hole. Avoid digging a well for the tree to get buried in. You don't want the bud union to be covered with dirt and weeds as you cultivate in the weeks to come.

Grey Aphids—Winter Visitors
Inspect your broccoli, cabbage and cauliflower plants carefully. There may be grey aphids lurking in their centers.

The first indications of something wrong are pale spots on the leaves. On the undersides of these spots you'll find a little cluster of grey, ash-colored aphids. Look tomorrow and the cluster will be twice as large. In a week, the plant will be severely stunted.

Aphids suck the juices out of the plant. In the early stages of attack you can rub the aphids out, using finger and thumb. In the last stages the clusters take over the whole plant and it's not worth saving. For in-between stages spray with soapy water and the aphids should fall off. If soapy water doesn't work, go to something stronger such as diazinon or Malathion. But don't eat your vegetables until a week has passed after such a spraying. Read the instruction label on the bottle before you buy any material to be sure it's what you need. The best control for such pests is to be observant and remove them before they do any serious damage.

Gray aphids go for tender growing shoots of winter vegetables. They don't bother to lay eggs, but give birth to live young. For this reason they multiply quickly. As soon as you see the first one, rub it out.

Winter Weeds
In the same manner, get rid of winter weeds before they become a nuisance. Every flower produces another 7 years' plague of seeds. Black Mustard and Wild Barley are currently growing strongly. The first is beginning to flower; the second is still a refreshing green, but don't be fooled. When Wild Barley turns dry and brittle, its seeds get into your socks and into your dog's eyes and ears.

It's easy to pull up the young plants, whose roots are shallow during their youth. This is especially true after winter rains that stimulated their growth in the first place, have softened the soil. While you are at it, pull up any other weeds such as Mallow, Shepherd's Purse and Sowthistle.

If you try to pull out these deep-rooted weeds from dry soil, they often break off, leaving their roots to grow again. Vigorous hoeing is also recommended, but if you are lazy or too busy, you have to resort to chemical weedkillers to get rid of them.

Fertilizing
Remember, ammonium sulphate is our general-purpose fertilizer for growing plants. We use ammonium phosphate when we dig the soil in preparation for planting. During winter, when the soil is cold, a more effective fertilizer is ammonium nitrate because it is soluble in cold water carried down by irrigations to the roots of plants. If they are cool-season growers, they readily absorb it. Leafy vegetables, such as cabbage, lettuce and spinach, ryegrass lawns and strawberries, benefit from light applications at this time of year.

Sprinkle half a pound of ammonium nitrate over a 100 square feet of moist soil and water it in. Water the plants' foliage to wash any chemical off the leaves. It will corrode them if you leave it on.

You get a very quick response from this fertilizer, even in cold weather.

January
WEEK 5

Mass, or mess, of last year's grape growth....

...can be turned into a tidy beginning for next season by pruning out 80 percent of the canes and arranging them to give each plenty of space.

A lot of wild growth was removed—just to let you see what you can save for next year. There's more work ahead.

Arms have been cut back, otherwise plant would grow into next one and crowd it. Each arm has four or five short spurs instead of 17 that grew last year.

Pruning Grapes

Grape planting, pruning and fertilizing can be done in January or February. Study a list of suitable varieties, like the one on page 148, before you plant more vines. Buy plants at nurseries or make your own from your neighbor's best plants or your own prunings. Grapes can keep you busy.

Grape pruning is special. For one thing it must be done, otherwise the plant runs away from you and becomes a nuisance. Grapes are vigorous plants and for that reason are particularly useful for summer shade. They leaf out in the spring as the weather warms. In the fall they shed their leaves and allow the winter sunshine to warm our outdoor areas. Grapes are a natural, automatically controlled, shade machine.

Before you start pruning, gather some facts. Read, ask questions, attend demonstrations, watch videotapes. Best of all, help a knowledgeable friend with his pruning. Ask questions and keep him talking. The first time is confusing—but it makes more sense as you gain practice.

You need to cut a lot—up to 80 percent of last year's growth, leaving about 40 buds to each plant. It's a lot of fun getting rid of that exuberant growth and becoming master of the situation again. It's as if you have asserted yourself and have taught that plant a lesson. Nevertheless, it's no good cutting away for the sheer delight of it. You should know what you are doing.

You cannot kill a grapevine by even the most rigorous pruning, but you can easily set back its production a whole year. The boss could be very critical next summer when the neighbors have tons of fruit and your family has none.

Grape vines are pruned to either a spur system or a cane system. Most grape varieties are pruned to a spur system. Your pruned vine appears to have a row of dog teeth to it—short stubs, each with only two buds. Ten spurs on each of the two arms of the vine give you 40 buds. Try to keep them evenly spaced and on top of the arms. There shouldn't be any spurs starting below and hooking upwards.

If you have a Thompson's Seedless or a Black Monukka variety, you must prune to a cane system. You want two canes on either side of the plant. Each cane will have about ten buds on it. This also totals 40 buds. The first five or six buds on each cane of these varieties are mere leaf buds. There are no fruit buds until farther out. If you prune either of these two varieties to a spur system, you unavoidably cut off all the fruit-producing buds. Your harvest will be small, even though the plant grows vigorously.

If you have an old vine, you must cut one or two canes back to a spur in addition to the four canes. These are renewal spurs that give you fresh canes for next year.

Get on with the job of pruning before winter rains and a warm spell start the sap flowing. This will be shown by swelling buds. If you are caught unaware and the plant begins its spring growth, you must go ahead and prune quickly. The copious flow of sap at the cut ends is sure to alarm you, but don't worry. Dripping will stop in a day or two and the plant will be little the worse for it. Make sure your loppers are sharp, and use a spray can of pruning paint.

Pick up all the prunings and sweep up last year's leaves and throw them away. You don't want powdery mildew to infect the new growth. This fungus survives winters on the canes and is easily recognized by brown patches on 1-year wood. It also rests among the leaf litter. Be clean and tidy.

Just to be sure, it's advisable to spray the young shoots as they emerge and until they are 6-inches long. Spray them with wettable sulphur once a week. Five or six sprayings might be carried out until the temperature rises to above 90F. Sulphur becomes corrosive at high temperatures.

Making Cuttings

If you are going to make cuttings from the prunings, select those that are free of mildew. Use 1-year-old wood that is tan-colored and about as thick as a little finger. It should have three or four

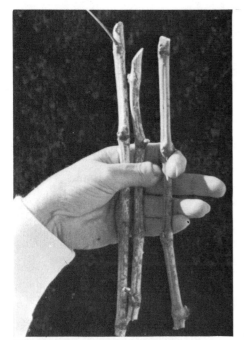

Nice grape cuttings of correct thickness and length. Note top cut is slanted and near a bud. Bottom cut is also close to a bud, but is blunt (square). If you drop cuttings, it's easy to tell which end is which.

Bundle of 10 cuttings can be stored in damp sand or wrapped in damp newspaper and put into plastic bag for a friend. If stored on their side, they won't begin to sprout as quickly as if they had been set upright. Some gardeners store them upside down in damp sand to delay sprouting even more.

buds on it and be about 9 inches long. Make the bottom cut straight across and close to the bud. Make the top cut at a slant. Then, if you drop the bundle, you will know which end is up.

Before the bottom end dries out, dip it in RooTone® dust, then shake off the excess. Nurseries sell this material in small packages. It doesn't keep forever and it's best used fresh.

One-gallon cans are suitable for growing grape cuttings, one, two or three cuttings to a can. Fill the can with a sandy soil mix made up of equal parts of sand, compost, perlite and vermiculite. Don't use manure or fertilizers.

Poke the cutting a third of the way down. Set the can in a sunny place and keep the soil moist. Next spring, the young plant can be set out in its permanent place. It will have exactly the same characteristics as the parent you pruned, so chose a good parent. Don't expect any fruit for three more years.

Irish & Sweet Potatoes

Adventurous gardeners like to try growing potatoes, both the Irish kind and sweet potatoes. Both can be grown in the southern desert, but there are limitations. If you are interested, now is the time to start.

Sweet potatoes are warm-weather plants. You may find rooted cuttings in the nurseries and even in seed catalogs at planting time, which is May. And then you may not. The best kinds for the desert seem to be Jewel, Centennial and Puerto Rico.

You'd be wise to start your own because sweet potatoes don't produce seeds.

Go to the supermarket and buy a sweet potato or a yam—really an orange-fleshed sweet potato—and set it upright in a glass of water with about half of the potato submerged. Change the water to keep it fresh and let the sunshine warm it up. Soon, little green or reddish shoots will appear and then these will develop roots that grow in

the water. Between now and April you will have a fine houseplant with shoots growing all over the windowsill. In April, separate these rooted shoots into 12-inch lengths and transfer them to small pots of soil where they stay a week or two until planted into the garden. Add in a little houseplant food when you water these plants so they gather strength.

Sweet potatoes are harvested late in the fall after the first frost kills the vines. Try and save some of the runners for another winter indoor plant—and next year's planting material.

Irish potatoes don't produce seeds, either. Go again to the supermarket and buy potatoes, some of which you will cut into egg-sized pieces. Dust the cut ends with sulphur to prevent rots from starting and keep these "seeds" in damp sawdust. After a while, the "eyes" will send out sturdy green shoots which are quite different from the long strings you find in an old bag of potatoes under the kitchen sink.

Sometimes nurseries stock "seed" potatoes in early January. The more suitable varieties for desert gardening seem to be Centennial, Red Pontiac, Norgold Russet, Kennebec and Red La-Soda. Don't try White Rose or Russet Burbank—they don't do well.

After about six weeks, the shoots will be firm rosettes of green leaves. It's time to plant them.

The same day you bought the potatoes, you dug a trench about 18 inches deep, in the garden. You put organic matter at the bottom of it and mixed it into the deeper soil, together with a little ammonium phosphate. You half-filled this trench in readiness for planting the sprouted potatoes and let it sit for a while.

Place the Irish potato sets with their rosette of green leaves about a foot apart in the bottom of the trench and lightly cover with soil; irrigate. As the green shoots grow longer, cover them with soil little by little until the trench is filled. It might take six or seven weeks.

Even after this stage, keep mounding up the stem with soil. Potatoes are not roots at all, but swellings on the sides

February
WEEK 1

Three-foot length of *rebar*—reinforcing bar used in construction—makes a good soil probe. It's one of the most useful tools a desert gardener can have. Because it won't go through dry soil, you can easily tell how effectively—deeply—you are watering.

Sweet-potato cuttings can be kept in a jar of water in a sunny windowsill and provide you with a house decoration until the weather warms up.

Next step is to get them into a pot of soil and harden them off before planting them outside in the garden. Cuttings rooted in water seem to be fragile and suffer when they are planted in soil.

of the stem. Mounding up with soil makes more room for the plant to grow these swellings—and you get a bigger crop.

You will not be able to grow full-size, mature, keeping potatoes because the weather gets too hot in July. The plant either gives up and dies or, in a flurry of growth, sends out green shoots directly from the developing potatoes. Remember, green potatoes are poisonous and your gardening efforts are in vain if this happens. Enjoy "new" potatoes before this inevitable disaster occurs.

Here's another way to grow both kinds of potatoes. Find some abandoned car tires—maybe four or five, but be sure they are the same size. Lay one on the ground and mark around it, using a stick. Take the tire away and dig the ground inside your scratch mark. Add in steer manure and ammonium phosphate. Put the tire back over the soil and place a few sprouted potatoes or rooted sweet potatoes on top of the soil. Put sawdust over them, leaving some green shoots to enjoy the sunshine.

As the shoots lengthen, add in a little sawdust from time to time and keep it moist. Add a tablespoon of balanced houseplant food to each gallon of water. Sawdust has no fertilizer value.

As you add more sawdust you will need to add another tire, and another tire and another tire—until you have a tire tower. See photo page 60.

In early spring, the tires' black color will absorb the sun's heat and stimulate early growth. Summer's heat will be too much for Irish potatoes and the tires should be whitewashed. If you are growing sweet potatoes, this is not necessary—sweet potatoes like heat.

If all has gone well, the tower will be full of potatoes at the end of the summer.

Every season is an abnormal one. Each year is different from the last, and this is one of the things that makes gardening interesting to experienced gardeners. Unfortunately, it leads to frustration and irritation for beginners. Just as you think you are getting used to things Mother Nature pulls a fast one.

Fruit-tree growers don't like a mild winter because they want their trees to get as much chilling as possible. A mild winter means deciduous fruit trees don't go into full dormancy. A February heatwave causes such trees to flower and sprout leaves before they have had their proper rest. Once this happens there's nothing you can do—you just have to go along with it and support that premature growth with a deep irrigation and an accompanying fertilization.

Large trees should have wide-spreading roots to support the tree during high winds. To make this happen, the irrigation well must be large enough to get moisture out to where the feeder roots should be. In this case, it's about where the little girl is standing. By providing a large-diameter irrigation well, you'll save water in the long run and you'll have a healthy tree.

Fertilization of Citrus Trees

In the desert, you shouldn't try to garden by the calendar. Of course, everything has to be done at the right time, but the right time often sneaks up on you—especially in the spring. The secret to success lies in being ready for what may come next.

February is one of the months set aside by calendar gardeners to "feed" their citrus trees. The other months, May and August, are are far enough apart to provide a regular supply of nitrogen to sustain steady growth.

The February application is best given before new shoots break out. Ammonium sulphate, spread over the surface of the soil and watered in with a deep irrigation, takes time to be changed into a nitrate form. This is absorbed by the tree's roots, carried up

the trunk, moved through the branches and out to the ends of the twigs where the new growth is starting.

If warm weather arrives without any notice, the new growth has to be sustained by nutrients within the tree's system. This is not always bad. Some gardeners overfertilize anyway, which means their trees have plenty of food reserves to sustain any premature growth.

If growth started up while you weren't looking, the big question is whether to fertilize late or skip it? The answer depends on the tree's appearance. If the leaves are dark green, don't fertilize this time. If the leaves are generally pale, give a fertilizer application, even if you are late. Don't take any notice of a few bright-yellow leaves—these are old ones dying and

ready to drop off. Don't fertilize flowering trees but you must irrigate them because they need water to fill the new growth.

You may be late by the tree's reckoning, though the calendar date for fertilizing hasn't arrived. Here is a reminder on how to fertilize a tree. It's a popular task as spring starts and it should be done properly.

Flood the soil underneath the spread of the branches, keeping the water confined by a little bank or berm scraped up from outside the tree's dripline. When you can push your soil probe 18 inches into the water-softened soil, turn off the faucet. Now scatter ammonium sulphate evenly, at the rate of 2 pounds to every 100 square feet, onto the moist soil. Open up the faucet again and continue watering until your soil probe easily goes down 3 feet.

The latter half of the irrigation carries the fertilizer down to the root zone that was premoistened by the first half. It's always a mistake to apply dry fertilizer to dry soil and then water it in. The result might be that you burn surface roots with too strong a solution of fertilizer.

Temperature Changes

"One swallow does not make a summer," is an old saying, not entirely appropriate to the desert. But it has some meaning for us. A week of warm sunshine in February doesn't mean that spring has arrived. Be prepared for more freezes before your plants can be considered safe.

Fruit-tree flowers are delicate and can be killed by a light freeze. If one is forecast, cover your tree at night with a light blanket or a heavy sheet—not plastic please—to protect it. Leaf shoots are hardier, but you don't want to lose your crop before it starts—at the flower stage.

Later in the month, it may be tomatoes—set out hastily and optimistically during an invitingly warm week—that need protecting. They can be covered with straw or newspaper, or a sheet or an inverted glass jar.

Be prepared for a day or two of gusty winds. They arrive suddenly,

February
WEEK 2

too, and very quickly dry out the soil and plants—especially those recently set out. February's weather is very uncertain. Be on guard!

Pruning After Frost Damage

Don't be in a hurry to prune any trees that were damaged by an earlier frost—even if they look terrible. We may get another one! Wait until spring has really arrived and the tree has put out new shoots, telling you how much of it was killed. Then make cuts just behind the dead parts to encourage side shoots where you want them to fill in an empty space in the tree's framework.

A normal, healthy, citrus tree is seldom pruned. Even a light trimming of the outer foliage takes away next year's crop because flowers are developed at the ends of branches. For this reason, most gardeners let their citrus trees grow to a natural shape—even if the lower branches sweep the ground.

There is an exception. Lemon trees grow vigorously this time of year and you can prevent their shoots from getting too long if you give each one a soft pinch. This makes the tree more compact because side shoots develop behind the pinch.

All you need for a soft pinch is finger and thumb nails. Keep them long and sharp for this springtime operation. Pinch an inch of soft growth off the ends of strong shoots before they get 5- or 6-inches long. New side shoots eventually grow fruit.

Insects

A warm February will bring out insects—good and bad—and you will see both of them on citrus trees. The good ones are, of course, bees that are busy working the flowers. The bad ones are tiny and barely noticeable. They are called *thrips,* and they rasp on the surface of fresh new leaves for the juices there. One or two thrips have no effect, but they seldom come in ones and twos. You'll see a bad infestation as a cloud of flying dust when you pass a tree that is newly leafing out.

You don't see thrips damage until two or three months later. The new leaves—much larger now—are twisted and misshapen. Such leaves still function well. They only *look* horrible.

Although repeated sprays of diazinon or Malathion will take care of them, most gardeners don't worry about controlling thrips because they know the bee population will be harmed by the chemicals. Without bees, you'll get only a minimal citrus crop.

Arbor Day

While on the subject of trees, it's well to know that there are two Arbor Days in Arizona. For the warmer lower desert areas it's the first Friday in February. For the higher elevations where they have a simple summer- and-winter gardening system, it's the first Friday in April. It's a very sensible adjustment from the conventional date back East, which would not be appropriate for the desert. It also tells us that the desert is not a vast, uniform area. Although it is uniformly dry, the varying altitudes affect the timing of gardening operations.

Arbor Day is a reminder to plant a tree and enjoy nature—a sort of Rite of Spring that relieves the monotony of grade-school life. But it's for grown-up gardeners, too!

Though January is the better month for most of the lower desert areas, you can still be successful if you plant a tree in early February. Don't stop at the traditional fir or elm but, instead, consider a pecan or a citrus tree or even a deciduous fruit tree—providing it has not leafed out already.

With water becoming more expensive as the years go by, it makes sense to get the most out of any tree you plant. It should give you shade in summer, allow sunshine in during the winter months, have a nice appearance, flower prettily and produce something you can eat.

Vegetable Bolting

When vegetable plants run amok, they're useless. Spurts of warm weather cause the staid cabbage, lettuce and even carrots and beets, to flower instead of continuing to develop leaves or roots. It's a natural reaction to the end of winter at a time of their development when they are halfway through their life.

These plants are *biennials:* they normally take two years to produce seeds before they die. Gardeners are not interested in their seeds, but in the halfway mark of the plants' development—stored energy of the first year's growth effort is what we choose to eat. In the wild, biennial plants use up this stored energy during their second year when they produce a woody stalk bearing a mass of flowers that turn into seeds.

New garden varieties have been developed to grow rapidly because we impatient people want a quick harvest. If they don't get a winter rest to slow their growth, these varieties do indeed grow quickly.

When there are sudden warm spells in February—a gradual increase in temperature doesn't affect matters—you had better be ready for a disastrous turn of events in the winter garden.

Cabbage plants that are coming along nicely develop a crack in the topmost part of the head, revealing the pale-colored, tightly packed leaves inside. At this point you can and should harvest the crop before things get worse. Salvage the crop before the flower stalk pokes out.

Lettuce does it a little differently and it's not so easy to detect. The leaves look good and they stay fairly tight, but when you get them in the salad bowl they have a bitter taste and are inedible.

Root crops—beet, carrot and turnip—also surprise you. Only rarely can you salvage their harvest because the roots become woody and inedible as soon as the flower stalks begin to show.

There's little you can do about this unfortunate weakness in winter vegetables because you have no control over the weather.

In August when you start your winter planting, it's safe to plant quick-

Clear plastic makes strawberry plants grow well in cooler weather. But weeds grow well, too!

growing varieties. The plants behave themselves and will be harvested in fine shape before Christmas. If you delay planting until October, your plants will simply sit still in the cold ground and react to February's warm weather by flowering prematurely.

The longer you delay planting in the fall, the more important it is to change varieties. Switch from quick-maturing kinds to those that grow more slowly. It's the only time in desert gardening that you give preference to long-season varieties.

February is an in-between month. It's the end of winter, but not quite spring, and certainly not the start of summer.

Deciduous fruit trees, with their new leaves and flowers, are at risk from sudden freezes. But they are the only plants in our gardens that show forward progress. Citrus trees that are bearing ripe fruit give the impression that growth is taking place. But, like grape vines, they are still dormant. Any day they will burst out in new growth.

It's a time when clear plastic becomes useful to a gardener who doesn't want to let things stand still.

Speeding Germination

If you want to intrude on Mother Nature and get things going a little earlier than she allows, try covering the ground with clear plastic. Sunlight passing through the plastic warms up the soil to your advantage.

First, here's a trick to get seeds to germinate quicker which means getting a head start on the warming spring weather. Make shallow trenches in your garden, running north and south, about 2-inches deep and 6-inches wide. Sow seeds in the bottom of the trenches: lettuce, radish, turnip, beet or any of the quicker-growing winter vegetables. Lay the plastic sheet on the ground over the trenches and hold it down with bricks in case the wind wants to blow it away.

Moisture evaporating from the soil condenses on the underside of the plastic and drips back. Germination is rapid and the seedlings stay moist without you having to water them.

This is a good system to practice, providing your garden is free of weed seeds. On the other hand, if your garden is full of summer weed seeds or nutgrass, plastic encourages their early growth, too. You'll have a horrendous

problem under the plastic as they vigorously compete with your vegetables. Removing the plastic to get at the weeds cools the soil again and the advantage of this system is lost.

If you expect summer weeds to be a nuisance, use this system to pregerminate their seeds and get them out of the way before you plant tomatoes, bell peppers, corn, squash and melons.

Wet the ground, dig it and cover your garden area with a sheet of clear plastic. Anchor it at the edges with bricks. The sun will do the rest.

In about three weeks there will be a mass of tender green weeds that can be dug into the soil as green manure together with compost, ammonium phosphate and soil sulphur in the usual manner. If you have nutgrass, then you should not dig it in again because it will merely multiply. Dig the ground with a fork and pick out the nutgrass plants.

If you are in the habit of reading statistics, you know garden sizes across the nation are shrinking. Gone or going are the days when people ploughed their gardens with mules or mechanically tilled them. Nowadays, we dig the soil by hand. Gardeners who live in condominiums and compact apartments or mobile-home parks may not even own a spade. A trowel is all they need if they garden in half-barrels and containers.

Shrinking garden space suggests that we work intensively using close planting and frequent fertilizing to get the most, in the quickest time, from the least space.

Vertical Gardening

Another way to get a lot from a little is to make your garden as vertical as you can. After all, air is free and it goes on for a long way. Make plans now to use it in your gardening program. Dig the soil along your chainlink fence.

Garden peas and snow peas lend themselves to vertical gardening. And cucumbers can be grown on strings up to 6-feet high. In the summer, there are all kinds of melons, winter squash and tomatoes that can be grown upwards instead of outwards.

February
WEEK 3

There's a confusing choice of organic matter at nurseries. If you don't have compost—you must make it yourself—it's perhaps better to stick with steer manure. Steer manure, like compost, is full of beneficial organisms. Don't be frightened by nurserymens' tales of steer manure being high in salts. It used to be so, but not now.

Organic matter, ammonium phosphate and sulphur is being thoroughly dug into soil. Mix well and dig deeply.

Don't delay your spring digging. It's better to have the soil ready ahead of the usual time for planting in case warm weather arrives early. Desert seasons are short enough. If we are late for any of Mother Nature's appointments, we invariably suffer by those seasons being shortened even further.

Although there's a lot of work to attend to this month, you'll have a good feeling after the main task of soil preparation has been completed. Digging the soil in readiness for a summer garden is a milestone at the start of the gardening journey.

Soil Preparation

The standard procedure for soil preparation is explained in Chapter 6. This is just a timely reminder. But let's go over it again—it's so important.

Dig deeply. As you dig, remove any overwintering chrysalids of cabbage-white butterflies, grape-leaf skeletonizers or squash-vine borers. Take out the white grubs, too. Here is your chance to get rid of nutgrass that lies deep in the soil as hard round nuts held to one another by slender threads. It's dormant now, but it's a bear in a summer garden. It's worse than Bermudagrass because it is more resistant to chemical weedkillers. Pull

out both of these summer nuisances as you dig. A fork does a more thorough job than a spade because it combs out long runners, whereas a spade cuts them into smaller pieces, each capable of growing again.

If you have a heavy clay soil, be sure to let it dry out before you dig it—or even walk over it. When you work a wet clay soil, it becomes very plastic and dries out into hard clods that don't crumble readily. You have to bash them into smaller pieces and this takes time. Fortunately, clay soils are not very common in the desert, but if you meet this handicap, treat it carefully.

Thoroughly dig in organic matter using 2 or 3 inches of compost or steer manure with 3 pounds of ammonium phosphate and 5 pounds of soil sulphur to each 100 square feet of garden.

Each time you work the soil, dig down to that undisturbed layer of a redder color and mix in an inch of it. This is a good way to deepen your garden soil gradually. Don't bring up too much poor subsoil at once. You'll dilute the soil's fertility if you do.

Shaping the Planting Bed

Rake the soil over to level it and shape a bed as long as you like, but no wider than 4 feet with a pathway of 2 feet between beds. You want to reach to the

middle of the bed to weed and to harvest without treading on the soil. You should be able to push a wheelbarrow along the pathway without brushing against plants. When laying out a first-time garden, give yourself plenty of elbow room.

Shape the bed with a rim around it about 3-inches high so water will not run off when you flood the bed. Don't build ridges because they dry out too quickly and draw salts to the plants. Ridges dry out nicely in places where the rainfall is heavy. In a dry desert, they dry out too quickly.

The bed with its new organic matter and fertilizer should be allowed to mellow for a week or so before you set out plants or sow seeds. If you are early with this task, so much the better. You could even cover the bed with a sheet of clear plastic to germinate any weed seeds present in the soil.

Scuffle any germinating weed seedlings, but make sure you leave the soil surface absolutely level. Then you will be able to flood the bed evenly to get vegetable seeds to germinate or plants to take hold. High spots in a bed mean dry spots; low places mean too much moisture. An uneven bed means uneven growth in your plants and a waste of water.

Use water to check that surface is level. A good lip around edges enables you to flood bed and give a deep irrigation.

Use rake to push and pull soil around until it is level. Spend time on this job so there will be no high spots that dry out quickly or low places where moisture stays too long.

Compost

All this soil preparation will have used up your old compost, but the new pile calls for your attention. Turn the pile of decaying leaves from last fall's crop. If a lot of steam comes off the compost, you'll know bacterial activity is

Crop residues decay if compost pile is kept moist. Bacterial activity produces heat, so you can easily tell if "things are happening" in the pile. Leave your soil probe in the compost. After you pull it out, feel probe. It may get so hot you can't hold it. If probe is cold, turn pile to let air get to bacteria so it starts working again.

taking place and all is well. On the other hand, no heat means no work— no work means no decomposition. Winter rains are usually sufficient to encourage bacterial activity, but if the pile is dry, sprinkle the leaves with water as you turn and aerate them.

At this time of year kitchen scraps include citrus rinds. They make excellent compost.

Citrus

If your grapefruit are thick-skinned and have a bulbous stem end, your fruit has the condition known as *sheep-nose*. Although the flavor and juiciness are unimpaired, commodity traders don't like the appearance of such fruit and it fetches a lower price. Sheep-nose might be an interesting piece of trivia for the dinner table when conversation lags. Anyone confessing to the crime should be advised to withold fertilizer from their grapefruit trees—and perhaps all their other citrus trees— this month. Too much nitrogen causes thick-skinned fruit.

Remember, February is the calendar

month for fertilizing citrus. But the point is you shouldn't garden by the calendar. Sheepnose tells you so!

You have a lot to do in February, but here's another little chore. It won't take a lot of time, and it could save you a lot of disappointment later.

Plant Ties

Take another look at all the bits of string that were used last year to tie plants, branches and shoots to tree-stakes, trellises, frameworks and supports. Ties that you made yourself, and ties made by a nurseryman on the plants you bought. I hope you didn't use wire—it really cuts into the plant. String is bad enough because, though soft, it doesn't stretch.

All your plants are going to experience a surge of growth during the next month or two—if they haven't started already. Don't forget, "growth" means fattening up a shoot as well as lengthening it. Don't let old ties strangle your plants. Loosen the ties. Better still, replace them with soft plastic that stretches.

February
WEEK 4

As the soil warms toward the end of February, you have an opportunity to sow in the ground seeds of winter vegetables such as broccoli, cabbage, lettuce, beets, carrots and turnips. This is your last chance until September. It's a short season before the heat is turned on in May, but there's time enough if you use quick-maturing kinds. Of course you gain time by setting out nursery plants of the leafy vegetables.

Don't be confused about this because earlier on I said to use the slower-maturing varieties for the winter garden. The situation has changed.

Winter Vegetables

Now, we have a short season of gradually increasing temperatures and longer days—a steady trend. Before, between October and February, we had cooling days with shortening daylight hours followed by lengthening days and surprising spells of warmth. It was an uncertain time and plants reacted in a correspondingly uncertain manner. For such unreliable times we expect specific characteristics in our vegetables.

A February planting of winter vegetables, which will grow until April or May, competes for garden space with a March planting of summer tomatoes, squash, corn and peppers. To overcome the dilemma, an energetic gardener really needs two gardens, one for a February planting of root and leaf crops that will take up space until they are harvested in May; the other for a mid-March planting of summer vegetables that will occupy the ground until fall.

Vegetables in Containers

Here is a partial solution: Save the ground for a mid-March planting of summer vegetables and, right now, set out plants or sow seeds of winter vegetables in containers.

Put the containers in a sunny place where their black sides gather heat from the sun which warms the soil inside and stimulates the roots to grow vigorously. You'll get a rapid return this way and you can measure the difference by comparing lettuce plants in the containers with a half dozen set out in the soil at the same time. In a recent cool spring, lettuce plants in containers were three weeks earlier—a worthwhile difference.

Containers smaller than 5-gallon buckets require more frequent watering. Plants become root-bound rather quickly, too.

You can also speed up your harvest of leafy vegetables by giving frequent applications of nitrate fertilizers. Ammonium nitrate and calcium nitrate are freely soluble in water, so they reach down to the plants' roots easily. Plants absorb nitrogen in the nitrate form, so these fertilizers are ready to use—they are the fast foods of the plant world.

A hose proportioner can be used to apply nitrate fertilizers at the rate of a tablespoon to a gallon of water. Do it every seven days or so, until the leaves become dark green. After that, back off to a fertilization every two weeks.

Vegetables in Bags

Another way to get a quick harvest of winter vegetables during a spring that isn't warming up fast enough is to grow the vegetables in plastic bags of soil amendment. Go to a nursery and buy several large bags of forest mulch, garden mixture or whatever it is called locally. Don't buy steer manure because you are going to put young plants directly in the mix. Steer manure will burn the roots.

Lay the bags in a sunny place, preferably on a board because you may want to move them later. Make sure there are drainage holes at the bottom of the bag—which was its side when you read the label in the nursery. Then wrap a sheet of black plastic round the bag, tucking it underneath without blocking the drainage holes.

Press and shape the top of the bag so it is flat. Use a cookie cutter to make eight holes through both pieces of plastic on the top of the bag. Slowly pour water through these holes until the bag is well soaked and water is coming out the drainage holes. See photo page 17. Now you are ready to plant through the plastic into the soil mix.

There will be a minimum of evapora-

Hose proportioner screwed onto faucet draws fertilizer from concentrated solution in jar whenever faucet is turned on. When you water with a hose, you supply diluted solution of nutrients to plants.

tion from the bag. The only moisture loss will be through drainage and plant use. However, keep an eye on the plants and prevent them wilting by timely waterings. In a couple of weeks time, after they have become established, you may include a tablespoon of houseplant food in the water to nourish the plants and get them growing quickly. But it will be the warmth of the sun—captured by the black plastic—that speeds up their growth.

After you harvest the vegetables, don't throw away the bag of material. Dig it into your next garden. What a saving!

You get another quick harvest if you plant vegetables in two or three old car tires laid on top of one another. Fill them with sawdust if you don't have any soil. Keep it moist with a nutrient solution. Your plants will do very well in the sunshine because the black tires absorb the sun's heat.

Citrus Trees

Citrus trees, especially lemons, look quite sick at this time of year before they start their new growth. Yellow leaves and bare twigs suggest to a lot of people that there is a blight or decline or a dreadful sickness going around. The trees are really all right.

Although citrus trees are evergreen, a single leaf doesn't stay on the tree forever. Evergreen trees are always dropping their leaves—look under pine trees for such evidence—but we don't notice it until some event like a cold snap makes it obvious.

It's interesting to know what is happening. When a leaf gets old, it gives up its nitrogen and that makes it turn yellow. The nitrogen is taken back into the tree and redistributed to the growing parts—the new shoots at the ends of the branches—that are, at this time of year, beginning to break out. If a lot of new growth breaks out, a large amount of nitrogen is drawn from the older leaves, causing many to turn yellow.

You can gauge the nutrient status of your tree by measuring the number of yellow leaves against the amount of new shoots breaking out. If things are too yellow, it helps to apply a nitrogenous fertilizer. Use ammonium nitrate at this time of year because you want a quick nitrate uptake of nutrients. You should prevent the rapidly growing new shoots from being starved.

Apply a small amount—say, 1/2 pound of ammonium nitrate to each 100 square feet—under the spread of the branches. Be sure there is plenty of moisture in the soil before you scatter fertilizer under the tree.

Citrus trees are supposed to sweep to the ground when mature. This bothers a lot of new gardeners. It's really better to let them sweep to the ground because that's where most of the fruit is produced in the early years. Avoid imitating people who trim their trees to make them look like lollipops on a white stick. If you let a citrus tree grow naturally, the sun won't reach the trunk, so there's no need to paint it white.

Don't worry about those brown leafless branches on the insides of a citrus tree. They are not dead. Don't prune them—they have leaves, and fruit, on their outer ends.

March
WEEK 1

Plant life begins to move forward in March. Although we may get several false starts to the real summer, every warm spell causes plants to grow. The danger is that there might still be a late frost, so don't be hasty in planting your summer vegetables.

Flowers on fruit trees may have already faded and young fruit is apparent. Early varieties are almost sure to have done this and now it is the turn of the later peaches and citrus.

Care of Fruit Trees

Be especially careful at such times. A warm spell should remind us to irrigate fruit trees. If we forget, the tree will be under stress when it is trying to develop fruit. The fruit readily falls off when the tree is under stress.

There's a deal of misunderstanding about the care of fruit trees at blossoming time. No matter what you hear, follow this simple guideline—keep the tree well watered and don't apply fertilizer.

Fertilizer, especially if too much is given at one time, acts as a shock on the tree's system. It is often enough of a shock to knock off young fruit.

March is a time of gusty winds, first from one direction bringing humidity from the California coast—then a dusty dry wind from the east. These winds provide shocks, too, and you must be sure to keep the soil from drying out. The best way to do this is to give good, deep irrigations down to 3 feet. Use the soil probe to make absolutely certain.

Destroying Olive & Mulberry Flowers

There are people who don't like fruit to develop on their olive trees. Later in the season the ripe fruit falls onto sidewalks and concrete patios and stains them. If you are one of these people, destroy the flowers and young fruit by spraying them with a solution called Olive-Stop® that you can buy at a nursery. Follow directions on the label and dilute with water. Spray the tree all over, wetting the flowers. Because olive trees flower over a period of time, it's advisable to make three or four sprayings and catch the first

This device saves you time. It takes up a strong nutrient solution from gallon jug and mixes it with water from hose. Irrigation water contains a tablespoon of nutrient in every gallon. "Feeding" as you water is a good concept.

blooming, the middle ones and the final blooming. If you like to cure your own olives, you should spray the later flowers to lighten the load on the tree. The fewer fruit on the tree the larger they will be.

This spraying will also be helpful to people who suffer from pollen irritation. You can use the same stuff to destroy the male flowers of mulberry just as easily.

Applying Fertilizer Through Leaves

New spring growth is tender and absorbent. If a tree is short of fertilizer, it can be fed through the young leaves. You make a mild solution, usually a tablespoon of fertilizer to a gallon of water, and spray the leaves thoroughly. This is common practice with grapes and pecans, both of which frequently suffer from a shortage of zinc.

Grapes will be ready for the treatment now, but pecans leaf out a little later. Apricots, citrus and peaches can all be fed in this manner.

Zinc Deficiency

If your trees have little leaves and, in pecans, soft, dark meats, zinc is probably the missing element. Spray with zinc sulphate. It's available at nurseries. There are specialized formulations of other chemicals, but you can take care of the common shortages by using a balanced houseplant fertilizer containing a range of nutrients. It's a "shotgun" approach to any particular shortage but if you are going to spray for zinc, you might just as well spray for copper and manganese and anything else at the same time. This is especially useful if you know some element is missing but are not sure which one. The deficiency symptoms are remarkably confusing, even to experts.

New leaves stay absorbent for about a month, and new leaves continue to appear. Nutrient spraying may be done every week in the spring for three or four sprayings.

It seems contradictory to apply salts deliberately even as plant fertilizers when we always try to avoid letting sprinklers spray plant foliage in the interest of keeping salts from the leaves. The difference is that salts in the irrigation water are harmful chemicals, whereas salts as fertilizers are plant nutrients. Nevertheless, be careful not to exceed the stated dose. In other words, don't increase the amount just because it's good stuff you are using.

Spray during cool evening hours rather than during the mid-day heat. Stop spraying when you notice a dark-green coloration to the leaves. There's nitrogen in houseplant food and you can easily give the plant too much. A strong color change is an unmistakable sign that you are overdoing it.

Even plants like strawberries can be watered and fertilized at the same time. It doesn't hurt them to fertilize while the fruit is developing—in fact it seems to help. And so we seem to be breaking our earlier rule—don't fertilize while the plant is developing fruit. However, strawberries are not lightly attached to the plant.

Using a Hose Proportioner

A convenient way to water and feed at the same time from the garden hose is to use a hose proportioner. This is a brass fitting that screws onto the faucet, and then the hose is screwed onto

There's a risk in having only one spray tank for insecticides, foliar feeding nutrients and weedkillers. It's much safer—and more convenient—to have a separate tank just for weedkillers.

it. A rubber tube attached to the side of this gadget is inserted into a gallon jug of water. A cupful of the appropriate fertilizer is added to the water in the jug. When the faucet is turned on, water passing through the hose draws the nutrient solution from the gallon jug to provide a solution equivalent to a tablespoon of fertilizer in a gallon of water—the original, standard strength.

When watering and feeding at the same time, it's important to use soluble fertilizers. Houseplant foods are usually soluble and are formulated to allow you to foliar feed. Make sure by reading the label. Sometimes houseplant food will contain urea—a useful and commonly used fertilizer—but it must be a pure form. Impure forms contain *biuret*, which is a harmful chemical when applied to foliage.

If you use a pressure sprayer to apply fertilizers to plants, remember to wash out the container when you finish spraying. If there's any extra mate-

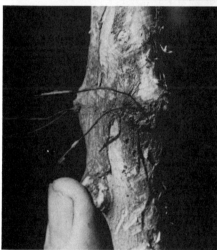

We tend to forget that plants grow fatter as well as longer. Above are examples of what happens if we don't check new spring growth on last year's branches. String or wire ties can completely cut through a branch.

rial in the tank, don't save it for next week's spraying. Fertilizers react with the metal of the tank and spray wand.

It's helpful to have two sprayers, one for foliar chemicals and another for weed chemicals. Label them—don't rely on your memory at a future date to tell you which one to use properly.

It's all right to mix insecticides and fungicides with foliar sprays, but never allow weed-killing chemicals in the same sprayer unless you do a very thorough washing out with soapy water and several rinses. It's really more convenient to have a separate sprayer for weedkillers, and use it for nothing else.

March
WEEK 2

Inspecting Plant Ties

Here's another thing to watch for when plants are growing vigorously because of warm spring weather. Stems thicken as shoots lengthen, though it's not so obvious. If you make any ties on new growth, make them loose so the stems don't become strangled. Inspect all the old ties and remove them if vines or trunks are being squeezed.

Take a look at any trees that were planted last month. You should have loosened the ties then, but new growth can be vigorous enough to tighten them again. When nursery ties squeeze a growing trunk against a stake, there's often an overgrowth at the top of the stake. If this is not attended to early on, there will be a scar on the trunk and damage done to the conducting vessels up and down the trunk.

It's a good practice to inspect plant ties all through the summer.

Don't Fertilize Blossoming Citrus Trees

Citrus trees all over town are flowering with gusto. Some gardeners might have been surprised by the suddenness of this manifestation of spring.

Take warning! You should not fertilize a flowering fruit tree. If you forgot to spread ammonium sulphate around your fruit tree at pruning time—don't play "catch up" in March. The addition of extra nutrients at this critical time can push off the flowers and you'll lose your crop. Wait 'til the next routine date in late May.

Don't spray your trees for citrus thrips—or nectarine thrips, for that matter— because you will kill good insects that pollinate the flowers of your trees. If the flowers are not pollinated because you killed the pollinators, you won't get a crop.

Another warning: You must water the trees to support the growth of flowers and leaves. Once they have started coming out you mustn't stop watering. Those recent rains didn't go into the soil very much—not nearly enough.

Strawberries are attractive to snails. If you keep soil surface moist all the time—an easy thing to do as plants come into bearing—snails remain to eat your fruit.

Insects

The spring season makes things grow, and it's not just garden plants. New leaf growth is tender and provides food for insects, particularly aphids. It seems we always have aphids in our gardens. During the winter it was grey aphids, largely feeding on plants of the cabbage family. Now the green, winged variety appears. You can expect black aphids and yellow aphids—all feeding on young tender growth.

Young grape leaves attract white flies and leaf hoppers. Leaves are full of sap and the surfaces haven't hardened, so insects find feeding easy and enjoyable. Later, their presence will be shown by lightly scarred silvery foliage. Quite possibly the insects will have dispersed by the time we notice the scarring.

If a cloud of little insects appears when you brush over the new shoots, you have a problem with leaf hoppers or white flies. The treatment is to spray with diazinon or Malathion. It's better to spray in the early morning or late in the evening to avoid the strong sunshine because the leaves are delicate.

Look in the strawberry patch. It's exciting to have the first flush of berries, most gardeners are keen to increase the crop by generous waterings. This provision of moisture, coupled with warming temperatures, is just right for snails and pillbugs.

If you can't hold back on watering enough to let the soil surface dry out to encourage snails to go deeper to where it's moist, you can trap them with stale beer.

Moist soil around plants simply invites them to become a pest. To stop them eating your fruit, you can pick them off—the snails, that is—and squash them. A cultural control measure is to water less frequently and allow the surface of the soil to dry out somewhat. Avoid using chemical controls on plants that are producing fruit that is ready to eat.

Good Insects

There are good insects starting up their life cycle as a result of the spring weather. Lacewings seem to follow the populations of leaf hoppers. This is

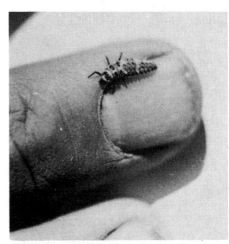

This little creature is a gardener's friend. Beginning gardeners don't recognize it as a larval ladybug. It eats more aphids than the familar spotted adult beetle.

Another misunderstood object: egg case of praying mantis, holding perhaps 100 eggs.

Too many fruit! It's not easy to thin them out to leave enough room for a few to grow to a large size.

Imagine space needed by full-size ripe fruit. If you can't do it yourself, get a neighbor to thin your fruit. It must be done!

quite natural because they comprise a large portion of the lacewing's diet. With their large lacy wings, emerald green bodies and bright golden eyes, lacewings are clumsy fliers but beautiful friends of the gardener. Don't spray them—they can and do help you.

Lacewings also feed on red spider mites—another pest of the moment. Ladybugs, too, like to eat red spider mites.

A word of caution is appropriate here. Don't get alarmed when you see an unfamiliar insect crawling over your plants in company with aphids, red spider mites, leaf hoppers and white flies.

This one will be a bit short of a quarter-inch long, broad-shouldered and tapering to a pointed tail end. It has the usual number of legs of all insects— six—but has no wings. It's body is mottled dull red and black, or grey. At first sight it makes you think of a miniature Gila Monster.

Don't spray this insect either. This is the larval form of the ladybug. It's a growing kid and eating like crazy. Because it doesn't have any wings, it just eats its way through the pests instead of flying away.

Adult ladybugs are notorious for flying away. In any case they are not particularly hungry when they are adult. It's a fallacy to think you can clean up your garden with a purchased pint of

them. Yes, you can buy them through mail-order catalogs, and you can sometimes find a cluster of them in the wild.

Now, if we could find a cluster of freshly hatched larvae, it would be a different story. However, with all biological pest control we have to ask ourselves the question, "What happens to our friends after they have eaten up all our pests?"

Praying mantises are another "good guy" insect. They usually appear a little later in the spring, but if you are watchful and know what to look for, you can bring them into your garden any time now.

Mantis egg cases come in two shapes, and they are plastered onto twigs of trees and shrubs. See above photo. They can be seen easily while the trees are bare of leaves. There's a long case, looking rather like a miniature loaf of sliced bread. Each 'slice' contains an egg—and there might be 50 of them. The other shape is an oval glob, tan in color, with the same sort of slight divisions showing.

Cut the twigs holding these cases and bring into the vegetable garden, sticking them in the ground between your plants. It won't be long before they start hatching. If all the eggs hatch at once, the youngsters eat one another unless a slight breeze scatters them. They eat the first thing they see, so let's hope it's aphids, red

spider mites or leaf hoppers and not their brothers and sisters.

Young praying mantises look just like little spiders unless you carefully inspect them. The adults are unmistakable with their front pair of legs held out in a praying attitude. Their nature, however, is one of preying. Keep one in the house on your plants near a window and watch them catch flies. Use a magnifying glass to give yourself a front seat at the original science-fiction movie.

Thinning Fruit

Let's get away from insects and go back to plants. Apples, apricots and peaches can be seen behind the faded flowers. If there are a lot of them, you will have to do some thinning. It's not easy to do, because you are rubbing out a part of the harvest. If you are a knowledgable gardener, you know some of the fruit is going to fall off on its own and some might be naturally thinned by dry winds, a late frost, shortage of water and other stresses.

Anyway, go ahead and do it—or get your neighbor to thin yours, and you thin his. If juvenile fruit stays on the tree, you'll harvest a heavy crop of little fruit and the tree will exhaust itself.

March
WEEK 3

See how roots all come from bottom of cutting. Cuttings of fruit trees with roots such as this are suitable for growing in containers where there's not enough room for a deep tap root.

New Plants from Cuttings

When people trim their roses, grapes, figs, pyracantha and oleanders they are often interested in starting new plants from the trimmings. It seems a shame to throw away all that good stuff. Cuttings can be made from these trimmings and no special equipment is necessary, but it calls for close atten-tion for a year or more if you are to fin-ish with sturdy plants. If you have a greenhouse or a cold frame where you can keep the temperature at 75F all the time and maintain high humidity, it will be a lot easier.

Move the cuttings from small containers into larger ones as the roots become crowded.

Should you admire a particular plant of your neighbor's and want to have one just like it, try your hand at mak-ing cuttings.

There may be a time when you need many plants. Perhaps you want to start a long hedge and think you can save money by creating your own plants. Perhaps the nurseries cannot find a particular plant for you.

With these situations you could well be ahead by making your own and you could get enjoyment out of the ex-ercise, too. However, under normal circumstances you'll find it more expe-dient, and less expensive, to purchase your plants from a nursery where you'll have a choice of plants. You'll also be getting a plant ready to put in the ground immediately.

Plants developed from cuttings have a fibrous root system as opposed to a tap root from a seedling, and are there-fore suitable for growing in half barrels and other large containers where root room is restricted.

Soil Mix

Prepare a soil mix to start cuttings in by using equal parts of sand, perlite, peat moss and vermiculite. Don't add in any fertilizers or steer manure be-cause they burn young, delicate tissues.

Don't try to root cuttings in water. Even if you are successful, the weak roots usually break when you plant them into soil. It's too much of a shock for the plant when you change it from a water medium into a soil medium.

Use any container larger than a pint size with drainage holes punched in the bottom. Large styrofoam coffee cups are readily available and inexpen-sive, but they are narrow-based and easily fall over when watered.

Tip cuttings grow quickest. You find these at the ends of branches and their growing point is indicated by lots of small, fresh leaves.

From this single growing point, new leaves emerge to make your new plant. You don't want very soft green twigs, but something with a bit of rigid-ity to it. Pyracantha, for example, doesn't have much tender growth and grape cuttings are usually taken when the plant is leafless.

Where to Cut

To obtain a more woody cutting, cut lower down the branch where the bark is a darker color and the stem thicker. These woody cuttings don't root so readily, or grow as quickly as do tip cuttings. However, they develop into a more bushy plant because new growth comes from the side buds in-stead of a single terminal bud. The ter-minal bud was removed when you made the first cut to get a tip cutting. The farther down you go on the branch, the more woody the material becomes and the harder it is to grow a new plant successfully.

Planting

No matter what the age of the wood you select, you should cut something about 5 or 6 inches long. Remove the lower leaves. Dip the lower end in RooTone® powder before the cut dries out. Tap the cutting on the edge of the table to remove excess powder, then quickly and gently poke the stem into the soil mix.

A hole made in the mix with a pencil will allow you to plant each cutting at about the same depth without scrap-ing off the RooTone® as the cutting is inserted. Place one cutting to each con-tainer with 2 or 3 inches of it in the soil mix.

Water, and set in a warm sunny place. Sunshine helps, but the warmth of the soil determines whether you get quick root growth or not.

Providing Warmth & Moisture

If you are planning to buy any equip-ment, make the first item a soil-heating cable. Spread the cable out and cover it with a sheet of metal. Then place the containers on the warm metal. Warm soil makes roots grow, even if air tem-perature is cold.

March
WEEK 4

Keep the soil mix moist. Reduce transpiration by bunching several containers close together. Sometimes, when leaves are large and numerous and when days are hot and dry, cut off half of each leaf when you make the cutting.

A plastic wrap around the cuttings or a plastic bag over each container and its cutting will hold in moisture. Be careful that this doesn't develop such a moist and still atmosphere around the cuttings that fungus and bacterial rots are invited in.

The best time to make cuttings is when, or just before, the plant comes into a flush of growth. This coincides with the usual pruning times in spring and fall. Cuttings taken at other times grow more slowly and require more care.

Keep your cuttings well watered, especially during dry, windy periods. Although you don't want the soil to stay too wet for any period, it is hard to overwater an open, free-draining soil mix.

Inspect the soil from time to time by poking a wooden stick to the bottom of the container to see if it comes out too wet.

Remember that a cutting already has leaves, is active, and is unsupported by a root system for at least ten weeks. Sometimes a cutting will grow new leaves without the benefit of roots. Don't disturb things by picking cuttings out of the soil to see what is happening.

Moving to a Larger Container

After a few weeks, turn the container upside down and give a sharp tap to dislodge the soil. Before the young roots begin to go round and round at the bottom of the container, it's time to transfer the cutting to a larger container. Good-sized roots will hold moist soil together during this operation, but work quickly and calmly.

Start adding Miracle-Gro® to the water just before the moving up operation. A teaspoon to a gallon of water is all you need. A week or two after the moving up, start using a tablespoon to a gallon. If the leaf color becomes too dark green, water with plain water.

There's little value in misting your cuttings unless you use distilled water. A misting with salty water puts salts on the leaves and the tender growing points. This causes growth to stop and sometimes it's the death of the cutting.

Take more cuttings than you think you need. Seldom does even a skilled gardener get 100% take.

Don't take cuttings from a diseased plant—you will be propagating disease as well.

Some plants that easily root from cuttings with the first being easier than the last are as follows: grape; fig; oleander; tomato; lemon and lime; cottonwood; geranium; desert willow; sweet potato; privet; rose; grapefruit; orange and tangerine; peach and apricot; apple; and pear.

March is often a confusing month for gardeners. We get promising spells of warm, sunny weather followed by sharp, cold spells, followed by warm weather again. Often there are gentle rain showers.

Good gardeners have their ground all prepared and are ready for planting. However, they are not seduced by the first warm spell that comes along—even if there are fresh young plants in the nurseries. They know unsettled conditions are a normal start to the summer season and they wait for the soil to warm up sufficiently. They might even use a soil thermometer poked in the ground to register the temperature at root depth. It's best to wait until the soil reaches 50F before planting tomatoes, the first of the summer vegetables to go in the ground.

If you are hasty and plant too early, you will discover that there is often no merit in it. An early planting in cold soil is quickly overtaken by a later planting in warm soil. Don't wait too long, though. There aren't too many days of good growing weather before late June when it gets too hot for pollination of summer vegetables such as corn, peppers and tomatoes.

Tomato plant will grow additional roots and become strong if you remove some leaves from its stem before planting. However, if you plant it deep, its roots will be in cold soil and they won't grow quickly. Put plant on its side in a shallow trench where the soil is warm. Its head in the air will quickly straighten up.

Give newly planted plant its own green-house. Cold winds will be kept off plant and, if you scrunch jar into the ground, cutworms won't find stem to chew on.

Wait until later to set out tomato cages to support wayward branches. During cold and windy weather, wrap clear plastic around them. Fasten it with clothespins and take it right round the cage. There is no need to cover top. When the weather gets hot, remove the plastic and put a sheet over top to provide shade.

Planting Tomatoes

A successful beginning can be assured by planting good-sized tomato plants. Remove lower leaves and bury stems in the soil. They will grow additional roots and be strong plants. Don't dig a deep hole, but lay plants on their sides in a trough. Their roots are at a normal depth of about 3 inches and their leaves are in the air, though at an angle for the time being.

By planting in this way, you use the upper, warmer soil. If you planted the tomato upright, you would have to place it deep down in cold soil in order to bury the stem where the new roots grow.

Another encouragement to newly set-out plants is to water them in with a starter solution using 1 pint per plant. You can buy such solutions at nurseries, but you can save money by using ammonium phosphate which is the same fertilizer you used when you prepared the soil a few weeks ago. Put a tablespoon of it in a gallon of water and shake well before using.

If cold weather follows, cover your plants with a 1-gallon glass jar. This acts as an individual greenhouse and, when it is pushed into the soil, it also provides a protection from cutworms. These caterpillars spend the day in the soil and at night come out to look for plant stems which they chew off.

You will have to take off the glass jars if the weather warms up, and put them over the plants again if it turns cold. Opaque plastic jars are not as good as clear glass jars.

Encouraging Growth

The name of the game at this time of the year is "keep 'em growing." Any cold period will check growth. This is even more applicable to bell peppers and eggplant—plants that like a little more heat than tomatoes.

Seeds of corn and squash also need help if the weather turns cold. Spread clear plastic sheeting on the soil between the rows or around the clusters of plants if you sow in groups, to get the most from the spring sunshine. Remember, it's roots you are growing at the beginning of the season. This is done by a warm soil, even if air temperatures are cool. After three or four weeks, take up this plastic and store it to use again in the fall when the weather cools.

Protecting from Cold

March can have us worried about our flowering fruit trees. Some late varieties of peaches and apples could well be flowering now, and so could some citrus.

Low temperatures merely delay flower opening. They won't hurt the trees. However, freezing nights are possible and you must be alert and ready for them. A freeze will kill flowers and a crop will be lost. It will also destroy recent new growth, which remains tender for a week or two after it has budded out.

On a freezing night, cover flowering fruit trees with a heavy sheet or light blanket. Better be safe than sorry. If you ignore frost warnings, you might lose your crop. It's a long wait until the next crop. Remember to take off the covering in the morning and let the sunshine warm up your trees again.

March can be windy, too. Winds can dry out the soil and the newly planted plants. Be ready with the garden hose. March showers are welcome, but don't rely on them to give your plants the water they need to make rapid growth.

Good gardeners are watchful at this time of year.

Nursery Tomato Plants Can Carry Sneaky Hitchhikers

If you buy your tomato plants from a nursery, give them a close inspection. They may be hiding aphids—little black things that suck juices from the plant. Get rid of them by spraying with a soapy solution—just ordinary dishwasher soap will do the trick. If you like, you can buy insecticidal soap from a nursery. And, if you want to use something a lot stronger, there's always Malathion 50 and diazinon.

April
WEEK 1

It's a widely held belief that modern man has lost contact with nature. He doesn't know how the stars move each night or from week to week. The phases of the moon go unnoticed. Buildings mask the spectacular rises of the full moon—when it looks to be bigger than a Greyhound bus.

Home gardening gets us back into the environment. At first we discover weeds, insect pests and other destructive parts of it. Natural happenings such as frosts alarm us. And in desert regions, a lot of people are dismayed when it rains.

But once you get interested in gardening you realize you are learning about your surroundings. You begin to see the reason for things, and you can make plans to take advantage of a situation that is developing right before your eyes.

Signs of Spring

Spring is one of those occurrences. When does spring arrive? We like to have calendar references, but this doesn't really help because every year is different—and there's no accounting for it. In the Midwest, gardeners put out tomatoes on Memorial Day because that's the start of spring there. But in the desert it's much too late.

For our desert gardening what sign shall we look for?

Over a general area there are the changes in day length. In other words, the mornings are lighter a little earlier. We may be still in bed and not notice this change. It's a lot easier to see that evenings stay light longer.

A week or two into March you will notice that the sun rises a little farther to the north each day and, if you are truly observant, you'll find that one morning it rises due east and the same evening sets due west. If you looked at your watch on that particular day, there were the same number of hours of darkness as there were daylight. You've passed the *equinox*—a sign of spring.

Song birds have been affected by the lengthening days and fill the morning air with their singing. There's another kind of singing, and most of us don't like it. City cats go a-courting—all

Soil thermometer shows temperature of more than 70F, warm enough for summer vegetables to be set out successfully.

Harvester ants are a sign soil is warming up, though they are a nuisance because they eat our plants.

through the night.

Some plants begin to flower, either little wild flowers or pesky weeds, depending on your point of view. Flowering is also influenced by warming temperatures, but it's changing day length that has the most influence. Look at your citrus trees now.

Temperatures get warmer, but only for a day or two, and then it gets cold again. March is a month of on-again, off-again. Sometimes April isn't much better—though it should be.

Carolina Jasmine is the first of our garden flowers to show itself in the spring. Newcomers liken it to Forsythia, though it's a different family. Banksia Rose comes next. Now it's the mulberry tree's turn. Before long there are any number of dormant plants coming into leaf or flower.

Even so, spring has not arrived—it's probably a false start. Don't rush into gardening activity. Officially, there's not supposed to be a freeze after March 31st at intermediate elevations. But that's a statement from a statistician, and it's almost certain he was not a gardener. We gardeners are waiting for warmer temperatures and welcome any reliable sign that they have come to stay.

In olden times European farmers judged the warmth of the soil by sitting on it—without the benefit of trousers—to determine whether to sow

their fields with spring barley. The present state of the art allows you to test the temperature of your garden in a more accurate—and more comfortable—way. Poke a soil thermometer 3 inches deep in various parts of the garden. Take an average. If the temperature is close to 60F, it's time to plant and sow summer vegetables.

Even so, it can turn cold again and you may be surprised. Look around the garden for natural signs of warming soil. Harvester ants may have been activated out of their winter dormancy to start their year's busy foraging.

Bee swarms tell us that spring is here and has come to stay. There are other signs, too, but they are less reliable. Bermudagrass lawns green up, mulberry trees flower, broccoli and lettuce bolt, and so on. There's a renewed activity around us.

If you are an absolute city dweller, there are human signs to look out for. They are interesting, but not reliable.

If you live in a college town, count the young people who carry tennis racquets to class. There's a formula that uses this number coupled with a constant and an adjustment factor for the incidence of out-of-state students that tells you when the time has come to plant your tomatoes!

Observe your neighbors on the roofs of their houses. Cleaning out evaporative coolers is a sure sign that spring

April
WEEK 2

has arrived. However, you should have already planted your summer garden when you see this. Reliably warm days got your neighbors on their roofs.

Now, there is one sign that you want to be careful of. If there are a lot of good-looking tomato plants in the nurseries, it doesn't necessarily mean spring has arrived.

It used to be difficult to find tomato plants in the nurseries at the right time—early March. For some reason desert nurseries were still tuned in to Memorial Day, and that's too late. Now the pendulum has swung back too far. Some nurseries have a good supply of plants long before spring has truly arrived. Don't be mislead by these early displays. However, if you feel in your bones that spring has arrived unusually early one year—and this does happen—go ahead and make an unusually early planting. Gamble a little; take a chance! We all know our seasons are short ones. Plant early and get strong growth and fruit set before hot weather comes to stay.

If you have misjudged or should a late frost hit the newly planted garden, you just have to buy another set of plants and start again. There'll be time, and there'll be plants in the nurseries. Don't plant too early though. Be cautious.

What sort of advice is that—if it isn't contradictory? Anyway, what's the right date for planting tomatoes? Nobody knows. Just watch the signs.

If grape tendrils grow ahead of terminal bud (arrow), it means plant has plenty of water and is in fine shape.

There's no problem with bunches getting tangled if you grow grapes on an arbor. They hang freely.

Taking Care of Grapevines

It's almost certain you are watering your grapevines well. Their springtime growth is so exciting that your natural reaction to the fresh greenery is to give the plant good irrigations. And that's good!

The January application of ammonium sulphate is really paying off now and the growth is exuberant, to say the least. A sign the plant is getting sufficient water is forward tendrils at the ends of new growth are longer than the new leaves. They are aggressively ahead, searching for something to wrap themselves around to support the plant in its onward journey to cover the trellis or arbor. It's a good sign.

Sometimes these tendrils act so aggressively toward one another that you have to separate them. Go in now and unravel the knotted cluster of new shoots and space them out on the trellis. You can use soft string to fasten them to the wires. Make ties rather loose because the shoots will fatten up later in the summer. Some gardeners, after tying the vigorous shoots to the wires, pinch out the tendrils to prevent further aggression. This is especially useful to prevent new flower clusters

being strangled.

While you are at it, rearrange the flower clusters so they hang free. It's a mistake to let them rest sideways between two shoots or squashed against a wall. If there's little room now, there will be even less as the clusters grow into bunches.

It's an advantage to grow your grapes on an overhead arbor because the bunches hang down naturally—free and clear. If they get caught up, it's easy for you to go in and release them.

If you think your grape vine is producing bunches too vigorously, simply remove some of them. A first-year production should have no more than eight bunches; some experts might say less. This allows strength to develop in the plant for future years.

If your grapes had mildew last year, you might need to spray the new shoots with wettable sulphur when they are 6 inches long. Spray every week until temperatures get over 90F. Sulphur becomes corrosive at such high temperatures. Spraying is preferred to dusting because you can get better coverage and it stays on the leaves longer. Also, spray the leaves with zinc sulphate if you think they are unusually small. Grapes, like pecans, seem to need a little extra zinc for healthy growth.

Lemon Trees

Another plant that grows strongly is the lemon. If allowed to do its thing, it will develop long sucker-like shoots that consume energy and reduce the fruit-producing potential of the tree.

Walk around your lemon tree and nip out the tender growing points with your finger and thumbnails. This soft-pinch pruning checks forward growth and stimulates side buds to break out early. Side shoots produce fruit and they are the start of new branches.

Summer Vegetables

In a late year when spring seems so reluctant to appear, gardeners are in a dilemma about planting summer vegetables such as tomatoes, eggplant and peppers. Plants have been available in the nurseries for weeks and they are usually in fine condition—inviting us to "go gardening."

There's no point in waiting any longer. You know summer will burst on us soon, and the end of June is unfailingly hot. We want our plants to be well established before this happens and able to take the heat. The dilemma is that the soil isn't really warm enough. Here's the trick to overcome that problem.

Remove the lower, older, yellowing leaves of your new tomato plant. There may even be some bumps on the stem, but don't worry about them. They are *adventitious* roots, a fancy name for additional roots that appear where we least expect them—in this case on the lower stem. We are going to use these bumps.

Dig the planting hole in the normal way to take the roots of the young plant. Make a sloping trench so you can lay the plant on its side with the leaves resting at soil level. In a day or two the top will have straightened itself up and your plant will look as if it had been buried—which it has. However, the true roots will still be in the upper warm soil and so will the bumpy stem. Your plant will soon have additional roots growing from the bumps.

Let's say you set the plant upright when burying it up to its neck of leaves. Then, the roots would be deep in the soil where it is cold and there would be little growth until things got really hot.

Another trick is to use a starter solution. This can be purchased at a nursery, or you can make your own. Put a tablespoon of ammonium phosphate in a gallon of water and shake well to dissolve it. Pour a pint of this solution into each planting hole—make lots of mud—when you set out your plants.

Some gardeners use vitamin B as a starter solution—it works. Others think phosphate is better because it's a nutrient. You probably have ammonium phosphate left over from soil preparation. Phosphorus encourages root growth and it's in short supply in most desert soils.

Selecting Plants

If you have grown your own plants, choose the better ones and throw the others away. There's little point in starting with poor material. If you buy at the nursery, become a picky purchaser. Those plants may have been on the shelves a long time. Bumps on the stems of tomato plants should not frighten you because you know how to make use of them. But examine the roots in their tiny compartments. If they are crowded, soft and black, and going round and round at the bottom, don't buy the plants. There are plenty more. Ask to see the latest consignment and examine the roots. Don't be shy about this. A good nurseryman will respect your concern about getting healthy plants.

Look at the color. If the leaves are pale green, the plants are suffering from a shortage of nitrogen. This was washed out of the soil-mix by waterings while the plants were waiting for a purchaser. Most nurserymen are good at watering their bedding plants, but it's an unwelcome expense to apply fertilizer while the plants are in their stores. Their business is to sell plants, not to look after them as if they were in a garden. Nor do they want

You probably have ammonium phosphate left over from soil preparation. Use a tablespoon in a gallon of water to make a nutrient starter solution. Settle in your new plants with a pint of this solution to help get the roots in contact with the soil. Many gardeners consider it better than buying vitamin-B stimulants.

their plants to grow too big.

When you finally get your plants in the ground—and it's still cool—cover them with a glass jar. This gives each plant its own greenhouse. You must be watchful and take the jars off if the weather gets hot at midday. Push the jars into the soil and you'll protect your plants from surface-crawling cutworms.

Protect Tomatoes in Wild Spring Weather

What a spring! Three or four weeks ago we had temperatures in the high 90s, but last week we had hail!

Gardeners who set out their tomatoes a few weeks ago and took care of them are smiling. Taking good care means keeping them out of the wind by setting up a shelter of clear plastic wrapped around a length of construction mesh with its squares. This, set around our plants, provides a sort of greenhouse to shield young plants from inclement weather.

Later in the year the plastic will be removed and the plant prevented from falling over by the mesh. This will cause plants to grow up into the air to save ground space, yet they will be full of foliage and flowers.

April
WEEK 3

Young lemon fruit usually drops off for one stressful reason or another before they reach size of lemon in left hand. Be attentive to your tree's needs until young fruit reach golf-ball size. After that you can relax a little.

Toward end of April, sun can get hot enough to burn tender leaves. Strawberries will continue to produce fruit if they are protected. Plastic materials that breathe are suitable covers from now on—even into full summer.

Citrus Fruit Drop

Expect a lot of young fruit to drop off citrus trees after they have flowered, or even while they are flowering. This is normal. Fruit trees produce far more flowers than they need to. It's sort of insurance against bad possibilities. Most of these flowers never mature into ripe fruit. It ensures a certain quality in what does survive to the end. From the tree's point of view, the end is a lot of seeds. From our point of view, the end is large-sized fruit enveloping those seeds.

Meanwhile, a lot can go wrong. Newly set fruit is liable to fall off after a shock such as cold winds, a sudden hot day or two, letting the tree dry out too much between waterings, adding too much fertilizer, or keeping the soil too wet. It's a time to take especially good care of your citrus trees. For now, those new fruits are very lightly attached. Once they have become bigger than a thumbnail, they seem to hang on better. When they are as big as a golf ball, they are usually safe.

Most of last year's orange crop will have been harvested by now, but if a few fruit remain on the tree, don't get anxious—just pick them when you need something good to eat. But they won't last much longer. Grapefruit will continue to improve in sweetness for another few weeks. Don't worry about your tree carrying old fruit, young fruit and flowers all at the same time.

Insects

Insects pollinate the flowers, so it's advisable not to get too eager with the spray gun during flowering. Citrus thrips have a bad reputation, but they don't do a lot of damage. The scars they leave on the skin do not spoil the inside of the fruit. In an effort to spray them out, you are almost sure to kill a lot of other insects that are busy pollinating the flowers.

Watering

Good watering is important at this time of the year. Continue to use the soil probe frequently to help you decide when to irrigate. You must irrigate flowering trees, but you should not apply fertilizer to them. Some gardeners get too anxious when hot weather starts and they overwater. Others become forgetful while they are busy with their vegetables—and trees suffer. A windy day can catch anyone by surprise.

Olive trees flower at this time of year. To some people this is a blessing because they look forward to a bumper crop in the fall. Others find it a nuisance because the pollen blows about and irritates them. There's a "magic bottle" for both kinds of people.

Nurseries sell a solution of plant hormone called Olive-Stop®. When it is sprayed on the flowers at a low concentration, some of them are killed so naturally they won't set fruit. If few flowers remain, the resulting fruit will be large. By adjusting the spray strength to the intensity of the flowering you can determine the kind of crop you want. You can choose a heavy crop of small fruit, a light crop of large fruit, or no crop at all. Some people don't like the fruit at all and become irritated when it falls and stains their sidewalks.

If you want to eliminate the crop entirely, you must spray several times because flowers are produced over a period of three or four weeks. Olive-Stop® can also be used on mulberry trees.

Strawberries

Continue watering strawberries for as long as they flower. You can help flowering and subsequent fruit production by a regular program of feeding-as-you-water. This means adding a tablespoon of houseplant food in each gallon of water at every other irrigation—less frequently if leaves are dark green. If your strawberry bed is large, feed through a proportioner device attached between the faucet and hose. It automatically draws fertilizer through tube inserted in a jug of nutrient—in a stronger solution, of course.

April
WEEK 4

As every pillbug and snail knows, strawberries are good to eat and fruit production continues through the end of June.

Irrigate deeply, to about 12 inches, so the soil surface dries out between waterings. Constantly moist soil invites pillbugs and enables them to live. They are not insects but *crustaceans;* they breathe through gills as do crabs, shrimp and lobsters. Their gills must be kept moist, otherwise they die.

Strawberries might need shading now. If you are growing them beneath a grape arbor, there will be enough growth overhead to keep the sun off the plants. As the sun gets hotter there will be more grape leaves—it's a nice arrangement. Strawberries out in full sun without the benefit of a grape arbor need shade anytime now.

Erect a wooden frame or use the construction mesh wire from your winter tunnel garden. Cover it with cheesecloth or shade cloth. White material throws off some heat and is preferred to the darker patio shade cloth. The covering will also help keep birds out of the bed.

Birds are persistent, but stupid. If you cover your fruit before it is ripe, they can't find it—or so it seems. On the other hand, if you try to protect your fruit after one or two birds have started to eat it, they will try their hardest to get through the netting or tear through paper bags.

Soil Mulches
We know that covering the soil on a summer's day will cool it and keep moisture in. Mulches of straw, compost and even pulled weeds, shade the soil and catch evaporating moisture.

So, why not use the old cooler pads when we carry out our seasonal maintenance chore up on the roof? They are flat, wrapped in nylon mesh to keep everything together, and a suitable size. Unfortunately, they are impregnated with salt from last summer's evaporation on the roof. Don't use them. If you want to, you can buy new ones for your garden!

Tomatoes planted a week or two ago in the belief that spring had really arrived, have grown slowly and will have started flowering. Perhaps the plants haven't much size to them, but we can't do anything about that—we must take care of what we have. And that means helping the flowers to stay on the plant and set fruit.

Avoiding Blossom Drop
One of the troubles of spring, as far as gardening is concerned, is the nights stay cold even though the days may be warm. Summer vegetables don't like it because it slows their growth. And if they are flowering, their pollen is not viable. This means the flowers fall off and no fruit will be formed. It's bad news at a time when your hopes are high. There's an easy way around this problem.

Buy some hormone-in-a-bottle from your nursery. Follow label directions and spray the flowers when they are fully open. Although the material is labeled for tomatoes—it is called *tomato-bloom set* by some manufacturers—gardeners have been pleased with the results on bell peppers and eggplant.

Pecan Trees
Pecan trees have started their growth cycle. They are usually late starters because they are a warm-climate tree, even though they require a moderate amount of winter chilling.

Follow the general rule concerning new growth. Water it and feed it. Pecans will have received the February ground application of ammonium sulphate, but there's an additional need to supply pecans with more zinc than other trees get. Putting zinc sulphate in the ground is not an effective way to supply nutrient. Our alkaline soils grab the chemical and it becomes unavailable to the plants.

Overcome this situation by spraying new foliage with a diluted solution of zinc sulphate—usually one tablespoon to 1 gallon of water. Repeat the spraying once a week as long as fresh new leaves appear. It might be four or five sprayings. It's best to spray in the evening after the sun has lost its strength so you don't burn the tender leaves.

Young leaf growth is soft and tender. It is the natural food of juice-sucking aphids. Pecans seem to attract aphids as much as roses. You can see them and you will notice they have left a shiny film on the leaves. Put Malathion 50 or diazinon in the zinc-sulphate solution and take care of two problems at once. Read the label for detailed instructions on mixing the two.

Irrigation
All our plants deserve a good watering toward the end of April. If it isn't already hot, it's soon going to be. Deep irrigations again! Tree roots have been extending themselves in the past few weeks.

Make your irrigation basins wider so the new roots at the ends of the branches continue to grow in moist soil. If you keep watering in a restricted circle around the tree, the roots will not move out into dry soil. Don't handicap your trees.

Fruit Thinning
As a result of your pruning of deciduous fruit trees in January, there's a lot of new growth. Leaves have grown out of those single narrow buds and some have turned into new shoots. Good! That's next year's fruitful wood on the way.

Even better, many of the fat, round buds opened up into flowers and most of those became small fruits. In some springs this doesn't always happen to our liking. Bees weren't busy enough, the weather suddenly turned hot and killed the flowers. Winds chilled them. The tree became too dry, and so on.

But, let's be optimistic for a moment and say there's lots of small fruit on the branches. They might even be touching one another in clusters. It all looks very good, so far.

Now you must remove most of those young fruit!

This is called *thinning.* But what you are doing is fattening fruit for harvest time. Most fruit trees develop more young fruit than they can successfully carry to harvest.

It's quite normal for a heavily laden tree to cast its surplus fruit later in the year when the stresses build up, in

Good way to tie tree to stake. It allows some freedom of movement in wind, but keeps tree from rubbing against stake. There's enough looseness to let trunk grow for a year without string strangling it.

Squash is a good plant with which to get children started in gardening. Big seed comes up in a few days. Plant grows quickly and you get a harvest before children get bored.

which case you get a small crop. Unfortunately a tree might cast them all off. Equally unfortunately, the tree might keep all its fruit—but they will be small. There's no telling.

You have to rearrange things on the tree so you get a lot of large fruit.

It calls more for determination than it does skill. Commercial peach growers hire high-school boys to knock the surplus fruit off with long sticks. You should do it more carefully.

Take a look at the branches and try to imagine each little peach, apricot or plum at the size you like to buy in the supermarket. Now give it room to grow by removing all the adjacent fruit that would get in the way of it reaching that size.

If you can't get up enough courage to do the job, ask a neighbor over to do it for you. Don't hang around nervously watching him and making coughing noises. Go over to his place and thin his fruit for him.

It's a tricky operation in some ways. If you don't take enough off, there'll be lots of little fruit at harvest time. If you take out too many, you'll get a light crop. If inclement weather follows, the tree might lose more fruit as a result of a sudden heat wave or a dry wind. Don't anticipate—do a good job.

Loosening Tree Ties

While on the subject of trees, take a look at the trunks where they have been tied to a stake. In a good spring with favorable growing conditions, these ties get pinched as the trunks fatten. Always make loose ties to anticipate this.

Fertilizing Vegetables

If you are new gardener or have started a garden in a new plot of soil, you may be disappointed with your plants' growth for the first year or two. This is despite the fact that you took pains to prepare the soil properly. Don't expect to make a good soil all at once. It takes a few years for the materials you add to desert ground to mellow. It will happen, but in its own sweet time.

Meanwhile, help your plants by feeding them as you water. Use a tablespoon of houseplant food in a gallon of water every time you irrigate until the pale green turns to dark green. Don't overdo it with the summer crops which are largely fruit-bearing. Too lush a foliage on tomatoes, cantaloupes, peppers and even corn, leads to reduced flowering.

Sweet Corn

Sweet corn that was sown several days

ago should be doing well if the soil is rich. Corn is a hungry plant and a thirsty one too. If it weren't so delicious it would be considered a *luxury* in our gardens. To get good results with corn, give it all you've got. This means supplemental fertilizing every three weeks after it has reached a foot high, and until it starts to flower. And water all the time until you harvest it. Even if you prepared the ground well, corn will respond to side-dressing with ammonium sulphate. Scatter a cupful to every 10 plants and water it in well. Keep the plants green and growing.

We can't afford to spend so lavishly on a long-term crop. For this reason, we must sow seeds of short-season varieties. Besides, as with many summertime plants, flowering must be completed before hot weather sets in. Poor pollination leads to empty kernels—and heat is the usual reason for this.

Center pair of cobs are poorly filled because heat killed pollen before it reached kernels. Left pair shows heat-affected exposed ends. It's better to grow varieties with fully extended leaves beyond ends of cobs. This keeps ends protected from insects and heat.

How 'Bout That Rain!

Rain is a kind of stimulant. Didn't you feel good during these recent rainy days? Rain gives us lots of gardening opportunities. Soft soil lets us pull weeds easily. There are a lot of black mustard, shepherds purse, mallow and foxtail plants that are setting seed. We should take care of them immediately. Apart from the foxtail that has shallow insignificant roots, they are deep-rooted nuisances that often break when we try to pull them up out of dry soil. When the soil is soft after a rain it is easy to get the whole plant—and with little effort.

April
WEEK 5

Winter's over—it must be, though it hung around a lot.

Clean-Up Time
Clean out all the residues of winter gardening—if they haven't already turned to dust. It's one of the basics of small-space gardening that you immediately plant something appropriate to the season as soon as you take out an old plant that has finished its productivity. Be that as it may, we tend to hang onto anything that has the slightest chance of giving us a last-minute yield.

We unwisely keep many wintertime plants long past their real usefulness. Beets start to flower along with carrots, spinach and turnips. Sugar peas and garden peas develop mildew—yet we are reluctant to bite the bullet. They should go. They should have gone two weeks ago.

Squash
Gardening is often all optimism. Now we are looking forward to abundant squash harvests. This is an easy thing to accomplish, even for beginning gardeners and the very young set.

Squash are good plants for children to start their gardening experience. The seed is big, it germinates in warm soil in a day or two, and it gives an abundant harvest in little more than a month of growth. You can see it grow.

There are many kinds of squash and you don't have to be particular about which variety to sow—they all do well. The favorites with most people are the zucchinis.

If you haven't tried the golden group of zucchinis, sow a few seeds for a pleasant surprise. The taste is really the same and so is the texture, but the big advantage lies in the color of the fruit. Instead of searching through all that prickly leaf stuff looking to see if you have any green squash, the golden kinds are visible from a distance. The green varieties are the same color as the leaves. It's easy to miss one and if you do, it will turn into a giant before the weekend.

Zucchini squash are best eaten when they are small and just a day two after the flower fades. Then they are tender and tasty. Keep harvesting them and the plant responds by producing more abundantly.

If you leave the fruit to get bigger, the skin thickens and the seeds develop and you lose gourmet quality. Old fruit needs to be cooked, whereas young fruit can be eaten raw and enjoyed in salads.

Leave old fruit on the plant and it will stop producing flowers. You lose all the advantages of quick harvests.

Many cookbooks tell you how to deal with the squash harvest, but even so, sow only a few seeds and two by two, not in a clump. Squash take up a lot of space and three plants are all you need.

If you want to eat squash all through the summer, sow a succession of seed every six weeks or so. A good measure is to sow the next lot after you have picked three fruit from the previous sowing. You might want to break a gardening rule that says, "Once you find a good variety, stick with it—don't chop and change." If you sow only one kind of squash, you are likely to get tired of it by the end of the summer.

If you haven't grown butternut squash, give it a try—it's delicious. A lot of people miss out on this plant because it's called *winter squash*. They think it should be sown in the cooler time of the year. Not so—it's a summer grower, but you eat it in the winter. In other words it's a keeper and that makes it useful. In the hot, sunny desert it's a fine replacement for potatoes.

Butternut squash is best sown after the soil has really warmed up and there's no doubt that summer has arrived. It's a sprawling plant and requires the same sort of room cantaloupe and watermelons need. Grow it on a fence if you don't have ground space. The fruit are not too big, but you'll have to support them in slings as they enlarge and ripen on the fence. New bush varieties don't seem to be nearly as suitable for desert growing as the original vining kinds.

You can eat the young fruit, but most gardeners like to let them ripen on the vine and harvest late in the season, even after the vines begin to die back.

Squash-Vine Borer
Now, there's a bad side to this success story. It's called the *squash-vine borer*.

This is perhaps the most irritating pest we have in the whole program of desert gardening. Squash seem easy to grow and it's so encouraging to start picking fruit only six weeks after sowing the seeds. Squash are strong and productive plants. One morning, we might discover the plants are wilting and a good irrigation doesn't bring them back. We are puzzled and a little dismayed. Then we become angry because close inspection reveals a soggy mess on the side of the stem. Inside there's a soft white grub about 1 inch long, eating its way along the stem and chewing up the conducting vessels of the plant—hence the wilt. The plant cannot use the moisture in the ground and its large leaves transpire at a high rate in the summer sun.

This is a disaster of the first magnitude. The plant is usually finished just as it begins its usefulness. If you catch the problem early on, try a little plant surgery. Slit the stem lengthwise, pry out the wormy grub, dust with sulphur and replace the two surfaces of the stem. Bind them together with a cotton bandage. Put a shovelful of soil over the repaired stem and water it well. In most cases this treatment saves the plant and it continues to produce.

A word of caution. There's sometimes more than one grub in the stem—make sure you get them all. Old plants that have produced a lot of fruit and have lost their vigor don't seem to respond so well as young plants. Even after repair there's the likelihood that more eggs will be laid and new grubs will get into your plants.

A number of gardeners try to avoid this pest by sowing a succession of seed—say every six weeks in the belief that young, vigorous plants withstand an attack better than old ones. This isn't the case. Nor is it true that eggs are laid only on older horizontal vines and not on young upright stalks.

Whenever you see a quick-flying moth buzzing like a bee around your squash plants—expect trouble. This red-tailed, brownish insect is the adult, recently hatched out of the chrysalid stage. It spent the winter in the soil and you should have destroyed all of these chrysalides when you dug your ground in February. If they were not squash-vine borers, they were something just as bad.

Look on the sides of the stems for pinhead-size eggs—maybe five or six. They are the same color as the stem, but they stand out like little balls. Wipe them off.

Don't try to control this pest with chemical sprays. Because the squash plant produces both male and female flowers, you need insects to do the pollination for you. There's no point in covering your plants with cheesecloth to keep the pest out—you will be keeping pollinators out, too.

Moths stays active all through summer, so don't relax. Some summers are a complete disaster because of this insect. Grubs infest all varieties, even butternut fruit is damaged. Fortunately, the moth leaves watermelon, cucumbers and cantaloupe plants alone.

Mixed Plantings

An old-wives' tale says you must not mix plantings of cucumber, squash, watermelon and cantaloupe because the flavors get mixed and even the shapes of the fruit are affected. Don't pay any attention to this story—such things don't happen. Go ahead and plant what you want. Your space is probably limited and you can't separate them enough. Insects—mostly bees—carry pollen from male flowers to female flowers up to a mile away.

Insects don't stay on one plant when they collect nectar and pollen. They move from male flowers of one plant to female flowers of another and unwittingly cross-pollinate them. Because of this, never save seed from plants with two kinds of flowers— even if you believe you have found a winner. Seed will invariably be mixed and usually downgraded. Always buy fresh seed from a good seed company to maintain good quality.

Once in a while you harvest fruit that isn't quite up to standard and some-

times it's downright bad. It's not because a cucumber was growing close by. It's because the parents of that seed became victims of circumstances beyond their control. It happens in even the best of seed companies.

Cucumbers like cool temperatures, so their immediate future is bleak because it could get hot quickly. They also need some shade and protection from wind. Cantaloupe, squash and watermelon like the summer heat and full sun, so their future is promising. Go ahead and plant all you want. Just remember that these plants take a lot of room and they need plenty of water. As with corn, they are not exactly an economical choice.

May
WEEK 1

In the desert, most varieties of onions flower before they develop a good bulb. Lengthening days of spring that follow a mild winter are responsible for this behavior. If you want big bulbs, select short-day types; there aren't very many of them.

Extra Watering

In May we notice how hot it's getting. The sun is higher and shadows are shorter. Days are longer, too—with the sun rising and setting more to the north. New parts of the garden are getting light.

Gardeners find their fluid intake has increased and they consciously increase the amount of water they give their plants. Nevertheless, the first hot spell usually takes us by surprise and plants wilt. We are reminded that summer is around the corner.

It's a time to watch our watering. Young fruit are on the trees. Apricots are almost ready and you shouldn't lose them. Apples and peaches are filling out nicely and they are vulnerable to hot, dry winds and rapid water loss. Newly planted trees are still establishing themselves and our summertime vegetables need a watchful eye. If they don't get a good watering, their first fruit will fall off and it will be some time before they start up again.

Onions Ripening

After a long period of growing imperceptibly, there's suddenly an onion harvest. Suitable varieties form a fine, fat bulb whereas those not suited develop a showy flower. The flower steals nutrients from the bulb and we get nothing to eat.

Two good kinds are Texas Grano and California Red. Both are "short-day" types—meaning they are suited to regions closer to the tropics where days are short—rather than northern states where summer days are long. They are also quick maturing. Kinds that grow well in the desert don't usually keep well. Don't plant a lot of bulbing onions. By contrast, the many kinds of slim-stemmed bunching onions do very well. They may be divided for both eating and planting at any time.

The best way to grow onions—after you've selected a suitable variety—is to sow seeds in boxes in September, transplant into the garden during January and harvest in May. Onions are greedy for time and garden space.

As bulbs begin to fatten, scrape a little soil away from them each week and let sunshine ripen them. As the stalks weaken at the neck and fall over, reduce watering frequency. Don't cut the stalks, but let them dry out on their own. After the bulbs are exposed—sitting on top of the ground as it were—they can be twisted off their roots and put in a cool airy place. They might store for a month or two, but not much longer. So eat them up with the outdoor barbecue meals the lovely weather allows us.

Garlic Ripening

Garlic and chives behave in much the same way as do onions. The seedlings are set out in January. They are cared for in the same way as onions, too.

It's especially important to let garlic completely dry out. The stalks will turn straw-colored, but don't cut them. If there are flowers, it's better to bend

Multiplying onions—those that bunch out of the base into several stems with somewhat swollen bases—are reliable producers in the desert. There are a number of varieties. Some are small like scallions; others are almost as large as a bulb onion. They produce throughout the year.

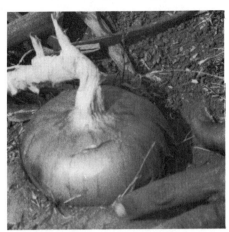

Here's a good bulb, at least for size. Unfortunately, it won't be a good "keeper."

the stalks over to stop the flow of nutrients reaching the seeds. The nutrients are needed in the bulblets or *cloves.*

If you harvest garlic before the cloves have thoroughly dried, they won't keep. They should be hard and the pointed ends quite dry.

Tomato-Bloom Set & Vibration

Tomatoes flower this month, but if nights are cool, they may not pollinate. Gently hit the plants' stems with a little stick early in the morning while the flowers are fresh. The vibration shakes pollen from the anthers onto the nearby pistel. Another remedy is to spray the flowers with a spray can of tomato-bloom spray. Read the precautions printed on the label—don't use this chemical indiscriminately.

Squash Pollination

The first summer squash plantings start flowering now and give us reason to rejoice. But something disastrous often happens at this moment. No fruit develops!

There are two reasons for this. The flowers you saw at first flush could have been all male flowers which will never produce fruit. Oh, they look the same as female flowers until you examine the stalk behind the yellow bloom. It's thin and long.

Female flowers are borne on the same plant and have a short, fat fruit immediately behind them. Unfortunately, the first flowers are often males and it

takes time for the females to appear. Once in a while the whole season passes and the plants simply won't produce female flowers—only males.

You can't do anything about it, although old wives say you should smack the plants, shout at them or pinch out the growing tips. Most gardeners, fearful of their watchful neighbors, simply pull up the plants and start afresh with a new sowing. After all, there's plenty of summer left for two or three more successive sowings.

Secondly, even if you have male and female flowers at the same time, it's no guarantee you'll have fruit. Pollination must take place and, if it's not done Mother Nature's way, you'll have to do it yourself.

Normally bees, flies and ants move from one flower to another during the early hours of the morning when the squash flowers are open. Pollination is incidental to their searching for nectar and pollen—but that's how things are arranged. The flowers drop off before the next day, no matter what happens. If pollination takes place, the fruit behind the female flower continues to grow and you harvest squash.

But if nothing happened that morning, the fruit that is already fully formed, though small, turns yellow at the end, followed by browning and further shrivelling. It looks just like a disease, which is what beginning gardeners think their plants have. "What do I spray it with?" they ask. "What did we do wrong?" "What shall we do?"

This is the moth that starts off destructive cycle of damage on grape leaves. Catch her and kill her before she lays eggs on underside of leaves.

You can see eggs at left and young caterpillars at right preparing to disperse. Pinch out whole clusters or whole leaf at this stage before caterpillars spread out.

It takes a little time for them to accept the idea that poor pollination is the reason for their misfortune. "The fruit was there . . . now it's dying. The flower must have been pollinated."

Well, it wasn't pollinated. And if you want fruit, it must be. And you'll have to do it yourself.

Early in the morning before breakfast, go out into your squash patch and look around. Make sure there are both kinds of flowers—females with a fat fruit behind them and males with their thin stalks. Pull a male flower from the plant and tear off the golden petals. You can eat them if you want—either fresh, or fried in batter.

You have in your hand a stalk with a golden knob on the end, and there's a mass of sticky golden crumbs on it. Rub these crumbs onto the center of the female flower where there is a similar knob, only this knob is divided into three little horns. Voilà! You've done pollination, and it didn't hurt a bit. Use one male flower to four or five female flowers. Do this every morning and you'll have a bumper crop of squash.

Five days later harvest the fruit while it's about 6 inches long. It's a mistake to wait for bigger fruit for two reasons. First, bigger fruit get woody and develop seeds. Second, the quicker you remove fruit, the more flowers you get.

Don't sow more than three seeds at each successive sowing. You'll get all the squash you can eat—but only if you pollinate.

After feeling pleased about this success and your control of a squash plant's life, you'd better take a close look at your grapevine. There may be a nasty surprise waiting for you.

Grape-Leaf Skeletonizer

Has the grape-leaf skeletonizer struck yet?

When you weren't looking, a small blue-black moth was flying around and laying clusters of eggs on the leaves' undersides.

After a few days, the eggs turn into pale caterpillars which spread out centrifugally. In no time they have skinned the leaf tissue and you can see light through it. They progress onto other leaves, eating voraciously as they go. Now they are readily visible, when before they were pale and inconspicuous. You see lots of 1/4-inch-long caterpillars wearing rugby jerseys—black and yellow bands. Behind them lies devastation.

Try to prevent this disaster by being alert and watchful during early May. Learn to recognize the moth. When you see her flying around, try to catch her before she lays any eggs. If you see any eggs on the undersides of leaves—they are laid 50 at a time and each one is smaller than a pinhead—rub them out using finger and thumb. If you don't notice them at first and they hatch out, pick off the whole leaf before the pale caterpillars start spreading over the plant.

When you see the larger, banded, caterpillars it's late—the damage has been done. But it's not too late to take action. Spray them with Dipel® which is a solution of bacteria that gives them a fatal stomachache. Or, use chemicals such as Sevin®, Malathion 50 or diazinon. If you don't like chemicals, shake the branches in the early morning when it's cool. The caterpillars will fall to the ground and won't find their way back.

Don't relax. This first attack is just the beginning.

May
WEEK 2

Cantaloupe, Squash & Cucumbers

Cantaloupe and squash like sun, so if you have spare ground, make a second sowing of these seeds now. They take summer's heat very well and you'll be able to sow a third, and perhaps a fourth succession before cold weather returns.

They are greedy on space and water, so don't grow more than you need. Perhaps three summer squash plants, four or five cantaloupe or watermelon, and four or five winter squash.

Winter squash grow during the hot summer months and you eat them during winter because they store well. They are a desert substitute for potatoes. It's not easy to grow keeper potatoes in the desert. Winter squash have long vines and will take up space until frost arrives. Keep pinching out the leading shoots to stimulate side branches that will produce more flowers.

There are many kinds of summer squash, so use different varieties at each planting—just to give you some variety in your meals. Successful gardeners easily get tired of squash.

Cucumbers are a relative of squash and cantaloupe, but they don't like the sunshine nearly as much. If you sowed seeds in March, you will be picking cucumbers any day now. It's too late for further sowings in May, but some gardeners take a gamble and sow the Armenian variety. Try to find a spot that enjoys afternoon shade and provide a tall trellis for the vigorous vine to climb. Slant the trellis rather than installing it upright. The fruit will then hang free and be straight. Fruit that gets caught up in an upright trellis is often misshapen.

Spinach Substitutes

Two other summertime vegetables are Malabar spinach and New Zealand spinach. Both can be sown any time now. Neither are true spinaches, but you eat the leaves and they are a good substitute because they grow so well in the hot months. Simply pick a handful of leaves whenever you need a fresh salad or mess of greens. Picking keeps the plants compact and freshly

Side shoots are called *suckers* by some people; experienced gardeners consider them to be extra leaves.

Ragged leaves and leaves with holes in them signal presence of a grub in stalk. Sometimes damage is bad enough to kill plant. Putting insecticide in funnel at an earlier stage than this will prevent such damage.

branched. The plants can be grown in pots or in the ground. Malabar spinach, with its large glossy leaves, makes a dramatic plant in a hanging basket.

Controlling Weeds

Don't let summertime weeds get started. They begin as small seedlings and we tend to ignore them just because they are small. Many of them root along their stems as they spread and become a difficult nuisance. Summer rains that come later cause these weeds to grow at an alarming rate. A large garden quickly becomes a demoralizing place if you let weeds get away from you.

A frequent light hoeing now takes care of weed seedlings and saves you trouble later.

Container Plants

Dry air and winds wreak havoc on container plants if they are exposed. It's worthwhile taking a look around for a more sheltered place for them. Put them where they will be shaded in the afternoon. Check their soil's moisture at the beginning of the day and watch to see if the plants wilt at midday.

Black-plastic containers absorb heat from the sun so much that plants' roots cook in hot, wet soil. You can get

around this problem by painting the containers white or wrapping aluminum foil around them. Keep them out of the direct afternoon sun.

Sweet Corn

Some gardeners worry about the basal suckers on corn plants. They consider them to be stealing nourishment from the main stem where the cobs are produced. They pull them off before they grow too big. Other gardeners think of them as beneficial additional leaves that pull more energy from the sun and make for a stronger plant—hence higher yields. It's the hybrid corn varieties that send out lots of suckers and, provided the soil is well supplied with nitrogen, there's no harm in them. Sometimes they produce a small, worthless cob.

Corn is a hungry and thirsty plant. Give good waterings and a tablespoon of ammonium sulphate to each plant every two weeks. Early in May watch out for the corn-stalk borer. This is a caterpillar that lives in the stem and eats the folded young leaves. The leaves appear at the mouth of the plant in a ragged way—sometimes so eaten up they don't open out at all and merely lay over.

When you see the damage, it's generally too late, so it's best to prevent it.

Cob that has poor leaf or husk coverage is like an open door. Pests, including corn earworm, easily get in and destroy kernels.

Some corn varieties have a long set of protecting leaves at the mouth of the cob and, as a result, the pest is less of a nuisance. It simply can't get in. Varieties with open ends to the cob are very vulnerable.

Once the damage has occurred, there's no point in worrying about it— you have to protect your harvest by anticipating it. As soon as the silks appear, apply three or four drops of mineral oil at the entrance to the cob. Eggs and young caterpillars will be smothered by the oil and the crop will be safe.

There's another cause of kernel loss and the commonest one in desert gardening. When temperatures reach the 100's, it's too hot for reliable pollination. Pollen grains falling off the top flowers (tassels) take their chances in reaching the lower female flowers (silks) and it's a perilous journey. They might be blown away by a strong wind. Should a pollen grain alight on the end of a silk filament, it still has a long way to go before it reaches the embryo—and often fails. Higher temperatures increase the rate of growth of a pollen tube and exhaust it before it finishes its journey. Very high temperatures kill the life-force in the pollen just as boiling water kills a seed.

It's too hot to sow any more corn seeds—until summer's end.

Long extended set of leaves effectively closes "door" to pests. When corn is in full silk is the time to put four drops of mineral oil at opening to keep out corn earworm. Varieties with few short leaves at end of cob are poorly protected and need treatment more than those with plenty of leaves protruding beyond opening.

Do this by putting insecticide down the funnel of the plant when it is about a foot high. A dust stays at the mouth of the funnel and a liquid trickles down to the insides. Take your choice.

Chemicals to use are Sevin®, Malathion 50 or diazinon. One application should be sufficient, but if you hear that it's a bad year for stalk borers, make applications every week or 10 days. Read the fine print on the label of the material you buy. Too many gardeners have carelessly exceeded the stated dose and burned the delicate tissue of the young leaves rolled up inside. If a strong solution gets on the growing point itself, the plant is finished—corn has only one bud.

If you don't like the idea of chemicals, try Dipel® or Thuricide® or B.T.—commercial names for Bacillus thuringiensis, a bacteria that causes terminal stomachache in caterpillars.

After you think you have taken care of the corn-stalk borer there's another problem waiting for you—corn earworm. This is the caterpillar you find inside the cob, eating the kernels. This caterpillar also comes from an egg laid by a moth. This time the eggs are laid at the mouth of the cob as the silks start to protrude. The caterpillars work their way down into the cob, under the enveloping leaves, where they are safe from birds.

May
WEEK 3

It's not the Merry Month of May if you are a desert gardener.

Insects

You never thought there were so many pesky insects. But before you rush for the spray gun, consider that most bugs are innocuous, some are beneficial and only a few are a nuisance.

The nuisance ones are the obvious ones. Let's start with the grape-leaf hopper. This small creature appears in hundreds on grape leaves and rasps their surfaces to give them a grey or silvery appearance. Photosynthesis is interrupted by them even though the damage appears to be slight. As you walk under the arbor, you can hear them jumping off the leaves at your approach. Don't ignore them. They may appear small and insignificant, but a heavy infestation can rasp leaves so severely that they lose moisture and fall off. The vine is trying to produce fruit, so replacing lost leaves is a strain on its resources. Spray with diazinon or Malathion 50.

A relative, the beet-leaf hopper, is a more serious pest because it carries the virus that causes curly top, or leaf curl, in tomatoes. It feeds on desert plants and as these begin to dry out and die, it migrates to our green gardens, bringing the virus with it. There are so many of them, and they come in waves, that spraying is not a feasible control. You could envelop your tomato plants in cheesecloth to keep the tiny creature out and, in the process, give some valuable screening from the sun, but this will not guarantee complete protection. Planting away from afternoon sun does help because the leaf hopper is a sun-loving insect. The best measure is to plant varieties resistant to curly-top virus.

Then there's the orange dog. This nasty-looking caterpillar comes from an unlikely parent—the beautiful swallowtail butterfly. The caterpillars love citrus leaves and do a lot of damage before you notice their presence. Be observant and pick them off as soon as you notice them.

You don't see tomato hornworms, either, until they have eaten a lot of your tomato leaves.

You certainly don't notice the arrival of the squash-vine borer.

Be alert to all of these possibilities in your garden. Don't relax a minute, because if you do there'll be a lot to cry about. As soon as you see something you know is damaging, take care of it.

This means catching a grasshopper in the cool of the early morning when it is sluggish. Or tracking ants back to their nest and pouring insecticide down it. Or using a butterfly net to capture grape-leaf skeletonizer and squash-vine borer moths before they lay their eggs.

Making Room

The start of summer means the end of winter, so we shouldn't spend any time with the remains of our carrot crop, or the onions, beets or lettuce left in the ground. Pull them out to make room for seeds of squash, cantaloupe, watermelon, okra and black-eyed peas.

All of these crops love the heat and grow vigorously, but they need a lot of water. As water becomes more and more expensive, you may revise your concepts of some garden crops. There's little point in spending time and money on growing something you can get cheaper on the roadside or in a supermarket from mechanized agriculture.

However, if you can grow vegetables out of season, or certain gourmet vegetables that aren't available in the supermarket, it's well worthwhile.

Additionally, there is the enjoyment you can get from overcoming the trials, tribulations and challenges of desert gardening. It's more satisfying than completing a difficult crossword puzzle. Everything you grow tastes better—it really does.

May
Week 4

With marbles for eyes that catch sunlight and a wicked grin that wobbles in a light breeze, cat is supposed to guard your fruit from birds . . . it doesn't!

Discouraging Birds

The way birds discover fruit and damage it before it's ripe is most irritating. We spend a lot of time and energy—not to mention money—on raising our own fruit and we have the right to enjoy it at its best. This means we should be able to leave it on the tree to sun-ripen as long as possible, but the birds won't let us. There are some fanciful ideas on the market that are supposed to keep birds from eating your fruit. They are not all that effective.

That original device, the scarecrow, is best made at home—though you can buy inflatable plastic ones. By

Inflatable owl looks ferocious enough, but birds try and chase it out of the garden by pecking it!

After pecking the owl, birds go to work on fake snake.

Home-town engineer found new use for old beer can. But flashing in sun and squeaky axle didn't keep birds away.

Bird psychologists recommended that hawk silhouettes be suspended from long poles. Their shadows and movement in the wind would—they insisted—be enough to scare away fruit-eating birds. It didn't work in the garden.

Only way to be sure birds don't eat your fruit is to keep them out of tree. Completely cover tree with a bird net. Use PVC tubing with a cross as described in text.

making it a family project you can at least get some fun out of the operation.

Scarecrows, stuffed owls, rubber snakes, children's toys, mirrors and shiny pie pans on a string don't work after a few days—the birds get used to them. Changing their position makes them effective a little longer.

The latest idea is a silhouette of a hawk attached to a long pole with a piece of string. Birds don't like the appearance of hawks and this one's shadow moving over the ground, say bird psychologists, is doubly effective as the sight of a hawk overhead. However, experience has shown that it's as effective as a stuffed teddy bear.

Another item, somewhat costly if ordered through a catalog, is a metal face of a cat with marbles for eyes. It's suspended on a string and, as it turns in the breeze, light shining through the eyes is supposed to frighten birds.

Birds even get used to interval-bangers that go off every now and again like a cannon. If you try these, you'll frighten the neighbors more than birds.

Dogs are no good, even if usually energetic and playful, but cats are very effective. The difficulty is to keep them close to your trees. In olden days gardeners would tether a cat to a long run of wire. That kept the birds off the fruit.

Using a Bird Net

The only thing left for us is the bird net—and it works. You can buy it at nurseries in varying sizes, but it's likely that you will need to sew two or three together. Completely wrap your tree because the net is no good just on top or halfway around.

To get the net over the tree easily, with its projecting twigs that catch everything, set up a plastic-pipe framework. Buy a fitting called a *cross* and four 10-foot-long plastic pipes for each tree. Fit, but don't glue them into the

cross and set the free ends on sticks in the soil to stop them sliding about. Anchor the bottom of the net with bricks to stop the wind from lifting a flap big enough to let in birds.

To be most effective, the net must be in place before the fruit starts to be interesting to birds. Once birds know there is fruit in a certain place they will try and try again to get to it. Half-eaten fruit puts out an attractive smell that brings more birds—and insects, too. It's nature's way of advertising a free meal. Pick all damaged fruit that is sending out a signal.

Some kind gardeners say that they don't mind the birds getting some of

Rock squirrels eat fruit, dig holes and steal vegetables. It's irresponsible to spread out poisoned grain and hope they eat it. Trap them and give them a drowning lesson.

their fruit. Half for me and half for them, is the notion. Such people don't know that birds take half of *each* fruit. If they took only half of the harvest you might get by.

Once apricots are harvested, you can move the protection to the peaches. Protect the earlier ones first and then the later varieties. Finish up with the apples. You don't need a net for every tree. You can protect the very light crop on a young tree by tying a paper sandwich bag—not plastic—over each fruit.

It used to be that the first ripe fruit escaped the attention of birds, but this is no longer true. It's also no longer true that birds ignore paper bags that hide grape bunches. Some have learned

To support over-burdened branch, make support of stiff wire. It slides up and down pole and is held in place by weight of branch.

that fruit is inside and now they tear them open.

Rock squirrels go for apples in a big way. A net doesn't hold them back, so you have to trap them. Box traps, baited with peanut butter mixed with oatmeal, catch them alive and you have to do the rest. It's humane in a way to take them far off and let them go, but this release of an extra animal in a balanced environment causes other problems, at least from an animal point of view. Throw the trap and its occupant into a barrel of water.

A tidy way to dispose of trapped animals is to put the trap, with its animal, in a plastic garbage bag and then introduce car exhaust fumes into it. Attach a length of flexible pipe to the exhaust and lead it into the bag.

Branch Support

After you have gotten rid of all the pests—an optimistic statement if ever there was one—you may have another problem. A heavy crop weighs down the branches so much that they break. Did you thin the young fruit enough? You have to support the weight with props. Bunches of grapefruit near the ground can be placed on bricks or boards.

Pruning next January will be influenced by such things. Remove long, weak growth and keep the tree as small overall as you can so a net can easily be put over it next harvest time.

Take a look at the grapevines and sort out the developing bunches. Let them hang free. If you have had a very good berry set, you may want to pinch out the bottom third of the bunch. This will help produce bigger berries—but don't forget watering while the harvest is growing.

June
WEEK 1

June is the month when we begin our gardening chores early in the morning because of daytime heat. It's stimulating to start the day with a drink of fresh grapefruit juice. Because the fruit is so ripe, it's possible to eat the fruit like an orange—it peels and segments so readily. Look at the thickness of the skin. It should be thin. If it is thick, let that remind you not to fertilize your trees so much this year. The fruit is now getting past its prime and you need to harvest what remains before it gets puffy. Besides, young fruit from the spring flowering needs all the tree's resources.

Squash Pollination

Early in the morning is when you carry out a daily chore on your squash

Male flower rests on a thin stalk.

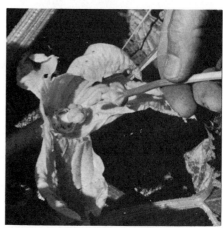

You can hand-pollinate female squash flower with de-petalled male flower. Pollen from one male flower is sufficient for pollinating four or five female flowers.

New gardeners are surprised to learn that fruit grows with flower and not as a result of actual pollination. Pollination sees it through.

If flower is not pollinated, fruit develops just a little more, but then rots at end. New gardeners think this is a disease when they first see it. Successive flowers will develop good fruit if polllinated. Plant is healthy.

plants—hand pollination. Sometimes the bees give your garden a wide berth and the smaller insects don't seem to do their stuff, either. Look for a good balance of male and female flowers and don't be misled by the presence of the young fruit behind the daily flower. The squash is there all right; it grows with the flower. But it simply refuses to develop if pollination doesn't happen. Then you get that rotting tip that looks like a disease—but it's not a disease.

Insects

While you are at it, inspect the stems of the plants for eggs of the squash-vine borer. They are laid two or three at a time on the outside of the stem. They are about the size of a pin head and can easily be rubbed off. If they remain, you have a much bigger task later on after they have hatched and burrowed into the stem and eaten up the inside. An ounce of prevention is worth a pound of cure. This is another daily task.

Stressed Tomatoes

Another fruit rot—on tomatoes this time—may be appearing now the weather is getting hot. It's hard for gardeners to accept this one, too. They ask, "What have I done wrong?" The ripening fruit shows a dark, corky, shriveled patch at the flower end of the fruit. You can cut this piece out and eat the fruit. You'll probably want to do this because this is the start of your harvest and you are all eager to get something back for your patient

This little grub, found in stem of plant, caused it to wilt and stop flowering. If not treated, it causes death of plant.

Sprawling tomato plant shades ground and humidity is trapped inside foliage. This ensures flower pollination and fruit set. Furthermore, fruit is shaded from strong rays of the sun and develops without splitting.

Watering basin needs to be enlarged so roots of tree expand into moist soil. Tree roots will not leave moist soil to go to dry soil.

Get bunches of early maturing varieties of grapes into paper bag before birds realize those clusters of marbles turn into something good to eat.

hard work during a difficult spring.

Blossom end rot, plant physiologists tell us, is not a disease, but a "condition." It's caused by stresses within the plant, not by a fungus or bacteria, even though the appearance strongly suggests it. The stresses are caused largely by irregular watering and high temperatures. Undoubtedly, bright sunshine and the general unkindness of June in the desert also have something to do with it.

The fruit's condition doesn't improve as time goes by, so if you have a lot of green tomatoes with a black end, you might as well pull them off and let the plant try again. Don't let the plant stay too wet and don't let it dry out too much, either. Don't give it shallow waterings. Try shading it to reduce stress.

Watering

It's best to deep-water all your plants this time of year. This means getting a reserve of moisture in the soil that lasts a long time. It also means encouraging deep roots that follow this moisture down and get away from the daily temperature extremes on the soil surface.

A sprawling tomato plant that shades the soil with its foliage seems to produce fruit longer into the summer than one that's been staked up and allows the sun to bake the soil around it.

Gardeners ask themselves and one another a good question at this change of season: "What's the best time of day to irrigate—morning or evening?"

If you irrigate in the evening, the plants have already gone through a bad day and you merely pull them back into a good state. Their wilt disappears and they look good again. On the other hand, if you water in the morning before it gets hot and stressful, your plants are more able to take the strain of mid-day heat. They will continue to grow and produce fruit. This argument is particularly apt if you make the mistake of sprinkling lightly and daily instead of giving that good, deep soak that lasts six or seven days.

Should you leave a garden hose out in the sun, don't forget it is full of hot water. Don't put this on your plants, but onto the compost pile or around a tree. Finish with cool water to keep down soil temperature.

Deep watering is always advisable, but especially on the trees and vines you planted in January. Their roots are just getting out of the planting ball and they will die if they meet hot, dry soil.

Enlarge the irrigation basin and use your soil probe to tell you when water has gone down 3 feet. Then all will be well. Gardeners who forget to do this let their trees lose the momentum of spring growth. With an unusually hot June there's also the danger of new growth dying back. Such a setback might mean you have to wait an additional year for the first crop.

Protecting Grapes

Early grapes are ripening—enough to make the fruit interesting to thirsty birds. The bunches aren't ready for us just yet, but if you don't bag them now there won't be anything for you next month. Birds work fast. Use brown-paper sandwich bags and staple them up at the top end of the bunch. There's no need to punch air holes—that will merely open the door for birds who will tear the holes larger. Don't use plastic bags because they sweat and cause the fruit to spoil.

June
WEEK 2

The sun gets too hot for many plants such as eggplant, bell pepper and tomatoes. Here's how to reduce intensity of sun's rays. Material breathes and keeps out insects, such as leaf hoppers which carry the deadly curly-top virus.

Grape Ties

While you are putting paper bags on the bunches of ripening grapes to protect your harvest from the birds, take a look at the ties you made in the spring. Let's hope you never used paper-covered wire. These are easy to use and look innocuous enough with their soft covering, but they don't stretch. Nylon string doesn't stretch nor does cotton string.

Why is this important?

Earlier on when you were training the shoots onto their wires, you were clever enough to make loose ties so future growth would not be pinched. Now you will be surprised to find the shoots thickened far more than you thought they would. It's possible that they are being strangled by their own energy. Paper-covered-wire ties might be so tight they are actually cutting into the shoot. It pays to take a careful look at all of last spring's ties and loosen them. Some may have to be cut.

One material that is suitable because it stretches, is the soft, green plastic ribbon that comes on rolls. There are thin kinds for soft plants and a thicker alternative for trees. Use the thin material for grapes.

New shoots will continue to develop during the summer and you should regularly guide these and tie them. Avoid a cluster of new shoots entangling themselves with their searching end tendrils.

Sow Seeds

There's a lot of exuberant growth during June. Sow seeds of squash, melons, okra, black-eyed peas, amaranth and yard-long beans. All of these love the heat and their seeds pop out of the soil in three or four days. It's very satisfying.

Shade Tomatoes

At the same time, high temperatures cause gardening grief. Tomatoes, bell peppers, eggplant and cucumbers slow their flower production. Some varieties stop completely, although plants themselves continue to grow vigorously. Those that continue to produce flowers don't set fruit because their pollen is killed by the heat.

There are two remedies for this state of affairs. First, provide shade for the plants. Even if you drape light muslin or cheesecloth directly on the plant, you will lower temperatures and reduce the sun's fierceness. You will also trap humidity around the plant, and this appears to be beneficial.

The second thing you can do is spray the flowers with tomato-bloom spray. First, read the instructions on the bottle. Don't use the spray too many times. The hormone stimulates fruit development without pollination so, as a side benefit, you get fruit with hardly any seeds.

Good gardeners select suitable varieties to overcome this summer problem. Cherry tomatoes can take the heat and will produce fruit continuously, but not everyone likes a summer full of cherry tomatoes. Plant breeders are developing bigger-fruited kinds of cherry tomatoes so the future looks promising. Meanwhile, don't try growing Beefsteak or Super Beefsteak. You'll be disappointed.

Yard-long Beans

Yard-long beans, mentioned earlier, are a wonderful summertime crop. They love the heat and sunshine and produce an abundance of long, green beans through the summer until they are killed by frost in November. There are a number of varieties that go by an assortment of names in the different catalogs. Look for Asparagus beans, or Chinese pole beans and you'll find them. This last name tells you that you must provide a trellis. It should be more than 6 feet high. Don't set it upright, but slant it a little. Then all the yard-long beans will hang straight and will be easy to pick.

And pick, you must. They grow vigorously and produce abundantly. The pods are best gathered before they harden into a string of beads. This calls for picking twice a week. Of course, you can let the seeds dry on the vine and have hard beans, but that's not the point. In summer, chop the tender beans for fresh salads. If you do steam the long pods, do so only lightly so they simulate asparagus.

You won't need a large acreage of this crop. A 10-foot row with plants 12 inches apart and trained up an 8-foot framework will keep you and your family well supplied all summer.

One gardener lost sight of his mobile home after planting a row of seeds on its sunny side. It turned into a heap of greenery. He couldn't eat all the beans. Many of them ripened and fell to the ground. The next summer he had to hack his way to the front door. He had the habit to go wandering with his friends, but he never got lost. It was easy to find home. Home was the biggest mound of vegetation for miles around in the hot, dry, brown desert.

June
WEEK 3

Harvest eggplant while there is a shine on fruit, upper right. Once shine has gone, lower left, quality is lost. Seeds become gritty and flesh loses its firmness. The best desert varieties are small-fruited Japanese kinds.

Heat Stress

In the dog days before summer rains break in July there's a lot of oppressive heat. It's common for shade temperatures to reach 105F and more. The sun is fierce and there are plenty of indications that plants are suffering. The obvious ones are wilting at the ends of new growth. Grapes give us a good example of this. Leaves drop off fruit trees and bush vegetables such as bell peppers and eggplant. Lawns show a characteristic dullness, followed by bluish-green patches that turn into straw-colored dead areas. Bad diagnosis calls this *fungus disease,* but it's not usually so and it's a waste of time and money to treat the area for a fungus. Treatment invariably requires the application of an expensive chemical—using a lot of relatively cheap water—and the cure is effected by the latter, not former.

Another common sign of heat stress on plants is a dull yellow patch in the center of a leaf. Sometimes this turns white and dead, right in the middle. Look for it on citrus leaves particularly, but it appears on many other trees that have shiny leaves. You'll find the same dead patch on ripening bell-pepper and eggplant fruit. It's sunburn, and it becomes worse if you let your plants go a day or two without watering. Be attentive.

Providing Shade

One thing you can do is move containers such as half whiskey barrels holding vegetables and dwarf fruit trees, into a shady place. Don't put them completely under a tree because they need morning sunshine and afternoon shade. You may have to begin watering them every day.

Shadecloth comes into its own now. The dark material should be attached to a tall framework so air moves over the plants easily. White shadecloth can come closer to the plants—even directly on them—because it reflects a lot of heat in addition to providing shade.

If you erect a tall structure, don't forget that the angle of the setting sun slants considerably. You will find the west end of your garden is in hot sun for a few hours unless you extend the shade 3 or 4 feet or allow the material to hang down 2 or 3 feet like a tablecloth. Make a scale model on a board and set it out in your garden before you start cutting any cloth.

Don't shade corn, squash, any of the melons, black-eyed peas, Chinese pole beans or okra. All of these enjoy the sunshine.

If peaches or apples are hanging at the ends of branches, you might put shadecloth over the trees. Protect bunches of grapes from the sun and birds by slipping a paper sandwich bag over them and stapling it at the top. There's no need to make breathing holes—the grapes are safe in the bag.

Citrus trees and their fruit can take the heat and sunshine as long as the trees are well supplied with moisture. You should have no anxiety about further fruit drop once the young fruit has reached golf-ball size. It's generally safe at that size, but don't be complacent. Watch the soil moisture and let the soil probe tell you when it's time to irrigate.

Insects

In years of ample rains when desert growth is luxurious, there is an accompanying large population of insects. When the annual weeds and flowers dry out and die, these insects migrate to the next green patch—our summer vegetable gardens. One particular insect, the beet-leaf hopper, brings curly-top virus with it.

Signs of this incurable disease begin to show in June—sometimes earlier—just as we start to pick the first tomatoes. An infected plant shows a wilt, stunted growth and poor flowering. Often these plants die, but occasionally they throw off the disease, struggle through the stresses of summer and revive to give us a fall harvest.

Plants in full sun are more attractive to the beet-leaf hopper than those that are shaded—for even part of the day. This suggests that shading offers some protection, but you will keep the pest out completely if you build a cage of cheesecloth around your tomatoes. Up goes the price of tomatoes! On the other hand, if you take your chances, you could have a complete disaster. Dead plants are a source of infection, but the soil can be used again when the danger has gone. Dead plants can be composted.

Harvesting Eggplant & Corn

How do you know when to harvest eggplant and corn? There's a tendency to let eggplant stay on the plant too long in the hope that you'll harvest a fruit as big as those you buy in the stores. The secret is to watch the shiny bloom on the fruit and avoid measuring its size. As soon as the shine becomes dull, the fruit is getting old. The seeds inside begin to harden and the flesh gets rubbery. The kinds that do well in the desert are naturally small-fruited ones—the Japanese varieties.

To be sure of getting a good cob of corn, make a daily inspection soon after the silks have turned brown and dry. Peel back a little of the enveloping sheath to expose the kernels. If they are plump and moist, the cobs are ready for boiling water. If the kernels

June
WEEK 4

are skinny, replace the sheath leaves and hold them with a rubber band. Look again in a couple of days, remembering corn ripens fast in June, especially when you water it well—as indeed it you must at this critical period. If the kernels are plump and hard and your thumbnail doesn't make much impression on them, you've lost the best. Don't give up, though. Today's varieties are super-sweet and you can enjoy them after the usual prime condition. In fact, some varieties don't seem to need any cooking. Shave off the kernels and eat them raw in a salad or, if you are under age, take the cob in both hands and bite away at the raw kernels. Don't waste water on a harvested corn plant—pull it out.

Plant sweet potatoes now. They love heat and sunshine. Not all nurseries stock young plants, so you may have to order from a catalog. Save some plants at harvest time and grow them during the winter as attractive houseplants in a sunny window.

It's the cicada grub that does most of the damage to plant roots. It lives in the soil for a year or more.

An unmistakable herald of approaching summer rains is the cicada. More correctly, we should speak of *them* because there's no such thing as *one* cicada. They sound off as if there are hundreds. June is cicada month.

Cicadas

"I've never seen anything like them," is the common cry. People must have short memories or the desert cities are full of new arrivals since last summer.

Cicadas live most of their lives in the ground as grubs, very similar in appearance to the June beetle grubs we turn up as we dig the vegetable bed. In the Midwest they are called *seven-year locusts*, but that's an inaccurate name in both aspects. It's not known exactly how long they stay in desert soils, but they come out in scores every June and climb upwards. You see their skeletons sticking to tree trunks, walls and even the front door. The split back tells you the live part has gone on, and your ears tell you that they are all over the place. It's the male sending out sexual signals that makes the racket to lure females to a tryst, after which eggs are laid.

It's the egg-laying that does some damage to our trees—either ornamental or fruit trees. The female makes a number of little incisions on tender twigs and places an egg in each. The result of this activity is the saw-tooth appearance of the terminal twigs,

After mating, this is the damage she does to tender twigs. Slits were small last year when she laid eggs in them, but grow with twig and often cause a localized die-back.

which often die back. It's a sort of gentle pruning and doesn't usually do a lot of damage to a tree, though it does leave it looking scorched at the edges.

The eggs hatch and fall to the ground. The little grub spends the next year or so, getting fatter by eating up vegetable material that might include roots of plants as well as decaying organic matter.

There isn't any worthwhile chemical control because cicadas don't stay in one place for long. They are 20 times the size of a house fly and a lot of poison is needed to overcome their hard protective exterior. There's little point in spraying the ends of tree growth because the spray evaporates quickly in the hot air and leaves little residue.

Nature's balance adjustment: Large wasp is called—rightly so—*Cicada Killer*. She makes her nest in the ground and drags adult cicadas into it to feed her young.

Thick mulch keeps soil cool and moist; plant roots benefit. But that's the best place for pillbugs, snails, earwigs and crickets on a hot summer's day. "You pays yer money and you takes yer choice."

Fruit pest has been hatching out in accumulation of fallen leaves and natural mulch. Soon, adults will be attacking ripening fruit and soft green nuts on pecan trees. Its appropriate name—*leaf-footed plant bug*.

Wasps

There is a natural predator of cicadas. It is appropriately called *cicada killer wasp*. It's the largest wasp in the desert and is capable of stinging the cicada as it flies around. The cicada body is brought to a hole in the ground and stuffed in to provide food for the baby wasps.

Wasps in general are beneficial insects—as long as you don't get stung by them. They eat aphids, mealybugs, red spider mites and other small insects that cause a nuisance to our plants.

Saving Water

Don't confuse twig die-back caused by cicadas with that caused by drought. They look similar and appear at the same time—that stressful, high-temperature period before the summer rains.

Constantly check the soil's moisture content at root depth with your soil probe. Just now, it's your best friend. Always give a deep irrigation down to the roots. Avoid the temptation to sprinkle a little in the evening when you get home from a hot, tiring day.

There are ways to save water. First, a deep soak puts water where it is wanted and promotes deep roots. Water won't evaporate if it is deep down. Second, conserve water you put on your garden by covering the soil with a straw or hay mulch. Mulch protects the soil from the hot sun and drying winds, and suppresses water-stealing weeds. Third, don't sprinkle and throw water high into the dry air where much of it evaporates before it falls to the ground. Fourth, shade the plants to keep them cool and slow their metabolism.

Unfortunately, a thick straw mulch often provides a cool and moist shelter with food provided to pillbugs, crickets and other insects. They repay your hospitality by eating your plants.

Then, there's the opportunity to reuse water from your bath, clothes washer and swimming pool. Provided that there's not a lot of sodium in these waters—from soaps in the first instance and as residue from chlorine powder in the latter—you can turn the outflows onto ornamental plants and lawns once in a while. Good water can be reserved for the vegetables and fruit trees. Your Cooperative Extension office will have a list of detergent soaps that are safe to use on the soil in your area.

Insects

The leaf-footed plant bug makes its appearance in June. It's aptly named because its hind legs have flattened sections that look like small leaves. The front end is the nasty part.

The bug feeds by sucking plant juices through its long piercing snout, and in the process introduces bacteria into fruit such as pomegranates, tomatoes and nuts such as pecans. These bacteria cause rot spots or, in severe cases, complete damage to the fruit.

June is a buggy month. Increased humidity can be blamed, but the one big monster insect of the desert hasn't appeared yet. It needs heavy drumming of raindrops on the soil to make it change from a 3-inch fat grub into an adult, giant, whirring beetle that scares old ladies and little children out of their wits.

Look out in July! The palo verde borer beetle is coming!

July
WEEK 1

Summer Rains

It often rains on the 4th of July—just to spoil someone's carefully arranged fireworks display. Never mind, you get a free display with all the lightning and thunder that seem to be just outside the window.

It's a desperate time, waiting for the rains to arrive. Temperatures reach 106F or more, forceful winds break off tree limbs and hurl corn plants to the ground. Desert plants and animals suffer from dehydration and we humans tend to neglect things.

We take care of our gardening chores early in the morning because it's the time we have the most energy. It's also the time when plants have their best moments. Make a point of inspecting them in the late afternoon when plants are most stressed. Their condition at that time of day, which is the worst time of all, will quickly tell you whether the soil has enough moisture.

Irrigating early in the morning is good. You prepare vegetable plants for the hard times ahead—2 or 3 o'clock in the afternoon. On the other hand, an evening irrigation—after the plants have had a hard day—merely brings them back to their early morning condition. With trees it's not the same. A good, deep watering can be given any time of the day because it's designed to last more than a week.

Birds are active at daybreak, too. If you see them around during the heat of the day, they are invariably after your grapes, tomatoes, apples, peaches or figs; anything that's juicy.

If you want a crop, you must keep the birds away. This means putting a bird net over your trees and paper bags on bunches of grapes.

Harvesting Fruit

In a hot, dry year, birds are extremely persistent so it's a relief to begin harvesting fruit for yourself. Beauty Seedless and Perlette

Summer clouds build up in a dramatic way and promise a good downpour. Although humidity increases, there's no guarantee rain will fall on your garden or part of town.

grapes are the first to be ready. Enjoy them. Anna and Ein Sheimer apples are ready during July. Don't leave them on the tree to get bigger, but eat Anna fruit while they have a pink bloom and before they turn a dull yellow. They are not good keepers in the best of years. Ein Sheimer are smaller, greener and more of a tart cooking apple. Hot sunshine on ripe fruit hastens its maturity to the point of it spoiling on the tree.

It's always good practice to pick up fallen fruit. It puts out a strong smell that attracts birds and insects.

You must be on constant alert for grape-leaf skeletonizer moths. They come and they go and even seem to disappear for a while, but they will come back. The tiny leaf hopper is also a summer-long problem on grapes. There are always a lot of them. Their rasping on leaves to get moisture and food causes the leaves to brown out and, in a heavy infestation, to fall off. Weekly sprays of diazinon will protect your grapevines from both pests and, provided you paper-bagged the bunches, you can safely eat the fruit soon after spraying and whenever it is ripe.

Watering

Keep irrigating all your plants in spite

of approaching rain. You quickly learn that summer rains are fickle and unreliable. Clouds build up beautifully, humidity increases, distant darkness and lightning gets closer, great winds stir up dust and thunder is loud enough to break the windows. Even so, you may not get a drop of rain.

When, finally, your patience is rewarded and the skies empty themselves, you still have to remain skeptical. How far into the soil did the rain go?

This is where your soil probe becomes useful again. Poke it into the soil to answer your question. You are likely to be disappointed. The storm was all flash and crash with no substance.

Keep on irrigating.

Storm Damage

Summer storms bring damage. If your fruit trees become heavy with rain and the winds are flying, it's likely that branches will be torn off. If young trees are not staked, they may be bent over. A corn patch can be lying on the ground after a storm. Tall palm trees attract lightning and are struck frequently. A lightning strike kills the tree and there's nothing to do except have it cut down and hauled away.

Damaged limbs and branches of fruit

July
WEEK 2

Summer-storm damage should not be repaired like this. Simply cut off damaged branch and let tree start over. Earlier pruning should be done to allow wind to blow through tree's foliage, not against it.

Rains on warm soil bring out mushrooms. These are edible meadow mushrooms, but gardener worries about another mushroom—Texas root rot.

Best place for containers during the rest of summer is in shade.

Branch, heavy with fruit, can be supported by your compost fork. It should not be in heavy use just now.

Or, make support of stiff wire. It slides up and down pole and is held in place by weight of branch.

Creating Shade

Although July is supposed to be a rainy month, it isn't always as wet as we would like. In between the storms there's still strong, damaging sunshine. Ripening fruit can be spoiled unless we shade it. Use muslin, cheesecloth or old lacy curtains and lay them directly on the plants if you can't find the time and energy to make a supporting frame.

In addition to the effort required during these trying times, there is a disadvantage in making a frame. A shadecloth structure gets caught up by the winds that precede rainstorms. As the cloth and frame bounces over your garden, it can do more damage than the good it did while shading tomatoes, peppers and eggplant.

If you merely lay the material on the plants, it does little damage should it be blown away and get caught on a fence or some trees.

Sunburn on grapes can be prevented by bagging them. You've already done this to keep off the birds, so you get a bonus. Apples, peaches and figs are not so easy to protect. Try the cheesecloth and keep putting it back when the wind stops.

trees should be cut off and the cut treated with pruning paint. It's seldom worthwhile to try to repair a broken branch. Even if it mends after being bound up, it remains a weakness in the tree. But if your tree is laden with fruit, prop up the heavily laden branches with a couple of forked poles until you harvest the crop.

Here's a case for summer pruning. Our January pruning caused additional growth, and that's the way we wanted it. However, much of that growth was renewal leaf branches which will produce fruit next year. If too much grew, aided perhaps by liberal fertilizing and watering, the thick foliage won't let the wind blow through the tree. It

gathers the force of the wind like a sail on a boat. Trees with underdeveloped root systems are often blown over. Before summer storms get started, thin out any congested new growth on your fruit trees.

If rain does fall, you can expect a lot of new mushrooms on the lawn. Usually they are edible meadow mushrooms, but be quite certain they are not poisonous toadstools before you prepare your free meal. Mushrooms and toadstools grow on the organic matter in the soil. They don't parasitize your plants. Unless you are afraid of them, there's no need to get rid of them.

When you select varieties of fruits and vegetables, always measure the plant's ability to shade its fruit with its own foliage. During winter months when you are reading the catalogs, pay attention to this characteristic. Color pictures, taken in cooler climates, show brightly colored fruit attractively sticking up in the air for all to see. During a desert July and August, we realize the importance of this self-shading factor. We wish we hadn't bought such kinds, or those that have to endure a whole summer before we can harvest them.

Plant Sunburn

Sunburn on leaves of evergreen plants such as citrus, privet and euonymus, becomes common in July. It's one of the reasons we shouldn't plant against the western walls of houses. A bronzed center on a leaf is the sign to fear. Trees that are short of water, even for an hour or two, sunburn most readily. Don't let your trees get hot. You can easily feel the heat on their surfaces and that's the signal to give them a good watering. Don't wait for them to wilt. Trees are like humans. They cool by sweating, so they must have the moisture to enable them to sweat comfortably.

Deep Watering

Advice is constantly given—perhaps to the point of irritation—to deep water your trees. This is important, but people forget or they have misconceptions about the operation.

You frequently hear them say, "Of course I water deeply. I have a root feeder that goes down 3 feet. That's how far down you recommend, isn't it? I made it myself out of a piece of piping." Well, that's not deep watering, not the best way. When you use one of these gadgets, you force water deep in the ground where it displaces soil and leaves great cavities. It should be called a *root disturber*. More often than not, the upper roots don't get the water they need. Don't forget that a good watering drives salts down through the soil and away from the roots. You have to start at the top of the soil to achieve this. Deep-root

"Deep-root feeder" gets water down deep, but puts it under root system and serves no purpose in washing salts past roots.

feeders, or whatever they are called, have no place in desert gardening.

Summer Fertilizing

Fertilizing during the summer does have a place in our program. We water a lot, and while we are washing down the salts we are also washing down the fertilizers we put there earlier. If we don't replace them now when growing plants need them most, we get pale lawns, sickly looking foliage, and trees that lose their vigor and strength.

Use small amounts of about 1 pound of ammonium sulphate to a 100 square feet every two or three weeks. Always apply fertilizers to moist soil and continue with the second half of the irrigation. If you throw dry fertilizer onto dry soil and hope the rain will wash it down, you may be in for a nasty surprise. Rain may not materialize and the fertilizer will be wasted. Only a little rain might fall, causing the fertilizer to be carried toward the roots as a concentrated solution that will corrode them. A lot of rain might fall and the fertilizer will be washed away in the surface runoff. Although it's welcome, seldom does rain fall in the way we want it to during summer months.

Harvesting Vine Fruits

On the joyous side of July, many beginning gardeners want to know when their vining fruits are ready to harvest. Often they pick a cantaloupe before it is ready in a frenzy of self-satisfaction that quickly turns to disappointment.

One general rule: Don't be in a hurry to harvest. The longer fruit stays on the plant, the sweeter it will be. There are always exceptions. Get eggplant before they lose their shine, regardless of size, and harvest summer squash a day or two after the flower fades.

Cantaloupe are the easiest to judge ripeness. The veins on the skin of the fruit become more prominent as the fruit turns from green to golden. When it is ready for harvest, it detaches itself from the stalk when you gently roll it along the ground. It *slips*—as the professionals say. If you have to tug to get it free, you have yourself an unripe cantaloupe.

Watermelon are the next easiest, though it calls for some scientific observation. For a few days, you've probably been thinking it's time to get that monster. You've placed it on a board to keep it out of the mud and you are fattening it with generous irrigations. The underside is white and flat. You're ready to do it. Don't! Size alone is no

July
WEEK 3

Best way to tell when a watermelon is ripe is to study the tendrils. There should be two or three back from the fruit that are hard and dry.

indication of ripeness.

Watermelons have little tendrils all along their vines. Use these as ripeness indicators. Close to where the fruit is attached, you'll find a dried-up tendril—somewhat like a brown little pig's tail. Go back, away from the fruit and toward the root and you'll see more of these tendrils. If there are three that are hard, dry, brown and curled, you have a ripe watermelon.

The non-scientific method of determining ripeness in a watermelon is based on old Chinese folk lore. In reaching these desert parts by word of mouth over the ages has, unfortunately, lost its accuracy. Tap with the knuckles, or slap with the hand—to begin with, you see, there's uncertainty in method—the fruit you think is ripe. If it makes a sound similar to that when you apply the same treatment to your head, the fruit should stay on the vine. If the sound is the same as when you strike your chest—fully inflated—the fruit may be picked within two days. If the sound is similar to that your stomach gives on being struck, you have waited too long and the fruit has lost its prime condition.

Sometimes you inadvertently carry out a destructive test on a watermelon. It unmistakenly tells you that you have a truly ripe one. As you proudly bring it through the kitchen door it falls out of your hands and crashes to the floor.

A ripe watermelon explodes as it hits the ground. An unripe one merely splits and lays there.

A word on *plugging,* which means taking out a little piece, looking at it wisely, and putting it back if it doesn't meet your approval. Look at the layer under the skin and not the colored, fleshy part. If the hardness extends an inch or so, you have a long wait for ripeness. When it's a quarter-inch thick, you're closer to your picnic.

Plugging is a messy, uncertain way to judge ripeness. The plug is supposed to go back into the fruit but, more often than not, you've opened the door to ants and other insects, and possibly molds.

Ripeness in casabas, Crenshaws and honeydews is not easy to judge. Use any method you like—and then wait a couple of weeks. Here are some ideas. Press the end of the fruit where the flower was—the end away from the vine attachment—and if it gives a little, the fruit is ripe. Smell the fruit early in the morning when it's cool. If it's more aromatic than that in the supermarket, pick it. If the bottom starts to flatten where it lays on the ground, it must be getting soft and, therefore, ready to harvest.

But don't be in a hurry—and don't worry. Even experts have been confounded in their haste to harvest.

Let your garden go fallow in summer and cover it with flakes from a straw bale. The wind won't pick them up as it will with shredded straw. A scattering of ammonium sulphate allows the straw to decompose—without it, any nitrogen in the soil will be used by bacteria as they digest the straw.

As soon as the soil is wetted down by storms, grubs of palo verde borer beetle come out of ground after a year or two of chewing on tree roots.

Palo Verde Borer Beetle

Last month we told you to get ready for the flying monster of the year—the palo verde borer beetle. It makes its appearance at night, though some appear to lose their way and turn up during the day, acting as if they were drunk.

The beetle is a 3-inch-long, shiny, brown creature with prominent feelers. It's a clumsy flier, attracted to the porch lights on a patio, street lights, anything white—even a pale human face recently arrived from the East. It doesn't attack the sunburned, leather faces of old-timers.

Where do they come from? Some years they are very common and are in everyone's yard. Other years it is hard to find one. All through the year they live underground as fat white grubs; the largest grubs this side of the Pecos.

What are they doing in the ground? They are eating the roots of your trees. Not just palo verdes, though this is the common victim. They kill trees such as mulberries, oleander, peach and plum. Trees that have been pushed along in their growth by frequent watering and heavy fertilizing so their wood is soft, are more likely to suffer than those living a more spartan existence.

When the thunderstorms of July beat their tattoo on the ground, the beetles emerge, leaving a hole the size of a broomstick handle. They fly around

Adult palo verde beetles fly around wildly at night, attracted to porch lights. They are easy to hit with a tennis racquet!

Green fruit beetles are more of a nuisance. They swarm onto ripening fruit and quickly spoil it.

for a week or two, find a mate, lay eggs and return to the soil—sometimes down the very hole they came out of. Then they die. Their eggs hatch and turn into grubs that burrow down in the moist soil until they find a root where they start feeding.

It's not known how long they live underground—maybe two years, perhaps more. One grub won't harm the tree very much but palo verde borer beetles don't come in ones.

A tree that is short of roots—for any reason—becomes a dry tree and loses its leaves. Twig ends die back, then the branches, then the limbs. In a year, the tree is dead, but you can't see the borers and you may not suspect their presence on the roots. The symptoms are common ones with many origins.

It's hard to dig down into the soil after grubs, large as they are, to find the evidence. You destroy the tree in the process. So you have to wait for the summer rains to see whether great holes appear under the spread of your tree. Holes the size of a little finger appear at this time, too. Cicada grubs

turning into adults and crawling out in just the same way, cause them.

The treatment is a sort of hit-and-miss operation, rather like throwing depth charges into the ocean to destroy a submarine you think is there. First, set a sprinkler halfway between the trunk and the ends of the branches. Let it run long enough so you can easily poke a probe 18 inches into the soil. Then take the sprinkler to the other side of the tree and repeat the process.

Next, sprinkle diazinon granules over the wet ground. Read the label on the container to know how much to use. Also scatter ammonium sulphate at the rate of 2 pounds to every 100 square feet. Continue watering to wash these chemicals deep into the soil. When you can poke your soil probe 3 feet into the ground, you've sprinkled enough. Let's hope you get all the grubs.

In any event, the watering you give the tree will help it. So will the ammonium sulphate because it helps root renewal.

It may satisfy you to pour liquid diazinon, diluted according to the label directions, down the holes. Don't forget that these are exit holes, showing where the beetle emerged, and it's only chance that any beetles are down there. But if one is down there laying eggs, the diazinon will take care of the next generation.

Green Fruit Beetles

Look out for the green fruit beetle, that iridescent beauty that destroys ripening fruit. The best way to avoid this pest is to plant varieties of fruit trees that ripen before the beetles appear in July. However, your trees may have been planted by someone else who didn't know and now you have to live with the problem.

Cover your trees with a sheet and spray the searching beetles with diazinon or Malathion 50 as they fly onto the sheet. Don't allow damaged fruit to send out attractive smells. Green fruit beetles are slow fliers, making a great whirring as they go. You can swat them with a tennis racquet if you want some exercise. One inven-

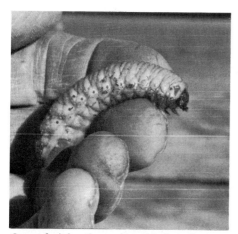

Green fruit beetles arrive with the rains. Grub stage has been feeding in heaps of organic matter such as your compost pile.

tive gardener sucks them off his fruit with a vacuum cleaner.

But you must empty the beetles out of the paper vacuum bag or they'll quickly chew their way out. Dump them into a bucket of water and give them a drowning lesson. That way, you know where they've gone—unless you are good with a tennis racquet.

These beetles spend most of their lives as 2-inch-long, white grubs, eating decaying organic material. They are in almost every compost pile. When you discover them and place them on the ground in what you think is the right way up—legs down—they roll over and wriggle along on their backs.

After that little trick, they stop being interesting. Put them back in the compost pile where they can chew up the bigger bits, but don't let them reach maturity and become a nuisance as a flying adult. Maybe it's best to feed them to the chickens. They're a delicacy, judging by the way chickens go for them. Or simply squash them.

Leaf-Footed Plant Bug

Yet another insect pest of July and the next few weeks, is the leaf-footed plant bug. The first part of its name is easy to accept when you look at the flattened hind legs. Being a bug, it sucks plant juices and, if this weren't enough, it introduces bacteria into fruit

as it pierces the skin. This accounts for rotted fruit and spotty pecan nuts later.

When this pest clusters on pomegranates, tomatoes, late peaches or grapes, use the same protection methods as you do for green fruit beetles. Above all, don't let rotten fruit put out a smell.

Declining Cucumbers

Due to the hot weather, cucumbers begin to decline even in the shade. The summer sun is too fierce. If your plants are producing some fruit, they are likely to be bitter. No one is quite sure why, and there's no antidote. Some kinds are worse than others. The best variety for the desert is Armenian. It's a big fruit—though it's better not to let it grow big—and sometimes the skin is thick. All other kinds are a summer disappointment.

Texas Root Rot

Now, just to round out the bad news, let's think about Texas root rot. This is the time of year it shows itself most.

I devoted a chapter at the front of the book to this disease, for it's a major nuisance. During July and August, it's likely to appear during periods of high temperatures and heavy rains that keep the soil wet too long. You will recognize these conditions as being stressful on trees and that's when the fungus overcomes its host. Texas root rot is in the soil and perhaps on the tree's roots all the time and a vigorous tree puts up with it until conditions become too stressful.

If the rains are heavy and continuous, don't keep watering your trees on the same old schedule. Turn off the automatic controls and water by hand according to the soil's condition. Use the soil probe to guide you.

If your trees show symptoms, carry out the treatment *at once*. Read Chapter 17 again and be ready for Texas root rot. Delaying the treatment can be fatal to the tree and disturbing to your peace of mind.

Drying Fruit

It's time for some good news. Perhaps you have more fruit—grapes, tomatoes, figs, peaches—than you can eat.

Bottling and canning isn't for everyone during the hot summer days unless you have outside facilities. Why not dry the surplus?

If the days are humid, it's not too easy. But on dry days, it takes just a week to drive out the moisture from ripe fruit, especially if it's thinly sliced. It's not the sun by itself that does the work. You need a movement of dry air to take away the moisture from any fruit. Several machines are available. These are really boxes of wire trays with good air movement. Those equipped with electric heater coils and small fans can be used on a rainy day, though they work better when the air is dry.

Sun-powered driers are also effective and cost nothing in the way of electricity. Make one yourself from plans found in a magazine dealing with energy conservation.

Grapes turn into raisins, figs can be dried whole, though it's better to split them. Peaches should have the stones removed, and tomatoes need to be sliced thinly. Squash, when thinly sliced and sprinkled with flavored salt, make wonderful chips.

If you like tasty treats, make fruit leather. Use a food blender to mix ripe, good-quality fruit with honey. Don't add water. Spread the paste thinly on waxed paper to dry. This works most satisfactorily when set on wire trays in a covered solar drier. Flies are kept out by window screen on all the openings that allow good air movement. In three or four days, you'll have a sheet of delicious, fruit-flavored confection that the children can't leave alone.

July
WEEK 4

Kill soil organisms by covering the soil for a month with clear plastic. It intensifies the sun's heat and cooks everything underneath.

Sterilizing Soil

The soil reaches its hottest temperatures during July and August. We can make use of this fact. The sun itself can be made to sterilize soil contaminated with weeds, especially troublesome nutgrass, and nematodes.

Let's call it *summer fallowing,* using clear plastic to generate additional heat. Of course, you have to stop using your garden for a while, but if it's a bit of a failure because of a build-up of pests over the years, now is your opportunity to tackle the problem.

First clear out all the dead plants and pull the weeds. Turn on the sprinkler to wet the soil down to 18 inches. Cover the garden with a sheet of clear plastic and let the sun cook everything under it. At first some weeds will germinate and established weeds will grow rapidly. But it won't be long before the heat becomes too much and they die. The same thing happens to soil organisms—both the good and the bad. If your soil has an excess of bad ones such as nematodes, snails, pillbugs, fusarium, verticillium and so on, the operation is worth it.

Leave the plastic undisturbed for a month. Put bricks on the edges to keep the wind from turning back the plastic and opening up the area to dryness.

After a month, remove the plastic, dig the ground to bring up the lower layers of infested soil, wet down the area again and replace the plastic for another month of solar cooking.

This is a cheap way to sterilize your soil and a way that doesn't pollute the environment. You can plant again as soon as you remove the plastic.

Chemical sterilization using Vapam® requires the soil to be cooler. That's usually when we want to be gardening and can't spare the ground for a month's treatment. Vapam® also affects the roots of nearby trees and you must be very careful when using it in confined spaces.

Tomatoes

Talking of plants that aren't doing too well in the heat, now is the time to cut back tomato plants. This doesn't apply so much to the cherry types, but most of the other kinds look miserable in July and August. They don't flower in the heat.

Cut back the top growth, leaving about a foot of stem to produce new leaves and branches. The new branches will produce flowers that set fruit in the cooling weather of September. Fruit production will continue until the first killing frost of November. You'll wonder what to do with all the green tomatoes.

In mid-July, sow tomato seeds. They will germinate quickly to give you plants big enough to set out in five weeks. Use houseplant food in the water to complement the warmth that causes such vigorous growth.

Because the days are warm in August and nights are cooling, newly planted tomatoes grow exceptionally well. They will start flowering in the cooler weather of September and give good yields until frost nips them in November and December. Even then, it's possible to carry over young plants during a mild winter or protect them in a greenhouse-like structure during a harder winter.

Last Vegetable Sowing

There's time enough to get harvests from a last sowing of squash, corn and black-eyed peas in late July. It's risky to plant longer-term plants such as watermelons or cantaloupe. Corn grows well in the hot days of July and August, but we have to wait for cooler nights to be sure the pollen isn't killed. These will come in September and October.

Sow corn seeds now and sow again in three weeks, and even a third time another three weeks later. You'll get a good crop over a period of time that will include Thanksgiving and, with some luck, Christmas. Remember to sow the seed in square plots rather than in long narrow rows. The pollen should fall on a nearby silk, not be blown away by the wind and lost.

August
WEEK 1

Only one month to go! That's what's in every gardener's mind in August. Nothing can be worse than this heat. Just the thought of September keeps us going. September is nice.

Most gardens look a mess in August. If anything has gone wrong, now it's underscored. Unsuitable tomato varieties look brown and useless. Corn is finished and stands forlorn. Squash-vine borer has most likely laid waste that department, too. Plants wilt at noon—even those that are supposed to like the heat. If you don't give a timely irrigation, they won't come out of the wilt and you'll lose them. Pay special attention to plants in containers. You may have to water them twice a day.

Taking a Break

It's time for a getaway vacation. Find somewhere cool and stay away as long as you can.

But can you afford to? Emotionally, as well as financially? The garden may be a mess, but don't you feel responsible for it and fear that your absence will lead to a bigger catastrophe?

Gardening in August is a change-of-seasons time and it's all right to take a break. You'll benefit from the change and come back with fresh resolutions and a lot of energy.

What's going to happen while you are away? Even with automatic watering systems there's a need for human surveillance. Something might break, storms may damage trees or blow them down, weeds may grow 6 feet tall if it rains a lot, pests can consume half a garden while you are absent. In addition, a neglected garden and landscaped area advertises your absence just as much as the heap of newspapers lying in the driveway or an overflowing mailbox.

Find a caretaker to look after things while you are gone.

Instructing a Caretaker

If you have a friend who knows your gardening ways, there isn't a lot of preparation required. Perhaps all that's needed is a reminder list and a walk around before you go. On the other hand, if you are encouraging a young neighbor to enter the work force for the first time, it's only fair to train him—or her—for the responsibility.

You need someone who is reliable—not clever. It's a fact of life that young people are not experienced and that's nobody's fault. They are energetic and work on impulses. This makes it advisable to make a list of things they should not do while you are away. For example, while a family was away for a vacation their youthful caretaker decided that a fresh crop of summer weeds needed spraying instead of being pulled up. His choice of 24D as the chemical, a fine mist to the sprayer, a breezy day and lack of attention, killed a nearby grapevine.

It's not fair to the caretaker to give instructions on the telephone, even if you make a list of things to do and leave it for him to find on the refrigerator door.

By all means make a list—it will be most helpful—and take it with you when you walk your caretaker through the jobs you want done. Actually do them because there may be some particular idiosyncrasy in your equipment, your way of doing things, or the way a certain plant has to be treated. Take this work walk a week or so before you leave. It gives him time to think about things and ask questions. Then, a day or so before you leave, work through the tasks again. Now he does the talking and you do the listening—don't interrupt—and you'll know if he has understood.

Give him the name of a backup person in case there are unforeseen troubles. A good gardening friend, even if he lives across town, is much better than your caretaker's parents. They may not even be gardeners, and surely don't want to take on additional responsibilities that are really yours.

Stress the need for personal safety, especially if you ask him to use power equipment. Here is a case where consultation with the parents is advisable. Do they want their child to use an unfamiliar power mower or electric garden tools or chemicals?

If he is to use your power equipment, give full instructions, let him try

Green fruit beetle is one of summer's pests. It is worse some years than others, but appears to be on the increase. This is one way to catch them. Old fruit puts out an attractive smell—at least to the beetles!

out and give a test. Don't let him use anything unless you are fully satisfied about his capabilities and the machine's performance. There are two points of view about friends being with him as he works: First, a friend is good to have when something goes wrong because it provides someone to go for help. Second, friends are a distraction and a temptation. Further, friends—especially little ones—are an added responsibility. They can easily be hurt if they get too close to things like a power lawn mower that throws out stones as fast as bullets.

It's good practice to encourage conscientious work by giving a bonus if all is well on your return. Say this before you go, but be careful not to give the impression that you will give him more if he does more. He might do far more than you want.

Well, perhaps there's so much to do that you decide to stay home and do it yourself. August can be a busy month

August
WEEK 2

for gardeners who are trying to keep up with conditions Mother Nature sends us and make plans for the fall.

Fruit Beetles

Figs, peaches, apples and grapes are ripening and humid breezes carry the smell of spoiled fruit downwind to the green fruit beetles. They come in droves, together with sour fruit beetles—those small, brown things that get into the open-ended figs and turn them sour.

Be clean and tidy. Pick off and pick up all damaged fruit and discard it. It may not smell to you, but it's a powerful attraction to insects who travel by smell for all of their activities.

Cover the tree or bag the bunches to keep the beetles out. Spray the insects with Malathion 50 or diazinon as they search for the hidden fruit. If they cluster anywhere, take the vacuum cleaner to them. Trap them before they get to your tree.

It's easy to make an insect trap. Take a gallon jar or can and place a funnel-shaped piece of window screening as the opening. A pair of scissors cuts it easily. Fasten it on with string or a rubber band. Put rotting fruit, watermelon rinds, or fruit juice in the jar—and wait. Green fruit beetles will come with their friends, walk down the funnel to the opening, fall in and be unable to get out. Dispose of them, clean the jar—an optional task because some gardeners think it's better to have a smelly jar than a clean one—and repeat the process until you have caught all the beetles in your neighborhood.

If all the gardeners in your neighborhood did this for a few years, there would be far fewer green fruit beetles to worry about.

Take vigorous axillary shoots from tomato plant that survived the summer.

Cutting Back Tomatoes

If you haven't already done it, cut back tomato plants now. It's your last chance. If you delay any longer, there won't be enough time for the plants to start anew, grow flowers in the cool of the year—yes, it is going to be cooler in September and October—and produce red fruit before frost kills them. Oh, there'll be lots of green tomatoes, but that's not the same. In fact it gives us kitchen problems because there are so many of them.

Get with it now. The bush-variety plants should be cut back, leaving about one-third in the form of short stubs, each bearing a number of side branches with leaves. The straggly cherry-tomato plants can also be cut back, but there is an alternative treatment.

Look over a cherry-type plant and spread the long branches on the ground, radiating outwards from the center. Where the stems have lost their leaves, dig small trenches and lay the stems in them. Cover with dirt, but leave the green, leafy ends out in the sunshine. Water widely to encourage the stems to grow new roots. Apply Miracle-Gro® at alternate waterings.

Whatever treatment you use will renew vigorous growth. Use the trimmings to make new plants. Take a strong axillary shoot—one that has developed against the stem where an old leaf stalk is—and cut it cleanly. It will be about 6 inches long. Dip the end in RooTone® powder and set it in a large styrofoam coffee cup filled with a light soil mix. Keep it in a well-lit place—not direct sunshine—all day and it will grow roots in a couple of weeks. It will be ready to plant in the ground at the beginning of September.

Ordering Winter Vegetables

September is going to be a busy month. Be ready for it. Start now by reading seed catalogs and placing your order for winter-season vegetables. Don't overlook the oriental vegetables, including interesting variations of broccoli, cabbage and radish. If you haven't tried them yet, you're in for a pleasant adventure in gourmet tasting. They are easy to grow, too.

Cicada Damage

Meanwhile, you may have noticed something wrong with your young fruit and nut trees. A number of dead branch ends with their brown leaves hanging on attract your attention. It's

Dip end of cutting in root-promoting powder and set in moist soil mix. Place cutting in a shady spot.

In a few weeks the axillary shoot has become a new plant, complete with roots. It should be set out in the garden as soon as the roots are this big.

enough to give you a fright because during summer rains it's natural to think of Texas root rot when you see something like this. These brown leaves look very much like the beginning of that scourge.

It's good to be concerned because you need to be alert to the possibility. But when you take a closer look, you find the brown leaves are the result of some physical damage. The stalk on which the brown leaves hang has a neat series of 10 to 15 fine sawtooth marks close together. Sometimes you see little white grubs in the crevices.

These grubs are bad news, but you can breathe a sigh of relief at this relatively slight damage. It's not Texas root rot after all.

Do you remember the loud squeaking-whirring noises all over your garden six weeks ago and the dead shell cases of some insect that started to climb your house walls and trees? That was the annual movement of cicadas from the ground where they lived as grubs, to the air where they flew around as "locusts" and began to make that irritating noise. The noise was not designed to bother you, but to attract the female cicada. The consequence of that episode is the little grubs you see in the damaged twigs of your fruit trees.

The damage isn't all that bad, but the danger is that next year's generation of cicadas is on its way to the soil. The

tree has been lightly pruned and it could even be considered a beneficial pruning because side shoots grow from such tip pruning.

If you are worried about the next generation, spray the dead twig ends with Malathion 50 or diazinon. Or better still, pinch them out grubs and all. As with all insect management, take measures as soon as you see any damage and know what the problem is. The longer you wait, the more likely it is the grubs have gone on their way to safety in the soil. You'll then have to resort to the treatment described on page 224.

Coping with Heat

What are you doing about the heat? Plants are going through a bad time. The least you can do is to keep the sun off their foliage and, thereby, lower their body temperature.

Of course you are watering—everyone realizes the necessity for this—but watering in itself is not enough. Providing the plant with water enables it to evaporate and cool off, but temperatures of more than 100F are a tremendous strain on anyone's system.

There's a danger in thinking that more and more water will bring down the plant's temperature. If you do keep watering every day, the danger will be in drowning the roots. They must have oxygen to breathe. If they don't get it, your plants will die.

Root Drowning

Symptoms of root drowning begin as dull, dark-green leaves that soon become *chlorotic*. If you remember that this means lack of healthy green color, you won't allow an overzealous salesman to compound your mistakes. It's a common error to assume automatically that pale-green plants need iron. There's no need to feel guilty and buy your plant an expensive present in the form of iron chelate to cheer it up.

True enough, the plant is short of iron simply because its roots can't breathe. Sometimes an application of expensive iron chelate does give a temporary improvement, but you can make a permanent change—as much as the weather will allow—by letting the soil dry out somewhat. When you next irrigate, water deeply, but let the surface dry out between times.

Reducing Surface Evaporation

If rains are inadequate during a hot August, water is uppermost in our minds. How do we keep our utility bills low? You can save water by reducing evaporation from the soil surface. Use your crop residues—and you may have lots of useful corn stalks that are otherwise no good to you—as a mulch over the ground. If you don't have crop residues, it's a good investment to buy a bale of straw and scatter it over the soil and in the case of strawberries, over the plants, too, to provide shade. It becomes effective when it's 3 or 4 inches thick. Don't pack it down. Just let it lay there and hope the summer storm winds won't blow it away. Put it back if they do.

Using Swimming-Pool Water

If you have a swimming pool, you may be able to use the backflush water on your plants. Have the water tested for total salts. Your swimming-pool-chemical salesmen will do this for you. If the figure is less than 800 parts per million, it should be safe to use on Bermudagrass lawns, eucalyptus trees and other arid-land plants. In this way you are saving the good-quality water for the salt-tender vegetables and fruit trees.

If your swimming pool has not been emptied for several years, the water will be high in salts because of the evaporation that takes place every summer. If you use liquid chemicals to provide chlorine, it's likely that the salts contain sodium—something you don't want to put on any plants, any time. If you have been using solid chemicals, then it's likely that the residues in the water are calcium salts which are not nearly as bad a prospect. In any event, don't spill the backflush water on the same part of the garden every time. Move it around so you don't fill the soil with unwanted chemicals.

Straw spread over growing crop in summer has several values. Obviously, it shades plants from heat of sun; it shades soil, too. Straw keeps moisture from evaporating and decays to provide humus that enriches soil's water-holding capacity and nutrient-exchange capabilities.

Your old friend the soil probe is always a useful tool. It tells you whether rain entered the soil or merely ran off. You may still have to irrigate in spite of heavy downfalls that are often localized and always seem to miss your garden.

Watering & Irrigating

After you have harvested apples, peaches and grapes, you can stop being so attentive about irrigating, but you musn't forget about it altogether. Trees and vines no longer have to carry a load of fruit that is 90% water, but they continue to grow and, therefore, need a given amount of water. Don't rely on it to be provided entirely by the rains. They're too fickle.

Use your soil probe to determine whether your plants are really getting their share of the rain. If storms prove to be mostly flash and crash, you had better irrigate.

August gives you an opportunity to test the latest in fertilizer notions from California. Grape researchers there assert that an application of nitrogen just after harvest ensures the nutrient reaches the branches where it is stored ready for springtime growth. They argue that a conventional application in February hasn't time to reach the opening buds and feed the rapidly growing shoots. It might be the same for deciduous fruit trees. Test this theory and see if your plants do better. Halfway through the next time you irrigate spread ammonium sulphate under the spread of the branches at the rate of 2 pounds to 100 square feet. Continue to water it in until you can poke your soil probe 3 feet down.

Weeds

Perhaps the rain is enough to keep your crop plants growing. Even a fickle rain is enough to produce a great crop of weeds. The humidity stimulates them so much that they easily grow to be 6 feet tall in undisturbed alleys and waste places. But not in your garden! Worry about these weeds because they are generating seeds for next year. Pull them up while the ground is soft. They come out easily, roots and all. If you put off the task and let the soil dry out, you're likely to snap them off at ground level. The roots will regenerate new shoots that produce seed close to the ground.

Rapid growth of summer weeds may exasperate you, but don't be hasty in turning to chemical controls. Large weeds call for a lot of poison and there's the temptation to use something strong and final instead of the usual leaf spray. Soil sterilants unfortunately come to mind.

They will do the job all right—and then some more. Soil sterilants last up to 10 years and damage everything in their reach. This may mean your trees—and your neighbor's trees—as well as the soil itself. If you sterilize your garden soil, you automatically handicap yourself in any gardening activity for many years. The roots of your fruit trees may be in the alley with the roots of weeds. It's better to stay away from soil sterilants. If the tall weeds that you pulled already have set seeds, it would be foolish to leave them lying around to dry out. They will simply shed their seed where you let them lay.

Immature weeds quickly die if you hoe them in the midday heat. It's easy if the soil is moist at the surface and

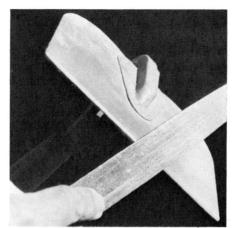

Another useful gardening friend at this time of year: Keep it sharp and hoeing out small weeds won't be hard work.

you sharpen your hoe blade beforehand. Take a file and smooth the edges until they are sharp enough to cut a piece of paper. Sharp tools make work a joy.

If hoeing in the noonday sun is not your idea of enjoyment, it's best to spray the weeds. Smaller amounts of weed-control chemicals will be needed on smaller weeds. There's a decided saving in material and you get a much quicker result in hot sun.

Avoiding Split Fruit

August rains have another effect that has a nuisance value. Ripening fruit splits. The hard outer skin of pomegranates doesn't stretch as the insides swell and the fruit pops open. It happens to navel oranges and tomato fruit. Such spoiled fruit has no value—it will not repair itself. It's best to remove it before it attracts a host of leaf-footed plant bugs.

Minimize this sort of waste by watering your plants carefully during the early summer. If you keep them short of water, the hot sun and dry desert air makes the skin of the fruit hard and rigid. It won't stretch when summer rains cause the inside to swell quickly. Unfortunately, no matter how careful you are about watering, you must expect a certain amount of split fruit. Navel oranges are notoriously prone to this weakness.

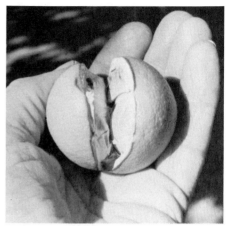

Fruit starts to split in August. Rains cause inside to swell, but skin is hard from strong sunshine and doesn't expand. Fruit is not ripe and will never improve. It's worthless. Remove it because its smell attracts insect pests.

New Citrus Growth

The rains bring on citrus flowers. This is exciting, but they usually drop off and don't set fruit—especially with young trees. If they do set on the larger trees, it accounts for the out-of-season lemons and oranges we find six months later.

New leaf shoots accompany the flowers and they grow well if the rains continue and humidity stays high. It's important to keep these tender shoots growing. If rain showers are sporadic, you will need to irrigate. Don't let this fresh new growth wilt during dry periods between showers. There's a great temptation to hope that enough rain fell last time and the next shower will come tomorrow. But it's seldom the case.

Insects

If July had its dry moments and the rains start up again in August, expect a second crop of insect troubles. A newly moistened soil stimulates pupae of grape-leaf skeletonizers and squash-vine borers to wake up and emerge. The first signs of trouble are the adults flying around looking for a place to lay their eggs. When you see them, start looking for their egg clusters. Rub them out using a finger and thumb, before they hatch. This will save you getting out the spray gun and using a lot of expensive chemicals.

Watch for a second round of adult moth of the grape-leaf skeletonizer. Kill her before she lays eggs.

Adult butterfly that leads to—and came from—orange dog caterpillar. Kill her, too.

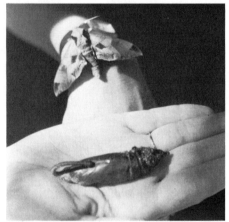

Spring tomatoes suffered from tomato hornworm caterpillars. After gorging on leaves, they rest in soil as hard-coated chrysalids. When summer rains stirred them into activity, they turned into adult moths. These lay eggs in September. Eggs turn into caterpillars that eat tomato leaves at end of season and the cycle starts over.

Don't Save Seed

Perhaps you've just enjoyed a super-tasting cantaloupe or watermelon, either from your garden or the supermarket, and you want to grow one like it. Don't save its seed. Plants like melons and cucumbers with male flowers and female flowers are always cross-pollinated and don't breed true. Seed from such plants saved from the garden always disappoints. It loses quality in the next generation.

Squash & Cucumbers

The beginning of August gives you an opportunity to sow squash seed in the last of a series that gave you abundant harvests all through summer. It's too late at the end of the month for guaranteed results. That's all right because there's plenty to do in the garden. Also, you may be getting tired of squash by now.

It's worth taking a chance with the squash relative, cucumber. Bear in mind that strong winds may stay through the end of September. Cucumbers, with their great paper-thin leaves, need a sheltered place and one not subject to bright sunshine in the afternoons. You will already have discovered that the phrase "cool as cucumber" has nothing to do with the way the plant grows. Summer's heat is usually too much for it.

Sow seed directly in the ground at the end of the month and give the seedling shoots something to climb up to 6 feet. Growth will slow with October's cool nights and the first frost in November will kill the plants. However, there's enough time for good harvests during the cooling months. It's worth trying varieties other than Armenian. They won't be bitter-tasting during early fall weather.

Chinese Pole Beans

Keep picking the Chinese pole beans. They are at their peak production in August and the more you pick, the more the plants produce. It's as if you are having a contest in which the plants always win. You cannot suppress their enthusiasm, so pick two or three times a week. Don't leave old pods on the vine to dry out, split and scatter seed. This tends to slow flowering and production almost stops. They will continue to produce abundantly until November's first killing frost.

Pecan Trees

Pecan trees show a bad side to their nature in August, but it's not their fault. The developing crop needs a lot of water for the small nuts to ripen and increase in size. August is the month when pecans have their highest water demand.

The insecure nuts show their disatisfaction with life by dropping off the tree. It may be that they weren't properly pollinated or perhaps they were damaged by insects. Perhaps the tree is short of zinc or there could be just too many of them for the tree to carry during this stressful month.

Nut fall can also happen if a well-loaded tree becomes short of water. Then it would be your fault for thinking the last storm gave the soil a good soaking when it merely wet the top 3 inches. You might also have been counting on the next good shower that has yet to come.

Pick up some of these fallen nuts and cut them open. Mostly they will be shriveled and half-formed—a result of earlier water shortage or poor pollination.

If the nuts are dark-spotted, it is because the leaf-footed plant bug attacked when they were soft. The bug's piercing mouth parts allowed bacteria to enter and cause a localized rot. If the nuts are dark and shriveled, the tree is most likely short of zinc. In which case, make a note to apply a spray of zinc sulphate on the emerging leaves next spring.

Sometimes the ground appears to be covered with fallen nuts. Recover your composure by looking up into the tree where, most likely, there are still a lot of good nuts securely attached. Nut fall is a warning. Irrigate your trees generously from now until the husks start to turn brown which indicates the insides have developed well and the harvest is near at hand. Remember to water 3 feet down and out to the ends of the branches.

Preparation for Fall & Winter

Sometimes August is a dismal end to the summer garden. Squash plants devastated by the vine borer and tomato plants turned brown by the heat are common-enough signs of things gone wrong. But August is also the beginning of another season and we can take heart.

All of a sudden gardening tasks take over our lives. There's tidying up to be done. Soil has to be dug. Soil mixes need to be prepared, put into styro-

Despite heat, end of August is a good time to begin gardening cycle again. Sow seeds now in ground or containers and you will have sizeable plants when weather cools in September. Warm soil will ensure rapid growth.

foam coffee cups and sown to seeds. Some seeds can go directly into the ground and, if we can find bedding plants in the nurseries, we set them out, too.

In spite of the heat and humidity, these are exciting tasks because they are all preparatory steps to the fall or winter garden. There's a lot of hope and optimism in the air. Fall and winter gardens are usually more succesful than those in spring and summer. And this is leading to a trend. If you want to be selective in your activities, join an evergrowing crowd of lazy gardeners who take it easy between June and August. It's very sensible of them, but they are not excused from gardening altogether. Their fruit trees and vines must be kept alive with needed irrigations, but these "new-wave" gardeners don't go looking for work.

They say it's not worth the water, work in the heat, fight against pests—and any other excuse that comes to mind—to produce an unreliable crop of tomatoes. They save their energies and garden space for an early start in August.

Now that August is here they clean up the summer weeds in their fallow garden, add organic matter, ammonium phosphate and sulphur to the soil, and dig the ground. There's no heart-wrenching decision to be made about saving the exhausted summer plants in the hope they'll produce

something before frost.

They go to the nursery, buy a few tomato plants and set them out. There isn't enough time for peppers and eggplant, but tomatoes will produce before frost if all goes well.

They sow sweet-corn seeds and bush beans in the newly dug ground. Any winter vegetable plants they find at the nursery get planted, too.

They make a soil mix and fill numerous coffee cups with it. Then they sow two seeds in each cup—only two because conditions for germination are so good there's no room for pessimism.

They choose seeds of leafy winter vegetables—lettuce, cabbage, cauliflower and broccoli, for example—that will produce plants to set out in the garden in six or seven weeks.

They don't overlook the oriental vegetables, either. These are refined versions of the cabbage family that have interesting flavors gourmet cooks enjoy using. Oriental vegetables are also easy to grow.

Those winter vegetables that produce roots, are sown directly in the ground later—sometime in September after the soil has cooled a little. So are garden peas and faba beans.

Bearing in mind the shortness of the seasons, it's important to choose quick-growing varieties. You'll be able to make another sowing at the end of September and spread the harvest into December and even January—in spite

September
WEEK 1

of cold weather. Remember that these vegetables were developed in places far colder than our mild desert winters. They grow quickly if given the chance.

In August, the soil is so warm that seeds germinate quickly and plants grow well in the sunshine. The nights are cool, so the plants get their rest in preparation for the next day's hard work of growing.

There's a temptation to sow seed directly in the ground instead of going through the coffee-cup process. This saves work and perhaps time, but you may regret it if you take the short cut.

Harvester ants become very busy in August. They strip foliage from plants and haul it back to their nest. They even appear to increase their numbers and start new nests. Their unrelenting industry—praised by Aesop—is a nuisance to desert gardeners and especially those gardeners who sow seeds in August.

If you have built up a high optimism and you can't stop—you've taken care of all your vegetable chores—try digging some planting holes for fruit trees. Admittedly, it's hard work, even if you start early in the morning, but it's good preparation for some pleasing garden operations in September.

Remember before your enthusiasm evaporates, a hole for planting trees should measure 5 feet square and be 5-feet deep. And you must get through any caliche you find. When you think you've dug enough, half-fill the hole with water and see if it has drained out by the morning. If it hasn't, there's more digging to be done.

Go for it—as they say.

Summer storms linger on into September. They are still localized, but increased humidity that is more widespread stimulates plant growth.

September is a delightful month for humans and a comforting one for plants, too. The summer heat is gone—or going—yet there's warmth in the sunshine. What makes the difference between the summer misery and pleasant weeks of fall is the cooler nights. A difference of 20F between day and night temperatures allows us all to rest more comfortably at night and work better the next day. Recent research in plant science has shown that plants—even cotton plants that are considered to be heat-loving, sunshine plants—do most of their body building during the night. This helps to explain why the fall weeks are so productive.

Citrus & Grape Growth

Don't be surprised to see fresh growth in grape vines and citrus trees. You might get a strong flowering along with new leaf shoots. Sometimes these flowers set fruit.

Budding On Citrus Trees

Take advantage of this fall growth in citrus and do a little budding on trees that you want to change or add on to. The spurt of growth stimulated by the cooling weather is sustained by vigorous sap flow up from the roots to the leaves. This causes the thin bark on the twigs to "slip" or open up easily when it is cut with a sharp knife.

Let's say you have a lemon tree that yields abundantly and you'd like to have a few oranges and grapefruit in addition to all those lemons. Just as the first fall buds begin to swell and before the leaves open or flower buds break, make some opening cuts on twigs whose bark is beginning to turn tan.

Freshly cut bud is neatly tucked into bark of twig. It should be secure. Wrap with tape to keep bud from drying out. Bud should be fixed and growing before weather turns cold. Too late and frost will kill young growth. Turn to page 124 for illustrations of complete budding process.

They will be a bit thicker than a pencil and the bark will cut easily with your sharp knife.

Into the slit on the twig, insert a freshly cut bud from a good-quality orange or grapefruit tree and push it downwards so it slides tightly against the inside of the bark. When snug, wrap it up with a length of soft plastic tape to keep the bud from drying out. Keep the tree well-supplied with water to sustain new growth. Your buds will be part of that new growth. Watch them carefully and, as they begin to swell, make a long cut in the plastic wrap to the side of the bud. This will open the plastic and allow the tender bud to grow out unimpeded.

Work in several more buds than you think you need because not every one will be successful—unless you are very practiced. The time available for this operation is limited and you won't have a second chance until spring. If you try again later in the fall, you may be successful, but the new shoots will be vulnerable to winter's cold. In any event, watch these shoots during the winter and protect them on freezing nights.

A number of experienced gardeners say fall budding is usually more successful than budding in the spring when mild weather can quickly turn to hot summer and dry out the new shoots.

There is a risk with fall budding. The onset of cold weather slows new growth and a sharp freeze can kill the young shoots. Be prepared for this by budding early in September to get as much growth as possible. Cover new growth with a blanket if freezes are forecast.

Cooler Nights

Temperatures cool because the days are becoming shorter and there's less time for the sun to heat the earth. Shortening days have a direct effect on plant growth too—often stimulating flowering. Many plants are *photoperiodic*, meaning they respond to the changes in daylength. September 23rd is the autumn equinox when the day is 12 hours long—equal with the night. So it's not just cooling temperatures

Your seeds of winter vegetables grow quickly and provide food for hungry caterpillars of the cabbage white butterfly.

that encourage our plants to come alive again.

In September there's still a hint of rainfall around. The desert can produce some dramatic cloud effects in the fall that may or may not give us worthwhile showers. We can be certain of high humidities that are good for plant growth.

Insects

Good weather for plants and humans is good weather for insects. Be prepared for insect activity. Look for and destroy grape-leaf skeletonizers, katydids, grasshoppers, orange-dog caterpillars, grape and tomato hornworms, and harvester ants. In the soil there's a stirring of white grubs and cutworms. Pick these out as you dig the ground in preparation for the fall planting. You'll enjoy digging if you start early in the morning while it's cool. Much of the enjoyment will be in your anticipation of success in growing winter vegetables.

We call them *loopers*, and they are hard to see because they are the exact same color as the food they eat—your leaves.

Coffee-Cup Seedlings

The seeds you sowed in coffee cups last month should now be growing strongly. Help them by including houseplant fertilizer in the water at every other watering. Start with a teaspoon to a gallon of water when the plants have four leaves and then use a tablespoon when six or eight leaves appear.

The plants will be big enough to set out during the second half of the month. This means you should not delay in getting the soil ready. As you dig there'll be Bermudagrass to pull out roots and all, and grubs to pick out. Then let the soil with its newly added steer manure or compost, ammonium phosphate and sulphur, lay awhile to mellow before you set out plants. Seed sowing comes even later.

Caring for Corn & Beans

Don't overlook the water needs of the corn and beans you planted last month. Daytime temperatures reach

These corn plants have already been side-dressed with ammonium sulphate. That and warm, humid weather made them grow. At this size they are ready for their last boost of nitrogen before they set cobs.

90F and clear skies tell us that humidities have suddenly fallen. Be alert and observant. React with a good, deep irrigation. You've got to keep your plants growing.

When corn is knee high, apply a side dressing of ammonium sulphate, about 1 pound to 100 square feet. Water it in well. You'll get a gratifying response in less than a week. At this stage of growth expect damage from the stalk borer. The first sign of the grubs' activity is a series of holes in the new leaves as they unfold out of the funnel. One small bite appears as a line of holes across the open leaf blade. A severe infestation shreds the leaves entirely. Should the single growing point, which is deep inside the stem and near to the ground be chewed into, the plant will stop producing new leaves and will never produce a crop. It pays to be watchful at this critical time of your corn plants' growth.

Dust or spray a small amount of diazinon into the funnel of the plants before they reach knee height. To be really sure, give three applications, a week apart. There's no telling whether the adult moth is laying eggs in the leaf funnel. When you see the stringy, damaged leaves it's too late.

Corn cobs with open ends allow the entry of corn earworm. The adult moth lays her eggs on the extruding silks and the caterpillars that hatch crawl down into the succulent kernels.

The awful damage they do—a complete hidden destruction of the crop—can be prevented by a barrier of four or five drops of mineral oil applied when the silks are fresh and green. As soon as you see the silks coming out, that's the time to make the application. Don't delay!

Sowing More Corn & Beans

Sow another plot of corn to make sure of a Thanksgiving harvest. Always plant your corn in square blocks. Pollen from the top tassels has to fall onto the lower silks at the appropriate time—within a week as a rule—to make sure of a full cob of kernels. Wind blows pollen away from plants that are in long thin rows, whereas it is caught between a mass of plants in a close square planting.

Sow another plot of bush beans while you are at it. They can go to the side of the rows of corn seeds, providing the rows are not so close that they keep sunshine from the beans.

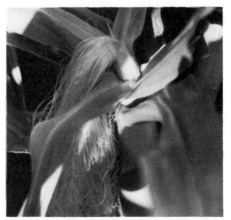

Long extended set of leaves effectively closes "door" to pests. When corn is in full silk is the time to put four drops of mineral oil at opening to keep out corn earworm.

Beans & Peas

Keep picking your pole beans and you will be rewarded with an even greater production. The more you pick, the more you get. This is a truism for plants that produce fruit except, of course, the one-time blossoming and fruit-set of trees. Green or snap beans are best eaten before the soft pod develops any *fruit*. Yes, beans are a fruit—botanically speaking. Don't wait for the pods to get knobbly enough to show the developing seeds inside unless you want to have a mess of soft-shell beans.

Recent plant breeding has almost eliminated the string bean from the seed catalogs—and a good thing, too. Young people don't know about taking a knife to the end of the pod and drawing off the fiber that runs to the other end before one can start slicing. Nowadays, there's a large assortment of snap beans—and even snap peas—with no strings attached to their fleshy pods.

Get ready to sow bean and pea seed out in the garden. Sow beans now while it's warm; peas later when it's cooler. You sowed beans in the ground last month as the first of three succession sowings that will give you a spread of harvests. Perhaps the soil was just a bit too hot and the germination rate wasn't too satisfactory. Nevertheless, you got several plants that are growing vigorously. If there are gaps in the rows, fill them in with additional seed. Your rows won't look picture perfect, but that's not the point. You want to eat beans over as long a period as you can.

Now is your opportunity for a second sowing in the series and you'll make the third toward the end of the month. In a normal year, things cool considerably after September and, although beans germinate nicely, you may not get much of a harvest before the first killing frost strikes in November. Always select short-term varieties such as Greencrop, Tender-green, Greenpod, Tenderpod. Such similarity in their names suggests a commonality in their breeding. They may not live up to their 55-day description, but they'll come pretty close to it.

Tomato & Pepper Plants

Your recovering tomato and pepper plants will benefit from a side dressing of ammonium sulphate. The beautiful weather encourages their growth and you can help them further by making sure they don't run out of nutrients. Most gardeners spent a lot of the summer irrigating extensively and this washed the soil clean of nitrogen. Remember, tomato roots spread out as much as the foliage before you cut it back, so scatter the dry fertilizer over the entire root area. Each plant should get about 1/2 cup every two weeks. Dry fertilizer always goes on damp soil and is washed in with the second half of the irrigation.

Look for more ground to dig. As the days go by you will more readily determine which plants are going to be productive. Those that survived the summer in a weakened condition might just as well be eliminated before you spend too much time on them. The old must give way to the new. Look forward to the forthcoming season with optimism. Don't dwell on "what might have been."

Container Gardening

One concept of additional garden space we often overlook is that of containers. Slowly recovering pepper plants in your old summer garden can be pruned back, dug up and put into 5-gallon buckets. During the forthcoming winter you can protect them from cold weather and freezes by moving them to a sunny part of the garden. The black buckets absorb the heat of the sun and the soil retains it through the night. If you have space for half barrels, you can make a summer-salad arrangement, mixing tomatoes, peppers, onions and lettuce all in the same container.

Strawberry Renewal

If you lost most of your strawberry plants during the summer—a very common situation—dig up those that remain and put them into 6-inch pots. Without breaking them, carefully dig up those plants that have strong runners and a bunch of leaflets on their ends and plant them in separate

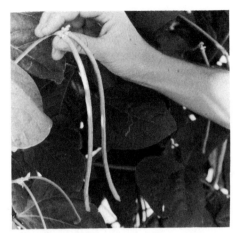

Chinese pole beans grow furiously and need to be picked every other day while they are soft and tender.

containers close to one another. Let the mother plant continue to nourish the young ones. Employ the usual nutrient solution, a tablespoon of balanced houseplant food in a gallon of water, to get good growth.

Improving Soil

Meanwhile, dig the ground and prepare it for planting your next strawberry bed.

Many gardeners would advise against using the same ground again after you have dug every plant out of the old bed. This is good advice because it gives your soil a rotational rest. Use it for some other plant and you won't be nearly as likely to keep feeding verticillium wilt or any other soil pest that attacks strawberries.

While the plants are out of the bed and being nourished in their pots by the liquid feeding, you have the opportunity to improve the soil by the standard procedure. Wet the soil down to 12 inches. Spread 2 or 3 inches of compost or steer manure but not chicken or horse manure. Scatter 3 pounds of ammonium phosphate and 5 pounds of soil sulphur to every 100 square feet of bed. Dig these into the soil, mixing them thoroughly down to 12 inches.

You have another opportunity if you know you have soil-borne diseases lurking in the bed. Don't be content with a suspicion. Take a dying plant to your nearest plant-disease clinic for a microscopic examination and positive identification.

If you don't pick often enough, beans lose quality. These beans have become stringy and beans inside show that pods have lost their tenderness.

Soil Fumigation

Soil fumigation is called for if soil-borne diseases are present. Go to your nursery and ask to read the label on a bottle of Vapam® to make sure it is appropriate for your purpose and situation. Read *all* the label—not just the stuff in big letters. Discover how long the process takes before you can set your plants back in the ground. Note whether the soil temperature is adequate for a good fumigation. You need to budget enough time to get your plants in the ground and growing before the end of the month.

If you don't have enough plants of your own, you can try the nurseries. As a rule they don't have suitable plants this early in the year—a pity! If you get plants from a friend, swap meet or patio sale, beware of the risk of introducing soil-borne diseases into your garden.

Citrus Fruits & Pomegranates

Citrus fruit and pomegranates continue to split because of good growing conditions. The insides swell, but the harder outer skin doesn't expand at

September
WEEK 3

the same rate. Something has to give. Remove damaged fruits before the insects, mostly sour-fruit beetles and leaf-footed plant bugs, get started on them.

Of course the citrus fruit is nowhere near ripeness. If you think it is edible, simply take a bite into the flesh and you'll quickly change your opinion.

How do you tell when pomegranates are ripe? To some extent the skin color is an indication, but not a very reliable one. Some kinds are pale-colored when ripe, while others are almost purple inside and out. The only way to tell is a taste test. Take one or two fruits from the tree and cut them open and sample them.

How do you tell when prickly pear fruit is ripe? It's the same story. Do a taste test and don't rely on last year's date.

There's no magic date that lets you start making jellies—some years are early, others are later.

If you don't find these items in a nursery, you'll have to special order them. Heavy end anchors tube in container. It also shuts off flow when you push it in, enabling you to control individual containers on a long run of tubing.

Another gardening item that may be hard to find locally: You can raise a lot of seedlings in a tray and save space in your greenhouse or hot bed.

Useful Equipment

The commercial nursery business is a competitive one. Whenever costs can be reduced, either in materials or labor, changes are made. Home gardeners are interested in those changes, but usually there is a time lag before new materials come onto the market in retail quantities.

At present, it's not easy to purchase small amounts of lead-weighted, drip-irrigation tubing used to deliver water to a 5-gallon container. This very useful device is inserted into the main irrigation tubing coming from the faucet—one at each plant container. It's possible to set 30 or so containers in a single or double row and irrigate them all at the same time from a single faucet. When you push in the lead weight, the water supply is turned off, so you can restrict water to a single container that is too wet while the other containers are being fully watered.

A plastic tray for raising seedlings is another commercial piece of nursery hardware that is available to home gardeners through retail nursery outlets.

It has 196 1-inch-square compartments that taper to a point to give a root depth of 3 inches. That's enough root room for one seedling for about four weeks of growth. At that age it's ready to set out in the garden. If it

happens to be too small, or your ground isn't ready, it can be transferred to a styrofoam coffee cup of soil mix for a couple of weeks more growth to reach the size you want.

Transplanting Seedlings

Many old-time experienced gardeners hold the notion that it's all right to transplant seedlings of leafy vegetables such as lettuce, broccoli and cabbage, but it's not possible to do this with root-producing vegetables such as turnip, beet and carrot. Their reasons are that such slow-growing, tender plants suffer from the shock of being moved out of a container into the ground. More strongly, they argue that the roots are invariably twisted during the process and give rise to deformed roots at harvest time. They repeat this argument when it comes to thinning crowded seedlings. The thinnings, they say, cannot be safely transplanted and are best thrown away.

Well, there's news for gardeners of this persuasion. It is possible to transplant root-crop seedlings out of a seedling row into their permanent growing bed. The plants will survive and their roots will not be deformed—provided you handle them very carefully.

Being careful means working in wet soil and gently separating the crowded seedlings, sand grain by sand grain. It

Harvester ants become very active, building up their stores of food for winter at your expense.

Birds, particularly sparrows, gobble up your seedlings. There's little to do except physically block birds with box of chicken wire over garden bed.

means handling the seedling by its leaves and gently lowering it into a hole deep enough to take all the root without bending it at the bottom of the hole. The moist dirt should then be moved sideways toward the roots and firmed against the plant without damaging the stem or burying the plant too deeply.

All this sounds like a surgical operation and this is a good way to consider the task. Work with a toothpick instead of a trowel, and don't hurry. Evening is better than midday so the damaged seedlings—you can't avoid some damage no matter how careful you are—have a whole night to recover from their stressful experience. Keep the soil moist all the time.

With the invention of the seedling tray, some intrepid new gardeners through enthusiasm and perhaps a blind ignorance, thought they would eliminate all this fine-tuned labor. After all, wasn't this the whole idea of the invention in the first place?

They had the effrontery to sow root vegetables in these tiny compartments—one seed to a square, correctly following instructions—and grew beautiful beet, carrot and turnip seedlings. Furthermore, they planted out these seedlings in their cones of root-filled soil and produced perfect-looking roots at harvest time.

You can do the same. You'll save yourself a bit of work, too.

Harvester Ants

The fall gives us good reason to use transplants in preference to direct sowing. Harvester ants are busy while the soil is warm enough for plant growth. They "go to ground" after the soil has cooled, but if we delay sowing on their account, we lose valuable growing time. Remember that our growing seasons are short. We don't want to be held back by harvester ants. Your seedling trays—begun in late August and continued through September—will be quite safe on a bench, high up from the ants. They will be safe from sparrows, too.

Lettuce

These pesky sparrows love lettuce seedlings and in some years prevent a successful establishment of this useful salad plant.

Many varieties grow well in the desert—all the looseleaf types, that is. Tight-head lettuce is not easy to grow and is seldom worth the challenge.

Even after caring for lettuce seedlings and getting them successfully transplanted, they are not entirely safe from sparrows or other birds. If you don't like the idea of feeding birds, the seedlings are best protected by covering them with a frame of small-mesh chicken wire.

At the end of September your first-sown seedlings should be set out in the garden plots. Work quickly and

carefully in moist soil because the air is dry. Small plants lying out in the sunshine are sure to suffer if their roots are exposed to the air too long. A minute at midday is too long. A cool evening is best because the plants will recover from shock during the night.

Beans & Peas

Large seeds of faba bean, horse bean or Italian bean, and those of English peas—including the new snap peas or Chinese edible-pod peas, should be sown toward the end of the month. They don't germinate too well in hot soil so wait until your soil thermometer reads around 70F at 2 inches depth. Bush beans that went in the ground earlier, prefer a germination temperature of 80F. So any late sowing of these legumes will produce a slower germination as the days turn cooler. Complete your third sowing of bush beans in the series before the end of the month.

Birds won't be a nuisance to these seedlings, but watch out for another pest, the cutworm. These caterpillars live in the soil during the day and assume the color of that soil, so it's not always easy to see them. At night, they come out of hiding and crawl over the surface looking for stems which they grasp tightly with their nasty bodies to get leverage as they chew through the stem at ground level. The next morning they are gone, but there's a row of

Use your rake to set out evenly spaced planting holes to get concentrated plant population. You can eat young seedlings earlier than usual as they begin to crowd one another.

As soon as seedlings become too crowded, eat them. Finally, you get many market-size plants in a small space. That's intensive and efficient gardening.

decapitated seedlings for you to get mad about.

Don't confuse cutworms with white grubs, which are also a nuisance. They stay underground to eat the roots of seedlings. Both can be controlled by spraying the bed with diazinon, Malathion 50 or Sevin®. Get the chemical an inch deep into the soil where the insects are lurking.

Faba beans and garden peas grow through a mild winter quite safely. They will begin to flower in the spring, early if they grew without interference from frost, later if they were nipped. Faba beans grow on a thick stalk to about 4 feet high and tend to have a short harvest period and then die. But, they are good! Garden peas need a support for their growth which can reach 6 feet high and they tend to produce over a longer period of time. The more you pick, the more they produce. It's possible to gather a light crop as late as the end of May before the heat kills off the plants. Both plants should be harvested before their pods turn dry and hard. The seeds inside are most tasty when they are immature.

Planting Fruit Trees

Here's a surprise for you! Dig some large tree holes and set out deciduous fruit trees. You'll remember from Chapter 15, how large a hole to dig. It's big, but it's worth it and the weather is cooling so you won't be exhausted.

What's interesting is that the soil is not cooling as quickly as the air temperatures. This makes it an ideal time to establish deciduous trees. Not so much for evergreen citrus trees because they can't take freezes but deciduous trees are going to lose their leaves anyway and they need a cool period. Read Chapter 23 on Deciduous Fruit Trees and their need for a chilling period to develop fruit.

Cooling air temperatures hasten leaf fall and the top of the tree will go dormant. However, the soil will stay warm enough to encourage new root growth, providing it is kept moist. Deciduous fruit trees are more easily established during a fall season than those planted in the spring. In the spring, suitable weather too quickly turns to hot summer. Young leaves scorch in the dry air and young roots are cooked in the hot, wet soil.

Sowing Winter Vegetables

Winter vegetables give us an opportunity to do some intensive planting, which, in turn, gives us an early harvest.

The trick is to sow seed thickly and directly in the garden as soon as you discover the ants have gone underground. A good way to get the right plant population is to press a rake into the soil until its teeth make 1/2-inch-deep holes. Pull the rake straight up without disturbing the row of holes

and set it in again, making a series of holes in a square pattern throughout your bed.

Sow one seed in each hole. Any of the winter vegetables are suitable, whether they are leafy kinds or root producers. The emerging seedlings will be about 1-1/2 inches from one another and will not become crowded for perhaps three or four weeks.

As soon as they touch one another, gently pull out the alternate plants and wash them ready for eating. Those that remain will grow stronger because the competition has been removed—for a while. Keep thinning as the seedlings grow and begin to touch one another—perhaps every three weeks.

In this way you get a quicker and heavier harvest from a smaller piece of ground. In due course, you finish with a harvest of full-sized root and leaf plants. The bonus is that you get a lot of extra food on the way as thinnings. They can be called *sprouts* and even *gourmet sprouts* if you wish.

September
WEEK 4

Insects

If it's good weather for humans and plants, it's good weather for the insects. They can be a last-of-season problem.

Insects seem to be as happy as we are about the end of summer. New growth coming on citrus and vegetable seedlings is a ready invitation to insects to be a nuisance.

Keep a sharp look out for the handsome, fluttering butterfly, the black-and-yellow swallowtail. Don't give it the benefit of a doubt. It looks attractive and its antics are amusing, but it is not showing off or trying to be clever. She is flying around looking for a citrus leaf on which to lay eggs. They sit singly on the upper surface of a leaf and are quite easy to see once you know what to look for. They are the size of a pinhead. If they are not eaten by wasps or other predators, the eggs hatch in a few days into quarter-inch-long, brownish caterpillars that start eating immediately. They prefer soft, pale-colored leaves and they do a lot of damage in a short time. When they become larger they are not so easy to recognize because they are a good imitation of a bird dropping.

This camouflage is not designed to fool human citrus growers as much as it is to avoid attention from birds. In addition, to make sure nothing bothers it too much, it can shake its head and put out a pair of orange horns and give out a nasty smell when it is stabbed or squeezed. Pick off these pests.

Grasshoppers do their final feeding and you see some pretty big specimens in the fall. Some of these will lay eggs in the soil and provide us with next spring's generation. Others will find a cozy place to spend the winter and lay their eggs in the spring after they come out. In either case, they are a nuisance and should be squashed when you see them. They are eating your greenery. Some years you will see lots of little green grasshoppers about 1/2 inch long on your newly planted seedlings. These are the last hatchlings of the year and are voracious feeders. Spray them with Malathion 50 or diazinon because these

First sign of trouble on your citrus tree—egg of the orange dog. Look for it during mild weather of September and pick it off before it hatches into . . .

. . . the orange dog caterpillar.

little creatures are usually too active and tiny to catch.

The larger ones are easily caught. Early in the morning when it's cold, they are sluggish and often sit prominently on the sunny top of a plant to get warm.

Cabbage loopers are harder to find. They are the exact color of the plant they are feeding on and align themselves along the leaf stalks when they rest. You need good eyesight to discover them before they do a lot of damage to small seedling leaves. As soon as you see pieces missing from the small leaves, make a thorough inspection of the seedling tray or the vegetable bed and pull off the creatures.

After noticing damage to their seedling leaves, many gardeners react automatically by spraying with diazinon or Malathion 50. They know that one or two tiny caterpillars can be missed on a visual check. The first warning you get is a white butterfly hovering around the seedlings. Don't let her lay any eggs.

Gray aphids start up at the end of September and stay with us through the winter. They begin in a small cluster, generally under a leaf of cabbage, broccoli, cauliflower, radish or turnip. They suck the juices out of the leaf and this deforms it into a pucker, which gives additional protection to

the insects. Although the pucker is on the underside of the leaf, the upper side shows a dull yellow spot, the sign you should recognize. Look underneath and rub out the colony with your finger and thumb. Don't delay and allow the colony to build up. A large number of them will weaken a young plant and make an older one inedible.

Slowing Growth in Fruit Trees

At this time near the end of the gardening year we don't want to encourage growth in our established deciduous trees and vines. They need several weeks of dormancy and usually don't get enough winter chill to produce a crop of fruit reliably next year.

The onset of cold weather usually starts plants into dormancy. A way to substitute for insufficient cold is to slow growth of grapevines, apricot and peach trees, for example, by reducing their water supply. The same tactic with citrus trees slows their growth and hardens the tree in anticipation of a freeze in November or December.

Continue to give deep irrigations, down to 3 feet, but lengthen the interval between waterings. Maybe every three weeks will be enough. Let the surface of the soil stay dry longer, but watch the young growth on the citrus and don't allow it to wilt for more than

September is time to start winter herb garden. Mints are vigorous spreading plants and are best confined in one-gallon container to keep them separate from one another.

a day. Although the fruit is ripening and filling with water, there is little risk of losing it at this stage of development. In fact the fruit, being full of water, acts as a reservoir of moisture and saves your tree from drying out too much. But don't let the dryness go too far.

With deciduous fruit trees and grapes, you have a good indicator of readiness for rest in the leaf color. Once the color starts to turn, hold back on the water. A good soak at the end of September might be enough for the remainder of the winter. Use the soil probe to keep your mind at rest.

Let's say you feel a great urge to irrigate your plants at the end of the season—after all the weather is beautiful and plants appear to want to grow. It's natural to feel this way.

It would be a great mistake to "feed" that growth with an application of fertilizer. It's also a mistake to irrigate frequently. Plants that should be going dormant will become tired because of their last-minute exertions and what growth they do make will be soft and tender to freezes.

Be tough-minded and put your plants into a resting condition at the end of September. Ignore the temptations of an Indian summer.

Winter Herbs

We are now in the season for setting out winter herbs. There are summer kinds and winter kinds and we change horses with herbs as the seasons change just as we do with flowers and vegetables.

A good herb garden can be planted in a half barrel—you don't need a lot of space. It's better to buy plants from a nursery because it's far too troublesome to grow herbs from seed, though it can be done if you insist. Herbs like a sandy, well-drained soil and the half barrel should be placed where it gets plenty of winter sunshine.

A little houseplant fertilizer in the water helps the new plants get established and growing strongly, but don't overdo it. Otherwise you'll get rank plants with poor aroma.

If you grow mints—and there are common, spear and peppermints—it's a good idea to keep the plants in their containers and plunge them into the half barrel. This keeps the roots within

bounds. Otherwise they intermingle to form an underground jungle that is hard to untangle. Mints like shade and plenty of moisture.

Parsley is a good herb to grow in a half barrel. It's ornamental in itself and you pick off the lower leaves as they become ready for salad or the pot. Two or three plants will keep you in fresh, nutritious, flavorful leaves all through the winter. Parsley goes to seed and stops growing when spring temperatures turn to summer heat.

Cilantro, or coriander, is another easy-to-grow winter herb. Others to try are chives, sage, thyme and oregano.

Remember that most herbs like plenty of wintertime sunshine. They also like a free-draining soil, not too rich. And once the plants are started, hold back on the fertilizers. Most failures with herb growing can be related to too much attention.

Like mint, watercress also enjoys shade and moisture. You can buy a bunch of watercress in almost any supermarket. Take three or four of the strongest sprigs and set them in a glass of water on the windowsill. Keep the water fresh and you will have roots in four or five days. Plant the rooted cuttings in a 5-gallon bucket of indifferent soil and keep them well-watered. Constantly pick the leaves and you'll get more and more growth until the top of the bucket overflows with greenery. Watercress is high in vitamin C—as high as any fruit—and it's only when you pick old leaves that you get the strong mustardy flavor. Young leaves can safely go into tasty sandwiches.

October
WEEK 1

October is an in-between month. The heat of summer has gone, but the cold of winter hasn't arrived. September's plantings and sowings are growing rapidly, but we know they will slow down in November. Last month's gardening hurry is over, but there are still a few things to be done before the quiet of winter.

It's a delightful time for gardeners. Warm, sunny days are followed by cool nights. It's pleasant for garden plants, too. They like to work during the day and rest at night, just like we do. Tired summer vegetables such as tomatoes, eggplant and bell peppers spring to life again. There's growth in citrus, grapevines and deciduous fruit trees, but this we don't particularly want.

Winter Vegetables

October is enjoyable to a gardener because the first harvest of winter vegetables is near. Bush beans sown in August are starting to yield. Lettuce can be picked. Radishes are being eaten, as are oriental vegetables. There's still lots of life in the Chinese pole beans and black-eyed peas. Everything in the garden is lovely and the future holds bright prospects. That is, with what we already have. It's too late to continue succession sowings of winter vegetables. They won't die, but they won't grow, either. They'll just stand there until the warm spring when they'll run to seed.

Selected Plantings

However, you can plant strawberries, Faba beans and deciduous fruit trees.

It's risky to plant citrus trees because the cold weather of November and December is likely to include damaging freezes. Although the soil is warm enough to encourage root growth and get trees established, it's safer to plant deciduous fruit trees now. You could have planted citrus trees in early September for a successful fall establishment, but wait now until March.

Strawberries

You may not be able to buy strawberry plants at the nurseries and they will be expensive if you can find them. If you

When someone gives you plants, always wash off soil just in case donor's garden is contaminated. Free plants are going to cost you a lot if they are infested with nematodes, fusarium or verticillium.

Faba beans are harvested in April or May. They are relatively slow growers and seed should be sown in October.

are lucky enough to have extra new plants from your own bed because everything went well during the summer—which it usually doesn't—you'll be able to plant up economically.

Perhaps you have a friend who has spare plants. Beg, borrow or steal some and patch up your bed if there are only a few empty spaces. If most of the plants have died, it's probably better to start a new bed. Dig deeply, add in organic matter and ammonium phosphate, and keep it moist for a few days. Then plant.

From now on the weather will be kind to strawberries—even through winter—and you'll have strong plants on the point of flowering when spring weather returns. People who put out strawberries in the spring lose this head start. Their plants give only a few berries before hot weather stresses them. Take advantage of fall's good growing weather and a week or two after planting, irrigate strawberries with a little houseplant food in the water. Get 'em growing.

Faba Beans, Lettuce & Radishes

Faba beans are a favorite of Italian gardeners and others, too, for that matter,

but are not as well-known as they deserve to be. Indeed, you may not find seed in local nurseries, so you'll have to write away for them. They are also called *broad beans, horse beans* or *Italian beans.*

You may find dried faba beans in gourmet food stores. Buy a small amount and try them for taste although they are best when freshly harvested and eaten as shelled beans. Dried beans grind into a tasty flour for flavoring soups and breads. The small round ones don't grow as well as the larger flat kinds. Among the larger kinds it seems that any variety does as well as another.

Although faba beans are legumes and improve the soil through their root bacteria, they won't do well in poor soil. Sow the large seeds 1-inch deep. There's no need to soak them, even though they are hard. Keep the soil moist.

Faba beans grow into woody plants about 4 feet high and send out basal shoots so give them plenty of room to grow. Unlike most members of the bean family, they need to be pollinated by insects. Therefore, it's a good idea to have a block of flowering

Bring containers into sunny part of your patio. Let them enjoy fall sunshine and they will produce for you.

Trim your summer vegetables that are in containers.

After this "haircut" they will send out new shoots if kept in a warm place. If kept in a cool, shady place, they will stay dormant until next spring. The choice is yours.

plants rather than long thin rows. Sow seed every 18 inches on the square.

If you don't have a lot of space in your garden, you can interplant with Bibb lettuce or radishes. These will be harvested before the faba beans get tall and crowded. The beans are slow growers in the early stages.

Moving Containers
Here's a light chore: You'll have noticed that the shadows are changing and the strength has gone out of the sun's heat. Move containers that are growing vegetables into a sunnier place.

Five-gallon buckets are easy enough, but half barrels are a struggle. If they are on a concrete patio, you can slip short pieces of iron pipe under them and roll them along to the new spot. If on grass or dirt, you'll need some friends to help you. Give the containers a quarter turn so plant growth is even, instead of it always reaching in the same direction for light.

Black-plastic containers usefully gather the sun's heat—especially in winter—and roots grow well in the warmed soil. As a result, so do the plants. It's a good way to extend the harvest of peppers, tomatoes and eggplant. Some gardeners even dig up such plants, trim the branches a bit,

and get a harvest all winter if it doesn't get too cold.

Of course, you can start your winter garden, or some of it, in containers. If you were unable to get things going last month, your October container plantings will catch up in growth because of the warmth they collect by being in a sunny place.

Planting Deciduous Fruit Trees
More and more gardeners are realizing that the fall is an excellent time to plant deciduous fruit trees, even though they are about to drop their leaves and go dormant.

Desert winters are seldom severe enough to freeze the ground. It's air temperatures that we notice and affect our garden plants. The soil actually stays warm enough to allow tree roots to continue growing. If you plant a tree that has been grown in a container at the nursery, in the sunshine, its roots are active and continue to grow in the new soil provided for it.

This is in spite of leaf fall. Actually, leaf fall is part of the story. If there are no leaves, there's no *evapo-transpiration*. That's a fancy name for water leaving the plant through the leaves.

The conventional time for fruit-tree planting is January or February—after the cold of winter. It's when the bare-

October
WEEK 2

root season starts. For many years, gardeners could only buy bare-root trees during a few short weeks in the spring. This is still the case in some parts of the country. However, nurserymen in the desert have developed a practice of planting bare-root trees they don't sell in the spring and holding them over as container-grown trees. There are no growing nurseries in the desert. All the trees are brought in from the traditional, cooler, growing areas.

There's another consideration related to our story. Many nurserymen got tired of living up to their guarantee with a replacement because of customers' failures with bare-root trees. They simply stopped selling them.

Failures occurred in the spring because the weather gets too hot too quickly. Trees' leaves come out because of warm weather and the lengthening days, but if the year starts off dry and windy, young trees' roots have a hard time getting established.

Unless gardeners give a lot of attention to irrigating their new spring-planted trees, the trees dry out quickly. This is especially true if watering is limited to a little area close to the trunk and is not deep enough. Even if good care is given, there's a danger of the heat of June and July causing fresh, new roots to cook in hot, wet soil.

None of this happens in the fall. The soil stays warm enough to keep roots growing. The cooling air and shortening days cause the leaves to slow down and drop off. The top part of the tree doesn't lose any moisture. Conditions are entirely favorable.

You'll find a fall planting of deciduous fruit trees very successful. The only snag is that you'll have to dig the planting hole during the hot time of the year—and that's no joke.

If summer's heat wouldn't let you finish digging tree holes, now's your opportunity. Don't delay. Your success in tree establishment calls for warm soil and November will be too late.

October can be a rainy month and we all know natural moisture from rain is much more effective than irrigations from the hose.

Rain is helpful in getting plants established. Those planted a few days ago don't go into shock and are stimulated to grow. If you have any late planting to do, it's fun to set plants into moist soil, even during a shower. We are almost guaranteed success. It's the same with seeds—they come up more readily. In addition, the general humidity favors plant growth.

Mushrooms

One kind of plant growth that alarms some people is mushrooms. "Where do they come from?" "I didn't have any last year—I've never seen them before." This is what we hear. Others, who are less frightened, want to know whether one can eat them.

It's difficult to offer advice on whether to eat mushrooms you discover on your lawn for the first time. See photo, page 221. Most are edible, even if they look horrible, but mushroom poisoning is a nasty experience. Books tell us the poisons don't work immediately. By the time you are desperately ill a few days later, you have forgotten exactly which mushroom you made into a gourmet meal.

Don't experiment with mushrooms. Go by experience. If you recognize a particular kind that you have eaten before, go ahead and enjoy it. If you have no experience, use someone else's—but don't get it over the telephone. Ask them to share a meal with you.

Soil mix is often made from forest products such as fir bark and composted sawdust. When you buy it, you invariably buy other parts of the forest, namely mushroom spores. These "hatch" when moisture and temperatures are favorable, to give us brightly colored clusters of miniature mushrooms. They only last a short time. Some people think they are nice—others think they are spooky. They don't harm houseplants. After all, they are living on the organic material in the soil mix.

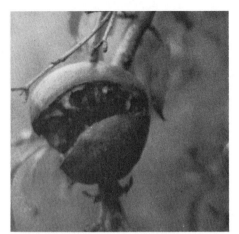

Citrus fruits are not alone in splitting. Ripening pomegranates do it, too.

Keep soil warm by laying down sheet of black plastic. Use clear if your garden is free of weeds. Cut holes through it for new plants. At top left are "cookie-cutter" holes made with sharpened juice can.

Plants already in garden can be kept growing by erecting framework over them and covering with clear plastic.

Citrus Growth

Warm October rain stimulates growth in citrus trees, even to the point of getting them to flower. Most flowers fall off, but sometimes develop into those out-of-season, maverick fruit that surprise us late next summer.

Navel oranges readily split at this time. The insides swell quickly, but the skin can't expand because, after a hot, dry summer, it has grown rigid. Split fruit never recovers. Take them off the tree because their smell attracts insects that further spoil the fruit by bringing in bacteria. Splitting is worse on trees that were kept dry during summer.

Avoiding Frost-Tender Growth

Here is an instance of not wanting our plants to grow, although conditions are favorable for them to do so. Good gardeners look farther down the road and see a freeze danger. Trees that have a lot of new growth on them are more susceptible to frost damage than those with hard wood.

Avoid soft growth on all frost-tender plants. Even on deciduous trees it's better to have hard wood because a severe frost will kill new twigs on dormant trees.

There's nothing we can do about winter rains and, in general terms, we like to have them. But we must manage our citrus trees carefully. Right now, don't irrigate them if the soil is moist. Let the rains determine how much they will grow, and hope for the best. Remember, in September you were advised not to fertilize any kind of fruit trees because of the possibility of fall rains stimulating them into unwanted growth. Do not fertilize again until February.

Grapes too sometimes start a fresh flowering and occasionally you get a light crop. Treat grapevines as you do citrus—get them dormant by denying them irrigations. If rain continues to fall, it's unfortunate that grapevines keep growing.

Semitropical fruit trees need protection from future cold. Deciduous trees need more cold than they usually get in the desert. This contradictory state of affairs can be resolved in both cases by witholding irrigations even though continued fall showers interfere. A wet autumn gives us a true desert dilemma. As temperatures continue to fall, plant growth begins to slow. And here is the dilemma: We want our fruit trees to rest, but also want our winter vegetables to keep growing.

Retaining Warmth for Vegetables

Resolve this one through temperature control. As long as the sun shines enough, the soil will be warmed. Catch and keep this warmth around your vegetables.

Lay plastic sheets on the ground between the plant rows. If you have a lot of weeds—another consequence of fall rains—use black plastic. Otherwise, clear plastic does a better job.

Toward the end of the month, you will get better warmth from a clear plastic sheet draped over a framework of construction mesh above the bed. This tunnel acts as a temporary greenhouse for only a little expense. You'll have to open up the ends on a hot day, but it will stay closed most of the time, retaining moisture and warmth. Keep it until spring and keep your plants growing all the time. A tunnel is particularly useful for strawberries.

Snails

Continuous fall rains means lots of snails. They go together. Where do snails come from? During dry times they burrow into the soil and seal their shells' entrance with a plug until moisture returns. But, where do they come from in the first place?

When you buy container plants grown in coastal California, look in the soil. That's where snails come from. Don't bring snails into your garden. If you see any, pick them off and crunch them.

October
WEEK 3

Once again, tomatoes begin to flower and set fruit. So do eggplant and peppers. August sown sweet corn is nearly ready to harvest and later sowings of September look promising for a Thanksgiving feast. Chinese pole beans continue to produce dozens of pods each day. It's a mistake to neglect picking them because they become hard quickly.

From now on everything in the garden will be lovely—until the first frost of the fall. Then all summer plants will suddenly come to an end.

Protecting from Frost
You can avoid this sudden demise if you dig up tomatoes, peppers and eggplant and put them into 5-gallon buckets for growing in a sheltered, sunny place. When it freezes, cover the plants with a sheet or bring them inside for the night.

Using a Greenhouse
If you have a greenhouse, now's the time to fill it up with end-of-summer plants in their 5-gallon buckets. If their foliage is luxuriant, cut back some branches a little. This keeps the plant in balance because it lost a lot of roots when you dug it up. The pruning will encourage new shoots to grow and, after a while, they will produce flowers. If the greenhouse is kept warm—around 70F day and night—the flowers will turn into fruit.

A greenhouse comes into its own during winter months. It's hard on the pocketbook to keep one cool during the summer. But in winter you trap the sun's warmth which costs you nothing, provided you keep the doors closed. You'll need a heater during December and January if you grow summertime plants. Tomatoes need nighttime temperatures above 75F to maintain production. A greenhouse lets you keep harvesting summertime plants, but cost of heating will be high.

Wintertime plants such as lettuce, beans and cabbage grow more quickly in a greenhouse than those outside and at little cost of heating because sun's heat will be enough. Later in winter you can start new plants from seed to prepare for spring.

In October we're coming to the end of Chinese pole beans. They've had a long "inning." Now you may want to let pods mature to give you hard beans. They're good in soups.

Green Tomatoes
Outdoor tomato plants will do well in the next few weeks, but be ready for the inevitable killing frost. It will result in buckets of green tomatoes. Ahead of time, select and study recipes on how to use them in pies, relishes, chutneys and jams.

Save some space in a garage or storage shed where you can hang up complete plants—roots and all. The fruit will gradually ripen on the vine for you. The alternative is to pick all the fruit, one by one, and store them in boxes of dry sawdust.

Pests
Back in the garden, there may be trouble. Your morning inspections may discover a few seedlings lying on their sides, with a neatly nibbled stem. This is the work of cutworms. These dark-colored caterpillars spend their days in the soil and nights crawling over your garden looking for something to eat. They are destructive to seedlings in the same way birds are to fruit—taking a bite here and a bite there. If they stayed with one plant and ate its leaves, half a plant would more than satisfy their appetite.

Control cutworms by spraying the ground, not the plants, with diazinon or Malathion 50 in the evening. When cutworms come up for their nightly

Dig up frost-tender summer vegetables in anticipation of that first surprise freeze. Grow them in a greenhouse or sheltered place where you can later cover them with tent of clear plastic. Use blanket on a freezing night.

feed they will be killed by the poison.

If you don't like chemical controls, wrap kitchen foil around the stem of each seedling—a tiresome task. Try placing a gallon glass jar over each plant and pushing it lightly into the soil. This will keep the pest out and also provide a sort of greenhouse to protect plant from the cold.

Harvester ants remain troublesome at this end of the season. They work furiously, gathering green leaves to store for the winter. Active at night, they easily strip plants and young seedlings before dawn. Take a flashlight and you'll be amazed at the intense activity that is all over by daylight. They leave a telltale trail of small pieces and maybe a few stragglers in the early morning sunshine, making it easy for you to discover their nest.

The next night, while all the ants are out cutting and stealing your plants, pour diazinon down the nest. The ants' compelling instinct to carry something home forces them to track the poison deep inside their nest.

Grasshoppers also have a destructive last fling before the frost. They are big and fat and not overly hungry, but a bite or two from them on small seedlings is all we need to regret their presence. October's mornings are cool and insects, being cold-blooded, are sluggish. You can easily catch them during

There aren't any moles in the dry desert. Moles eat insects. This varmint eats roots of plants. It's called a *pocket gopher* because of pouches on either side of its cheeks. Your roots go in those pouches.

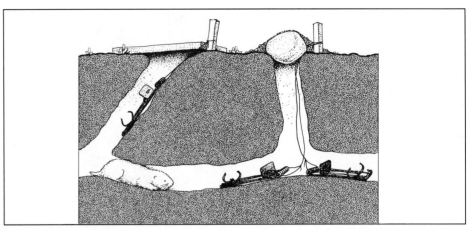

Methods of placing traps for pocket gophers: Single trap in lateral tunnel, left; hole dug with shovel and two traps set in opposite directions in main tunnel, right. Traps should be fastened with wire or cord to stake tall enough to be readily visible. Block light by covering opening(s) with a board or rock, or fill with dirt.

the first couple of hours of the day. Hit them with a stick or smash them underfoot.

If they are left alone, they will lay eggs that *overwinter* in the soil and hatch out next spring. Sometimes grasshoppers, though old and fat, will survive a mild winter. We all hope for a chilly November and December to kill off a number of pests.

We also like to have sufficient cold to provide deciduous trees with the chilling they require. We don't always get this and, if we have the old varieties, there's always a loss in yield and performance. On the other hand, a mild winter means our citrus trees will not be damaged and the fruit will be safe.

Gophers & Rabbits

Gophers spend the summer *estivating*. This is a word similar in meaning to hibernating, but it refers to inactivity during the hot time of the year. Who can blame a gopher for doing this?

However, we put a lot of blame on gophers that come out of this resting period. October's cool gives them a lot of energy to tunnel all over the place, bury our new plantings and eat the roots of tomato and pepper plants that have in their turn, recovered from summer's heat.

It's not effective to put out poisoned grain, hoping the gopher will eat it. It's a dangerous and irresponsible thing to

do. You might poison a pet, some birds or perhaps a curious child who tries out the colored grain.

It's not effective to drown out the nuisance by leaving a hose running in a tunnel. You simply waste water because it comes out the other end of the tunnel to cause a flood. The tunnels can be quite long and the gopher—if it is washed out of its passageway—runs off while you are not looking.

Some people try to gas the animals by sealing all the holes but one. Then they attach a hose from it to their car's exhaust. This might work as might "gopher bombs" you buy in nurseries—but you never know.

You can protect your plants in gopher country by wrapping the roots in chicken wire. Dig large planting holes and line them with a box of 1-inch-mesh chicken wire. Of course any roots that grow through the mesh will be at risk and there are times when the gopher climbs into the box and has a feast.

Other animals eat gophers. If you don't like to have snakes, owls, hawks and coyotes living with you, then get a cat—but don't feed it to the point of fatness and laziness. A well-instructed cat makes a great gopher hunter.

Two interesting tricks might be tried. The first involves buying or making one of those animated windmill things on top of a pole that you stick in the

ground. The vibrations of the windmill, especially if you incorporate a little man beating on an anvil, are carried to the ground through the pole. The gophers think an earthquake is taking place and they scamper off! At least that's what the salesperson tells us. But the salesperson can't tell us what to do when the wind stops blowing!

The second trick is to surround your garden with a planting of castor beans. It is said their roots are a deterrent to gophers. Castor beans are a summertime plant and gophers are more active in the cooler times. Some gardeners say this doesn't matter because the roots send out their smell even when dead. Other sceptical people think such gardeners pour castor oil down the tunnels when no one is looking.

If you don't own a good cat, you have to trap gophers. Garden stores sell traps. Ask the salesperson to show you how to set them. You need to buy at least two. You don't know which way the animal is traveling along its tunnel so you set one pointing this way and the other pointing that way. Select a currently used run as shown by a fresh heap of dirt the gopher pushed up, and exclude daylight from the disturbed soil with a board or rock, or fill hole with dirt. Wear old gloves so you don't leave your scent. Inspect

October
WEEK 4

Best way to rid your garden of gophers is to trap them.

Gopher tunnels act as drainage tubes and can divert a lot of irrigation water from your garden. Fill them in.

Encouraging Dormancy

If a fall season is mild, suggesting that winter will be mild, there's reason to worry a little on behalf of our citrus trees.

Because of cooling temperatures and shortening days, our trees put on a spurt of growth—they might even flower a little. This encourages beginning gardeners to invoke one of the cardinal rules regarding fertilizer applications—namely, support new growth when it occurs by applying a nitrogen fertilizer.

Normally this makes good sense, but at the end of the year when the next few weeks are sure to bring freezing nights, we don't want to encourage or assist new growth. Ignore fall growth in your citrus trees. Don't be tempted to help it along. *No fertilizing.* Remember, new growth is frost-tender.

Less-Frequent Irrigation

Encourage your trees into dormancy by watering less often. Their water requirement diminishes with cooling weather, so it will be quite safe to change a 10-day irrigation interval into a 14-day one. Watch the condition of the new growth carefully and allow it to wilt just a little before you water again. As the month progresses, try for a 20-day irrigation interval.

Resist the temptation to be kind to your trees by catering to their apparent growth needs. Ignore the mild weather that prompts such kindness. When the first frost of the year strikes, and indeed it usually surprises us in mid-November, you'll be glad you were tough-minded in October.

Don't forget that you still irrigate deeply using the same amount of water each time. It's just that you reduce the amount of water by lengthening the interval between irrigations. You are controlling new growth, instead of letting it run away with itself.

There's another benefit to controlling growth by less watering: Let's say you disregard this advice and go ahead with frequent irrigations. Oranges and tangerines that are getting close to ripening, will continue to expand because of the increased availability of water. Unfortunately, the skin, which

daily and dispose of the bodies. Use them to train the cat.

Another pest of the moment—in fact most of the year if you live on the outskirts of town—is the cottontail rabbit. Misguided people who feed them call them *bunnies.*

Your garden plants and landscaping plants are full of moisture. That's why rabbits go for them. You can't blame them—really.

It's useless putting out blood meal, moth balls, pepper, hair from the barber shop, or chemical deterrents. They last for a day or two in the dry desert air and the wind blows them away.

Coyotes and birds of prey eat rabbits. And so do cats. But most dogs don't—not even if you tell them to.

The only effective thing to do about rabbits is to surround your garden completely with chicken wire. Buy it 3 feet wide with small mesh and bury 6 inches of it so the varmints can't squeeze under it. Don't ever leave the gate open!

Rabbit's eye view of thriving garden. There are too many to trap and they can't be discouraged. You just have to surround your garden with chicken wire.

Grey aphids are a winter scourge. They don't bother to lay eggs, but produce live young. Stop them before they reach plague proportions by pinching out affected parts of plants.

has been hardened by the summer sun, doesn't stretch any more and the swelling fruit splits. Nobody wants split fruit. It smells and attracts gnats that bring in bacteria which start decay and spoil the fruit.

Pecan Trees

You have to keep up an irrigation schedule with pecan trees in spite of the coming cold weather. Nuts must continue to get water so they fill out well, otherwise there will be a number of shriveled nuts instead of plump ones. If the trees become badly short of water, there will be a premature nut fall.

A number of beginning gardeners mistakenly take this as a sign that the crop is ready for picking. They start knocking the remaining nuts off the tree just at a time when they need to stay on in order to fill out. In any event, it's best to harvest your crop from the ground. Let the nuts drop when they are ready.

Snails

If we have rain in October, expect a lot of snails. A night of gentle rain brings them out in dozens. And on a cloudy morning you catch them far from their hiding places. Step on them and crunch them, or buy them from your children at ten for a penny. You can increase the rate to a cent apiece when

the children get bored with their collecting. It's easy money anyway, and it stays in the family.

Most of the time snails live underground, hiding among ground covers. Vinca beds are great places for snails in a resting condition. They see no point in coming up to be blasted by the desert's hot sun and dry atmosphere. However, when these conditions are changed by gentle fall rains or frequent irrigation and cloudy weather, they pop out all over the place.

Keep the soil surface as dry as possible by irrigating less frequently, and in the morning so the sun dries everything out. Remove excess shade caused by low branches of trees and shrubs. Snails are a part of the natural chain of destruction, but will, unfortunately, eat young seedlings when they are tired of decaying vegetation.

Snails can be enticed by beer and become trapped or drowned in it. Lay a beer can with a little beer still in it on the ground so the opening is at ground level. The snails go in—but they don't come out. See photo page 194. Put the can of snails in the trash for a journey to the dump.

If you are not a beer person or prefer to drink your can dry and empty, there are snail baits at the nurseries. A lot of gardeners don't like them because they look like cat food or breakfast cereal. You are supposed to sprinkle them around your garden for the snails to bump into. Although they may have a component attractive to snails, many people think the poisonous pellets are too attractive to children, birds and pets.

Aphids

Here's another little worry for the gardener. Aphids get a second chance at being destructive. Their opportunity is new growth on plants occasioned by the mild weather. There may be a repeat of springtime populations—green, brown and black—but they are sure to be joined by grey aphids. You find these especially on cabbage-family plants.

At first, it's a small, ash-like cluster at the growing point or on the underside of a young leaf. In a day or two the population increases and it's obvious the plant is under stress, but the cause may still be hidden. See photo at left. It pays to inspect your young plants closely and rub out the first pest invasions. Once they get into a broccoli head or a cauliflower there's little to be done except serve the vegetable with a lot of cheese sauce.

November
WEEK 1

There are obvious signs that summer is coming to an end. The days are shortening and temperatures are falling, but winter is not here yet! Summertime plants slow their growth and leaves of deciduous trees start their color change, though they don't drop off yet.

We can't do much about the summertime vegetables except to consider digging them up and preserving them through the winter in containers placed in a sheltered environment. They will be planted out again in the spring.

Preserving Heat for Winter Vegetables

We can do something about the newly planted winter vegetables. They must be kept growing.

This means you have to preserve heat that reaches them from the sun. You can cover individual plants with gallon glass jars, but you'll need a lot of jars to do this. Another way is to bend a length of fiberglass over the row of plants or seedlings. When you close the ends with a board, you'll keep out sparrows that tear out lettuce seedlings.

You can also use panes of glass fastened together to form a box, over a row of plants or seedlings.

Old windows, a sheet of clear plastic, anything that lets light through can be placed over the plants. Just keep the material off the leaves to avoid sunburn—or even frost burn at night.

Winter rains are gentle and widespread compared with localized summer storms. Moisture soaks into ground and overcast weather keeps it there. There's little evaporation.

If you want to buy such panes together with their special fasteners, look in seed catalogs for *cloches*. This is a French term for covers.

Another device—a result of the plastics revolution—is called *Wall-of Water*®. It can be bought through the catalogs. It is a large tube made up of a number of little tubes that are filled with water from the top. They are tricky to fill and to keep upright, but once erected they allow light to reach the plant through the water. The water is warmed during the day and releases heat during the night. You'll need a lot of tubes if you have a large garden.

Keep the soil warm by laying clear plastic on the ground between the rows of vegetables. Provided the roots are growing—and they need warm soil for this to take place—the tops will also grow, even in cold air. Clear plastic will encourage weed growth, whereas black plastic will not. Contrary to what you might think, black plastic is not as effective as clear plastic as a soil warmer.

Then you can build a temporary greenhouse or tunnel of clear plastic over the whole bed. See photos page 258.

Small Amounts of Fertilizer

If your winter vegetable plants are growing, you can extend their activity by using small amounts of ammonium

Black plastic warms soil, retains moisture and keeps weeds down. At top of photo where plastic did not cover ground, there are weeds.

New plantings of strawberries were made through plastic in October or even September. They grow well on less irrigation and without competition from weeds.

Even seeds can be sown in November with help of clear plastic. Trenches stay warm because wind is kept out and moisture is kept in. Sun warms soil and seeds germinate rapidly.

Old windows placed over new garden act as a greenhouse and make plants grow during winter months.

All plant growth slows during winter and so does bacteria that change ammonium fertilizers into available nitrate. Ammonium nitrate becomes winter favorite because part of it is immediately used by winter vegetables. Ammonium part will be changed by bacteria later when soil warms.

Because ammonium nitrate is very soluble in water, it can be applied through garden hose to growing plants. Proportioner lets you nourish your plants every time you irrigate them.

nitrate fertilizer. Don't think, however, that you can bring dormant plants back into growth.

Scatter dry fertilizer on the soil around plants at the rate of half a pound to every 100 square feet. Water it in well, washing any fertilizer off the leaves. It will burn the leaves if left on. If fertilizer is washed into the growing point of a lettuce or cabbage, it will kill it.

Another way to apply soluble fertilizer is to put a tablespoon of it into a gallon of water and use this solution to irrigate plants. Better still, put half a cupful of ammonium nitrate in a jar and use the hose proportioner to suck it out as you sprinkle the garden.

Keep your plants growing, even into cold weather, with such a feeding every 10 days or so.

Faba Beans & Peas

It's getting late for more seed sowing or putting out plants, even if you go to the trouble of following the previous suggestions. The exceptions are—fortunately there are always exceptions— peas and faba beans. Both of these plants prefer cool soil and, if you sow their seeds at the beginning of November, they will germinate if the soil is not too wet. They will grow slowly during the winter and then put on a burst

of growth early in the spring. This will provide you with a harvest that starts in January and goes through to April. These plants are fairly frost-resistant, though some damage may be done to early flowers. If you let the winter go by and sow their seed in January, you'll get a short harvest and a light one.

Taste-Testing Citrus

Tangerines are getting ripe. It's time to taste-test the Algerians. Winter Navels also might be tested. Don't go by the fruit's color alone. If the fruit tastes good, it's time to eat it.

Birds, Gnats & Citrus Fruit

A new pest is developing in the desert. Birds are eating, or at least spoiling, our citrus fruit. If the winter is a dry one, it's hard on birds and they turn to whatever choices are left open to them. If you grow citrus, you'll discover that thrashers, sapsuckers and woodpeckers punch a hole in the ripening fruit.

You may not actually see it happen. All you see is a hole, as if a child had stuck a pencil into the fruit. Around the hole are a number of small gnats. Although such small insects couldn't possibly have made such a hole, that's the conclusion a lot of people jump to.

The gnats are attracted by the juice

smell. They bring in bacteria which start to decay the fruit. In a short time the fruit is spoiled.

Pick off such fruit and, if the damage has been done recently, eat it. Badly damaged fruit should be thrown away. Don't throw it on the ground to put out a strong smell to attract more gnats.

Keep the birds from your tree by covering it with a fine-mesh net. These can be bought at nurseries in varying sizes. Unfortunately, bird nets also catch birds and lizards, and they may die because our inspection trips are not frequent enough to prevent it.

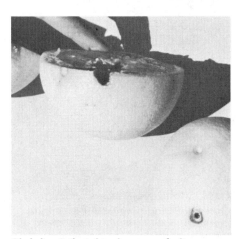

Birds learn that ripening grapefruit are a source of moisture—citrus-flavored!

November
WEEK 2

Small seedlings need to be thinned when they start to crowd one another. If roots are intertwined, snip off stems with scissors at ground level without disturbing those that are left. Water with houseplant fertilizer using one teaspoon to a gallon.

Out in the garden your closely planted winter vegetables need to be thinned. This makes room and gives you a meal.

Eggplant are frost-tender and this one was left out a day too long. To save, cut off damaged branches and put container in greenhouse or sheltered place. Perhaps it has not been killed and might send out new shoots.

Thinning Seedlings

If you have direct-sown lettuce, beets, radishes, cabbage, cauliflower—in fact any of the wintertime vegetables—in the ground, thin the seedlings before they crowd one another.

Most gardeners prefer to put out transplants in the fall. But, a direct seeding can be succesful because soil temperatures are favorable and the young plants grow well. You can lose seedlings to harvester ants and sparrows, but if you did sow seeds in September, it's time to thin them. If they are allowed to compete with one another, they will be weak and spindly, and subject to disease. Give young plants plenty of space to grow.

Don't throw away the thinnings—eat them. In fancy restaurants they are called *gourmet sprouts.* You might as well eat them at home. Wash them, roots and all, and mix them into a salad, sandwich filling or side dish.

Pecans

Some pecans are ripening enough to fall off the tree, but don't let this get you excited. The first falls are generally poor-quality nuts—those that are not fully filled or are insect-damaged. Wait for the main crop which is still on the tree. And don't go climbing up pecan trees. Wait for the ripe nuts to

fall off on their own. Pick pecans from the ground.

The first frost of the year will send a lot of nuts down. The freeze won't hurt them, but they will be nuts that are nicely filled. Don't be in a hurry to eat them either because green nuts have the same effect on your stomach as green apples.

The First Freeze

Often the first half of November is mild and pleasant. The weather changes imperceptibly—getting nicer every day. Then all of a sudden we get a sharp freeze. Be ready for this event which seems to have some connection with the full moon, because it's going to be a killer.

It comes at a time when a lot of summertime vegetables begin to grow again after their summer misery. Even fruit trees and vines unwisely get going again. All new growth will be killed.

Save eggplant and peppers from the disaster, cut them back and dig them up. Grow them through the winter in 5-gallon buckets of good soil in a greenhouse or a sheltered place. You won't get much production from them until April, but new plants set out at that time won't produce until late June. You'll get a steal on the season.

Green Tomatoes

The big effect of the frost will most likely be lots of green tomatoes. Too many, perhaps. You'll have to get out your cookbooks and make chutney, relishes, pickles, jams and pies.

Individual fruit can be wrapped in newspaper and set aside to ripen in its own time. Put some fruit in a warmish place for quick results and others in a cool place for later. Some gardeners pull the whole plant out of the ground—roots and all—and hang it in a cool, airy place for the fruit to ripen.

If we don't get a frosty mid-November surprise, plants will continue to grow unharmed, although their growth will be much slower. Bush beans should continue to please. Pick frequently to encourage them to keep producing flowers and pods. Help them with a side dressing of ammonium phosphate using a teaspoon per plant, but scuffle it into the soil carefully without damaging the roots. Then give a good irrigation to wash it down.

A plastic tunnel over the beans will keep them warm and growing. In a favorable year, they'll grow all winter.

November
WEEK 3

That first frost probably surprised you. Nevertheless, you must have been comforted in the knowledge that summertime trees are safe as long as they are not growing. And, being the good gardener that you are, you held back on irrigating and fertilizing a few weeks ago, so your trees didn't suffer.

Infrequent Irrigation

Continue to give your citrus trees deep irrigations and let the surface soil dry out between waterings. Don't let ripening fruit frighten you into frequent irrigations. Obviously, we musn't let the trees dry out to the point where fruit shrivels and drops off. The trees' water need is greatly reduced during cool weather and you shouldn't encourage new growth by overirrigating at this time. It can easily happen if we get a few warm days.

Deciduous fruit trees should receive the same treatment. Freezing will not hurt them unless they still have active growth—they should not. They need a long resting period. The sooner it starts, the better. Drying out deciduous plants is one way to add to the dormancy usually induced by cold temperatures. In the desert, we don't have enough cold, so help it out with a little induced dryness and hope it doesn't rain.

Split Fruit

A sign that fruit trees got too much water earlier on becomes evident now. Pomegranates and oranges continue to split their skins.

If summer rains were heavy and the soil became saturated, and you kept up a summer schedule of irrigations longer than necessary, the fruit grew in size. You might have been pleased at the time, watching the fruit get bigger.

In the desert, growth is rapid, whether it be fruit swelling or shoot lengthening. Unfortunately, fruit skins become hardened by sunshine and lose their elasticity. The internal swelling is too much for the inflexible outside. Something has to give and the fruit splits.

Next, the smell of the juice attracts insects, usually leaf-footed plant bugs,

gnats and sour-fruit beetles. These 1/8-inch-long, brownish "vinegar beetles" carry bacteria on their feet and soon a fermentation or rot starts. Pick off all split fruit and put them in the trash can or compost heap. Left lying around they are an attractive nuisance.

Dealing with Summertime Plants

Now we come to a dilemma: What shall we do with summertime plants that were not hit by the frost? Shall we save them or pull them up to make room for wintertime vegetables?

Even if we had a mild start to winter, we know to expect more severe and damaging freezes in the next few weeks. In fact, we won't be free of them until mid-March. Shall we gamble on fair weather and keep our summertime plants alive?

Remember that last spring, eggplant, bell peppers and tomatoes took a long time to get established and produce a harvest. A similar long wait next spring can be avoided. Preserve your old summer vegetables through the winter by putting them into 5-gallon buckets before the frost gets them. Plant them next spring side by side with your usual new plants. We can even hope that a mild winter will allow plants to continue production. It has happened before—so our neighbors tell us.

Cut back the straggly top growth to short main stubs. Such a pruning, as does all pruning, encourages new growth. On that growth we find flowers that turn into fruit in the spring.

There's nothing outlandish with such thinking. There's a tempting economy in the idea. Go ahead—do it, but weigh the consequences first.

The Danger of Continuous Cropping

Desert soils start by being free of harmful bacteria and fungi. When we grow plants continuously in the same soil and keep watering them we provide food for these organisms. The longer we grow them, the more the organisms multiply and the weaker our plants become. The organisms are now soil pests—killers.

Care of the soil is part of good husbandry. It's best done by growing different plants each year in the same plot of ground. Sometimes the soil has to lie fallow in an effort to starve out a disease. Crop rotation—resting the soil from continuous cropping with one kind of plant—makes a lot of sense.

It's hard to get rid of soil diseases. And they make a garden plot worthless.

Pick lower leaves when you need greens for a salad. Lettuce gives better continuous yield this way.

November
WEEK 4

Deciduous shade trees provide wealth of organic matter every fall. Instead of throwing them away, sweep up leaves and turn them into valuable compost.

Prepare your compost bin for oncoming harvest of leaves. Here, each panel is 3 feet square and held together with pegs at corners. It's easy to move frame of stout chicken wire or something similar, and get to finished product from a summer's collection. This will be dug into soil in readiness for your spring garden.

Cutting Back Asparagus

Asparagus plants begin to look a little weary in November. Some years this does not occur until really cold weather starts or it coincides with the same sharp frost that knocks nuts off the pecan trees. Asparagus plants have grown satisfactorily all through the summer in full sun. It's now their turn to rest.

As soon as asparagus leaves begin to turn brown, stop watering. Dormancy can be induced by drying out plants and they will benefit because they need it.

Cut off all leaves, right down to the ground. Be sure the plants are dormant, otherwise the cutting will act as a pruning and cause fresh growth. We don't want new growth until spring. This is important! If you sense the plants are not quite dormant, don't risk a cutting back.

Let the bed stay dry. Withhold manure until spring just in case we have a wet winter. Let asparagus rest.

Deciduous trees will be dropping their leaves soon. Think compost. Get the frame ready or perhaps make a new one.

Disposing of Ashes

The first cold snap, if it is a sharp one, sets people to lighting fires in their houses. It's a nice Thanksgiving gesture to their friends and a comfort to themselves. What's not so comforting is the ashes. What to do with them?

People from Eastern states remember putting fireplace ashes on their gardens. Ashes supply potash, a plant food, and make an acid soil sweeter.

Our desert soils usually contain sufficient potash and they are already too alkaline. Putting ashes on a garden makes things worse—not better. Don't do it. Send the ashes to the dump even if it seems wasteful.

Home-Grown Fruits for Thanksgiving

You will enjoy your Thanksgiving dinner more if you grew the vegetables and fruits. Citrus on the tree won't be ready except, perhaps, Algerian tangerines. However, what's wrong with serving home-canned apricots and peaches? Or offering your own applesauce?

There's an apple variety called *Ein Sheimer* that grows well in the desert. It makes a wonderful applesauce that is more solid and chunky than the mush you usually find in a can. Ein Sheimer is self-pollinating, so you don't need to plant two trees. It's a good yielder and vigorous tree. Prune severely. Keep the tree small and it will fit into a small yard or patio. You'll also be able to put a net over the whole tree and keep the fruit for you and your family—not the birds.

Fun with Sweet Potatoes

If you have a sweet potato or two left over from the holiday feast—and don't particularly want to eat another for a long time—you can give the children an interesting indoor-gardening assignment.

Get them to slice the root lengthwise. Dust the flesh with sulphur to prevent decay. Place the two halves, flat-side down, in a shallow pan containing a sandy soil mix or even plain coarse sand. There should be drainage holes in the pan. The sand should be 3 inches deep to allow strong roots to grow in it. Put the dish in a sunny window and keep the sand moist and warm. Remember, sweet potatoes are hot-weather plants. Some people grow the potato in a pan of plain water, but you must keep the water sweet by changing it often.

After a month or two trim back the new shoots or train them up on a framework. The old root shrinks as its food reserves are used up by new growth. Then you start putting houseplant food in the water—the usual tablespoon in a gallon. Luxuriant leaf growth calls for a lot of nitrogen. You'll have to supply it because there's none in the sand or water.

If your children are imaginative, they can train the more vigorous shoots up strings attached to the ceiling. Of

Frost will get this mass of sweet-potato vines just as you are ready to harvest roots for Thanksgiving dinner. Before this happens, take some vines for next year's crop. You may not be able to get rooted cuttings from your nurseries next May.

Root cuttings in water and use as house-plants for a couple of months. When soil warms up in May, set plants outside.

course, they can't move the dish now, so they should have selected its permanent place in their room. Encourage the vines up the strings, then guide them along horizontal strings to the corner of the room. When the vines reach the corner, tell them to make a left turn and then another, and another until they come back from where they started.

You will have a green room and an enjoyable sense of achievement.

Next April, take slips off the room plant and put them in pots of sandy potting soil. In May or June when the soil is well-warmed and when the slips have a bunch of strong roots on them, set them out in well-prepared soil. Fertilize and water—and there's your own sweet-potato bed!

In years past you may have yearned for one of these and been disappointed when you discovered that local nurseries didn't have any plants in early summer when you needed them. Remember that we have short seasons in the desert, so you must plan ahead and start early. You can't get seeds and the plant doesn't make any, so get an early start in your warm house.

December
WEEK 1

Here's a nice leaf fall, but compost bin is already full. Leaves are soft and readily break down. There will be room in bin after a week. Don't try to make compost in a pit. You exclude air and bacteria don't work well without it.

It's the fall season, but leaves stay on the trees until the first hard cold snap hits. This often happens in mid-December.

Compost from Leaf Fall
Don't let those leaves go to waste—pick them up. Mulberry leaves rapidly decompose into wonderful organic matter. There's little use for the material during winter, but in six or seven weeks you'll be digging the ground for your summer garden. You'll want compost then. It's a lot less expensive than steer manure and other prepared organic materials you find in the nurseries.

Be ready for this leaf fall. Compost is best made in a wired frame above ground, even though a lot of books mention compost pits. Some people try to make it in plastic bags and garbage bins. If you want good, quickly made compost, you must allow air to reach the bacteria that break down the vegetable materials. No air means undesirable bacteria get to work. They make a smelly soggy mess instead of a light crumbly leaf mold.

Some years we get enough sharp frost to knock off all the leaves at once. That's good for people who aren't too keen on sweeping up be-

You get different grades of compost, depending on age of pile. Material on table is ready for digging into garden, but material in sieve needs to be returned for further decomposition. It is suitable for a mulch to shade soil in summer.

Decomposition rate can be gauged by heat transferred to your metal soil probe left in pile. Great bacterial activity shows as a hot rod—too hot to handle!

Any goat interested in organic gardening can be trained to use the compost pile as a bathroom.

cause it's once and for all, and they can handle that. But if it happens that way, your bin is filled to overflowing.

From a compost-management point of view, it's better to have the leaves fall down over a period of time. The first filling of the bin settles and makes room in a few days. Besides, a carpet of colored fallen leaves looks nice in the sunshine. They don't herald the weeks of deep snow you experienced back East. Raking is a gentle, satisfying activity and an activity for all ages.

Keep the heap of collected leaves moist with an occasional sprinkle. They will heat up in a day or two from bacterial activity. Temperatures of 120F are easily reached. These will kill weed seeds and some disease organisms. Use your soil probe to gauge the heat developed. It can get too hot to hold, but if it stays cold, there is no bacterial activity. The bacteria may need moisture, so you need to water the pile. Or the bacteria may be too wet and short of air so the pile needs to be turned. If you want compost in a hurry, simply turn the pile to provide oxygen for the bacteria. Turn once a week, keep the pile moist and you will have usable material in six weeks.

You can add in any vegetable material from the kitchen, but don't use your compost pile as a garbage heap. Meat scraps invite vermin, tin cans and plastic don't decay, bottles are a danger.

Some gardeners value homemade compost so much that they buy bags of leaves from neighborhood children who have raked them up from other people's yards. Buy leaves—and help a child through Christmas. Help your garden produce more next summer. Plenty of organic matter in the soil keeps it moist and that saves on your water bill.

Tunnel Gardening

The first cold snap reminds us that plants must have warmth if they are to continue growing. Cold is welcome because of deciduous fruit trees. These trees need their rest if they are to produce. But we want our winter vegetables to keep growing.

In home gardens, tunnel gardening has come to stay. It's something borrowed from commercial vegetable growers who lay clear plastic over their growing plants during winter.

To make a tunnel, you need a framework over the vegetable bed. This is most easily done by using construction mesh, the 6-inch-square material, to make an arch. Go shares with a friend

to get a discount price. Cut off 10-foot lengths from the 100-foot roll you buy. Rolls come in widths of 5 or 6 feet.

A 10-foot length makes a nice arch over a 4-foot-wide bed. This can be neatly covered by a roll of clear plastic 12 feet wide and 4 or 6 mils thick. The extra 2 feet on the plastic enables you to anchor it down along the sides with bricks.

You need extra material at the ends to let you close up the tunnel. Add 10 feet to the length of the bed when you buy the plastic. Fold and hold the ends down with more bricks. Four arches of mesh will be enough for a 20-foot-long bed.

On sunny days, keep the tunnel closed and allow moisture to build up inside. Moist air absorbs heat and holds it better than dry air. You'll save water, too, because moisture condenses on the inside of the film and drips back to the ground.

Keep the tunnel closed all the time, but watch your plants to make sure they don't get too hot, or the closed, warm atmosphere doesn't encourage aphids or molds. On really hot days open up one end—or perhaps both—to ventilate and cool things. Don't let the soil dry out. You'll have to watch carefully and tune in to the weather.

To keep them warm put your containers into tunnel of plastic if you don't have a greenhouse.

Tunnel, besides conserving sun's heat, helps with your water bill. Water evaporates from soil, but plastic prevents it from blowing away.

Redwood lumber, corrugated fiberglass and pair of hinges make *cold frame*. Use it during cooler months for raising seedlings.

Use tunnel for the next three or four months of cool weather to keep wintertime vegetables growing vigorously. In early March you can use a tunnel to start summertime seeds such as corn and squash. Set out early pepper and tomato plants, too. A tunnel lets you capture the sun's heat to make a microclimate 20F or 30F warmer than the outside. You change winter into spring and spring into summer.

Using a Cold Frame

If you are handy with hammer and nails, you can make a *cold frame*. This is basically a glass-covered box in which you grow seedlings and young plants prior to setting them out in the garden after the weather warms up.

Like the tunnel, it's a sunlight-trapping device, so build it to face south. Make the front wall as low as possible to let in the sunshine. Keep the lid on during cool weather, but slide it off a little when things get hot. If you don't have a sunny place in your yard, there's little point in making a cold frame—unless you want to turn it into a hot-bed.

Making a Hot Bed

A *hot bed* is a cold frame with a soil-heating cable installed. The electric company now provides the heat in-

stead of the sun, but don't forget that plants need good light to grow strongly. There should be some sunshine available. Old windows make good covers. Make the walls of old boards, bricks or blocks. It's a temporary structure, so don't get fancy. Just make it functional. Make the front wall 1 foot high and the back wall at least 2 feet high. Slope the side walls making them airtight with the lid.

If you can't find any old windows, you can make the lid cheaply from corrugated fiberglass. Start with an 8-foot length and make two 4-foot lengths by

Offset winter's cold by wrapping bag of soil mix with black plastic. Put in a sunny place and plants grow quickly.

cutting across the middle. Place these side by side to give you a 4-foot-square top for your structure. Frame it with 2-inch X 2-inch redwood and hinge it at the back if the walls are wood. If the walls are brick, you'll have to slide the cover to get ventilation. A loose lid can blow away, so hinges are preferred.

Spread the soil-heating cable on the ground and cover it with hardware cloth to protect it from sharp tools. An inch or two of soil over the hardware cloth spreads the heat and retains it, but it takes height from the inside of

Old windows placed over new garden act as a greenhouse and make plants grow during winter months.

Use compost pile's heat to grow winter vegetables.

Even a glass jar over plant helps it to grow. Jar also keeps out cutworms that live in soil and birds that fly into your garden. Birds love lettuce.

the structure. Some gardeners spread 8 or 9 inches of good soil mix and grow their seedlings directly in it. Tall plants go to the back and seedling trays go to the shallow front.

You have the same responsibilty as with the tunnel to make sure things don't dry out or get too hot. It's not a hard task, but keep an eye on things.

Planting in Soil Amendment

Yet another way to make the most of the winter sun is to plant directly into a bag of soil amendment, such as peat moss or potting-soil mix. You don't even open the bag. Don't use steer manure, it's too strong. Details are described in Chapter 7.

Plants can be set out in your compost pile. This can be either the new one that is steaming away with fresh leaves, or the old one that has been livened up with a layer of fresh leaves. You are looking for heat and new organic matter will provide it.

Containers can be moved into a sunny, sheltered place where they will gather daytime heat that will carry plants through the night. If the nights turn frosty, cover tender, young plants with a light blanket.

Winter vegetables that were set out in mid-October will grow quite well during December, but it will be slow growth and a little disappointing. They

can be helped by placing a glass gallon jug over each one if you don't want to go to the trouble of making a tunnel. This will provide an individual greenhouse for each plant, keeping it warm and protected from cold winds. You may need a lot of jugs for a large garden. A glass jar pushed into the soil also keeps cutworms from the plant.

It's not worth setting out plants or sowing seeds at this time of year. It's too cold in spite of the sunshine and a comparison with the rest of the country under snow and sleet.

Citrus Fruit

As temperatures drop, citrus fruit turns from leaf-green to orange or yellow. All of a sudden there's fruit on the trees.

This appearance is pleasant and exciting, but it doesn't mean the fruit is ripe. The color change is stimulated by falling temperatures, not the amount of sugar in the fruit. If you don't believe this, just take a fruit or two and discover for yourself what it tastes like.

Algerian tangerines are the first citrus fruit to ripen—sometimes at Thanksgiving, but certainly at Christmas. You have to watch them carefully because they don't last long and are all over soon after the New Year. Once you've carried out a taste test and found tangerines to your liking, don't delay eating them. They don't keep, either on or off the tree.

Navel oranges begin to ripen in December and so do Minneola tangeloes—one of the best citrus for home gardens. Grapefruit won't be at their best until March or April, in spite of their appearance.

Lemons and limes will be ripe, although some may still be green. We are so used to store-bought lemons looking bright yellow that we forget they have been treated to bring out the color. Don't go by appearances—do a taste test. If the fruit is juicy, go ahead and enjoy it. Lemons store on the tree very well, even after the fruit turns yellow naturally. So don't hurry to eat them all because they will still be good in March.

Preparing for a Freeze

The color change in citrus fruit gives us a reminder to get our frost-protection materials handy. It's hard to believe that such beautiful sunny days can go hand in hand with freezing nights—but they do. And a freeze comes quickly. Don't be caught unprepared.

Get a number of light blankets or heavy sheets ready. Second-hand stores are good places to find them if you have none of your own at this time. For each tree you want to protect, you'll need a light bulb or two, a metal bucket and an extension cord.

Grapefruit on the inside of tree are safe from frost damage. Light bulb placed on ground under tree will warm inside of tree during freezing night. Only outer foliage will be damaged.

Hawk silhouettes suspended over garden are supposed to frighten sparrows off lettuce and sapsuckers away from ripening grapefruit. See if it works!

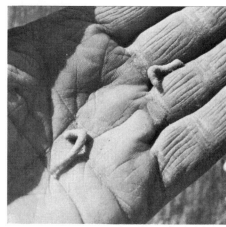

Why don't birds eat caterpillars? You have to pick these things off cabbage and lettuce yourself!

Watch your thermometer and compare your temperatures with those at the airport and the forecasts. Be aware of what's going on. Be ready at short notice to cover your trees and set out the light bulbs. Read the chapter on Frost Protection, page 153.

Protecting Citrus Fruit from Birds

Around this time of year you may see funny things happening to your ripening citrus fruit.

Fairly large, neat holes appear in the fruit and there are clusters of little brown gnats at the entrances. Gardeners who notice this for the first time are puzzled. Those little gnats couldn't have made the big hole—yet there's no large insect around to blame.

Of course, the gnats arrived after the hole was made and they continue to spoil the fruit because they are carrying bacteria. They were attracted to the fruit by the aroma of citrus juice. The holes were put there by thirsty woodpeckers who have learned that there is good stuff inside those brightly colored balls hanging on certain trees in our yards. They do it more every year.

Besides covering the tree with a bird net to provide a barrier between fruit and bird, there's not much that can be done to protect your harvest. You may need a large net, but if your tree is too big, you can completely protect one or two limbs and let the upper fruit take its chances.

Traditional bird-scaring devices, including the scarecrow, pie-pans, rubber snakes, stuffed owls and so on are largely ineffective. They work for a day or two, but the birds get used to them.

The latest device developed by bird psychologists is a black cut-out of a flying hawk that you suspend on a long pole over a tree. As it waves in the breeze its shadow is supposed to scare away the bothersome birds.

Any damaged oranges and grapefruit should be removed from the tree because more gnats will be attracted by the juice smell. If you find the fruit soon after it has been damaged, you can eat it. But bacteria carried by the gnats soon starts a decay.

Birds can be kept away from ripening fruit if you spray the whole tree with Sloanes® Linament. Add two tablespoons of linament and a dash of detergent to emulsify the mixture, to a gallon of warm water. This spray certainly protects pyracantha berries from birds. If you are doubtful of its value on citrus, you might want to spray a branch or two and hope that the smell will envelop the whole tree. Otherwise, you yourself might be deterred from eating the fruit.

Pests & Winter Vegetables

If you have winter vegetables such as broccoli, cabbage, cauliflower and lettuce, there might be something nasty lurking on them. Have you been vigilant lately?

Take a close look in the heart of the plants and on the back of the leaves. See photo page 261. That's where grey aphids hide when they first attack plants. The early appearance is one of a puckered leaf with a pale blotch on it. Aphids are on the other side sucking away the juices. Grey aphids look like a speck of wood ash lying in a cupped portion of the leaf. That's their way of hiding. A spotty paleness and crinkling of the leaves will tell you something is wrong. Later on, the wilting plants show complete stress and the pests are obvious by their masses.

In addition, take a close look on the mid-rib of each leaf. That's where the slender-bodied looper caterpillars line themselves up. Because they have just eaten your plant's leaves they are an identical green color and hard to see. Take your time.

As soon as you find these pests, remove them. Don't wait for tomorrow because they will be twice as destructive.

You can rub them out using a finger and thumb. Or spray them with soapy water if the plants are close to harvest.

December
WEEK 3

Grey aphids quickly become nuisance in winter. As soon as you see them on plants of cabbage family, pinch them off even though you have to sacrifice a leaf or two.

If the plants are still young, spray with diazinon or Malathion 50. These chemicals have a short residual life of about 10 days, but read the label before you use them to determine safety margins.

Gardening has slowed considerably. Whatever is growing is growing slowly. And there's little that can be set out at this time. Active people want to be doing something—and there lies a danger.

No Pruning or Fertilizing

Don't start pruning deciduous plants. The best time is when the sap is really down, which will be sometime in January or February. If you start doing it now, there's a likelihood that each cut end will drip sap. That sap is sugary. Any disease spores that alight on it will happily germinate and grow into the branch, causing such problems as slime flux or sooty canker.

Don't fertilize any plants that are starting to go dormant. There's a temptation—especially if December is mild—to look at young growth and think it needs help. The truth is quite the contrary, some plants need to stop growing. Deciduous fruit trees and vines need a rest—and a long one, if possible. Citrus trees need to be hardened off against forthcoming freeezes.

If you cannot contain your energy, go and dig some planting holes. They are going to be 5 feet square X 5 feet deep, so do a little reconnaissance before you start digging.

Look around to be sure your tree won't grow into a driveway, wall, path or powerlines. It shouldn't hang over your neighbor's fence. This will surely cause problems in the future even if you have the nicest neighbor right now.

Fruit trees should be enjoyed at all seasons. Plant them where you can see the blossoms. Perhaps use them to screen out something unsightly. But don't let them hide a pleasant view. In other words—think. Don't act on an impulse. In December you have time to think.

Deep Irrigation

Part of the "so little to do at this time of year" syndrome is that there isn't a great need to irrigate. Normal winter rains are gentle and long-lasting. Even if they don't fully materialize, our plants seem to get by quite comfortably because of the lower tempera-

There are many kinds of lettuce and they do very well during winter months, withstanding freezes.

tures that are not low enough to stop growth altogether.

Winter rains soak into the ground because they are gentle. In some years the soil is well-watered with the purest water—and quite deep down. If you have been having salt problems, caused by overfertilizing or salty water, or by stingy irrigating in summer when the water rates were high, now is your chance.

Leach those salts farther down by a good deep irrigation—even if the plants themselves don't need it. A deep watering will do far more good in wet soil than it will trying to get through dry soil first. Furthermore, the salts are already in solution from the rains, meaning they are more easily carried through the soil and away from the root zone.

If winter rains are continuous, the weather is usually warm and vegetables that were set out in September continue to grow nicely. You'll be rewarded with a good harvest.

December is a most satisfying month if we get normal rains. Of course, we are always taking a gamble with the weather. It can be nice today and terrible next week.

Lettuce

A few Decembers ago, a number of gardeners took a gamble with lettuce.

If it's too cold outside, you can grow fresh vegetables that are full of vitamins and nutrients in a jar on a kitchen windowsill. Week-old sprouts are tasty. Mung beans are at left; alfalfa at right. Change water daily to keep it sweet.

Parsley does well in winter. You don't need a lot, so a half barrel is enough garden space.

The newspapers reported earlier in the fall that something had gone wrong with commercial lettuce plantings in southern California. Home gardeners sowed lettuce seeds.

They germinated well and grew very nicely to reach harvesting size just as supermarket prices rose to double than normal. It's rare that you succeed at playing the futures market in your home garden, but lettuce does its best for you in winter.

Usually, the first seed is sown during late August and thereafter at monthly intervals. The first harvest is ready mid-October and the succession of sowings gives you a continuous supply until May. It's a really useful and productive crop for the cooler months of the year.

Although lettuce prefers cooler temperatures, we get a little impatient with its slower growth during the month of December.

We can overcome this to some extent by using ammonium nitrate in place of the usual ammonium sulphate. Use a little less because it is stronger—33 instead of 21 percent.

Pale plants will green up within a week and their size will increase, too. A gentle application, say a teaspoon shared between three or four plants per plant every two weeks, will really push your crop along.

Head lettuce does not grow nearly as well as leaf types. And there are many from which to choose. Change from one variety of leaf lettuce to another as you make successive sowings, and you'll have an interesting variety of salad food.

Head-lettuce varieties take 75 days—or more—to mature, whereas leaf types need only 40 days or so. We are back at that principle of desert gardening that says you have a number of short seasons to use. You may want to read Chapter 2 again. In any event, use quick-maturing varieties.

Birds go for lettuce seedlings in a big way. Protect the rows with a cover of chicken wire. You shouldn't have trouble from harvester ants in December, but there may be cutworms in the soil. These come out at night and crawl over the surface until they meet with a plant stem they cut off before going to the next plant. You may have to purchase lettuce seedlings from a nursery to maintain your interval planting if birds and cutworms get the better of you.

Remember, you only fertilize plants that are growing or are about to grow. If your fruit trees are starting their dormancy, don't keep them growing by applying fertilizers. Even try to dry them out by witholding an irrigation.

But don't overdo it. Roots must remain moist if the tree is to survive.

Christmas Gifts for Gardeners

Start thinking about Christmas gifts for your gardening friends. You may have to write away for certain items.

First, know the level of your friend's interest or competence. It would be a mistake to challenge him too much by giving him a plant or seeds that don't grow well in the desert. This is especially the case with children who have just started an interest in gardening. Don't smother that enthusiasm by starting them on difficult projects.

A good choice for a child is a sprout kit. It can be made at home or there are fancy ones to buy from the stores. Glass mason jars with wire-mesh lids let you drain the water. A selection of seeds, such as alfalfa, mung beans, cabbage and radish, can be found at a food store. Don't buy packets of seed from the nursery. They are often coated with poisonous chemicals—green, blue or pink—to protect them from soil diseases.

Fruit trees make wonderful gifts. You will find them in the nurseries as container-trees. These will survive being left on a doorstep overnight. The problem of wrapping such a gift can be overcome by using a gift certificate

December
WEEK 4

Ordering from Seed Catalogs

Seed catalogs begin to arrive in late December. At last the seed companies have realized that desert gardening has a different time frame from the Eastern states. Even so, there's still the invitation to get the free bonus offer by ordering before May 15th.

Here in the desert we've usually got everything planted by that date. We order tomato seeds in December and sow them in mid-January.

Catalogs always have been a beautiful stimulant. As we sit by the fire, we are so encouraged by their colorful pictures that we forget the difficulties of desert gardening. We plan our "next time round" with enthusiasm and optimism. There's never a bad word in a seed catalog.

Don't go overboard because of new varieties, although they may be better than the old strains, And it's nice to know plant breeders are working on types suitable for home gardens. These new varieties have not been fully tested under desert conditions. Until recently we had to take leftovers from commercial field varieties that were developed for one-time harvesting. Expensive machinery obliged the farmer to gather as much as he could in one pass. He didn't want to pick a second or third time. He likes *determinate* plants.

A home gardener, on the other hand, likes to pick a little something every week of the year from *indeterminate* plants.

Look for these words as you read a seed catalog.

Although the catalogs are wooing home gardeners, they are looking at the centers of population—the old ones, not new. This means desert gardeners have to be particularly choosy in ordering their seeds. Many of the All-American winners are not suitable for desert gardening.

For example, a few years ago new sweet-pepper varieties were praised because they displayed their fruits well above the foliage. A picture showed a gardener gazing admiringly at his colorful fruits. Here in the desert, any fruit that shows off in this manner gets badly sunburned and is quickly ren-

Watercress becomes available in supermarkets during December and spring. It is easy to root in water. After strong roots have formed, transplant into soil, preferably in a container. Then harvest an abundance of salad greens, high in vitamin C. As spring weather warms up, move container into a shady part of the garden.

that allows your friend to choose the tree and select the variety.

What could be nicer—for the receiver, at least—than a Certificate of Promise? A promise to dig a planting hole measuring 5 feet X 5 feet and 5 feet deep. And to fill it up again!

A friend living in a townhouse is sure to appreciate a half whiskey barrel, especially if it has been sanded, oiled and drainage holes drilled in preparation for planting.

Bags of potting soil are not very exciting, but they are useful and often very welcome. A bottle of insecticide might offend, but a pump-up sprayer is another story.

It's always nice to own good-quality tools, but we often buy the "bargain" kinds for ourselves. Buy your friend a

good set of hand tools that will last a lifetime. He is sure to take care of them. And you've turned him into a better gardener without him knowing it. Good tools are a pleasure to own and a joy to work with.

A minimum-registering thermometer that records "how cold it got last night" will be appreciated by the methodical gardener as will a rain gauge by the optimist.

A soil-heating cable is a good gift for the gardener who likes to grow his own seedlings.

And then there's the magazine subscription. Or better still, a good desert gardening book!

dered useless. Choose vegetables that keep their fruit tucked well under the foliage.

Ignore superlatives like *jumbo, giant* and *colossal* because those kinds are usually slow growers. Don't be influenced by statements like "the biggest fruit we've ever seen" or "the sweetest, juiciest, etc."

There are a lot of good varieties from European countries. Their seeds do well in the Midwest where growing seasons are long. They don't do so well in the desert where seasons are short. Surprisingly—at first—varieties from Canada do well in the desert. On second thought, they have short growing seasons, too—occasioned by snow, whereas ours are caused by heat. An ideal plant begins to produce early and maintains that production through thick and thin or, in other words, *in spite of weather changes.*

Seed companies can't tell you about this. They haven't carried out a trial planting in your backyard. Nor do you have the resources or time, but your local Land-Grant college could be doing it for you. Ask their Extension Service Agent for information about locally planted variety trials.

Look for more than total yield. Instead, choose a variety that will give early and sustained production throughout the summer months. There's little point in having no yield most of the year, then a great heap of tomatoes all in one week.

It's the same with beans, melons and squash—or any vegetable that produces fruit.

Of course, you want good flavor, but catalogs cannot tell you this. Flavor is a personal thing. You must experience it yourself.

Recently, catalogs have begun to use a number in parentheses after the variety name. This tells you how many days after planting out or sowing seed it will be until the first harvest. It's a useful piece of information. Don't ignore it.

Go back and read Chapter 2, page 5. Count the days of the variety you think you would like to plant, and of the season available to you. Match them up.

For example, if there are less than 100 days of good growing weather—neither too hot nor too cold—it is unwise to try a variety that needs more than 100 days to bring in its first fruit. Production should continue, of course, long after that first glorious day.

Good seed catalogs are a useful guide. So is your garden diary. You can read back and discover what did well for you. You can avoid repeating a mistake.

If you haven't kept a diary, do so. It will help you a lot. Make a New Year's resolution right now.

There's satisfaction in eating your own vegetables at Christmas Dinner, especially if they are freshly picked. Leafy vegetables such as cabbage, lettuce, broccoli, cauliflower, and perhaps Brussels sprouts are all possibles. So are beans, carrots, beets, turnips and snow peas.

Fertilizing

Keep your vegetable plants growing by fertilizing with ammonium nitrate in small, frequent amounts—a teaspoon for two or three plants every two weeks. Always apply dry fertilizer to wet soil—preferably halfway through an irrigation. If you scatter dry fertilizer over the plants instead of carefully putting it on the ground, be sure to wash off any crystals that rest on the foliage.

To keep your plants growing during cold weather, erect a construction-mesh arch and cover it with clear plastic. See photo page 258. Tuck in the ends to make everything airtight.

Moist air trapped inside heats up very nicely. During hot days you will have to open the ends to ventilate your temporary greenhouse.

If you get freezing nights, cover the structure with a light blanket as the sun goes down. This retains heat accumulated during the day. Remove the blanket in the morning after the sun shines on the bed.

If you succumbed to a seed-catalog's blandishments and selected a variety that exposed its fruit above the foliage, you would have lost this crop of green tomatoes. Plants with plenty of foliage and fruit tucked underneath are safe from summer sun and winter freezes.

Use December as a study month. Besides vegetable seeds to choose, there are fruit trees to consider. If you are going to plant bare-root trees, which are less expensive than container-grown trees, you must have everything ready for the rush that inevitably occurs.

A number of new varieties that require a minimal amount of winter chilling are becoming available. These are something you should take notice of. They are very suited to our desert conditions.

Visit your favorite nursery and ask to see his order catalogs. Read the descriptions of fruit-tree varieties. Talk with him about them, and place an order. Go and dig the planting holes to keep you out of gardening mischief. Remember, you should do no pruning in December and no tree fertilizing, either. There is less watering to do. Dig those holes! Be ready in the New Year.

Happy New Gardening Year!

29

HYDROPONICS—GARDENING WITHOUT SOIL

Growing tomatoes in an NFT system. Nutrients in lower tank are pumped to the left end of sloping channel. They flow back—nourishing the roots—then splash into the tank, oxygenating the solution. Top tank is a reserve with a float valve to make sure there is enough solution. Covers reduce algae growth and channel is covered for same reason. Timer determines when pump operates. Stakes driven into ground support top-heavy, tall tomato crop.

All of the many hydroponic gardening systems have two basic factors. The first is that you "work with water" (from the Greek *hydro* = water + *ponos* = work). Second is that you don't use any soil.

Its emerging popularity is a direct spin-off from recent space-age research and development where closed-environment capsules include everything that man and woman need on their journey to Mars and beyond.

Water-conservation and recycling concerns also make hydroponics interesting to a lot of people.

It's a growing field—if you'll pardon the somewhat contradictory pun.

Do-It-Yourself Method Appeals to Handyman Gardeners

Hydroponic gardening is not an exclusively science-fiction activity—it's something any of us can do as long as we take a little care with it.

You can buy ready-made units—all you have to do is add water and nutrients and follow directions. Or you can improvise and save money by using materials available in any hardware store and tailor them to your own circumstances.

Appealing Features

You won't have to dig or weed, and you'll get clean vegetables —the

strawberries won't need washing!

You can forget about poor soil and caliche, and you'll get more produce from less space because plants will be closer. Plants will grow faster and you can program them more tightly. Your garden can be placed on an apartment patio or balcony. It can be folded up when you are evicted by a wicked landlord and set up again in your new apartment the same day. Wheelchair gardening becomes a possibility when you set the unit on a bench. Your garden can be outdoors but a greenhouse will enable you to grow crops "out of season." In winter it's easy to heat the water that bathes the roots, and this gives you faster production than a conventional garden in cold soil.

Hydroponics May be the Answer to Future Water Shortages.

Continuing urban growth creates tremendous demands on our limited water supply and distribution systems, especially in the desert. Our gardening practices are affected by the increasing cost of water, plus use limitations being imposed on city dwellers. Hydroponics might well be the answer to these constraints.

At present we measure crop yields in tons per acre, but when a shortage of water becomes the limiting factor it's not unreasonable to think of measuring production in pounds per 100 gallons of irrigation water. When that day comes we'll find that hydroponics is a tremendously more efficient growing system than conventional irrigation farming.

Plants don't grow well when irrigated with water that is full of salt—from natural sources as well as treatments—and both farmers and gardeners find that growing a crop becomes more difficult when water

Growing tomatoes in a "Flood-and-Drain" system of 5-gallon buckets of aggregate resting on ground in a greenhouse.

Flood-and-drain system: Growing tank filled with coarse sand is watered by raising nutrients bucket. Nutrients flow through a garden hose and irrigate the plants from below. When sand is wet enough, bucket is lowered and nutrient drains out, drawing air with it. Gravity does the work!

When it's time to wash salts out of the sand, irrigate gently from above. Don't wash the plants out of the sand with a sideways blast of water.

quality falls below a certain level. We are approaching that level in the desert southwest.

Hydroponic gardening, by recycling smaller amounts of good-quality water, will ensure a supply of fresh nutritious vegetables.

This situation occurred during the second world war when the allied forces occupied tropical islands. Food could not be grown in the thin soils with the available salty water. Hydroponics structures were built, good-quality water was distilled from seawater and fertilizers were flown in. It was an expensive undertaking, but bountiful crops of good-quality vegetables were grown.

By the way, hydroponically grown vegetables don't taste of chemicals. In a taste test you couldn't tell which tomato came from a traditional garden and which came from a soilless one.

Basic Hydroponic Systems

The first system is called *flood and drain,* where plants are grown in containers of inert material called *aggregate.* Plants are set either singly in buckets or bags, or grouped in large troughs. A nutrient solution is poured over the aggregate and either drained out and discarded (the non-returnable) or collected in a tank and pumped

back over and over (the recyclable). Aggregate includes any solid non-reacting material such as gravel, sand, pumice, broken bricks, styrofoam, charcoal, perlite, vermiculite, rockwool, and so on. Units can be horizontal or vertical.

The second system is called *Nutrient Flow Technique* (N.F.T.). It uses a sloping trough with a stream of nutrient solution bathing the plant's roots as it goes by. The solution is used over and over. Roots simply lay in the flowing solution and don't provide any support to the plants. You have to provide support with string or netting of some kind.

From these basic systems, all sorts of developments are possible.

It is wasteful to discard the chemicals after a single use, so most systems have a number of growing containers draining into one another and finally into a collecting tank. Then the nutrient solution is pumped back to the beginning. The pump can be controlled by a timer and a float valve maintains a proper solution level in the tank.

More Sophisticated Systems Require More Monitoring

Hydroponic systems don't grow plants all by themselves, they have to be watched closely. Don't think of them as a means to avoid work.

Greenhouses are the same—they don't do the work either. Things can

go wrong more quickly in greenhouses and with hydroponics than they do in a conventional garden, where the soil provides a considerable safety margin regarding moisture and nutrient levels. When you combine hydroponics with a greenhouse you *doubly* increase the chances of things going wrong if you become careless.

Don't Overlook Basic Plant Needs

Hydroponic systems do not circumvent the basic needs of plants.

- You must grow vegetables in season (unless you use a greenhouse where climate can be controlled).
- Grow summer vegetables in summer, and winter vegetables in winter.
- Plants need light, so your hydroponic structure must be placed where they will get it—and not too much either.
- Plants need protection from strong desert winds that dry them out.
- Hydroponic systems won't overcome the effects of freezes (unless they are in a greenhouse) but during milder winter weather you can speed up plant growth by warming the nutrient solution that flows over the roots.
- You must monitor the solution's nutrient levels and Ph. Their supply is critical to plant growth and you have absolute control over them. Get things right by monitoring the solution all the time.

One tomato seed is placed in each of the rockwool cubes and kept moist by misting with good-quality water or by soaking from below. When a plant fills the rockwool cube, transfer it to a bigger rockwool cube and put that onto the nutrient-fed rockwool bed shown at right.

NFT: Simple gravity "feeding" system does not require electricity. Plants grow on a slope and nutrient falls into a collecting bucket. This is hand-emptied into the top bucket with its six delivery tubes. Cucumbers grow in cubes of rockwool sitting on top of a bed of rockwool—that's all! The right end of this rockwool bed is higher, so the nutrient drains to the left. The nutrient solution readily siphons out of the bucket if it is placed a little higher than the mat.

It's not long before roots come through top cube into rockwool bed. See photo at right.

How to Provide Correct Nutrient Levels

Before you start adding nutrient chemicals to the water you must make sure that they will not be altered by reacting with any part of your system. Don't let the nutrient solution come into contact with any copper tubing, brass fittings or metal containers. Even concrete growing boxes release calcium which upsets the balance.

Salty water will make some nutrient chemicals unavailable to plants, so don't use it. Plastic containers, storage tanks, tubing and valves are most suitable for hydroponic systems. And plastic is cheap.

The growing medium itself must be free of chemicals. It's a good practice

NFT: Cucumbers growing in rockwool cubes placed on a rockwool mat. These few plants have grown extra-large leaves because the nutrient solution was a little strong. See leaf photo, page 269.

to wash it thoroughly to make sure any chemicals are rinsed out. Washing takes care of chemical contamination but you also have to think about biological contamination. Use a 10% Chlorox® solution in the wash to remove fungi and bacteria.

You don't even want a smidgen of soil in the system, for it will react with the chemicals and upset the nutrient levels, and there is the danger of it contaminating the medium with harmful organisms.

Manufactured redwood tower filled with vermiculite and peat moss has 35 holes for plants—in this case strawberries. Submersible pump sits in nutrient tank below. Tube takes nutrients to the top and it trickles down through the medium.

Nutrient spray reaches over the aggregate's total surface. A slow drip would moisten only part of it. Note absence of metal—everything is nonreactive plastic.

One solution increases acidity, the other alkalinity.

Nutrients to Add to the Water

In conventional gardening our vegetables obtain their nutrients from the soil. In a series of complex chemical processes that rely on useful organisms, the soil builds up nutrients, stores them and releases them to plant roots. When yields are inadequate we boost the soil's chemical content by adding fertilizers. The application—usually more than a plant needs for the moment—is stored in the soil and our plants take their nutrients as they require them. In this two-step process the soil acts as a buffer—a sort of safety valve against sudden changes and excesses.

Hydroponic systems have no buffering safety margin. Nutrients are applied directly to the plants roots, so you have to be extra careful not to overdo it and kill your plants—

or underdo it and starve them. You cannot afford sudden changes and excesses!

Hydroponic systems are too delicate to let you make up your own mixtures from garden fertilizers—even from pharmaceutical-grade chemicals.

Furthermore, the "complete" houseplant food fertilizers are not fully complete nor are they properly balanced for hydroponics growing—they will be too acidic or too alkaline, even if you get the nutrient balance nearly correct.

This means that you have to buy specially formulated mixtures from hydroponic stores.

You Need a Storage Tank

To avoid spending a lot of time mixing up small amounts of nutrient solution, select a 20- or 30-gallon plastic tank that does not allow light in. The nutrient solution will grow algae if light gets in, and algae will change the nutrient balance. Plastic garbage cans are just about perfect.

Use plastic fittings so the nutrient chemicals don't contact any metal. All the fittings and tubing must be nonmetal.

If you place the tank at a higher level than the plant troughs or containers the solution will siphon itself out unless you have a valve in the tubing between the tank and the plants. Then you have to remember to turn the valve on and off. It's easier to place the tank at a lower level, use a submersible pump to pump the solution to the topmost plants and let the containers drain into the tank.

Follow the Manufacturer's Directions!

The chemicals you buy are very soluble in water. Read the directions and follow them carefully. It's often a teaspoon to a gallon of good-quality water, but it could be something else!

Solution Must Be Tested

If the solution is too strong it will burn the roots. If it is too weak, it will not nourish the plants. If the acidity/alkalinity is wrong, some of the nutrients will not be available to the plants and they will not grow.

Each plant has its optimum nutrient level which is measured as the Conductivity Factor, or C.F. For example, lettuce levels should be between 8 and 12, whereas tomato levels should be between 22 and 28.

Hydroponic reference books list the C.F. for vegetables. Be sure to consult one for this vital information. Do not try to grow two plants with widely different C.F. requirements in the same strength nutrient solution.

In addition, each plant has an optimum range of acidity/alkalinity, measured on a pH scale. Neutral is 7.0 with lower figures indicating acidity, and higher figures indicating alkalinity. Fortunately many plants share the same pH level of 6.3. If the solution varies too wide of this mark, the nutrients in the solution can't be used by the plants and they don't grow—no matter how much nutrient is offered. pH keeps the solution comfortable for

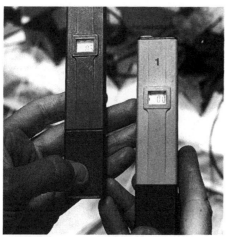

These digital meters quickly and accurately read the levels of pH and C.F. Just dip them into the nutrient solution and observe the reading.

Simple tank of aggregate is watered by gravity from gallon jug on right. It works like the chicken watering trough that fills itself when the water level falls enough to let air into upturned jug.

"Burnt" margin of this large leaf is evidence that the solution is too strong.

plants in the same way a thermostat keeps a house temperature comfortable for humans.

Several plants sharing the same pH range allows us to grow a variety of plants with one solution and without worrying about its suitability for any particular one of them. We don't have to pay attention to pH as closely as we do with the C.F.

Monitor the Solution Daily

Commercial fertilizers start with the right C.F. and the right pH. When plants are growing quickly—and with hydroponics they do so all the time—they absorb the nutrients and change the strength and the balance of the solution that remains in the tank.

Daily monitoring is recommended, both for pH and for C.F. It's important that you know how quickly the plants are using up the nutrients.

If your system runs short of solution and the C.F. and the pH are still within range you simply add more solution of the right strength. Mix a teaspoon of fertilizer in a gallon of water and "top-up" as required.

How to Measure Nutrient-Solution Strength

You can buy battery-operated "measuring sticks"—one for C.F. and one for pH—that show the results in digital fashion (numbers). Just dip them in the solution and they read out immediately. On the cheaper side you can use color guides for pH measurement—such as litmus paper and

swimming-pool test kits. However, if you are color-blind you'll have difficulty in deciding whether the reaction has turned bluish-green or greenish-blue.

Nutrients Nourish More Than the Crop Plants

Algae are undesirable plants that take advantage of the nutrient solution, and they alter its balance and concentration.

If the storage tank lets light into the solution you'll discover that algae turn it green. If the water is warm, then algae will grow quicker and thicker. Avoid this problem by keeping the solution in the dark.

Don't use clear plastic tubing between the nutrient tank and the growing containers because that's where algae can get started. It will travel forward to the growing medium and backward to the tank.

If nutrient solution is poured over the top of the growing medium and there is sunlight there, algae will grow on the surface. Even with Nutrient Flow Technique troughs you'll find algae growing wherever there is light.

Because of this nuisance it's usual to cover everything as much as possible with black plastic to keep the light out.

Algae will be reduced if you flush clean water through the system every fourth time you "top up" the tank. Should you use algicide chemicals they will affect the pH and the C.F., requiring you to readjust the strength of the solution.

If algae becomes too much of a nuisance you will have to close down the system, clean it thoroughly and start again. It's best not to let it get started.

How to Get Started—Seed Selection

If you have a system inside a greenhouse, use greenhouse varieties of seeds. If your system is outside, use garden varieties. In either case choose quick-maturing kinds because they are smaller and more productive than the long-term varieties. The right strategy is to have a rapid turnover of plants that you harvest as soon as possible. The small gourmet-type vegetables are of high quality, quick growers and readily available.

At present there aren't many vegetable varieties that have been selected solely for hydroponic growing. One day there will be, but for the present the ordinary varieties do well enough.

How to Get Started—Seed Sowing

A tray with an inch or two of a mix of equal parts vermiculite and perlite, or vermiculite and crumbled sphagnum peat, makes an excellent starter box for the first week of a plant's life.

After that, an individual seedling, an inch or two tall, can be picked out from among its companions and set into a plastic basket containing the same mix.

Another way is to sow a single seed in a small cube of rockwool and after seven or eight days it can be set into

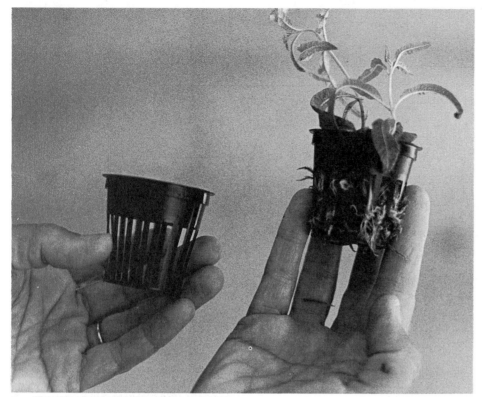

Seedling planted in plastic baskets ready to be grown in an N.F.T. system. The baskets are set into holes in a floating styrofoam plank in an open-trough system or into holes in a closed-tube system.

Axillary shoots on a tomato plant are vigorous and provide new planting material when you want to start a new generation of plants. Take them from your most-vigorous plant—they will perform in exactly the same way as the parent from which they are cut.

the small plastic basket.

Plastic baskets are used in N.F.T. systems. Rockwool cubes are used in flood-and-drain containers where the aggregate is too lumpy for small seeds. Large seeds such as corn and beans will germinate very well in large-size aggregate. Where you have small-size aggregate—such as chat or coarse sand—you can sow small seeds directly into it.

However, you don't want to use valuable growing space for germinating seed and raising seedlings—they are best grown separately and transplanted when ready.

How to Get Started—Cuttings
There are times when cuttings—say of tomatoes or New Zealand spinach, that produce more quickly than seed—are preferred. Start them in the same way—in a vermiculite/sphagnum tray, a plastic basket, or a cube of rockwool.

Planting Into the System
With flood-and-drain containers the rockwool cubes are set directly in the aggregate and the roots grow out of the cubes into the aggregate. If you put several plants in a large growing container all the roots of all the plants will intermingle. This doesn't matter until you want to remove one or two old plants that are not producing. Then you'll find yourself tugging out the roots of vigorous plants and disturbing them.

This doesn't happen when you put one plant in one container—such as a two-gallon-size plastic bag. At the end of the plant's productive life you simply dispose of the bag and its contents—unless you need to salvage an expensive aggregate.

N.F.T. systems have either an open trough (letting light in) or a closed tube (keeping light out) to carry the nutrient solution. For example, ordinary house gutter (plastic) makes a good trough, but all troughs need a sheet of black plastic to keep the nutrient solution in the dark—otherwise algae grows in the system.

Open troughs are fitted with a floating strip of styrofoam that has holes made in it for plastic baskets. The closed tubes also have holes drilled in them for the plastic baskets.

The baskets are set into the holes so they rest just above the nutrient solution. It's not long before the roots leave the basket of sphagnum peat and are bathed in the nutrient solution as it passes by.

Rockwool cubes can also be placed in the holes. The roots soon find themselves in the nutrient solution.

Importance of Oxygen on the Roots
It's important to remember that plants' roots need oxygen.

Gardeners know that their soil must have good drainage and if it is constantly wet, their plants drown. In the same way, plants grown in soilless conditions—in water all the time—are in danger of being drowned.

This means that you must oxygenate the water, and it's easy to do.

With N.F.T. systems you let the water fall with a splash to the next lower tube or trough.

With flood-and-drain containers the action of flooding and draining drives air through the aggregate.

You can make sure that the nutrient solution is oxygenated by using an aquarium aerator with its bubbling tube in the nutrient tank.

How Often and Fast Should Solution Flow?
With N.F.T. systems you need a slope of 1 in 40 (1:40) to get a good flow of nutrient without tearing off the roots.

With flood and drain, gravity is all you need—with adequate drainage holes in the bottom of the container.

You can let your system run all the time, or you can run it intermittently—

a minute on and a minute off—with the purpose of aerating the roots, but you must not let the roots dry out—even for a moment. A little experimenting with the timer will determine how long a "dry" interval you can allow, but don't forget that this will change as the seasons change, as your plants grow, and as you replace the old ones with new. Some people run their system during the day and not at night.

Plants growing in a container of aggregate have a reserve of moisture that allows a longer interval between waterings. There's less of a safety margin with plants growing in a nutrient flow.

When large plants are growing rapidly and during sunny days (and also during windy days if your system is outdoors) you'll have to run the system more often than with small plants in a protected greenhouse during cloudy weather.

Your best measure is to watch the leaves for wilting and the aggregate for wetness—and then make a judgement. Conditions change from week to week, so you must make frequent reassessments and just as frequent readjustments.

Large growing trough divided into individual containers for corn. This prevents the plants' roots growing into one another. This is an excellent site for extending the season—in spring or fall—when temperatures are barely warm enough for corn. South-facing brick wall gathers the sun's heat and releases it during the night, keeping the corn growing.

What Happens When There's a Power Failure?

Hydroponics systems are dependent on electricity—the pump keeps the nutrient solution moving, the aerator keeps the water oxygenated, and the lights in an indoor situation keep the seedlings growing. It can be a tragedy if the electricity fails!

If the pump stops you can safely flush the system with water from a hose. Plants will be quite happy for a couple of days on plain water. However, water from a hose isn't "plain" at all and it will upset the chemical strength and balance if you let it recycle through the holding tank. Therefore, drain the hose water away from the nutrient tank.

Splash the hose water as much as you can to get oxygen into it. Make sure the temperature is the same as the nutrient solution—which should be in the 77F (25C) range for best results. Any sudden change of temperature will stress the plants and perhaps damage the roots.

A few hours without lights won't hurt your mature plants but seedlings should be quickly moved into full day-

light without subjecting them to severe temperature changes or strong dry winds.

Your plants will continue to grow during a power failure and continue to use up nutrients in the solution—changing its strength and balance.

When repairs have been made and everything is back to normal, use your testing equipment to see how much adjustment you have to make to the solution.

If you are handy with things electrical, you can rig an automatic switch-over to a 12-volt pump powered by a back-up automobile battery kept charged with a trickle charger. This could keep your hydroponics system functioning normally during a power outage of up to several hours. You could use a manual switchover if someone visits your garden area at least a couple of times every day.

Hydroponics Won't Eliminate Pests and Diseases

Hydroponically-grown plants aren't immune to pests—there's the same risk in "catching" something as there is in a conventional garden. When you get plants from a friend, or buy them

from a nursery, look at them closely—you don't want to bring home aphids, spider mites or caterpillars. It's better to avoid these problems by raising your plants from seed yourself.

Plants grown outdoors can have pests and diseases blown onto them but you can pick off the insects and pinch out diseased leaves and fruit. A greenhouse is a protected place, where you manage the environment to get the maximum growth from your plants. That same environment (and that same management) grows pests and diseases—and they can grow rapidly.

Take the usual gardening protective measures. Try predator insects (see the Chapter on Alternatives to Poisonous Chemicals), pick off the big pests, blast off with a water spray, use soapy water and, as a last resort, use insecticides. Don't let chemicals change the nutrient strength and balance.

In a greenhouse, mildew can be prevented by good ventilation and by growing resistant strains—which is the way to go if your system is outdoors. Because you are gardening without soil, there's no risk from soil-borne diseases.

Homemade tower of 5-gallon buckets tied together. White plastic "lips" keep aggregate in tower and enable you to plant easily. You may find it helpful to line the buckets with plastic and only create an opening just big enough for the seedling. This keeps the aggregate from spilling out of the bucket tower.

Desert Extremes Also Affect Hydroponic Gardening

The extremes of the desert environment affect hydroponic gardening even though we have eliminated the problems associated with a difficult soil.

We still have short seasons, and we adjust to those by using quick-maturing varieties—just as we do with gardening in the soil.

The wonderful spring and fall weather is good for conventional gardening—and good for outdoor hydroponic gardening, too. There is the "dead" season of mid-winter to contend with and we adjust in conventional ways by making a temporary covering of clear plastic over outdoor plants. There is plenty of warm winter sunshine to be trapped by this method but hydroponics gives us another way to keep plants growing during cold weather. Warm the nutrient solution to 86F (30C). This is a good measure to take even if you have your system in a greenhouse.

Summertime can be severe on hydro-ponic systems if the water gets too hot—and it will if the nutrient tank is exposed to the sun all day. Roots can't grow away from the heat nor can they get relief from protective mulches as happens in a conventional garden. Indoors and out, shading the nutrient tank and the solution will be helpful. But don't shade your corn, squash and other sun-loving plants.

How to Grow Tomatoes in a Hydroponic System

Four or five plants is all that a family needs to grow because you can get a pound of tomatoes a week from one plant grown on a vine system, in either drain-and-flood (aggregate) or N.F.T.

With an aggregate of equal parts vermiculite and peat moss in a two-gallon plastic bag you can use an intermittent flow (something like five minutes four times a day and turned off for the night). With a N.F.T. system you'll probably run the system 24 hours a day.

If you use lava rock or gravel, you'll have to irrigate more frequently because they don't hold moisture in the same way as peatmoss and vermiculite. Pumice, on the other hand, does hold water well.

If the aggregate container drains to the ground (you are not recycling the nutrient) make sure that a little liquid flows out the drainage holes. If the ground under the bag is dry, the inside is probably dry too.

When you squeeze a handful of the peat moss/vermiculite mix and it drips liquid, your plants are properly supplied.

Use a locally recommended variety of tomato for outdoor growing and select a greenhouse variety for out-of-season production. Raise your own seedlings. Don't buy plants that may be infected with pests.

Plants must be trained up a support system (usually a strong string) and the axillary suckers pruned out as they develop, otherwise you'll have dense bushes with too much foliage. Furthermore, there'll be too much stalk and stem for your plants to carry nutrients to the developing flowers and fruit.

When the plant begins to bloom, cut off the top to check its growth. Keep pruning out the axillary suckers to direct energy into fruit production. The plant will grow 8-feet tall, with not much foliage on its single, unbranched stem. When there are no leaves on the lower three feet or so, drop the whole plant on its string and wind the lower stem round and round without breaking it. Place the coils in the aggregate, where they will grow new roots very quickly.

You can do the same sort of thing in a N.F.T. system. Drop the long stems and lay them in the trough. They will grow additional roots in the nutrient flow.

In the desert, even in a greenhouse, tomato fruit is subject to sunburn, especially if it is grown this way with a minimum of foliage. Shading during summer is essential. Harvest the fruit at a deep-pink stage and let it ripen on a shelf indoors. There will be little loss of quality and you are "making room" for fruit to come on later.

Outdoors, and to some extent in a greenhouse, summer temperatures cause the plant to stop producing flowers. Those that are produced will not pollinate in the heat. Even in mild weather you'll need to shake the flowering plants to effect pollination and ensure fruit production. A gentle tapping of the vine with a stick is all that's needed, but it's needed every morning.

No matter how careful and attentive you are, a hydroponically grown tomato plant won't go on producing at a high rate. It needs to take a rest, even when the temperature is suitable. Don't get upset when this "pause for breath" occurs.

The final pause occurs after about 20 weeks of growth. Take the bag of peat moss/vermiculite which is now full of roots and put it on the compost pile for your conventional garden.

When you want a new set of plants, cut axillary shoots from your best plant and root them in a bag of aggregate. This is a much quicker way to get a new crop than starting again from seed.

If you grow tomatoes outdoors, an extra-strong support for the vines should be set in the ground. Desert winds are strong and gusty and the whole system will fall over if you rely on the bag of aggregate for support as you do in a greenhouse.

This stronger support lets you keep more foliage on the plants and that helps to shade the plant. You can't keep outdoor plants cool like you can those in a greenhouse.

How to Grow Cucumbers Hydroponically

You grow cucumbers in much the same way as tomatoes, but they require a different kind of pruning. You want as many side branches as possible because that's where the fruit is produced.

After the flower has set fruit (no pollination is required with the preferred European varieties) pinch the side shoots to concentrate the nutrients in the developing fruit, instead of them nourishing further lengthy growth. When the vines reach the top of the greenhouse, allow them to tumble over and hang down. Wrap them around the string so they don't become too heavy and go wandering off in the wrong direction.

How to Grow Root Crops Hydroponically

Root crops have to be grown in containers of aggregate—they don't do well in a N.F.T. system because their roots need anchoring.

How to Grow Top-heavy Plants Hydroponically

Cabbage-family plants, eggplant and peppers all become top-heavy at maturity. They need root anchorage. This means they must be grown in containers of aggregate (drain-and-flood)—not in N.F.T. troughs.

How to Grow Strawberies and Lettuce Hydroponically

Both of these crops can be grown in either aggregate containers or in N.F.T. systems. Use the small, quick-maturing, lettuce varieties—and there are plenty to choose from. Grow lettuce seedlings in a tray of vermiculite and sphagnum peat and replant them as you need them into plastic baskets full of the same mix. Another way is sowing one seed in a small rockwool cube. Set the seedlings into the aggregate, or into holes in a styrofoam strip floating on the nutrient solution in the trough.

Final Considerations

Hydroponic gardening is not a way to avoid the intricacies of desert gardening, any more than a greenhouse is. In fact, it adds to them. But you can do it!

This is a new and more-productive way of gardening that will give you a lot of pleasure once you master the details. It will give you plenty of opportunity for masterful control and it will broaden your understanding of what plants need and how they function. It's a fun way to garden. And it's the gardening of the future!

Small container growing lots of summer vegetables—many more than a conventional garden would allow. A golden zuchinni is ready for harvest.

With small, portable hydroponics units you can carry your garden wherever you want it. The top of a garden wall is the site for this gardener's efforts. These use aggregate supplied with nutrient from the attached gallon jug. They work like the chicken watering trough that fills itself when the water level falls enough to let air into the upturned gallon jug.

INDEX

House Plants Want to Grow

House plants want to grow and you should accommodate their growth by paying them a little attention. Some house-plant gardeners observe four times in each year as a sort of ritual for care and attention. They use the four main holidays of the year as signs—Christmas, Easter, Labor Day and Thanksgiving. These are conveniently spaced quite evenly as calendar dates. Also, they coincide with the seasonal changes.

Just now (November 20) our days have shortened and will continue to shorten a little. It's a time when plants normally begin their rest. However, houses become *hot* houses at this time of year and the plants respond by putting out a little growth. That is, unless their growth pattern is determined by day length alone. It's time to trim out the dead stuff and to train any new growth—such as on climbers like Hoya—into the desirable shape.

It's time to give a "feeding" to support the growth encouraged by a warm room. It's advisable to move a plant into a more sunny window, because the safe northern window of summer is now too dark for plant growth. Trim out all the dead stuff. Separate a clump of plants crowding a limited space in a container where they've spent too many years.

House plants readily sicken during the winter months because we forget that they have slowed down in their growth and yet we continue to water them on a summer-time schedule. Dormant plants don't need so much water as actively growing plants. Reduce the watering.

Adapted from one of George's weekly columns in the *Tucson Citizen* dated November 20th.